10

THE FBI-KGB WAR

THE FBI-KGB WAR

A Special Agent's Story

ROBERT J. LAMPHERE and Tom Shachtman

Random House
New York

Library of Congress Cataloging-in-Publication Data

Lamphere, Robert J.
The FBI-KGB war.

1. Lamphere, Robert J.   2. Intelligence officers—
United States—Biography.   3. United States. Federal
Bureau of Investigation.   4. Soviet Union. Komitet
gesurdastvennoĭ bezopasnosti.   I. Shachtman,
Tom, 1942–   . II. Title.
HV7911.L325A35   1986   327.1'2   85-19407
ISBN 0-394-54151-0

Manufactured in the United States of America

23456789

FIRST EDITION

Book design by Carole Lowenstein

In memory of Maxine and George

—ROBERT J. LAMPHERE

Acknowledgments

I would like to acknowledge with appreciation the help I have received from a number of people. My friend James J. Angleton, formerly of the CIA, has been both helpful with and critical of some of what I have written. Several former special agents of the FBI have assisted me on certain details: Ernest Van Loon, Hollis Bowers and Lawrence McWilliams. Most important was the work of my former secretary, Elaine Mourey, who spent many hours of her time in research, typing and editing my original manuscript. Our editor, Bob Loomis, has been patient, friendly and unfailingly knowledgeable. Finally, my literary agent and friend, Kathy Robbins, deserves special thanks for her criticisms, wisdom and long-lasting support.

—ROBERT J. LAMPHERE

Contents

THE FBI-KGB WAR

1
UNFINISHED BUSINESS

IT WAS ONE OF THE EVENINGS in the week between Christmas and New Year's Eve of 1944. In New York City a fine snow was falling, and it was cold and dark. Mayor Fiorello LaGuardia had ordered that New York's lights be turned out so that the city wouldn't provide a bright backdrop against which German U-boats might spot moving merchant ships. I was on the streets of the upper reaches of Manhattan, one among eleven hundred special agents of the FBI who were taking part in one of the largest manhunts the FBI had ever mounted—a search for an armed German saboteur who had been landed in the United States by U-boat and whom we believed to be somewhere in New York.

Small groups of people passed me, on the way to and from seasonal parties. For the party-goers the war was far away, though in Europe the Battle of the Bulge raged and in the Pacific fighting was fierce on several fronts. An Allied final victory didn't seem quite so assured as it had a few weeks before.

I should've been at a Christmas party myself—after all, I was twenty-six years old, single, employed, and a young man in a city that had sent most of its young men to war. But no such luck. I trudged through the snow canvassing every two-bit hotel and rooming house,

and cursing quietly to myself. Agents had come to New York from
as far away as Baltimore, and Assistant Director E. J. Connelly—a
tough taskmasker whom many in the FBI feared—had flown in to
take charge of the search. Each agent had a few streets to cover. I
don't know how many times I asked if anyone had seen a thin,
good-looking man, five feet ten inches tall, mid- to late thirties, who
spoke English with a noticeable German accent.

Erich Gimpel was our target's name, and we already knew quite
a bit about him because his fellow saboteur William Colepaugh had
been caught and had told the FBI of their mission. Earlier in 1944
Colepaugh, an American seaman with pro-Nazi sentiments, had
jumped ship in Portugal and made himself available to the Third
Reich. He was taken into Germany, enrolled in an Abwehr (German
army intelligence) group, and teamed with Gimpel. Erich Gimpel
had been born and raised in Germany; after a long residence in Peru
he had been repatriated at the outbreak of hostilities, in 1939. The
two men were extensively trained, then were taken across the Atlantic in a U-boat and were let off in the vicinity of Bar Harbor, Maine,
on November 29, 1944.

Nobody would have known of their arrival without a few lucky
breaks and some dogged research. On December 3, 1944, a British
freighter was torpedoed not far from Bar Harbor. That in itself was
not significant, but it gave the FBI reason to believe a U-boat was in
the area. The FBI also had learned from the navy that in an earlier
offshore torpedo incident, a U-boat had carried a spy. Believing this
new U-boat might also be ferrying spies, the FBI began a manhunt
in the Bar Harbor area. Through our usual tenaciousness in talking
to everyone in the vicinity, we located a sheriff's son and a woman
who had seen two men they did not know near Bar Harbor. The hunt
was intensified; by this time, however, Gimpel and Colepaugh were
in New York City.

They moved between small hotels and a rented apartment in a
building purposely picked because it was constructed of wood and
brick—steel would have interfered with their plans to operate a radio
transmitter. The Abwehr had given them ninety-nine small diamonds, sixty thousand dollars in cash, two guns, microdots, false
identity cards, ink for secret writing, and other espionage parapher-
nalia. Colepaugh wanted to go on a spending spree, but Gimpel
wanted to get on with their assignments. The German was beginning
to hate the turncoat American. He tried and failed to buy parts to
construct the shortwave transmitter, and then returned to the apart-

ment to find Colepaugh gone, together with the suitcase, the money, the diamonds and the guns. After leaving the hideaway Colepaugh had checked the suitcase and its contents at Grand Central Station, and looked up a male friend who lived in Queens. There he stayed, drinking and talking, until late at night, and in the morning confessed to his buddy that he'd come from Germany on an espionage mission. Soon Colepaugh was in the FBI's custody and began to spill out his experiences with the Abwehr.

The manhunt started in earnest. Agents immediately went to look for Gimpel and for the bag at Grand Central Station. Both were gone. Gimpel, a shrewd man, had figured out what Colepaugh had done and told the attendant in the Grand Central luggage room that he'd simply lost his claim check to the suitcase. He described a few clothes that he knew to be at the top of the bag. The attendant opened the suitcase, saw the clothes and didn't look underneath them—which would have disclosed the guns and diamonds. Gimpel took the bag and vanished.

I had grown tired of looking for Gimpel, or, as he was also known, "Edward Green," and after checking out my allotted number of streets I went back to FBI headquarters, on Foley Square in lower Manhattan. It was midnight, but the place was buzzing: anytime E. J. Connelly ran an operation, everyone worked at least eighteen hours a day. I told "Markey" Best, a friend who was the agent making street assignments, what I thought of wasting my time in an area where I was certain the German was not going to be found. Markey asked, with a twinkle in his eye, if I'd be interested in becoming a jailer. "Hell, yes," I said.

The prisoner was Colepaugh, and he was being held in a seldom-used small detention center on the top floor of the U.S. Courthouse at Foley Square. I was put in charge of the four-to-midnight shift, and had two other agents working with me. None of us liked Colepaugh; to us he was a traitor and a man without even the courage of his pro-Nazi convictions. His backbone had evaporated before he left Germany, when he had sat through the Allied bombing of Berlin, and he had already decided not to take part in the sabotage assignment when he got off the U-boat in Maine.

We maintained a suicide watch on Colepaugh: I had an agent observing him at all times from a post just outside his cell, and we had taken away his belt, necktie and shoelaces; we even cut up his food before serving it to him on paper plates. I spent most of my time in a center room that controlled the access both to the outside corridor and elevator, and to the cell block. There were a half-dozen units, and we had Colepaugh in the one farthest away from my command post. At least the cells in this historic building weren't in the cellar, like dungeons; it was cold enough close to the roof.

Colepaugh was singing like a bird. He told his interviewers that Gimpel's wife and children were in Peru and that Gimpel bought newspapers from that country in a subway-level newsstand in Times Square that specialized in foreign publications. Two FBI agents watched the spot at every hour of the day, and on December 30 saw a man who matched Colepaugh's description of Gimpel except that his hair was the wrong color. The man saw the agents looking at him and started to turn away, and the agents stopped him. That evening I had two prisoners. I put Gimpel in the cell nearest to me so he wouldn't know we had Colepaugh, who was down at the far end of the hall.

Having been on duty at one distasteful task on Christmas Eve, I was on the job in my new position on New Year's Eve, and the clock had already crossed over into January 1945 when I left the cell block and headed uptown to the hotel I called home.

For forty-five dollars a month I had a single room in a midtown hotel, and few amenities; one of those I'd grown used to was the hotel's bar. I stopped in. Most of the people there were drunk and sloppy; the air was stale, the streamers and decorations had begun to droop from the walls. I heard snatches of conversation about teenage sensation Elizabeth Taylor in *National Velvet,* and about Judy Garland, who was appearing at the Astor Roof, a nightclub which I liked to frequent but which I obviously wasn't going to see much of for a while, until I was finished with my prison guard duties. At the bar were two young ladies who also had rooms in the hotel. One of them was nominally my girlfriend; both of them were chatterboxes, but good-looking.

"Been working again?" my girl inquired. I admitted I'd been downtown. Neither of the ladies needed a drink, but I sure did, so I ordered a round for all of us, then sat sipping mine as the ladies joined forces and raked me over the coals. My ridiculous long hours. My infatuation with the work. My disinterest in having a good time. My close-mouthedness.

Suddenly the notion came to me that they'd be astounded to know precisely where I'd been until midnight on New Year's Eve, and amazed to know whom I'd been guarding. Of course I could reveal nothing about German saboteurs, and I don't think I really wanted to say much about them to these ladies, anyhow. As their chatter continued, I looked around the room and muttered to myself, "You dumb clucks—don't you even know there's a war on?"

A day or so later a doctor who was sent in regularly to examine the two men told me that Gimpel, the German, was so depressed—certain he was going to be summarily executed—that his heart was weakening. He suggested that I talk to Gimpel and help him out of his depression. Now, in the FBI that was just the sort of thing one did not do lightly; we were under strict instructions not to talk to prisoners about anything except their confinement. I took the request to Al Belmont, then our ASAC (assistant special agent in charge) of the New York office; Belmont checked with Connelly—the two men were currently handling the interrogation of the prisoners—and received permission for me to chat with Gimpel as long as I stayed away from discussing his case.

I'm a good talker, but this was a difficult assignment. Going into the cell, I sat down near Gimpel, who must've thought I'd come to ask him what kind of sausages he wanted for his last breakfast. He was very down, but he had to listen to me and I knew he understood English. For a time this conversation was a one-way affair, but little by little over a series of evenings I began to convince Gimpel that he wasn't going to be shot on the spot. Ours was a system of laws, I told him, and he'd have a military trial and, in all likelihood, an appeal, and he'd be represented by counsel throughout this procedure. Because the trials would take some time, even if he were to be found guilty and sentenced to death, it wasn't going to happen tomorrow at sunrise.

Gimpel began to relax and talk, and when he did, I came to admire the man rather than to resent what he had tried to do to the United States. I began to understand that he was basically a German patriot who had gone into enemy territory to attempt a near-impossible mission. Unlike Colepaugh, Gimpel had not betrayed his country; rather, Gimpel had undertaken a dangerous assignment in its service. I wondered: If the circumstances had been reversed, would I have had the courage to go into Germany and perform a similar mission?

Gimpel, being a smart man, had figured out that there was another prisoner down the hall, and that it must be Colepaugh. Once he requested a favor of me. Motioning to the end cell, he begged me, "Chust put me alone vith dat other von for fife minutes!" He made a choking motion with his hands. I shook my head and told him to cut it out, but respected his sentiments. I probably hated Colepaugh as much as he did; to me, there was nothing lower than a man who betrayed his own country.

We now had four agents assigned to the cell block for my shift. One evening I stationed the newest man to watch Gimpel, told another to sit near Colepaugh, and sent my third subordinate out for our dinners; meanwhile, I remained in the command center and cut up the food that had previously arrived for the prisoners. After finishing the preparation, I lifted a paper plate in each hand and carefully opened the door from my control room into the cell block. As I went in, I said to the new man who held the door open, "Don't let that door close!" He thought I was joking, and let the door slam shut. I stared at him in disbelief. "You stupid son-of-a-bitch," I said, "now we're all locked in here too!" I showed him that the door from the cell block to the control room could only be opened from outside the block. He was amused. I, realizing the consequences of his actions, was aghast. Soon the fourth agent would return from downstairs with our dinners, and when he discovered that he was unable to get into the control room from the elevator, he'd raise the alarm; that would bring people running, and would inevitably result in my having to face that tough bastard Connelly.

I gave the food to the prisoners and came back to the steel-mesh door. Stripping off my belt, I worked it through the mesh and then tried to loop it over the outside doorknob so I could open the door. As I tried and failed many times, the wet-behind-the-ears man kept telling me the stratagem wouldn't work. I swore at him and instructed him to pull on the door at my signal. On about the twenty-fifth try I got the knob, opened the door and got back in the control room just in time to let in the fourth agent as he arrived from the elevator with our dinners.

Now I had only one worry. The whole circus had taken place out of Colepaugh's sight but directly in front of Gimpel's cell. Later that evening, when I had settled myself on the bare chair, I said to Gimpel, "Erich, you didn't see anything."

He replied soberly, "Do not vorry; I vill not tell." I relaxed. Then he asked, "How did you get dat thing vith your belt?" I buried my face in my hands. We both laughed.

I guess that broke the ice, because that night our discussion ranged far and wide. We spoke at length about the war. To my mind, it was far from over, but Gimpel saw things differently. Germany was as good as beaten, he said, and the war in Europe would be over in a few months. He prophesied that the defeat of Japan would take the Allies only a few further months. In the postwar period, though, the United States had better watch out, he warned, for there would be no real peace because the Soviet Union would seek to dominate the world. He advised that the Allies' best course of action would be to sign a separate peace with Germany's military leaders, and then for the Allies, augmented by Germany, to face down the Soviets. Hitler would be no problem, Gimpel believed, because the Germans would take care of Hitler themselves. All the United States had to do was agree to an immediate cease-fire; then Hitler could be eliminated and the Russians could be thwarted.

I recognized his words as German military propaganda, particularly the end of the scenario. In fact, Gimpel told me that part of his mission here had been to advance the idea of a separate peace between Germany's military men and the United States. But the idea of a coming clash between the Western democracies and Communism struck me as being a true evaluation of the future, not empty words.

Weeks later, Gimpel and Colepaugh were turned over to the military, and from then on the FBI had nothing to do with them. Colepaugh received a lengthy prison sentence, and Gimpel was sentenced to death. President Harry S. Truman reduced that to life imprisonment and later pardoned Gimpel so he could go back to Germany after the war. Still later, when Truman made a trip to Germany, Gimpel sought him out and thanked the President for his kindness. I admired Gimpel's gesture—and never forgot his warning about the shape of the postwar world, and the inevitable clash between the West and the Soviet Union.

2

BEGINNINGS

IN AMERICA the Lampheres go back to 1669, when George Lamphere was one of the original settlers in Westerly, Rhode Island. A descendant, my paternal grandfather, lost an arm in the Civil War; afterward he was chief administrator for the Treasury Department, and wrote the first book on the organization of the federal government. Later on he moved to Minnesota to publish and edit a pioneer newspaper. His son, my father, was intelligent and quick-tempered. In the 1890s the two men had an argument, and my father went west to become an itinerant miner. He roamed the hard-rock mining camps of Montana, Idaho and British Columbia until he met the American-born postmistress of a small mining town in southeast British Columbia and married her.

I was born in 1918 in the Coeur d'Alene mining district of Idaho, the middle child of three, and grew up in the small town of Mullan, where my father had become a leaser. This was a man who leased the rights to mine someone else's underground ore deposits—silver, lead and zinc in this area—and who hired hands to do the actual work. Many times before, my father had risen to the position of shift boss, but his temper got in the way of further advancement; being a leaser, in control of his own operation, was more suited to his personality. In later years he also became a consultant to companies that had financial interests in ores and deposits.

Mullan was a tough little town. The inhabitants came from a variety of national backgrounds; the predominant group was composed of Finns. Most of us boys learned a few choice swearwords in Finnish, and I grew up with tough kids (though I never considered myself one of them) and had my share of fights. A little professional boxing instruction helped me in those tiffs. My father and mother expected all three of us to do well in school, and we did. I liked nothing better than to go up into the hills with my dog and wander about on the ridge-line, out of sight of people from dawn to dusk. I learned to hunt, to fish and to enjoy reading.

The University of Idaho counselor tried to talk me out of an accelerated program that would bypass the usual bachelor's degree and earn me a law degree in five years, but I stubbornly pointed out that it was listed in the catalogue and that I was going to do it. To help defray the expenses, during the summer I worked in the mines. The first time, my father made sure I got every dirty job available so he wouldn't appear to be playing favorites; succeeding summers, I worked deeper in the mines, and for the larger company that owned them. I preferred working down in the hole because I was treated more as an equal. The air was stale, hot and humid, and we twisted the sweat out of our socks when we got home at night. In the depths there were more fights. Twice I had to face down other men; I didn't like that, but my father heard of one of the incidents and it seemed to impress him. The other miners started to cajole me into joining the union until they realized they didn't want a boss's son at their meetings.

Tough situations in the mines were counterpoint to the intellectual jousting at the university. From both I learned the importance of talking to people on whatever level they were functioning, an insight that stood me in good stead in later years.

In 1940, after a short illness, my mother died. I looked at my father —a man who had been in chronic poor health all his life—and knew he would not long survive without her. The realization triggered a decision that rather than finish my last year of law school in Idaho, I'd go elsewhere, get a job and finance the year myself so I wouldn't have to take any more of my father's dwindling supply of dollars. In Washington, D.C., with the help of a senator's administrative assistant, I became a clerical auditor in the procurement division of the

Treasury Department. It wasn't much of a job, but it enabled me to complete my degree at night at the National Law School (now part of George Washington University).

During that year I visited my father once but, at his request, did not return for his funeral. I didn't have enough money to take the cram course for the bar exam, but somehow managed to pass the exam and was admitted to the Washington, D.C., bar in 1941.

Eight years of the New Deal had brought considerable amplification of the federal government's role in the country, but before World War II began for the United States, Washington was still a somewhat sleepy southern city. In 1939 President Franklin D. Roosevelt had given FBI Director J. Edgar Hoover jurisdiction over all espionage matters, and the FBI had begun to expand at a rapid rate. The Bureau was looking for candidates, and I was seeking experience. I reasoned I'd stay in the FBI for two years and then, with practical knowledge under my belt, I'd be better able to open up my own law office or go into a business.

The FBI was known as an elite outfit. At a time when most adults had never gone to college, FBI men had graduate degrees; they were taller than the norm (over five foot seven); and they were exemplars of good upbringing and high moral standards. If I was somewhat attracted to the FBI's "crime-busting" image, I was more attuned to the idea of being among the very best, and wanted to measure up to the high requirements for membership in the Federal Bureau of Investigation. My parents were dead, my hometown was left behind, and for me, the past was rapidly receding. Maybe I needed the structure the Bureau would provide, and perhaps I just sought a way to test myself. Either way, the FBI was a good choice.

To be admitted to the class of new agents one had to pass a written exam, be recommended after an interview by an experienced Bureau official, and survive an extensive background check. Later on, when I conducted such "new applicant" checks, I understood how thoroughly the FBI evaluated the family, schooling, experience and moral fiber of those who wished to carry one of the Bureau's gold badges.

Fifty of us began classes in Washington, D.C. I was the youngest, and more than a bit brash. Instructors told us 10 to 20 percent of the class would wash out. We were issued what was repeatedly described as "Bureau property"—credentials, badge, two briefcases (one with a secure lock), various manuals, and a .38 pistol. Only God would be able to help us if we lost this Bureau property. One morning we were given exactly sixty minutes in which to buy a Western-style belt to hold up our holster, a snap-brim hat, several white shirts and other appurtenances of the well-dressed FBI agent. During this time we were also to pack for our trip to Quantico, Virginia, and eat lunch. Along with most of the other novices, I managed this trick somehow. In his haste, one guy left his Bureau-property briefcase in a taxi, and was crucified for the blunder.

At the FBI training center on the Marine base at Quantico, we began intensive study—classes were from 9:00 A.M. to 9:00 P.M. Monday through Saturday, with a half-day on Sunday. I believe the FBI packed more into sixteen weeks than a college offered in a year. And unlike most boot-camp experiences, the Quantico program was directly relevant to our later work in the field.

If the training was superb, it was also purposely difficult. After only two or three of us passed the first exam, we were told that we were the dumbest bunch ever to be allowed near a gold badge, but that because so many of us had failed, there'd be a makeup exam on Monday. We crammed all weekend, only to find the Monday test was easier than the one we'd failed; the first one had been a deliberate move to scare the hell out of us.

Two ideas were continually drummed into us: pride at membership in an elite organization, and fear of failure. Eventually these two became completely intertwined and inseparable feelings. Inculcation of fear began on our first day, and dread of our superiors' wrath never let up during my whole career in the FBI. We were constantly afraid of earning the displeasure of Hoover—who, we learned, could fire any of us at any time for any infraction of the multitudinous rules that governed the conduct of an FBI man, on or off the job. Unlike other government employees, we in the FBI were not covered by many civil service protections.

We were expected to be better in every category than ordinary lawmen. We knew more about firearms. We knew how to behave in the courtroom—to stand erect to take the oath, to testify impartially as to the facts in simple language cleansed of legalisms that might confuse the jury and in a voice loud enough so that all might be able to hear. It was to be "Yes, sir," and "No, sir," to all citizens, regardless of their station. To a much greater degree than most policemen and many prosecutors, we knew and continually reviewed the wording, intent and details of all the statutes the FBI had in its purview. We submitted all our own work to rigorous examination; we developed facts and legal evidence in such a way that their validity would be self-evident; we wrote our reports with logic and clarity.

In the classes we learned about fascism, Communism, the Ku Klux Klan and other extremist groups. We attended lectures on the Abwehr, the Russian KGB and GRU, and the intelligence agencies of "friendly" countries. We were instructed in jujitsu and in the lifting of fingerprints off various surfaces. We worked the Bureau's cameras. We spent time in the well-known FBI laboratories, which performed tests for our field agents and for police departments countrywide.

Training. Discipline. Pride. In Hoover's hands, fear had a salutary purpose: to build a strong and remarkably incorruptible organization. Fear made us tougher, proud to be able to endure and live with the strict standards and stringent discipline of the FBI. Our self-esteem became interconnected with the FBI's image, and we took strength from our membership in the organization. We believed in the mission of the Bureau—to defend the nation from enemies without and criminals within—and we believed in ourselves, the highly trained special agents who could accomplish the difficult tasks set for the FBI.

As I look back on my classmates and on the agents with whom I worked in my first few years in the FBI, I can see that we were, in a phrase, middle Americans. Many came from small towns in the Midwest, the South and the West; most of us were Protestants, with only a sprinkling of Jews, though with a good percentage of Catholics. With rare exceptions, we were all white. We were a politically conservative bunch, and extremely patriotic. We believed in, and reflected, the views of Director Hoover and much of the FBI hierarchy —we were anti-Nazi, anti-Communist, anti any of the "isms" on the right and the left. Fervent admirers of hard work, discipline, high moral and ethical behavior, we were entirely convinced of the supremacy of the American system of laws and economics. If we were "straight arrows," we were proud of being so.

Near the end of our training we were assigned to the Washington, D.C., field office, then on K Street, for two weeks. We were chafing at the bit to work as special agents, but weren't yet allowed that honor. First we had to be apprenticed to an experienced agent and learn how to fill out forms—registers for signing in and out, the number 3 card to record an agent's whereabouts at each moment and the case on which he was working, and myriad other memos, forms and reports.

At Quantico we'd been told that it was our duty to inform superiors of infractions of the FBI rules by other agents. One rule prohibited people from taking a coffee break—that was stealing time from the job, "fraud on the government." We learned, however, that Washington, D.C., field agents didn't tattle about this sort of infraction, and that those agents who did tell tales were dubbed "submarines" and wouldn't last long in the FBI.

While in the field, agents were obliged to call in every two hours for messages if they were not at their permanent residence telephone number. Should one go to a movie or to a girlfriend's house, the name and number had to be left with the office; there were tests in which these emergency numbers were called. I always found that this rule weighed heavily on me. As committed to the FBI as any man could be, I didn't need a watchdog. Neither did most good agents. During my fourteen years in the Bureau, I always had the feeling that someone was looking over my shoulder, checking up on what I was doing and how I was doing it. In fact, some of the FBI discipline verged on thought control. The unfortunate impact of the stringent disciplinary system was a damping of the spirits of the men in the FBI.

One Sunday I was on my way to the movies when I decided to drop by the Washington field office. There I learned that the Japanese had just raided Pearl Harbor, and was told to report to the streets on the perimeter of the Japanese Embassy. For me and for many of my fellow agents-in-training, that infamous Sunday was our baptism of fire. Our tasks were to keep the Japanese diplomats inside the grounds of the embassy until arrangements could be made for them to leave the United States, and to prevent any Americans from venting their anger on the Japanese within the gates. This patrol work lasted two weeks, after which we returned to the classrooms of Bureau headquarters to finish up our apprenticeship; then we were individually assigned to field offices around the country.

My assignment was Birmingham, Alabama. That was FBI policy at work: send a new agent to a field office as far away as possible from the site of his upbringing, and see if he'll sink or swim. In Birmingham the special agent in charge (SAC) told me a few horror stories about mistakes made by previous men in the northern Alabama territory I was to take over, and then turned me loose, suitably warned about failure, to work on a variety of cases. Every day I faced something new. I investigated a supposed murder at a new defense plant in Huntsville. I went along on a raid of a series of brothels near an army base in Tennessee. I took part in searches of the homes of enemy aliens (they were proscribed from owning such things as shortwave radios, guns and telescopes). I helped look into suspected sabotage in coastal dockyards. We were supposed to develop as generalists, and the work in Alabama was well suited to that concept. I enjoyed it tremendously; the job kept me going at every moment, and the tasks were interesting, multifaceted and challenging.

I was having a ball, and looking back, I think I know why. In the smaller towns and cities—indeed, in most of the United States in 1942 —the FBI agent was a king. The prestige of the Bureau was at its height, and as an agent I was treated with a deference far out of proportion to my age. I had a large, efficient and powerful organization behind me, and I could call upon its resources. Citizens of all levels of society gave me their attention when I called, and local and state police afforded me friendship and respect. My credentials and gold badge were often as much authority as I needed to make an arrest; in many instances, my gun was superfluous.

In Alabama I learned the finer points of the FBI system. Locating fugitives, a difficult task, brought one commendatory attention. Early on, I was lucky and found a fugitive. Then an occasion arose on which I was able to do my SAC a good turn. After three months he rewarded me by sending me to work with the resident agent in Mobile, a suboffice under his jurisdiction. It was a small promotion. In Mobile I enjoyed an even wider latitude and responsibility for the investigations I conducted.

After seven months in Alabama, I was feeling comfortable with the job and, not incidentally, earning more money than I ever had in my life—$3,200 a year. Since I was on the road a lot, where my expenses were paid, I was able to bank some of that salary. To a boy raised in the Depression, money in the bank was a wonderful comfort.

I was just getting settled where I was, becoming familiar with my territory and the people in it, when word came down that I was being transferred to the New York field office, which was sorely in need of more agents. My previous visit to New York had not been all that pleasant, and I shared the distaste for the big city that most small-town people have. It was a wrench for me to go to New York, but of course I had to go.

. . .

New York in 1942 was raucous, frantic, ultramodern. I missed the gentle pace of the South. One bewildered mistake in the city subways and you ended up in Brooklyn rather than in the Bronx. To step off a curb and into traffic was an adventure. The most surprising thing to me was how blasé New Yorkers seemed about the war, despite continual reports of German submarines as close as twenty miles from the city.

I took a room in a hotel near Gramercy Park. It was small, and I ate most of my meals in restaurants. Footloose, I began to enjoy the city's distractions, becoming a frequent visitor to Café Society Uptown and Downtown, the Astor Roof and other nightclubs. I exercised in the gym at the Downtown Athletic Club, which had a special wartime rate for the FBI. I joined a makeshift FBI basketball team and played games against local colleges; in a season of having college guys run my pants off, my weight dropped to a new low.

The New York field office was the FBI's largest and busiest, with one thousand of the Bureau's seven thousand agents, and, instead of a SAC as its head, a full assistant director. I found I had less latitude and personal responsibility for cases than in Alabama, and worked on a squad with other men. I didn't much like that, or the "new app" investigations on which I was put for a while. Fortunately, I was then transferred to more interesting work.

The FBI believed in loading its agents with cases, and every case required a lot of paperwork. A report had to be rendered on each case every forty-five days. A towrope that had been lost from a government tugboat became as much of a paperwork burden as finding an out-of-state murder suspect.

It seemed to us that, as others have later documented, Director Hoover continually sought bigger and better statistics for the Bureau; each year there had to be more investigations handled, more fugitives located, more convictions, more property recovered. To some degree we agents were forced to choose among the cases that awaited our immediate attention. We usually applied our energies to those we felt had the greatest potential, and gave less attention to others; even on the "back-burner" ones, though, we filed periodic reports after covering one or two minor leads.

In New York, in three and a half years, I made between four hundred and five hundred arrests, mostly on Selective Service cases. That's a large number of arrests, and an indication of how much time I spent on the streets. I learned that in New York, displaying your credentials wasn't the automatic door-opener it was in Alabama. In

New York, FBI agents were forced to be more ingenious—and maybe a little tougher. Frequently, when I started an interview, nobody knew anything about anybody; I often wondered whether any New Yorker would admit to having seen his or her neighbor in the previous six months. So I asked nicely, cajoled, wheedled and got tough with people in proportion to how they treated my inquiries.

A few times I had to tell a recalcitrant man that we'd have to continue our interview downtown since he wasn't cooperating with us where he was; usually he then agreed to give us the information before we actually made the trip. Another ploy that I had occasion to use on certain questionable people was to say that if they refused to cooperate, the FBI might have to look into *their* affairs after we'd finished with the matter in hand.

This sort of pressure was only to get us information; after we'd obtained it, we'd leave the interviewee alone and go on our way. Actually, obtaining information often proved more difficult than making arrests. I remember once that two of us went to arrest a man in Brooklyn who was a known member of the Toledo Purple gang, and who was wanted on a murder charge. As soon as we told him he was under arrest, he said we'd have no trouble with him. He even offered to help us fix a flat that our car developed; we declined his gracious offer of assistance.

Incidentally, we arrested that man, not on the murder rap, but rather because he was in violation of the Selective Service Act.

Most of my arrests had to do with Selective Service Act violations, and occasionally draft dodgers had other charges pending against them; we attempted to have the most serious of the charges prosecuted, regardless of jurisdiction. New York Local Selective Service Board Number 1, on whose cases I worked, had more delinquents than any other local board in the country because of its location, astride the Bowery (New York's skid row) and Chinatown.

Not all the draft cases consisted of dodgers. I assisted in the first case of a Selective Service Board member to be prosecuted for selling his influence to keep people out of the army. In another important case, by diligent investigation we broke up a ring of eleven guards at the Brooklyn Port of Embarkation who were pilfering and reselling materials that were supposed to go to the war effort in Europe.

At times, however, in spite of such interesting matters as German saboteurs, draft dodgers and thieving guards, I'd get the feeling that I was missing the war. Maybe, I thought, I should quit the FBI and join G-2 (army intelligence) or naval intelligence. FBI agents were exempt from the draft, and some outsiders felt agents were shirking their patriotic duty by staying in the FBI rather than being in the military. In fact, some agents made clear their intentions to leave the Bureau when the war was over. One time, in the midst of thoughts about the front lines, I got a letter from my brother Art, who told me he thought I was doing more for the war effort in the FBI in New York than he was doing in the service as he sat on a deserted Pacific atoll. That helped.

Having worked many Chinese-American draft cases, I came to know Chinatown better than any other FBI agent in New York City. I developed contacts within the various family groups and the On Leong Tong, the Hip Sing Tong and the Chinese Merchants Association, who assisted me in straightening out Selective Service mix-ups. In Chinatown there were many men who'd changed their names in order to get into this country, then changed them back once they got in.

My contacts in the community helped me solve one big case, that of a shakedown of Chinese merchants by a renegade U.S. Treasury agent by the name of Thomas John Whelan. This guy would make unannounced visits to Chinese merchants during which he'd check the books, ostensibly for records of Social Security payments on behalf of the merchant's employees. Invariably finding that no such payments had been made to the government, Whelan would threaten the merchant with jail—unless he got five hundred or a thousand dollars to forget what he'd seen. A dozen merchants had been hit before I got wind of the shakedown. With cooperation from the Chinese Merchants Association I managed to stop the scheme and to arrest Whelan, but he never went to jail. The political connections that had gotten him his job in the first place served to delay the trial for some time. In fact, it wasn't until seven years after I had arrested Whelan—long after I'd transferred to Bureau headquarters in Washington—that the bribe-taker died of a heart attack; he was still under indictment, but his case had never come to trial.

I was reluctant to go to the Soviet Espionage squad. I liked criminal cases, and after working on some as interesting and personally rewarding as the Chinatown shakedown, I wanted to continue doing them. On criminal cases you could do a good job and have a sense of completion. Soviet Espionage was Siberia time: the enemy just went on and on; when you got rid of one spy, another would take his place. How would you get satisfaction? And another thing: the cases handled by the SE squad seemed to be mostly old ones on which little was breaking.

Actually, my initial attitude toward Soviet Espionage was similar to that held by many of my fellow agents. Only a small fraction of the New York field office—fifty or sixty men out of a thousand—was concerned with Soviet espionage, and few agents outside the squad really knew or cared much about Soviet spies.

Then there was the supervisor of the squad, Bob Granville: he happened to have been a year ahead of me in the University of Idaho's law school, and I'd known him almost all of my life. I and many others in the field office considered Bob to be one of the careful and cautious types. I didn't know if I really wanted to work for him.

There was also the problem of physical surveillance. I hated to do that, and it seemed that physical surveillance was a lot of what the SE squad did. There were some men who actually liked such work; it kept them out of the office and out of trouble. After three and a half years in the FBI, I could at least understand the attitude of those who liked standing in doorways and sitting in Bureau automobiles. There were agents in the Bureau who did what was asked of them, kept their heads down, handed in a lot of paper and initiated very little. Fortunately, the majority of the FBI's agents were, by nature, hard workers and damned good at their jobs. These men wouldn't take no for an answer; they were curious, patient, painstaking and thorough in their approach to cases. These were the agents who often could and did make the difference between success and failure.

I wanted to be with the aggressive ones, not the men who liked surveillance—and I didn't start liking Soviet Espionage until I found that my friend Don Jardine, one of the good men, had started working with Soviet Espionage months before I was assigned to the squad. Jardine and I had been colleagues on General Criminal and on Selective Service; we had survived a block of ice dropped at us in Harlem. Jardine was a big man, a lawyer from Minneapolis–St. Paul who seemed to get a lot of enjoyment out of life. On the job he made many wisecracks and seemed to be a frustrated race-car driver: good behind the wheel, he loved nothing better than racing New York cab drivers for a one-space-wide lane between cars. He put more than one cab up on a curb but never scratched the paint on a Bureau car.

Jardine and some of the others taught me that a Soviet Espionage man could be ingenious as well as aggressive. Once, the squad needed to know what was in a suspected Soviet agent's briefcase. In what might be described now as James Bond style, the squad pulled a classic switch. Locating a copy of the man's briefcase, they substituted it for the original while the guy was at a conference, photographed the contents of the real one and restored the original to its position. The man never even noticed that it was gone.

Years later, when I had more experience in the FBI, I came to appreciate in retrospect how good the agents on the Soviet Espionage squad really were. They were quite a bunch of young men, eager for action and willing to go to any lengths to do a good job. To the outside world, then as now, they were faceless foot soldiers in an unseen war, and history doesn't know their names. But to me they were excellent comrades-in-arms, people on whom I relied in a fight that consumed every ounce of our intelligence and energy.

My closest friend in the Bureau became Emory Gregg, a practicing attorney in Battle Creek, Michigan, before he joined the Bureau in 1942. Emory was another big man, strong and thick-chested; both of us were intolerant of stupidity and had tempers that didn't always stay under control. It was Emory who assigned agents to physical surveillance duty; he knew I disliked having to do such work on a regular basis, but understood that I could be counted on to work odd hours, evenings and weekends to fill in during emergencies. Francis X. Plant was another good friend; as Whittaker Chambers later characterized him, he was a "walking archive of the identities, features and peculiarities of Soviet agents." The fact that he could relax and go to sleep in a car just by putting his head back always amazed me. Jack Ward, a Boston Irishman with a dry wit, later became our historian of Soviet intelligence. John Malone, another dedicated man, rose quite high in the Bureau hierarchy; he used to tip his hat when he passed a Catholic church, and didn't quite know what to do when several of us Protestants started to do the same. Scotty Miller was a Texan, and bright; he was good at long interrogations, and you'll see his name on some important ones later in this book. Harvey Rath was another gem, but we lost him: he was so intelligent that after he'd designed a baby crib gadget while out of the office recuperating from an illness, he was hired away from the FBI by a toy manufacturer.

We were the up-and-coming idealists of the squad—but in early 1945 we were just a bunch of young agents, and hardly recognized the impact of what we were trying to do. To me, especially, the whole field was new, and I was only beginning to love its challenge.

Knowledge of the Soviet threat to the United States, and of my task in trying to counter that threat, came to me in stages. For example, before joining the SE squad, as with most people in the world, I'd never heard of an "atomic bomb." However, on coming on board the squad I was made privy to the secret of the Manhattan Project, principally because we were trying to stop an ongoing Soviet effort to steal atomic bomb information. Knowing in part what the bomb could do—nobody really knew the totality of it then—made me doubly aghast at the possibility that the Soviets might be able to obtain its secret from us by stealth.

When I came on board, my colleagues on the squad were watching a Soviet agent named Arthur Alexandrovich Adams; months before the first atomic bomb was due to be tested, he had gotten Clarence Hiskey, an employee of the Chicago radiation laboratory, to give him some atomic-bomb-related data.

The FBI had learned a good deal about Adams, who had apparently been in and out of the country since 1927, but couldn't move against him for lack of legal evidence. However, he could be tailed, and since he lived in New York, that task fell to my squad. Our agents followed Adams around the clock. The problem was that he was well aware of the coverage and kept a low profile. Once he even tried to make his escape from the country; avoiding our surveillance, he got all the way out to Portland, Oregon, and a pier that would have taken him onto a Soviet ship. On the dock, though, he saw some waiting FBI agents and simply reversed his footsteps and took the next train back to New York.

I may have been a neophyte, but the blanket surveillance of Adams and the half-dozen people associated with him seemed to me rather useless. The man knew he was being tailed, and wasn't going to renew his contacts. Wasn't that a waste of manpower?

Adams, of course, wasn't the only Soviet agent trying to obtain atomic secrets. We had hard evidence that American Communists working with Soviet consular employees in San Francisco had tried to get data from the laboratory of J. Robert Oppenheimer. Some of the people involved in the unsuccessful effort had New York connections, and our squad handled them. (More about one of these in a later chapter.)

Then there was Andrei Shevchenko, an engineer for Amtorg, the Russian commercial trading company—which, like Tass, the Soviet Government Purchasing Commission and the Soviet consulate, was (I learned) a cover for many spies. Shevchenko was gathering classified information from American citizens in Buffalo and in Philadelphia. It didn't concern the atomic bomb, but it did deal with aircraft production and other military matters. The FBI knew of his activities because the Americans whom he'd approached had told us of his overtures. Now Don Jardine was running these people as double agents against the Soviets. I watched and learned as Don carefully fed Shevchenko certain data—and then was as upset as the rest of my colleagues when, after Jardine had amassed enough evidence to convict Shevchenko, Justice consulted with the State Department and the decision was made not to arrest Shevchenko but to allow him to leave the country. International political repercussions were feared if we arrested and tried a Soviet national during wartime when Russia was our ally—though I've never understood to this day what we had to fear from exposing a spy.

Adams and Shevchenko, who both worked for the GRU (Red Army Intelligence), were actual Soviet spies whom I could see right there in front of me in New York City, toiling away against the interests of the United States. This was no faraway or invisible enemy, it was two trained spies on my doorstep. My attitude on the Soviet threat to our security began to change as I was confronted with particulars such as the existence of these two Soviet agents. The danger was visible and palpable. It was a strange feeling to realize that only a handful of people in New York knew about these Soviet spies—but that realization only made me feel my responsibilities more keenly. I knew they were spies, and it was my task to try to do something about them, no matter how frustrating the attempt might be.

I thirsted for more details about the Soviets, our allies and adversaries. I remember that we were trying to arrange for the defection of another Amtorg employee, a man who was about to be called home to Moscow in disgrace. Punishment and possible execution awaited him there; even so, the man told the White Russian who was our persuader that he couldn't bring himself to defect at the last moment, because he wasn't sure that he could "make it" in a capitalist society. What sort of system produced that effect on people?

I read our own reports on what recent defector Victor Kravchenko, a Soviet Government Purchasing Commission employee, had told the agents on my squad. I was struck by his description of the Soviet system with its rigid security and lack of freedom; he painted vividly the horrors of living under Communism. I could see what the future might hold if the Soviets succeeded in their struggle against us. My impressions were fortified by reading such books as Arthur Koestler's *Darkness at Noon*, and by reports of the Soviet purges of the late 1930s. The idea that Stalin could have ordered the liquidation of tens of thousands of people, of the entire upper echelon of the Red Army, and of almost all of the old Bolsheviks, and banished millions to Siberia, astounded me.

I sought impressions of Soviet intelligence everywhere I could find them. When on a surveillance with a more knowledgeable agent, I'd steer the conversation to the background of a case and sop it up. For instance, at one point we were still looking into people who'd been associated, many years earlier, with Robert Switz, a wealthy American who'd operated for the Russians in the United States and in France in the 1930s, together with Lydia Stahl and spymaster Valentin Markovich. Switz had also been connected with a separate attempt to obtain American Panama Canal defense information through Robert Osman. After Switz was caught, he confessed and led authorities to twenty-nine others in the United States and France, some of whom also admitted their activities. We were still tailing a few of the people in Switz's orbit to see if they were active. Hearing about such people as Switz, I'd make it my business to go into our office, after hours, and read files. I was determined to understand the structure, intent and threat of the KGB.

Espionage and underground networks were ingrained in the character of the Soviet regime, it seemed. For years prior to the 1917 revolution the leaders operated secretly; once the Bolsheviks seized power they made espionage and a secret police force important elements in their own government. This force shifted names many times, from the OGPU to the NKVD, the NKGB, and the MGB before it became the KGB; through all the nomenclature changes it retained the same dread character while its power increased until it was a dominating force in Russian society. By the 1940s the organization encompassed border guards, railroad police and forest patrolmen as well as men who peered over the shoulders of Russians inside the country and those who spied on foreign countries. The KGB became the entity closest to what George Orwell described in *1984* as the "thought police." It was believed to have massive dossiers on Russian citizens and on all members of foreign Communist Parties. It controlled the "Gulag archipelago" and the whole of Siberia. Its functions included and went far beyond those performed inside the United States by the FBI, Immigration Service, Customs Department, border patrols and the National Guard, and outside the United States by the Central Intelligence Agency (CIA). The KGB virtually controlled the embassies as well as the various trading corporations, press service offices and other Soviet links to the outside world. It was known to have an experienced assassination division.

In the late 1940s we in the FBI had only partial glimpses of what later arrests and defections would document about the KGB. But we knew even then that there were KGB rings operating inside Germany, Switzerland, France, Holland, Belgium, Sweden, England, Australia, Canada and the United States—just to cite cases that have subsequently been made public. Consider the example of Sweden: all during the 1940s five KGB networks there worked to pass to the U.S.S.R. every single detail of Sweden's national defenses. When some of the spies were caught, it was learned that the Soviets also had saboteurs and explosives hidden inside Sweden, and in case war broke out between the two countries, the Soviets could have immediately knocked out the Swedish railroads and communications facilities to gain a decided advantage in the conflict.

Gradually, in my mind, the image of an amorphous, omnipotent KGB began to resolve into that of a dangerous adversary that operated with specific human beings as agents—some of whom had brushed very close to the FBI. In a later period there were 400,000 employees and 90,000 officers of the KGB worldwide, but most were concentrated inside Russia. As might be imagined, only the most trusted and experienced officers were sent to such sensitive areas as the United States.

It seemed clear from our files that much of the KGB's espionage in the United States in the 1930s and 1940s could be traced to two Soviet "residents," Vassili Zubilin and Gaik Ovakimian. When I was a young agent, I read up on them, and later—indeed, throughout my whole career in the FBI—I spent my time chasing after their handiwork. These men became something like totems for me, symbols of the adversary whom we were forever trying to locate and eliminate. Although they were people of the shadows, they were not faceless; I learned their faces, and tried to discern what I could about their characters.

The one who troubled me most was Gaik Badalovich Ovakimian, whom the FBI had pinpointed as head of the KGB's activities in the United States from 1933 to 1941. He had vanished before I even came into the game, but for many years I tracked the agents he had put into place. He was often referred to as "the wily Armenian," and it was a measure of his slipperiness that it was never completely clear whether or not he really was an Armenian.

The official documents showed that Ovakimian was born on August 11, 1898, in Russia. Rather small and stocky—five foot seven, 165 pounds—he had a medium-dark complexion with dark-brown hair and blue eyes. He was educated as an engineer, and spoke somewhat broken English as well as German, French and Russian. He was married to a woman named Vera, and they had a daughter, Egina. In the 1930s the FBI had uncovered an extensive industrial espionage operation tied to a man named Armand Labis Feldman, who was connected to Ovakimian. Then his name cropped up in conjunction with a case that originated in England with a man who had a false passport in the name of Willy Brandes.

As we later learned, Ovakimian's recruits were scattered as far afield as Mexico and Canada; some of his exploits involved forged passports and attempts on Leon Trotsky's life while the former Soviet leader was in exile in Mexico. Americans whom Ovakimian recruited or controlled described him as charming, serious, sympathetic, well read in English literature, knowledgeable in science, and a man who inspired loyalty in his agents. He must also have been agile and politically aware, for he survived the great purges of the late 1930s which decimated the upper ranks of the Russian espionage services.

Ovakimian was known to be in close contact with Jacob Golos, the head of World Tourist, Inc., a Communist-dominated organization in New York. In May 1941, the FBI closed in on Ovakimian and arrested him; he was charged with being a foreign agent who had not registered as such with the Department of Justice. At that point the Bureau had identified a number of his agents, and might possibly have rolled up several of his networks—including Golos and other people at World Tourist—but international considerations intervened. The State Department knew that a half-dozen Americans were being detained in Russia, and struck a deal whereby they would be exchanged for Ovakimian. As a result, the KGB man was allowed to leave the United States in July 1941.

Ovakimian might well have laughed at us over that one, for by the time of his deportation Germany had attacked its former ally, Russia, and several of the Americans in the deal were captured by the advancing Third Reich and never reached the United States. As I recall, none of the Americans in Russian hands had been spies, and in any event, the Russians welched on other parts of the deal and did not return to us the Americans whom the Germans missed. The whole affair was a mess, and my colleagues in New York who handled the case were thoroughly disgusted with the State Department over it. Later, reading over the 164-page summary report on Ovakimian, I was impressed by how much the FBI had been able to find out about the man—and was depressed by the fact that we had been forced to let him go.

Vassili Zubilin—alias Zarubin, alias Luchenko, alias Peter, alias Cooper, alias Edward Joseph Herbert—was another character from the shadows. All evidence pointed to the notion that he became the chief KGB resident in the United States after Ovakimian's departure. Zubilin and his wife, Elizabetha, were veteran KGB officers whose espionage activities dated back to the 1920s and had taken them all over the world. Zubilin was stocky and blond, with a broad-featured face and a manner that, according to those who had dealt with him, could be alternately pleasant and menacing. He operated from a position as third secretary of the Russian embassy in Washington.

As to his exploits, he seems to have been more of a "fixer" than Ovakimian, but perhaps this is because it was in this role that the FBI had caught more glimpses of him. We knew people who had worked with him at various times in Hollywood, San Francisco, New York and Washington. He was involved in everything from using a film company as a front to funnel money to clandestine activities, to attempted atomic espionage. Zubilin's personality seems to have been more outgoing and less cerebral than Ovakimian's—but both men survived the purges. Zubilin's name cropped up in a number of cases, and during my time in New York we charted his comings and goings and tailed him when the manpower was available. We tried to learn what he was doing; most of the time we didn't know. In later years, after he had left the United States, we heard that he had been made a general in the KGB, and that he had died an alcoholic.

Trying to counter the work of Ovakimian and Zubilin was a task full of frustration and repeated failures, with only occasional and partial successes—a pattern reflective of the difficulties the FBI experienced in fighting the KGB at the outset of the postwar period. In this intense but nearly invisible combat, counterintelligence was playing catch-up ball; the Soviets had built up an early lead and the FBI, new to the endeavor, was not as knowledgeable or as sophisticated as the enemy.

One evening in 1946 my friend Emory Gregg and I were bemoaning the fact that although we knew the top GRU man in New York (Pavel Mikhailov, the consul general), we had not been able to identify the leading KGB agents. Emory and I were aggressive and young, and had a lot of ideas for actions the Bureau ought to be taking against the KGB, but we didn't have much clout within the organization because we were just foot soldiers. This night we resolved to try something new.

The FBI thought that the U.S. headquarters for the KGB was in the Soviet consulate on East Sixty-first Street, a block off Central Park, and believed that the top KGB man, called the "resident," was in that consulate. Our knowledge of the Soviet espionage system suggested that while strings were ultimately pulled from Moscow, the New York resident had the power to develop targets of espionage, to enforce discipline within his own ranks and to insist on full reports from subordinates. Under the resident's direction, coded cables would be sent to Moscow (more bulky papers went in a section of the diplomatic pouch), and at his behest logs were maintained which noted the location and substance of all meetings between espionage agents and recruits. We knew a lot about the resident's job, but we didn't know his identity.

I went to see old Mr. Boguslav, a friendly White Russian émigré who had a son in the FBI and a warm spot in his heart for all special agents. Through having spent hours and hours as a translator of materials that our coverage on the Soviets provided, Boguslav came to know many of the personalities of the Soviet employees. Boguslav had two candidates for KGB agents—Stepan Choudenko and Anatoli Yakovlev, both middle- to low-level officials who were accorded a respect by other employees that was out of proportion to their official status. For instance, "Bullet-head," the close-cropped doorman who we were sure was a KGB man, was quite deferential when these men entered or left the premises. And both of them seemed to have greater freedom than usual to come and go as they pleased—most of the Soviets stayed at their desks and were highly restricted in their movements.

Boguslav's choices fit the pattern of what we knew about the KGB, and we opened investigations into both Yakovlev and Choudenko, logging their movements, taking new surveillance photos of them, noting who talked to them. Though these were not all-out investigations, they did give the men more attention than we'd previously been able to pay to them.

In the evenings, or at other odd times, when I had extra hours of my own, I'd tail Yakovlev. I got no pay for this, nor did any of the other special agents who pitched in, though we did get overtime credit, which was important in the Bureau system. It was just a guess made by a couple of aggressive young guys and an old White Russian, but we gave it everything we had. Another SA and I would pair up and follow our man around.

It became clear quite quickly that Yakovlev was a professional in the intelligence game. He had seemingly casual but very effective ways of checking to see if he was being followed. He'd never fully glance over his shoulder, for instance, but would stand at street crossings, or look into a store window from such a position that he'd be able to tell if someone behind him appeared too often. These "natural" moves only became obvious when we observed Yakovlev make them several times in the course of half an hour. The disadvantage for Yakovlev of this kind of checking behavior was that it precluded the use of truly evasive maneuvers such as going in one door of a hotel and out another, or going up one department-store escalator and down the next, until anybody tailing him had either been definitively "made" or lost.

One evening in early 1946 another agent and I waited in a car for Yakovlev to come out of the consulate. If he emerged and went to his upper Manhattan apartment, we said to ourselves, we'd quit for the night and go home. Yakovlev appeared, nodded to Bullethead, and walked down the street away from us, chatting with another consular employee. He was recognizable even a block away by his full head of hair, a lock of which was usually falling down over his forehead. He was a young man, not much older than we were, with a wife and twin girls who had been born in the United States. He seemed almost too boyish to be a top KGB man. Getting out of the car, we followed the two Soviets; each of us took a side of the street and we kept only a loose rein on them, not wanting to be made.

It was near twilight. Yakovlev and his companion strode along the border of Central Park; this was the elegant part of town, with rich old brownstones on the side streets, and hotels like the Plaza and the Pierre along Central Park South and Fifth Avenue. We passed well-dressed men coming home from their offices, walking in that purposeful way that many New Yorkers seem to affect, regardless of the time of day. In this world there are striders and strollers—Yakovlev and his fellow Soviet were strolling, this night. I guessed where they were heading: to a Swedish smorgasbord restaurant that was a favorite watering hole for visiting Russians. Many of them liked to fill up on the restaurant's generous portions; there was still near-famine in Moscow, but in New York, now that the war was over and rationing was behind us, the smorgasbord was bountiful.

The main attraction was a huge turntable on which the platters slowly rotated; half the turntable was behind the kitchen wall, and partially empty serving plates would disappear into the wall while new, full ones would emerge on the other side. We allowed time for the Soviets to enter the restaurant, to go around the revolving smorgasbord and to find seats, and then we went in ourselves and got our dinner. As we were on our own time and not the Bureau's, the check wouldn't be put on any expense voucher, but we didn't care. I had the feeling that something would happen this evening, though I didn't know what.

In order to finish our meal and go back out onto the street before the Russians did, we had to hurry. By the time Yakovlev and his companion left the restaurant, we were waiting for them, out of sight. At the door the two men separated and Yakovlev headed downtown. We let the other man go and followed Yakovlev by foot all the way to Times Square.

I'd tailed a few people to Times Square for the FBI. Back in 1942, I briefly followed a suspected German spy who liked to frequent the area to look at the prostitutes, but who never seemed capable of bringing himself to approach any of them; I'd thought about paying a hooker for the guy and shoving her in his path, just to put him out of his misery. But Yakovlev wasn't looking for a prostitute. We discovered he was heading straight for the one movie theater in town that showed Russian-language films. I noticed that it was a featuring a documentary about the Red Army's triumphant parade in Moscow after the close of hostilities in Europe.

Yakovlev bought a ticket and went inside. After a few minutes we followed and found seats several rows behind Yakovlev, in the middle of the theater. The place was about one-quarter full. It seemed simple to keep Yakovlev in view, and I became engrossed in the film —all those marching men, those women in kerchiefs, those battle-scarred tanks. A few minutes later I was startled to discover that Yakovlev was gone. Hurriedly we looked around the darkened theater and spotted the telltale shock of hair in a seat nearer the screen. He had just changed seats. I was relieved; at least we hadn't lost him.

But the seat to which Yakovlev had moved seemed an odd choice —well forward, and over to one side. It wasn't as good a place from which to view the film as the first seat had been. I didn't take my eyes off him during the remainder of the film. He didn't brush against anyone, didn't speak with anyone, and generally appeared to be doing nothing of interest. When the film ended, Yakovlev left the theater and took a subway to his apartment. We followed him to the building, and then went home ourselves. There had been nothing unusual about the evening except that strange shift of seats in the movie theater. That bothered me, and I wondered why he had made the move.

Shortly thereafter, Yakovlev left the United States. He returned briefly in the summer of 1946, and then went home again and never came back to the United States.

Four years went by before I was able to know definitively what had happened that night in 1946 at the movie theater. We in the FBI had become more sophisticated and aggressive in counterintelligence, and by 1950 began to make headway against the KGB. I was at FBI headquarters and was personally and very deeply involved in the investigations that uncovered the atomic espionage of Klaus Fuchs, Harry Gold and David Greenglass, because I was working with deciphered KGB cables that allowed us to penetrate the enemy's secrets.

That summer of 1950, when we broke into the network of people surrounding Julius Rosenberg, I finally came to fully understand Yakovlev's actions in the movie theater. David Greenglass told the FBI that his brother-in-law, Julius, had once confided that he used to leave messages and material for his Soviet controller underneath one particular seat in the theater in Manhattan that showed Russian-language films. In the lingo of espionage, that night Yakovlev had probably been emptying a dead drop.

We also found out that summer that Yakovlev had been the KGB controller both for Harry Gold and for the Rosenbergs. In the realm of counterintelligence, though, there are many things one never knows for sure, even long after the battles have been fought. For instance, I never did prove to my own satisfaction that Anatoli Yakovlev was the KGB resident in New York—he may have simply been one of the resident's top employees. Whichever, Yakovlev did plenty of damage to the United States during his tenure here. So it is with more than a bit of chagrin that I look back on that evening when I watched the film of the Red Army parading through the streets of Moscow, and didn't fully understand how close I was brushing to an important espionage transaction between a KGB controller and one of his agents.

3
TWO DEFECTORS

I N THE FALL OF 1945 there were two defections from the
ranks of Soviet espionage in North America that sent
shock waves through all of the Western countries' intelligence agencies, and through the Soviet intelligence establishment
as well. At the time I was only peripherally involved in the matters
of Igor Gouzenko and of Elizabeth Bentley, but these cases were so
important, and impinged on many of my later cases in so many ways,
that I want to describe them briefly here, as they appeared to us at
the time.

We in the FBI learned of the defection of Soviet GRU cipher clerk
Igor Gouzenko in Ottawa, Canada, a few days after it happened in
September 1945. The story was this: Gouzenko had been planning an
escape almost since the day he arrived in Canada in 1943; in the
summer of 1945, he made a clumsy mistake and was reprimanded by
his superior and by Moscow GRU, which demanded that he be sent
home. Knowing of the orders that he was to be returned to the Soviet
Union, on the evening of September 5 Gouzenko sorted through
many secret telegrams in the embassy's cipher room and lifted out
those he had previously dog-eared as important; these he stuffed
inside his clothes, together with some key pages from his superior's

handwritten diary. Then he managed to make his way out of the embassy without incident.

The next twenty-four hours were a nightmare for Gouzenko, because neither the Ottawa *Journal* nor the lower-level bureaucrats at the Canadian government's Department of External Affairs were prepared to believe his story. One of the most telling things, to me, was the attitude of the Canadian government, as revealed in a later-published diary entry of the time by Prime Minister W. L. Mackenzie King: the idea that the Russians might be spying on Canada came as a complete shock; the PM wasn't sure that Gouzenko ought to be taken into protective custody because he feared such an action might make Russia break relations with Canada! So it was not until the following night that Gouzenko was taken in hand by the Royal Canadian Mounted Police—and that happened only as the Russians were in the process of breaking down his apartment door in order to take him back by force.

In a secret hideaway Gouzenko was debriefed by the RCMP, aided by officials from the FBI and from British Intelligence. His accusations, and the papers in his shirt, showed that the security of Canada, Great Britain and the United States had been breached in many ways. The GRU had had spies in the Canadian Department of External Affairs' cipher room, as well as in various branches of the Canadian military and the Canadian National Research Council—all of which worked closely with their counterparts in the other English-speaking democracies on radar, on the new RDX explosive and on aspects of the atomic bomb. For example, the telegrams Gouzenko carried revealed that British scientist Alan Nunn May, while working in Canada, had handed over to the GRU many pieces of research about the atomic bomb, as well as an actual sample of U-235 which had probably come from an American laboratory.

Other telegrams showed that the GRU had organized many "cells" in Canada which reported to Gouzenko's superior, Colonel Nicolai Zabotin, through "cut-outs," or intermediaries. One such telegram requested information on two dozen different technical subjects, all military related. In answer to this one, a Zabotin recruit in the Radio Branch of the National Research Council was asked to get details on a photo flash bomb and some special lenses being developed for aerial photography at night. The initial request was in July; by late August, Zabotin could announce to Moscow that he was sending a courier to Russia with seventeen "top secret documents (English,

American and Canadian)" amounting to seven hundred pages, all of which dealt with secret scientific and military-research topics.

Another target was strictly military information. An August 1945 telegram directed Zabotin to have someone find out about the transfer of American troops from Europe back to the United States and to the Pacific, and to establish the locations of certain U.S. armored and infantry divisions.

The pages from Zabotin's diary were his handwritten notes of a briefing he'd been given by his immediate predecessor as GRU chief in Ottawa. These pages gave details on how people in the "net" had been recruited. Nearly all had come from within the ranks of the Canadian Communist Party; many, though not all, were Jewish and, the diary said, had been recruited by an appeal that suggested that in the dark days of war, Jews should be made to believe that Soviet Russia was the only country really fighting the anti-Semitism of Hitler.

Even though Alan Nunn May had been quickly identified from Gouzenko's material, authorities in the Western democracies decided he should not be arrested immediately because some of the telegrams detailed proposed meetings in London between Nunn May and a new Soviet contact, and the intelligence services wanted to see if these rendezvous would take place. When no meetings occurred, Nunn May was taken into custody, and later confessed to his part in the espionage. In Canada a dozen other people were also apprehended, and some of them confessed as well. Almost two dozen Soviet nationals, now known to be spies, were sent home. It was an enormous national issue in Canada, and shock waves reached the United States and Great Britain.

It was a few months, though, before those arrests were made, and in the interim I became briefly involved in one peripheral aspect of the Gouzenko case. The cover name and identity of a longtime GRU agent residing in Los Angeles on a false Canadian passport were the subject of some of the material from Zabotin's files. "Ignacy Witczak" worked as a teacher at the University of Southern California and set up clandestine GRU networks along the West Coast. We never knew his real name, but he came by the cover name in a circuitous way— the real Ignacy Witczak's passport had been taken from him by the Soviets when he went to fight with the International Brigades in the Spanish Civil War in the mid-1930s; in 1945 the GRU used this old passport to obtain a new one for their man in Los Angeles through the machinations of Sam Carr, one of Zabotin's spies but also a high official of the Canadian Labor-Progressive Party. When Gouzenko defected and Sam Carr disappeared, "Witczak" got itchy. FBI agents in Los Angeles followed him to New York, where the tail was turned over to agents from my squad—but "Witczak" had discovered the surveillance and quickly lost us.

We put fifty or sixty men out to watch his logical departure places. I spent a long and uncomfortable night at Pennsylvania Railroad Station, but it was my colleagues at the bus terminal who spotted "Witczak" as he was trying to get on a bus and leave the city. They practically surrounded him. He was a smallish man with glasses, and immediately panicked and started to run away. While the other agents kept up with him, one man got a message to the field office, and then to headquarters, describing the situation and asking for permission to bring in "Witczak" for questioning. Headquarters notified the RCMP, which asked that we *not* bring him in, lest we somehow jeopardize the cases that were just then being developed for prosecution out of the Gouzenko defection.

At nightfall "Witczak" checked into an upper Manhattan hotel. Even though it was freezing, teams of FBI agents waited all night long for him, out on the streets. They were convinced that their quarry was so nervous that if he'd been picked up he would have immediately collapsed and confessed. However, they had been ordered not to do anything like that.

My friend Don Jardine was one of those who spent the whole night on the streets, and by morning he was tired, cold and irritable. By contrast, "Witczak" had regained his composure during the night and seemed convinced that the FBI was under orders not to touch him. Coming out of the hotel, he went right up to Don Jardine and said, "Hope you had a good night's sleep."

"Get away from me, you little bastard," Jardine retorted.

"What would you do, hit me? You can't do that."

"Get moving," Jardine replied.

"You don't dare hit me."

Jardine hit him, all right, a slap across the face that sent "Witczak's" glasses flying. He picked up the glasses and hurried away. Later he headed for the train station, where he caught a train for Los Angeles. On "Witczak's" return there, West Coast agents followed him for a couple of months—though at a greater distance. After the arrests in the Gouzenko case had been made, "Witczak" managed to disappear; presumably he went back to Russia on a Soviet ship. Years later Emory Gregg, who'd become an expert on the GRU, was able to trace some of "Witczak's" prior West Coast operations; working with data unearthed by Los Angeles agents, Emory and his associates located people in California who'd worked for "Witczak," and obtained confessions from some of them.

In the fall of 1945, also, the FBI got its own break against the Soviets, one of almost equal magnitude to the defection of Gouzenko. When Elizabeth Terrill Bentley came to the FBI, her information was startling—she had been a KGB courier for some years, and had carried secret data to the Russians from U.S. government employees in the OSS, the Air Force, the War Department, the War Production Board, the Foreign Economic Administration and the departments of the Treasury, Agriculture and Commerce. This was a staggering penetration by the Soviets. Bentley's initial confession was of such moment that Director Hoover sent a digest of it immediately to the White House and to top government officials, on November 8, 1945.

My colleagues on the Soviet Espionage squad in New York, who had taken down this initial confession, were looking forward to a long series of debriefing interviews with Bentley. But almost immediately, the case was taken away from my squad because of internal politics within the Bureau. The "major case" squad that had been cleaning up matters relating to wartime German and Japanese espionage was running out of work, and the Bentley case was taken away from the experts in Soviet espionage and given to this other squad. My colleagues were disgusted at this bureaucratic move.

For much of my career in the FBI, the Bentley case intrigued me; her name kept coming up in many investigations I pursued; finally, in the 1950s, I was put in charge of the voluminous Bentley files and came to know them intimately.

Elizabeth Terrill Bentley, a well-bred New England Vassar graduate, had joined the Communist Party at the same time she began work for a master's in Italian at Columbia University, in the early 1930s. She refused pressure to work for KGB agent Juliet Poyntz Glazer, but while working in the Italian Library of Information she was shocked to discover that this organization was a fascist propaganda outlet, and offered to document her charges about it to the Communist Party. At first the CP seemed uninterested in her idea until Bentley met a man who told her that spying on the Italian library was important and that he would gladly receive any information she cared to bring out. Jacob Golos didn't make much of a first impression on Bentley—to her, initially, he was "a small, stocky man in his mid-40s . . . rather colorless and shabby"—but as she began to do secret work for him, she fell in love with him and found that he was "quick, keen, incisive . . . powerfully-built." To Bentley, Golos was "the ideal Communist."

A Russian-born, dyed-in-the-wool revolutionary, Golos was also a member of the inner circle of the CPUSA, and a KGB man. His cover was a travel agency, World Tourist, set up with Party funds furnished by Earl Browder. Golos used Bentley as a mail drop from Canadian Communists Sam Carr, Fred Rose and Tim Buck, as a contact person for the Arenal family (Mexicans, two of whose members killed Trotsky's bodyguard) and as a courier. In 1940 the World Tourist offices were raided and Golos was publicly linked to a false passport ring. Afterward Golos, whose health was deteriorating, let Bentley take over some of his duties as a controller of agents.

In this new capacity she met with such people as chemical engineer Abraham Brothman, who photocopied some of his blueprints and secret industrial processes for her to give to Golos. She began receiving material from Mary Price, a secretary to Walter Lippmann, who gave Bentley copies of material from the newsman's private files.

In 1941 the FBI arrested Gaik Ovakimian, who was Golos's superior (although Golos had never known Ovakimian's name). As a result of the arrest, Golos and Bentley were tailed for a time by the FBI, and had to lie low. Once the State Department had let Ovakimian go back to Russia, they resumed their activities.

When Germany attacked the Soviet Union in 1941, many American Communists asked Party officials how best to aid the U.S.S.R. Some were told to deliver secret materials to CPUSA officials. Among the volunteers were Russian-born Nathan Gregory Silvermaster of the Farm Security Administration, and his wife Helen; together with their many friends in government, they formed a network that gave material to Golos through Bentley. At first, in bimonthly runs to the Silvermasters' suburban Washington home, Bentley would bring back copies of documents; later she carried developed microfilms of documents; still later, as the volume increased, Bentley hauled to New York in her knitting bag as many as forty undeveloped rolls of microfilm at a time, along with lists of what documents had been photographed. The Silvermasters boasted that two of their sources were White House counselor Laughlin Currie and Assistant Treasury Secretary Harry Dexter White.

Bentley said she'd carried information on new planes for the Air Force, troop deployment, new explosives, reports on economic and political affairs in Asia and Latin America, and the secret letters home of the American ambassador to Moscow. As the war wore on, Bentley's sources multiplied. Mary Price nominated a new one, Major Duncan C. Lee, an assistant to OSS chief William Donovan. Joseph North, editor of the Communist monthly magazine *New Masses*, suggested William Walter Remington of the War Production Board, and Remington suggested Bernard Redmont, a Latin American affairs analyst. Louis Budenz, managing editor of the *Daily Worker*, furnished information coming from OSS consultant Louis Adamic. Bentley learned from Golos that Cedric Belfrage, a British Information Service officer in New York, had passed to him an instruction manual for British Intelligence agents. After Golos's death in 1943, Bentley also met a large group of men centered around Victor Perlo of the War Production Board, including John Abt, Harold Glasser and others who worked for Senate committees and executive branch departments.

She also knew about certain sources she had never actually handled. For example, in the summer of 1942, before Golos's death, she learned about the existence of a cell of engineers who reported to him. Here's how she told this to the FBI in 1945:

> I recall that on one occasion while I was driving through the lower East Side of the City of New York with GOLOS to keep a dinner engagement, he stopped the car and told me he had to meet someone. I remained in the car and saw GOLOS meet an individual on the street corner. I managed to get only a fleeting glimpse of this individual and recall that he was tall, thin, and wore hornrimmed eyeglasses. GOLOS told me that this person was one of a group of engineers and that he had given this person my residence telephone number so that he would be able to reach GOLOS whenever he desired. He did not elaborate on the activities of this person and his associates nor did he ever identify any of them except that this one man to whom he gave my telephone number was referred to as "JULIUS." However, I do not believe this was his true name. I received two or three telephone calls from JULIUS telling me he wanted to see GOLOS and relayed the message to GOLOS.

Once the "Julius" caller roused her early in the morning because he had "lost his Russian contact and wanted to enlist GOLOS' aid in getting re-established." Bentley thought "Julius" lived in the Knickerbocker Village complex in New York.

After Golos's death on Thanksgiving of 1943, the Russians soon insisted that people such as the Perlo group report directly to them, and by the spring of 1944 Bentley no longer acted as a courier to the Perlo group or to the Silvermasters; she believed, though, that these groups were reporting directly to the Russians. "Bill" replaced Golos as Bentley's own superior, and in October 1944 "Jack" replaced "Bill." "Jack" didn't seem to be Russian; he spoke English with a Brooklyn accent, and he and Bentley got along well. Bentley asked to see a higher-up, and "Jack" took her to meet "Al." Over dinner, "Al" announced that the U.S.S.R. had awarded her the Order of the Red Star; he also proposed that they sleep together. Bentley refused both honors. By January 1945 she was entirely out of being a courier and contact person for the KGB. Later in 1945, when she came to us, the FBI asked her to arrange a dinner with "Al," whom we had identified as Anatoli Gromov, first secretary of the Soviet embassy in Washington, with the hope that she could be turned back against the KGB. However, at the dinner Gromov talked only in pleasantries, and there seemed to be no chance of Bentley's rejoining the espionage apparatus.

Bentley had named more than eighty individuals as Soviet sources or agents, and said that a dozen different government agencies or government-associated groups had had their information stolen and delivered by her to the KGB. Because of the importance of her charges, Director Hoover had felt duty-bound to alert the White House, Cabinet officers and other top officials of her main accusations. But in the process of spreading Bentley's information throughout the upper echelons of the government, many of those whom Bentley had named learned of the accusations and had a chance to cease any questionable activities. And when hundreds of agents in the New York and Washington field offices mounted massive and intensive physical surveillance of all those who'd been named, this, too, had the effect of alerting the suspects and spurring them to cover their tracks.

In hindsight, these moves appear massive and clumsy, but Bentley's accusations were a pressing problem for counterintelligence in 1945–46, and the FBI had to do something about them quickly. The initial investigations did corroborate details of Bentley's stories—for instance, Harry Dexter White was observed to keep up extensive contacts with those in the Silvermaster network; the Silvermaster home was discovered to have a photo lab in the basement, as Bentley had said; people as diverse as Brothman, Perlo and Belfrage all worked in the positions and matched the descriptions Bentley had given of them; four people whom we'd suspected of being KGB agents were identified by Bentley from our photos as her former spymasters.

The problem was that, unlike Gouzenko, who brought out evidence in the form of telegrams and pages from Zabotin's diary, Bentley had nothing to backstop her stories—no documents, no microfilm, not even a gift of Russian origin which might have been traced. So very little in the way of prosecutions could be mounted, based on her recollections.

Privately, some of us were exasperated and thought we knew what could and should have been done with Bentley. I believe that very early the FBI could have forced things by moving in aggressively and interviewing everyone connected with her; in this way we might have gotten some of them to break, or to contradict one another's stories. We also could have obtained warrants and searched the Silvermaster home and the apartments of the Perlo group for evidence. No such actions were taken at the time. In addition, a number of leads were not pursued to their logical ends. For example, a cursory investigation of Abe Brothman turned up a business partner, Jules Korchein, whom the FBI thought for a time might be "Julius." But when agents discovered that Korchein didn't live in Knickerbocker Village and didn't precisely match Bentley's description of her nighttime caller, the investigation was dropped. Had a list of Knickerbocker Village tenants been properly perused, the name of Julius Rosenberg would have turned up, a man with the name of Julius who did fit Bentley's description; more about that in a later chapter.

Partially as a consequence of Bentley's charges, in the spring of 1946 there were many firings and enforced resignations in the State Department, the OSS, the Office of War Information and the Foreign Economic Administration. At the time, the public knew nothing of Bentley's role in all this, and in fact, Bentley was enjoined from saying anything in public for several years because she was a witness before grand juries. In 1947 one such grand jury was empaneled in New York specifically to investigate her accusations, and called such people as Abe Brothman and a business associate of his, Harry Gold —but indicted no one. It was not until the summer of 1948, after this grand jury had finished its work, that Elizabeth Bentley made her sensational debut before the House Un-American Activities Committee, and became known as the "Red Spy Queen."

After that, Bentley's accusations were ridiculed in public because only William Walter Remington, of those she named, was successfully prosecuted in this era. It's important to know, though, that later sworn testimony corroborated much of what she'd told the FBI. For example, both Whittaker Chambers and Nathaniel Weyl independently named members of what Bentley termed the Perlo network, and Chambers named others who Bentley had said were in the Silvermaster group. Other important corroboration came from the various testimonies of Louis Budenz, Bernard Redmont, Duncan Lee and the wife of William Walter Remington, Ann Moos Remington. Also, Katherine Perlo, ex-wife of Victor Perlo, wrote an anonymous letter to the FBI, which she later acknowledged, that backed up Bentley's naming of Perlo and his associates as being involved in espionage.

That spring of 1946, after the Bentley affair's initial phase, we in the New York office's Soviet Espionage squad felt frustrated: we were near and yet so far. Igor Gouzenko and Bentley had shown that Russians were operating all around us, but we were unable to counter their efforts.

While on surveillance, or after hours, Emory Gregg and I would get specific about our complaints as we watched the Bureau, on the one hand, squander its limited counterintelligence resources while, on the other hand, it refused to be very aggressive in pursuing certain kinds of leads. From the time of Arthur Adams to the days of Bentley, the "watch and wait" philosophy had gotten us nowhere.

We believed we knew what needed to be done. In near-dormant cases or those about to be closed for lack of evidence, we wanted to call a halt to useless physical surveillance and to interview all suspects and their contacts. We wanted to throw manpower at good cases and to close those cases that were unproductive. New cases were opening up every month, and we could easily absorb double the manpower we already had on the squad. We weren't doing enough to cover Soviet personnel. We needed to use more electronic equipment— microphones, telephone taps, remote devices. We felt hamstrung, facing an enemy that did not fight by rules of decency or fairness; we believed the FBI had to become more aggressive in counterintelligence against the Soviets or we would lose the war with the KGB.

4

GERHART EISLER

I N LATE 1945 Don Jardine decided to leave the FBI and return to practice law in the Minneapolis–St. Paul area. I inherited many of his cases, among them that of one man I knew well because Don and I had spent a fair amount of time tailing him. This was Gerhart Eisler, a small, balding, bespectacled man of forty-eight who looked like a bookkeeper. With his young wife, Brunhilda, he lived in a thirty-five-dollar-a-month third-floor walk-up in Long Island City. He spoke with a German accent, as did many of his neighbors, and like many of them also, he had contributed blood during the war. He had also been an air-raid warden.

You could set your watch by him. He'd leave his apartment early in the morning and walk in a distinctive, unhurried way to a newsstand, buy the New York *Times* and catch the IRT subway into Manhattan. To the casual observer he might have seemed ordinary, but on close examination one could notice in his manner a hint of arrogance and a quiet confidence. For Gerhart Eisler was not an innocuous commuter; ever since he had gotten off the boat in New York in 1941, the FBI had been tracking him because he was an agent of the Comintern.

The Communist International, or Comintern, was devoted to furthering the revolution in countries other than Russia, and to keeping foreign Communist movements in line and subservient to Moscow. Stalin had nominally dissolved the Comintern in 1943, but its people were still doing the same jobs, all over the world.

Real interest in Eisler had picked up in 1943 as a result of another, entirely separate investigation in which the FBI overheard important conversations in San Francisco between an American Communist and a Soviet vice-consul. Steve Nelson, the American, told Soviet Vice-Consul Gregory Kheiffets about his efforts to recruit scientists at the Manhattan Project, and also spoke of the dissolution of the Comintern. In effect, Nelson offered a "Comintern apparatus" then functioning on both the East and the West coasts, through Kheiffets, to his superior Vassili Zubilin, the man whom we believed to be the KGB resident for the United States.

Historically, there had been some direct transfers from the Comintern to the KGB and the GRU, and so the FBI opened a series of investigations. Some concerned Nelson and led us to other veterans of the International Brigades, which had been put together by the Communists to fight in the Spanish Civil War. An organization called the Joint Anti-Fascist Refugee Committee was deeply tied in to these veterans; it raised money for several hundred thousand survivors of the partisan groups from that war. The FBI knew the JAFRC to be a Communist front, and Gerhart Eisler, who went to its offices in Manhattan every morning like clockwork, to be a Comintern man. Eisler didn't appear to do much for the JAFRC, yet received from it a monthly check for $150, made out to "Julius Eisman."

When not at the JAFRC, Eisler met with some of the foreign Communists who swarmed the city, just waiting for the end of the war in Europe so they could catch a boat and get back to their own countries. He even turned up when we weren't expecting him. One day a colleague and I were watching two important Italian Communists who were believed to have Comintern connections, and Eisler met them on a street corner; the three men talked long enough for us to call an FBI photographer to come and record the scene. We wondered what language they were using and what subjects they were discussing. Another time I thought Eisler was going to have a clandestine meeting, and followed him to the Eisenhower victory parade; but he was only meeting his wife, Brunhilda, and I ended up watching the parade virtually over their shoulders.

We became convinced that Eisler was not involved in Soviet intelligence, but believed he was still a major Comintern "rep," active in political affairs. In mid-1946 we received word that the Eislers were making plans to go to the Soviet Zone of Germany, and had applied for and secured the exit visa required before a temporary resident alien could leave the U.S. Many questions were raised by Eisler's answers on the application. He wrote that he'd first entered the country in 1941—but we knew he'd been here illegally in the 1930s. He swore that he'd never been a Communist; that, too, was a lie.

I would have been perfectly happy to have Eisler disappear behind the Iron Curtain. However, I decided not to let him go without a personal interview, an action in line with the more aggressive moves that Emory Gregg and I longed to have the FBI take in such cases. After obtaining permission for an interview, I telephoned Eisler at his apartment in Queens and suggested that it would be a good idea if he came in to see me. When he said he was preparing to leave the United States, I told him I was well aware of his travel plans. Apparently deciding that if he avoided me, the FBI might interfere with his departure, he agreed to come in.

Eisler showed up in a nondescript gray suit, a dark shirt with a collar that was too large for him, and a quiet demeanor. I asked Frank Plant to sit in on the interview. After a few gentle questions from me, Eisler started to portray himself as an anti-Nazi German who had merely been a refugee in this country during the war and who sought nothing more than to go home again. I let him run, waiting to see how much he'd tell me before I weighed in with tougher questions. He spoke of his father—Austrian, Jewish, a philosophy professor who'd written thirty books. Three Eisler children were born in Vienna before the war: Gerhart in 1897, his sister, Elfriede, a few years earlier, and his brother, Hanns, a half-dozen years later. Eisler traced his schooling, his service in the Austrian Army during World War I, and his work as a journalist after it. He didn't say he'd been a Communist, but that he'd been "much in sympathy" with the Party in Austria and in Germany. From 1922 to 1927 he'd traveled in Europe, and was in China from 1927 to 1929—a wanderer who became so openly anti-Nazi that the Third Reich put his picture and short biography into an anti-Semitic book. He had been to Spain as a propagandist for the Republican troops, then had been captured and sent to a French refugee camp. He'd come to the United States in 1941, he claimed, only because the war had blocked his through-passage to Mexico. While here he had worked with a German-language newspaper, had received money from Hanns (who was now a Hollywood composer), had worked odd jobs including writing part of a book, *The Lessons of Germany.*

The portrait of the wandering idealist was wholly misleading. Eisler had said nothing about having fostered revolution in the United States, China and Europe for two decades. He hadn't mentioned writing inflammatory articles for the Communist press or the receipt of money from the JAFRC, both under assumed names. To listen to him, you'd have thought he never harmed anyone or wished ill of the United States.

The time for gentleness was over. I quickly pushed him to admit his work for the JAFRC and asked if he'd ever endorsed checks under the name "Julius Eisman." "I do not care to answer," he told us in reply to this question and to why he hadn't reported the Eisman money on his tax returns, or why he'd written articles under pen names such as "Hans Berger." (One of the statements on the exit visa was that he'd never used an alias.) I asked why he hadn't told Immigration in 1941 that he was a Communist; he'd lied, he said, in order to have refuge from the Third Reich. He criticized U.S. government agencies that in 1941 had detained him and tried to prevent him from entering the United States, and were now interfering in his attempt to leave the country.

At the conclusion of our interview I wrote up a report and added it to the Eisler files; I was just waiting for the day when the Eislers would sail and I could close out the case.

Then everything changed because Eisler's name became public. Louis Budenz, the longtime managing editor of the *Daily Worker*, broke with Communism and in the fall of 1946 made a spectacular speech, which exposed the inner workings of the CPUSA and named, as the "Number One Communist in the U.S." the man who gave theoretical direction to the Party, a "Hans Berger." When Budenz made his charge, Eisler's luggage was at the pier, and his ship was due to sail in a few days. Two days after Budenz's speech, the New York *World-Telegram* discovered independently of us that Hans Berger was Gerhart Eisler. The publicity pushed the Justice Department to revoke Eisler's exit visa and look into his case.

We had known a lot about Eisler, but had no independent evidence that he was acting as a Comintern representative until Budenz confirmed our suspicions. Then, suddenly, instead of being the subject of a modest FBI investigation, Eisler was headline news. James McInerney, the number two man in the Criminal Division of the Department of Justice, was a former FBI agent, and when he saw my report in the Eisler file, which the Bureau sent him, he decided to come to New York and talk with me. Big, bluff and articulate, Jim was a great guy and we hit it off well. The Justice Department, he explained, had to do something about Eisler, and it was clear to him from the files that there was a *prima facie* prosecutable case against Eisler for having made false and misleading statements on his application for an exit visa. McInerney wanted me to take the wraps off and conduct a no-holds-barred effort to develop information for criminal prosecution of Eisler. I am now going to relate at some length the story of Eisler and the people around him. I do so not only because the tale is fascinating but also because it has many details that are echoed in later, better-known cases—Coplon, Fuchs, Gold, and the Rosenbergs.

It was a time of increased public attention to the matter of Communism. The 1946 off-year elections were colored by allegations about the influence of Communists in government and on foreign policy. The House Un-American Activities Committee (HUAC) was in the midst of a probe of the JAFRC, and because of their refusal to submit the organization's financial records to scrutiny, a number of JAFRC board members were charged with contempt of Congress. In early 1947 the HUAC called Eisler himself to testify.

Eisler came to the committee's hearing room direct from his Ellis Island detention cell; he was accompanied by attorney Carol Weiss King and a phalanx of reporters. In a show of bravado, he refused to be sworn as a witness unless he was allowed to make an opening statement. When the committee wouldn't let him make the rules, Eisler would not testify. He was voted in contempt. HUAC member Richard M. Nixon, in his maiden speech before the House of Representatives, asked the House to cite Eisler for contempt of Congress. The House did so.

I could only read about Eisler's HUAC appearance in the papers because I was deep into our no-holds-barred investigation. I wanted to know about Eisler's activities here during the 1930s. Many former American Communists, reinterviewed at my request by various FBI field offices, identified him as having been at the center of some major labor unrest and industrial violence during the Depression years. William Odell Nowell, a black man, had met Eisler at Moscow's Lenin School, where Eisler taught the rudiments of preparing for revolution, and had also seen him in the United States, where Eisler went under the name of Edwards.

Under the name of Brown, in Cleveland and other midwestern cities, Eisler had worked to undermine legitimate unions and to set up Communist-controlled organizations whose aim was not better working conditions but social agitation; one former Communist told us that Eisler had come back from a trip to Moscow with specific instructions for American Party members to infiltrate the newly formed CIO. Former Communist Joseph Zack Kornfeder told us how he had tried to prevent Eisler from subjugating the labor movement, and that Eisler had had him thrown out of the CPUSA for his interference. Another former Communist, Sam Diner, told the FBI that Eisler had acted in concert with Harry Bridges to stir up dock workers in the San Francisco strike of 1934 that paralyzed the city. At one meeting Diner was given a pistol, and a box was placed under a window. The idea behind both items was to protect Eisler; in case of a police raid, the pistol would be fired and Eisler could use the box to jump out the window to safety. Manning Johnson, another former Communist, told of Eisler's exploits, which crossed national boundaries: Johnson had arranged for "Edwards" to meet in Buffalo with Canadian Communists. He also recalled that in CPUSA National Committee meetings, when Eisler rose to speak a hush would descend over the delegates and everyone would listen carefully to what the Comintern rep had to say.

Earl Browder, the CPUSA leader, had known Eisler since he had preceded Gerhart as Comintern rep in China, but didn't want to talk to us about him. Whittaker Chambers, not yet well known, might also have given us information about Eisler, but didn't. In early 1947, when another agent and I went to the offices of *Time* and had a few words with him, Chambers was closemouthed. He denied that he had known Eisler or "Edwards." Years later, Chambers wrote that as editor of *New Masses* in the 1930s he had known Eisler as the "Edwards" who contributed articles to the magazine—but in 1947 he wouldn't tell me that.

Legally, the most damaging thing uncovered in our investigation was right in the State Department's files. On August 30, 1934, Eisler had met Leon Josephson (co-owner of Café Society Uptown and Downtown) at a cafeteria, and had gone with him to the State Department's New York offices, where they filled out a false passport application. The application was in the name of Samuel Liptzen (a staff writer for the Yiddish-language paper *Morning Freiheit*), but they attached Eisler's photograph to it. As with all such applications, this one stayed in the State Department's files long after the passport itself had been issued. Eisler had used the false passport for foreign travel, which he arranged through Jacob Golos and the World Tourist organization. In the 1940 raid on the World Tourist offices, the FBI had obtained records that, seven years later, told me of Eisler-as-Liptzen's travels in the 1930s.

I personally interviewed one potential witness who was quite close to Eisler: his sister, Elfriede. Her small Manhattan apartment was cluttered with books, magazines and foreign newspapers, which she used in her work as editor of the anti-Communist newsletter *The Russian State Party.* She was a middle-aged, bitter and intense woman with tousled gray hair and a thick German accent. In her youth, at the time of the Russian Revolution and World War I, she had become a Communist and received "Card Number One" of the Austrian Communist Party. Gerhart, who had been demoted in the army for spreading Socialist propaganda, soon joined her in the Party. At that time he was "bookish, athletic, gay, moody, tender, insolent, hard to manage, a strong lover and hater, with frequent outbursts of temper." In 1920 they both moved to Germany, where he became an editor of the Party paper *Rote Fahne* and she was elected chairwoman of the Berlin branch of the Party. Her star was rising. She began to shuttle back and forth to Moscow, meeting with Lenin, Stalin, Trotsky, Bukharin and Zinoviev.

By 1923 Germany was on the verge of revolution; monarchists and Hitler's fascists on the right, and Communists on the left, all prepared for insurrection. There were two failed *putsch* attempts that year—one, well known, by Hitler, and the second, almost forgotten now, by the Communists. Hitler went to jail after a publicity-generating trial; the Communist party was outlawed in Germany. As Elfriede (who became "Ruth Fischer") later wrote, about 1923, "Hitler presented nationalism in proletarian disguise and this captured the imagination and energy of the masses . . . [whereas] Communism . . . definitely proved its impotence."

Elected to the Reichstag, Ruth was unable to take her seat and went into hiding for a year until restrictions on the Communists were relaxed. *Time* characterized Ruth the deputy as

> a sneerer and a snarler. She sits on the far left of the House, inter-rupting Streseman, Ludendorff and Tirpitz with cries of "Phooey." She is fat . . . and addresses the House with a vaudevillian shimmy that is unique.

In the next several years the lives of Ruth and Gerhart diverged. Called to Moscow after Lenin's death, Ruth fell afoul of Stalin and was held a virtual prisoner in a Moscow hotel for ten months, and was then expelled from the Party. Gerhart overreached himself in a plot to bring down the general secretary of the German Communist Party, and was also called to Moscow for punishment. But Gerhart did what Ruth refused to do—he publicly denounced Zinoviev and the Comintern leadership, and agreed to adhere strictly to the new Stalinist line. He was then sent to China.

According to Ruth, China changed Gerhart; he became tougher and more withdrawn. His mission there was to direct the liquidation of the opposition to the Communist movement. This became the subject of Bertolt Brecht's 1931 play *The Measures Taken.* (When the play opened in Berlin, it had music by Ruth and Gerhart's younger brother, Hanns.) The play suggested that lying, secrecy and other "moral" sins were laudable if done in the service of Communism; strict loyalty was the greatest virtue; the play's oft-repeated lesson was in the lines "Sink into the mud, embrace the butcher—but change the world, it needs it."

In 1933, when Hitler came to power, Ruth escaped from Germany on the last train. In Paris she went to stay with Hanns, who drew aside a curtain and revealed Gerhart, whom she had not seen in several years. The Eisler family reunion began well enough but degenerated into acrimonious debate. Gerhart boasted:

> Germany is through for a while. New York will be the new center of the Comintern outside Russia. We will change our line in the States completely. Until now it has been an unimportant sideshow. . . . We will do a big business with Roosevelt before I am through.

Beyond this point in time, Ruth knew little of Gerhart's activities— only enough to believe that he had become a man who ignored Stalin's murders and spouted the Party line, while she herself had grown to hate Stalin and all he did to eviscerate the pure cause of Marx, Engels and Lenin.

Ruth Fischer had given me a glimpse of Eisler, but I believed another person in the New York area could, if she talked, tell me more about Gerhart as a man than anyone else. Hede Massing, born Hede Tune, had married Eisler at the age of seventeen in 1920 and divorced him shortly thereafter, but had remained close to him down almost to the present day.

For some time the FBI had known of Hede and her third husband,

Paul Massing. Both were suspected of having been Soviet espionage agents in the 1930s, but the Massing file had been closed for lack of evidence of criminal wrongdoing. I decided to reopen it.

Hugh Finzel, who'd been in the same training class as I, had handled the Massings' files. I wondered, with him, which of the Massings to interview first. He had no clear preference, so on a hunch I opted for us to go and see Paul Massing.

An economist at a social research institute, Paul was distinguished, erect and completely uncooperative. He believed that the FBI had kept him from becoming a citizen by giving derogatory information on him to the Immigration and Naturalization Service. Actually, Paul was right about that, but when the interview was drawing to a close and he had told us nothing of value, this talk of citizenship made me a bit hot under the collar. Standing to leave, I said with some vehemence that becoming a citizen was a privilege, not a right, and that Paul had lived safe and secure in the United States during the war, whereas if he'd stayed in Germany the Nazis would long since have killed him.

As he ushered us out of his book-lined study, Paul said nothing in response, but I later learned that my estimate of his probable fate had hit home, for when I called Hede to come in to talk about Gerhart Eisler, she raised no objections.

A tall, middle-aged, carefully dressed woman, no longer the striking beauty she had obviously been in her youth, Hede was still attractive. My early questions were so discreet that she leaned over the table to Finzel and me and said, "You don't need to be so delicate, Mr. Lamphere. I am very willing to tell you my story." Tell it she did, in many long interviews over the course of the winter of 1946–47. Of these interviews, Hede would later write that they had been, though polite, a "terrific ordeal," because it was hard to "pour your heart out to a stranger, to face yourself, your crumbled illusions, your misconceptions—it is like a psychoanalysis without reward."

Once more I heard about the cafés of Vienna, the home of the Bohemian life in the days at the end of World War I. Gerhart was a playwright. Hede was an actress, tall, slim, with reddish-blond braids, all of seventeen and on scholarship at the theater conservatory. She and her younger sister, Elli, came from a broken family. When Hede met Gerhart at a café it was as though she had "struck a whirlwind and was hopelessly and helplessly tangled and engulfed." Within weeks he had separated her from a weaker boyfriend, made her his mistress, and taken her to live with his family. The Eislers gave her warm family surroundings and intellectual stimulation. Hede never fully understood the Marxist doctrine, but implicitly trusted it and believed it to be humanitarian.

Hede and Gerhart moved to Berlin in 1920 and married—for convenience, he said, not because of bourgeois convention. In Berlin she starred in plays and he wrote editorials for *Rote Fahne*. Socially, they saw only fellow Communists. (I was reminded of Bentley's similar comments about the all-embracing environment that Communism provided—answers for all questions, jobs and lovers for true believers.)

By the time of the 1923 upheaval, Gerhart and Hede had grown apart, and Hede passed rather easily into the hands of wealthy Communist publisher Julian Gumperz, an intellectual Marxist who had been born in the United States. Her sister, Elli, moved in with them; Elli was fifteen, bright, beautiful, and "quite a self-centered little animal, wild and untamed." When Gerhart lost his job, Julian suggested he, too, take a room in the Gumperz house, and soon Gerhart and Elli were lovers. Hede took this as a compliment to her and a solution to the thorny problem of providing the great revolutionary with a suitable wife.

Hede and Julian made frequent trips abroad. In 1926, in New York, Hede met Helen Black and other Communists and worked as a "cottage mother" in an orphanage until her American citizenship papers came through, after which she and Julian moved back to Germany. At the university in Frankfurt-am-Main they met Paul Massing, an outdoorsman and agricultural economics student whom Julian thought a "rare combination of peasant boy and intellectual." Hede and Paul were both tall, Nordic-looking, passionate and romantic. They fell in love, and Julian let them go, helpless to stop their affair.

By this point in the interviews, Hede had become completely absorbed in telling me her story. I wanted her to feel comfortable enough to tell me details of her later espionage activities, but our relationship was often disturbing to me because it was based on a deep confession during which Hede's own perspective on her life changed dramatically. She was no longer young and attractive, but she was vivacious, and her coquettishness and wit were much in evidence during our sessions. It was easy to see why many men had desired her. She told me once that sex was no longer important to her; I doubted that.

In Berlin in the late 1920s the Massings and the Eislers saw one another frequently and led parallel lives. Gerhart and Paul played chess and Ping-Pong; then Gerhart was summoned to Moscow, and Paul went of his own accord to study agriculture. Languishing in Berlin, Hede had dinner with Richard Sorge, who later became one of the most successful Communist spies of the era. Sorge, formerly a Comintern man like Gerhart, had spirited his wife away from an older man, just as Paul had taken Hede from Julian. At dinner he convinced Hede that espionage was heroic and glamorous and that she, too, could do important things for the Party. He took her to meet "Ludwig," a man she discovered she already knew as a regular customer of the Gumperz bookstore, where she had worked for a time.

"Ludwig" was Ignace Poretsky, sometimes known as Ignace Reiss, a charming, erudite man who inspired near-fanatic loyalty on the part of Hede and many other agents. Together with his childhood friend Walter Krivitsky, "Ludwig" was a mainstay of Russian intelligence and had been so since the early 1920s. On his instructions Hede dropped her attendance at local Party meetings, provided details and evaluations of promising prospects, located "safe" apartments for agents and set up "mail drops" where messages could be exchanged—in short, she learned the rudiments of courier work. She did not use this knowledge right away, however, because she joined Paul in Moscow. When Gerhart came back to Moscow from China he was so arrogant that Hede could no longer speak with him. But then he had a heart attack, and she softened and visited him in the hospital.

In 1932 Hede and Paul both returned to Berlin and began to work for "Ludwig"; they told new recruits that espionage for the Soviets was really fighting against fascism. Paul organized in the universities, while Hede, with her American passport, ferried Jews and Communists out of Germany and into Czechoslovakia and Russia.

At the time Hitler came to power, Hede was on a courier mission from Moscow to Paris, carrying Comintern money in a false pregnancy outfit. In Paris she learned that the Nazis had thrown Paul into the concentration camp at Oranienburg; she hurried there with Communist underground help and watched for him from outside the barbed-wire enclosure. He yelled at her to go away and said he would join her when he could.

In Paris a KGB man gave her the torn half of a cigarette box-top as a signal by which to recognize her new superior in New York. Once in the United States, Hede disobeyed her instructions to stay away from obvious Communists, and moved in with Helen Black.

Gerhart sent Earl Browder to see her. Browder kept asking if she had any money for him, and Hede wondered if he'd produce the other half of the cigarette box-top. They were both disappointed in the meeting.

During the next several years, Hede served as a recruiter and a courier in the United States under a succession of mostly cruel, sloppy and incompetent Soviet superiors; one used to come into her apartment, drunk, discourse in a maudlin manner on his friends who had been liquidated, and then pass out on her floor. Others spent too much money in department stores and displayed other faults inimical to espionage. But during these years Hede recruited two men, both from the U.S. State Department—Noel Field and Laurence Duggan. Neither would pass documents to her, but both agreed to give her oral reports every few weeks. Alternating with trips to Washington were Atlantic boat crossings on which Hede carried packages for "Ludwig"—microfilm, she believed. (I wondered if Hede had become the replacement for Robert Switz as "Ludwig's" transatlantic courier.)

In New York a superior asked her to secure U.S. passports for KGB agents—and for this task she turned to Gerhart Eisler. He sent her, in turn, to Jozef Peters, a dark, heavy-set Hungarian of many aliases who had connections to the American Communist underground. Peters obtained many passports for her—once, a document that included an entire family. With this story, Hede added to our understanding of Gerhart Eisler's activities in the United States during the 1930s.

During these years, as well, Paul came out of the concentration camp, crossed with Hede to the United States, and wrote the first inside account of Hitler's terror, which attracted attention when it was serialized in *New Masses*. In an introduction to the book version, Lincoln Steffens wrote that the author "did not yield or peach, but held silently, grimly, to the line of his conviction." It was Paul's courage that helped Hede obtain the introduction to Noel Field, and the Massings and the Fields became good friends. In 1935 Paul decided to return to Europe, and did underground work for the KGB in Switzerland, slipping into and out of the Third Reich. Noel Field tried to follow this route and took a job with the League of Nations in Geneva—but "Ludwig" rejected him as too flighty to be his agent. Walter Krivitsky, however, put Field to work in his own Soviet apparatus.

When Hede was assigned to work with a boorish, profligate Russian in New York who was a close associate of some high Kremlin official, and when she was ordered to sit for weeks watching the apartment of Ludwig Lore, a CPUSA founder and columnist for the New York *Post,* she realized she was moving far away from her personal goal of fighting fascism. The idea of the Spanish Civil War (where Gerhart was serving) exhilarated Hede, but the knowledge that many German Communists whom she had known were being tried and executed in the Moscow purges depressed and confused her. She went to Europe, where an equally downhearted "Ludwig" gave her twelve thousand dollars which she was to put into New York bank accounts for his eventual escape.

Hede later learned that in mid-1937 "Ludwig" was summoned to Moscow and his wife, Elsa, went in his place, an action that bought him some time. In a Moscow café Elsa saw Gerhart—scheming, a friend said, how to get himself out of Moscow and back into Spain. "Ludwig" then broke with the apparatus in an open letter to Stalin, after which he went into hiding. Krivitsky, ordered to take a hand in locating and executing his lifelong friend, declined the task and started laying plans for his own defection. In New York two Soviet superiors hung around the Massings' mailbox, waiting for them to receive mail from "Ludwig." Finally the "open letter" came. It read, in part:

> The letter which I am addressing to you today I should have written . . . when the Sixteen were murdered in the cellars of the Lubyanka. . . . I kept silent then. I raised no voices of protest at the subsequent murders, and for this I bear a large responsibility. My guilt is great, but I shall try to make up for it. . . . Up to now, I have followed you. From now on, not a step further. Our ways part! He who keeps silent at this hour becomes an accomplice of Stalin, and a traitor to the cause of the working class and of Socialism.

Reading the letter, Hede and Paul embraced in excitement; the words, Hede said, burned into their souls and freed them from their bondage.

A "very important comrade" whom they had not known, but who was referred to as "Helen," came to see the Massings. She wanted to know why they wished to be released from Soviet service. She labeled "Ludwig" a traitor and a Trotskyite, hammered at the Massings about the necessity of adhering to the Party line, and asked them to go to Moscow. "What if I don't want to go?" asked Hede. "Helen's" response was a threat, which took on added meaning when newspapers reported that a man, later identified as "Ludwig," had been machine-gunned on a lonely road in Switzerland. Paul, the good Communist, decided he'd obey orders and go "home." Against her better judgment, Hede gave in and agreed to accompany him; she didn't want him to go to Moscow alone.

I asked Hede why she and Paul hadn't come to the FBI then. In 1937, she said, they feared the FBI more than the Soviets. However, she only went to Moscow after leaving a trail and excercising extreme caution. She bought her own Intourist tickets so she and Paul could live in Russia as American vacationers. She asked American friends to write them in Moscow. She insisted on crossing aboard a German ship, not a Russian one. She had Paul leave a deposition with a New York lawyer and instructions for it to be opened in a year should the Massings fail to return. Last, she refused the false passports that "Helen" proffered and used her own American and Paul's German passports.

On the voyage, Hede got a glimpse of "Helen's" passport, which depicted her as part of a family. Using these data in 1947, we found the first hard evidence that "Helen"—who was Elizabetha Zubilin— had been in the United States with her husband, Vassili, in the 1930s.

"Peter" (Vassili) joined them at a Moscow hotel; the Zubilins' interrogation of the Massings alternated with dashes of Moscow social life. The couples went everywhere together. "Peter" tried to curry favor by telling Hede that her report on a boorish microphotographer had sent the man to Siberia; Hede only shivered at the implication.

After three months, in January 1938, Hede saw Herta and Noel Field in another Moscow hotel, and latched on to them. Noel was cold—a clear indication, Hede thought, that he was now engaged in espionage. While the Fields were in the Massings' room, Hede called her New York superior, who was also in Moscow, told him who was with her, and demanded her and her husband's passports and visas. Noel turned pale, Paul said, "This will be the end," but while the four were still munching caviar the superior arrived with the passports, other papers and reservations on the next morning's train to Leningrad. A day later the Massings were out of the U.S.S.R.

Hede considered it a miracle to escape Moscow at the height of the purges. During this dark period hundreds of thousands died and millions were sent to Siberian forced-labor camps. The entire old order was decimated, including most of the espionage services and the upper echelon of the Comintern. Gerhart Eisler probably avoided death only by becoming a complete Stalinist tool. Abroad, renegade espionage agents such as "Ludwig" were ruthlessly eliminated; even in New York, Juliet Poyntz, who had tried to recruit Bentley, disappeared under mysterious circumstances. Hede always considered it amazing that she had been in Moscow during the purges and survived. I, too, thought it incredible that the Massings, who knew a lot, were able to escape.

The Massings bought a run-down Bucks County, Pennsylvania, farm and took in paying guests. In 1939 they read about the purges and the murder of "Ludwig" in a series of *Saturday Evening Post* articles by Walter Krivitsky. Certain old "movement" friends now shunned the Massings; Hede concluded those who did so were still working for the Soviets. Then came the Nazi-Soviet pact of 1939 and the onset of World War II—a turning point for Communists outside Russia. After the pact, only hard-core believers could stomach doing espionage work for Stalin, the partner of Hitler. Hede and Paul turned completely away from Communism.

Toward the end of 1941 Walter Krivitsky was found dead of a gunshot wound in a locked Washington, D.C., hotel room; an awkwardly worded note said he had committed suicide. Hede and others familiar with espionage thought it probable that Krivitsky had been murdered, like "Ludwig," by the KGB.

During the war Vassili Zubilin came to visit the Massings and halfheartedly tried to re-recruit Hede, who spurned his offer and thought it had been made chiefly to see if the Massings would maintain silence about their old contacts. Both Hede and Paul applied for government service and were turned down. Hede got a sensitive job anyway—making gun mounts for Todd Shipyards in Hoboken, New Jersey—and Paul joined the social research institute. Hede saw a bit of Gerhart Eisler and of Julian Gumperz in New York during the war; ideologically speaking, neither had changed much. Gerhart had divorced Elli and married Brunhilda, another young woman he could indoctrinate. Hede drew closer to such anti-Stalinists as Elsa Bernaut, "Ludwig's" widow.

Toward the end of the war she made a trip to Washington to warn Larry Duggan to get out of Soviet espionage; he was noncommittal. In 1945 Hede saw the Fields in New York and deduced from their behavior that both were still in the espionage apparatus and weren't going to come out. Having tried and failed to persuade the two Americans whom she'd recruited to leave Soviet service, Hede felt relieved of personal responsibility to them. I came to believe that this, rather than Paul's urging, was the ultimate reason why, when I called her to speak to us about Gerhart Eisler, Hede Massing was finally ready to tell her story.

At the end of March 1947 I attended an Alien Board hearing in New York at which Gerhart Eisler appeared. Under Jim McInerney's sharp questioning Eisler admitted even more of his past Communist activities than he had when I first questioned him. Eisler made these admissions, I believe, because he was outraged at being held as an enemy alien—he thought the statute should apply only to Nazis— and perhaps reasoned that if he admitted past Communist activities he'd convince the hearing board that he was not an enemy in the sense that Nazis were enemies. Perhaps he didn't even realize that his answers supported what the government would now charge, that he had made false statements on his exit visa application. Those were the charges on the indictment leveled against Eisler two weeks after the hearing. A trial was set for the early summer in Washington, D.C.

As I prepared for the trial, my colleagues continued to interview both Paul and Hede Massing. They were now separated. Hede later claimed that their break had begun as a result of their trip to Moscow in 1938, but it was clear to me that her long act of confession had completed the process. Paul's interviews with my colleagues were quite different from mine with Hede; he wouldn't tell the FBI anything about his antifascist work in Switzerland, claiming that it had in no way damaged the interests of the United States. He refused, he said, to endanger the reputations of any with whom he had worked in the underground in the prewar years. It was a stance that we in the FBI could and did respect. Now, convinced of Paul's anti-Soviet feelings, we told the INS that Paul had cooperated with us. Shortly thereafter, Paul Massing became an American citizen.

A man from the Unitarian Church's worldwide organization came to see me about one of their employees in Europe, Hede Massing's recruit Noel Field. I told him I wasn't permitted to say anything about Field, since the matter was under investigation, but I suggested that the day would come when the church would not want to have Field associated with its endeavors. Allegations had begun to surface that Field was a KGB agent; I neither confirmed nor denied them. Soon, though, Field was fired by the church organization and went behind the Iron Curtain. In Czechoslovakia he was arrested and charged with being an American double agent. He never returned to the West.

That spring there were "Free Eisler" rallies in New York. Hanns Eisler was also in the news. The HUAC discovered that Hanns had lied as he'd entered the country in 1941, and that he'd used his connections with American liberals to have Eleanor Roosevelt write to then Under Secretary of State Sumner Welles in an attempt to obtain permission for him to enter the United States. Mrs. Roosevelt's intercessions had been shunted aside by Welles, but the HUAC made much of the matter and pressed for Hanns to be deported.

Life magazine dug into the Eisler story. One of its reporters found Elli and Natasha in Stockholm, where they were penniless and very bitter about Gerhart's having abandoned them. Arthur Koestler had little good to say about Eisler, either. He'd been at the French detention camp Le Vernet with Eisler, and told *Life* that when the detainees' families sent some precious goose fat for Christmas, Koestler had shared his, but Eisler ate his goose fat alone, under his bed. Eisler also told Koestler and some others who had long since abandoned Stalinism that after the war, "When the time comes, we will cut your throats in the first five minutes," because they were no longer sufficiently revolutionary and had let their consciences sway them from Communism.

In the late spring I traveled down to Washington, newly married, to prepare for the Eisler trial. My wife and I took a room in a little residential hotel that was within walking distance of the federal courthouse and the Justice Department headquarters, and I stretched my government *per diem* as far as it would go to try to cover expenses. After New York, downtown Washington was incredibly hot and muggy.

But this was the chance of a lifetime for me—a big case on which the FBI and I in particular were very well prepared. Jim McInerney pronounced himself too busy to handle the courtroom presentation, and U.S. Attorney William Hitz took over the case. Bill Hitz was the son of a judge, and had attended Princeton and Harvard Law School; I was still a young FBI man from a small mining town in Idaho—but we got along very well together. We worked jointly to decide which witnesses to call for the trial. As a matter of fact, we worked so well in tandem that when, in pretrial maneuvering, the defense counsel moved and the judge agreed to have all government witnesses excluded from the courtroom until they had testified, Hitz decided that rather than using me as a witness, he'd prefer to have me sit with him at the prosecution table as a sort of associate counsel. That way my intimate knowledge of the case and the evidence would be instantly available to him throughout the trial.

If that was unusual, I didn't pay it much mind; I'd just done the most thorough job I could imagine doing, and sitting at the prosecution table was the result.

Another thing that I could hardly have imagined when the case began: by the time the trial opened in July 1947, Communism was the issue of the day. Loyalty screening of government employees had begun. Bills to outlaw the CPUSA had recently been before Congress —only J. Edgar Hoover's testimony that such measures would make martyrs of the Communists had killed them. The Truman Administration's determination to contain the spread of Communism had come to testing points in Greece and Turkey, and the Marshall Plan was just being introduced as a way to stop Russia from taking over Europe. Many people believed, as columnist David Lawrence wrote, that U.S.–Soviet relations were in a dangerous drift toward war. Eleven Communist leaders had been convicted recently in New York, and their appeal process was reported in the newspapers every day.

This, then, was the setting for the trial of Gerhart Eisler, the first major case in the United States to involve an international Communist figure. The press gallery was full, every day, and most major papers carried stories on the progress of the trial. Eisler's defense attorneys were public figures, Abraham Isserman and Carol Weiss King, both prominent in the National Lawyers Guild, which often provided counsel for accused Communists.

As the trial opened, the jury was chosen carefully. It was made up of seven men and five women, of whom half were black.

The government's case, which we presented in rapid order, was very strong. The indictment was narrow—false statements made on the exit visa application—and we had witnesses and evidence to back up the contention that Eisler had lied on it many times. Former Communists Joseph Zack Kornfeder, Manning Johnson, William Nowell and Louis Budenz told of Eisler's inflammatory activities here in the 1930s and 1940s, which had been performed under assumed names. Ruth Fischer and Hede Massing testified about Eisler's long history as a Communist and Comintern man. Helen R. Bryan, executive secretary of the JAFRC (who was considered a hostile witness), had to admit under oath that she had paid Eisler under the name of

Julius Eisman. We introduced as evidence the 1934 passport application with Liptzen's name and Eisler's photo attached. Looking back, perhaps we were guilty of overkill, but there was intense public interest in the case and we were determined to prove that Eisler had indeed lied to the government about his Communist past.

In cross-examinations the defense continually tried to impugn the integrity of the government's witnesses. A break for the defense came when Manning Johnson testified that he'd set up a meeting in Buffalo in the 1930s between Eisler and two Canadian Communists, one of whom he said was Sam Carr—who turned out to have been in jail at the time of the meeting. We sat Johnson down to look at over a thousand photos until he identified another Canadian Communist as the one who had met Eisler. Helen R. Bryan was turned to advantage by Isserman, who used her as a friendly witness to testify that she knew Eisler mainly as a dedicated antifascist, and that she believed Eisler was sending the money she gave him to help refugees in Europe.

Since Bill Hitz wanted me in court at all times, I couldn't testify about my interview with Eisler. But Frank Plant could. The only problem was that Frank didn't remember it too well because he'd only sat in on it at my request and had let me do all the talking. The defense used a legal maneuver to limit what Frank could testify about; in a voir dire examination by the judge, out of the presence of the jury, it was decided that Frank's testimony would be restricted to certain things that were "admissions against interest" made by Eisler.

After the jury returned, Frank was on the stand during one entire morning. At a lunch recess I remembered one additional "admission against interest" that Eisler had made in the interview, but which we hadn't arranged for Frank to mention in the voir dire. After the recess, Bill Hitz asked the judge if he could ask two additional questions of Frank on this subject. The judge agreed, and Frank proceeded to fill in the blanks—but then courtroom tempers flared. Isserman and Carol King attacked Hitz's handling of the case, Isserman saying, "I charge that this whole procedure is in bad faith and savors to me of something more." Pointing at me, Carol Weiss King screamed, "This is all a frame-up by you!" There was an uproar, and in it I retorted, "You're a goddamned liar!" Hitz jumped to his feet and asked the judge to admonish the defense attorneys, which he did.

Until the next recess I sat silent at the counsel table, wondering if the reporters would print my remark and, if they did, what the Director's reaction would be. He'd fired more than one agent for inability to hold his tongue, or for saying words that did not uphold the dignity of the FBI. During the recess I bolted to a telephone and called a Bureau official to tell him of the incident; he said he'd write a memo to the Director about it. That evening I opened the Washington *Evening Star,* and my heart sank. Newbold Noyes's report on the trial included both Carol King's accusation and my rejoinder. But when the Director got the memo about my actions, he wrote across the bottom, "The agent is to be commended," and in due course I received a letter commending me for having defended the integrity of the Bureau when it was under attack at the trial.

Each day after court I reported to Bill Harvey, who was the headquarters supervisor in charge of the Eisler case. Harvey was odd-looking, with protruding eyes and a pear-shaped body. His voice was like that of a bullfrog; once you'd heard it—and the intellect behind it—you never forgot it. The resident Bureau expert on counterintelligence, Bill had been so busy handling the Bentley case that I'd been pretty much left alone on Eisler. In our meetings he'd offer a few suggestions, but little more.

The Communist press made much of the fact that two of our witnesses were black, implying that the black jurors would be sympathetic to the black witnesses. Eisler's lawyers tried to make one of our black witnesses, Manning Johnson, fall into one of the oldest cross-examination traps. When Johnson was asked whether he'd talked to anyone about his testimony before the trial, he said he hadn't. Well, of course Johnson had talked both to Bill Hitz and to me in our pretrial meetings, but we had not, as the defense implied, told him what to say on the stand. After a recess, we had to put Johnson back on the stand to correct his testimony and to say he'd talked to us but that his answers had not been coached—however, some damage to his credibility had been done.

Joseph Starobin, the soft-spoken foreign editor of the *Daily Worker,* testified for the defense that he and Eisler had made up the name Hans Berger, but that he, Starobin, had actually written the Berger articles from ideas by Eisler.

Starobin was also covering the trial for his paper. I read the *Daily Worker* and observed that as the trial went on, the paper became progressively more vituperative in response to the rising mountain of evidence against Eisler and the increasing likelihood of his conviction. The paper never lost an opportunity to point out that it was no crime to be a German Communist—or, for that matter, an American one. By August 3, 1947, Starobin was writing:

> This has been more than a trial: it has been the dissection of the rotting tissues of American society today. Here, petty spies and pretentious informers have been manipulated as the puppets of ambitious district attorneys working with the FBI chiefs, who in turn are the bought agents of respectable steel magnates and coal barons.

Starobin predicted that the blacks on the jury would vote for conviction in order to keep their government jobs.

In the midst of a sweltering heat wave, on August 5, Gerhart Eisler took the stand, dressed in his shapeless gray suit and blue shirt with its too-large collar. His statements strained credulity: "I never in my life was a member of the Communist International. I never in my life went anyplace in the whole world as a representative of the Comintern." He said he hadn't lied when he put on his application that he'd first entered the United States in 1941 because his other entries were just visits; he said he wasn't a member of a group that advocated the overthrow of the U.S. government because he was a *German* Communist, and each national party was separate, distinct, and not controlled by Moscow. As to what he'd done with the exit visa application, why, even Mr. Lamphere had said to him, "I don't know. In the same situation I might have done exactly the same as you did."

This was a lie, but an opportune one for us. It gave me the legal opportunity to take the stand as rebuttal witness. First I testified in detail as to precisely what Eisler had told Frank Plant and me. Then came the cross-examination. It was crucial for the defense to derogate me as a witness, and it was nearly as crucial for the government's case that I bring out a number of points that the prosecution had previously been unable to make.

This part of the trial was a battleground, and I thoroughly enjoyed the fight. Isserman demanded one-word answers to "when did you stop beating your wife?" questions. I continually qualified and expanded on what I meant, and would not answer with a simple single word. Isserman began to drift into questions about what might or might not be contained in the FBI's files on Eisler, but I refused to respond. It was getting on toward lunchtime, and I was hungry. Just before the recess Isserman and Hitz got into an argument as to whether or not I should be required to answer a question in this area. Glancing over at the judge, I finally said, "Your Honor, if I was allowed to answer that question, my answer would be 'I don't know.' " Everyone laughed and we recessed for lunch.

In the afternoon Isserman returned to the attack, determined to discredit me. By now I was quite comfortable in the witness chair; I had the facts on my side, and he couldn't shake them. At last Carol King realized that Isserman was not helping his case by cross-examining me, and I was excused.

The Communist press, of course, had its own view of things. Whereas to *New Masses* Eisler was "clean-cut . . . calm . . . mellow," the magazine said that government witnesses would eye Special Agent Lamphere uncomfortably, as if I would get them next if they made a mistake. Lamphere, the magazine said, was "too pleasant" to the point of being sinister. One weekend Bill Hitz and I went fishing, and I got a bad sunburn; I sat in court for a week with my collar hurting my sunburned neck. Perhaps it was this red neck that pushed Joseph Starobin to write a full-page article for the *Sunday Worker* of August 10, 1947, which began this way:

> There are plenty of FBI men in the courtroom here at the trial of Gerhart Eisler. They are easy to spot as they sit on the polished benches and smile in the cool hallways. But the real presence and guiding role of the FBI in this case is very open and unashamed. Alongside the U.S. attorney, William Hitz, there has been sitting all during these weeks the special FBI agent Robert Lamphier [*sic*], who's had more to do with this fantastic frame-up than any other man.
>
> Baby-faced, but hard-lipped, this character has behaved as the government's special counsel, leaning over to prime the prosecutor, fishing into his black bag for papers and notes, and his red neck visibly flushes as the defense counsel unravels the whole abysmal story of what the United States government tried to do with Eisler.

To me, this article was a badge of honor. It meant that we had succeeded in making our case, for it was a last, desperate attempt by the Communist press to ready its own readership for what they now believed would be an adverse verdict. The attention paid to me in this article was most flattering; I've always been proud of it.

At least the Communist press was right about one thing. After only a few hours of deliberation, the jury brought in a guilty verdict. As court was adjourning, I said to Eisler, "Gerhart, do you think you got a fair trial?"

"Yes," he responded, "a fair trial but an unfair indictment." We would have talked further, but his attorneys didn't want the newspapermen to overhear anything that might prejudice an appeal. It was the last time I saw Eisler in person; in a way, I almost liked him—his bravado was astonishing.

Though the government asked for $100,000 bail, the judge set bail at $23,500, which Communist front groups put up, and Eisler was freed pending appeal. The FBI now tailed him, but keeping track of a man who knew he was being followed was not as easy as following a man who didn't know you were after him.

In May 1949 the Polish ship *Batory,* en route to Europe, radioed to the United States that it had a stowaway from the States on board whose first-class passage had been paid. It was Gerhart Eisler. He had gotten away from our surveillance. According to *Time,* Carol King almost exploded when she heard that Eisler had jumped bail, causing the confiscation of the money raised by the front groups.

The United States asked Great Britain to hold Eisler for extradition, and Scotland Yard men carried a kicking and screaming Eisler off the *Batory* in Southampton. Eisler had been convicted of something approaching perjury in the United States; perjury was a crime specifically covered in the Anglo–U.S. extradition treaty, but Eisler's British attorneys convinced the court that under British law a false oath was not perjury unless it had been taken in connection with a judicial proceeding. Eisler made a triumphant return to the *Batory.* In later years he was seen teaching at the university in Leipzig; he became chief of the Information Office in East Germany, and in 1962 was named chairman of the East German State Radio Committee.

In the summer of 1946, when I first came face to face with Gerhart Eisler, the United States' wartime friendship with Russia was still evident in Russian War Relief rallies and newspaper cartoons that showed a smiling "Uncle Joe" Stalin. By the time Eisler took the stand in 1947, there was severe strain between the two countries. The Eisler case served somewhat as a bridge between the era of wartime alliance and the era of the Cold War. More important, it revealed to the public just how closely the CPUSA was tied to Moscow—despite the American Communists' efforts to show their distance from the Soviet Union. The Eisler case also conclusively demonstrated that organizations such as the JAFRC had been used as fronts to hide and to finance international Communist representatives. And within the FBI, the Eisler case showed the hierarchy that an FBI security investigation could lead to a successful prosecution if Justice was willing to take and hold an aggressive course of action.

Finally, the Eisler case was important to me, because it changed my career. After the trial Jim McInerney asked me to come into the Justice Department as an attorney, to work on internal security matters. However, McInerney's was not the only offer I received. Bill Harvey said to me that new blood was needed on the counterintelligence desks at headquarters, and asked if I would informally sound out some of the people on the New York Soviet Espionage squad about coming down to Washington. Harvey's request was an absolute breach of Bureau procedure—under the usual circumstances, only those men thought to have administrative ability were transferred to headquarters—but what Harvey wanted was men with experience in Soviet espionage, not managerial acumen. I talked to a few of my colleagues in New York, but only Emory Gregg was interested—and I put his name down with mine as wanting to come to Washington to be a case supervisor.

I declined Jim McInerney's gracious offer and told him that my loyalty was to the FBI. After clearing up a mountain of paperwork in New York, I moved down to Washington with my wife and reported to the new, intense and difficult assignment of supervisor in the Espionage Section at FBI headquarters in Washington, D.C., in the fall of 1947.

5
HEADQUARTERS

I T WAS WITH SOME REGRET that I left New York and the work of a special agent in the field, which I enjoyed, because I wasn't sure that I'd like my new job of supervisor, sitting at a desk day after day. But in September 1947 my wife and I drove to Washington; we'd been married only a few months, though I'd met her on my first assignment, in Birmingham. We took up temporary residence in a room on East Capitol Street; we'd signed up for an apartment in a new complex being built in Silver Spring, Maryland, but it wouldn't be ready for another month or two. Washington was still in the summer doldrums, and our small room was stifling and muggy at night. We'd wake up in the mornings with our pillows damp with sweat.

The main thing I wanted to know about headquarters was whether by being here I could make any real difference in the Bureau's war against Soviet intelligence. That was why I'd taken this new job, and as soon as I could I sought out my friend Emory Gregg, who had preceded me to Washington by a month while I stayed in New York cleaning up the paperwork accumulated during the Eisler trial. Emory said he'd found a number of supervisors at headquarters who shared our aggressive ideas, and he was confident we'd be able to push things along. In fact, there was an awareness at headquarters of a need for more than seven supervisors in the Espionage Section (as a result of new breaking cases); it was part of the reason we'd been transferred. I discovered that it had been the lack of an adequate number of supervisors that had often made Emory and me, as field agents, feel as if the information we were sending to headquarters was disappearing into a bottomless pit.

It was a surprise to me that Bill Harvey, the man who'd approached me about coming down to Washington, was gone from the FBI and now worked with the newly formed Central Intelligence Agency. Evidently Harvey had run afoul of the Director in a unique way. At a party Harvey had drunk too much, and on his way home parked in Rock Creek Park and fell asleep; when he didn't come home, his wife Libby raised the alarm, which resulted in the episode's being brought to the attention of the Bureau hierarchy. Hoover fired Harvey, and that was too bad, because his drive and intelligence were the CIA's gain.

Instead of Bill, I dealt with a man who was almost his polar opposite in terms of personality, Lish Whitson—a quiet, studious researcher who was also an expert on the Soviets. Lish was the Espionage Section man who served on all the interagency committees. The chief of our section was Pat Coyne, whom I'd known briefly when I was in Birmingham, and with whom I'd had extensive conversations during the Eisler trial.

Emory's job was to handle the coverage of Soviet Military Intelligence (GRU) cases; mine was to work with another new supervisor to set up coverage of the Soviet satellite countries. In the field, we both had been the recipients of letters from supervisors down here telling us how to conduct investigations, what to do and not to do, criticizing our performance, and so on. We hoped that as supervisors we wouldn't have to write such letters, and in general I always preferred not to tell a field agent how to handle an investigation, but rather, in my letters, repeatedly emphasized the objectives of an investigation and what sort of results I wanted to see in the agent's next report.

We handled a lot of paper at headquarters—mail from the field offices, from other agencies, from private citizens, from within headquarters—but that wasn't the only difference in being a supervisor. We also had to handle the bureaucracy. In the field we were active agents dealing with specific investigations, and we weren't involved much with the superstructure of the large organization that the FBI had become. But at headquarters the bureaucracy was at our elbows.

We were in the Espionage Section of the Domestic Intelligence Division of the Bureau, which, along with the Criminal Division, supervised all the field investigations. On the administrative side there were divisions that handled the files, training, inspection, personnel, the vaunted FBI laboratories, fingerprints, equipment—and we were constantly bumping up against these in our push to investigate the Soviets.

I soon learned that one of my main jobs was to keep the people up the line informed on what was happening in the various investigations that I was supervising. In general, for me, that meant keeping Mickey Ladd apprised of what was going on. D. M. (Mickey) Ladd in 1947 was the assistant director of the Domestic Intelligence Division of the FBI, and soon thereafter became head of all investigative operations, which made him the number three man in the hierarchy —the most powerful position behind the Director himself and his close associate Clyde Tolson. When I first met Ladd he was in his forties and getting a little paunchy; he had almost no jawline left. His manner was disarmingly friendly, but this was deceptive, as he could turn tough at a moment's notice. Ladd understood power and was extremely knowledgeable about intelligence, particularly the organizational aspects. Wary of the burgeoning of the CIA, he worked to strengthen the FBI's relationship with other U.S. intelligence agencies and helped draw the Bureau closer to the British.

I admired Ladd, and he came to like me and to respect my work. He could be tough on subordinates, but was equally as tough on himself, working many long hours and even devoting his social life to furthering the FBI's contacts in the intelligence community. Many of my colleagues were critical of Ladd because they felt he didn't go to bat for his own men when the Director was on a rampage; I viewed it differently, and saw that while Ladd sometimes suffered a few casualties when the Director was angered, he knew what he was after, and in his own subtle ways could wait out the storm and then quiet and influence the Director as no one else could. In particular, I saw him do this time and again in regard to our own wishes to be more aggressive against the Soviets in counterintelligence—and understood that Ladd was our most important advocate up the line.

That brings me to the Director. Whereas in the field the Director seemed a distant figure, at headquarters a supervisor felt his presence all the time. I found out very quickly that everything at headquarters revolved around J. Edgar Hoover; sending memoranda up through the hierarchy was part of keeping the Director abreast of all investigations. And, of course, everything that went out to the field did so over Hoover's signature.

Director J. Edgar Hoover was a tough man to work for and to keep satisfied, but I greatly respected him. He was an immensely able man who understood power and politics, and who could keep himself informed on a large number of ongoing investigations by dint of his prodigious memory and his unyielding will.

As most great men do, Director Hoover had his faults and idiosyncrasies—but he was indeed a great man, and while in this book I am at times critical of his actions, I must emphasize that I greatly respected the Director and the organization he built.

In general, we junior men were in the FBI because we believed in many of the things that Hoover did—such as the fervent observance of the law of the land, and the need to protect the United States from the ideologies of the right and the left. We admired his actions taken against the Nazi Bund, the Ku Klux Klan and the Communists. However, Hoover also believed that the organization he had built, the FBI, should repulse all attacks on it, whatever their source—and it was particularly in this area that he made mistakes, most of them in the years long after I had left the Bureau.

I've always been puzzled by the accusation that the Director possessed too much power and that Presidents were afraid to remove him, supposedly because of his "personal and confidential" files. It was his long memory that they needed to be wary of, as I'll show in a later chapter when we see how Hoover locked horns with Harry S. Truman over Harry Dexter White. To me, the fact that no President chose to get rid of Hoover with a stroke of the pen indicates not that the Director was feared, but that the various Presidents recognized Hoover's value to the nation as head of an incorruptible agency.

We in the FBI did fear him—every member of the organization did, from top to bottom, for he was as rough on his top men as he was on the lowliest of new field agents. For example, none of the top people would dare leave headquarters in the evening before they got quiet word on the telephone that the Director had left the building. Every winter when the Director went to La Jolla to enjoy the California horse-racing season, he made it a habit to become angry about the progress of major investigations and to give tongue-lashings to his subordinates by phone, just to keep them on their toes while he was away from his desk. The problem was that such reprimands often resulted in extra work for supervisors like me.

For instance, a short time after I arrived at headquarters, the Director inaugurated a "Special List" system. He kept everyone at headquarters alert by reviewing incoming teletypes and memoranda on important cases, and commenting on them in the margins, sometimes with questions we would have to answer. When a piece of mail came down from the Director's office with a tag that said "Special List," we were to drop everything and answer the Director's questions. During the day we'd be prodded from above on these lists, and if the answers weren't ready by quitting time we'd stay as long as it took to obtain them, even if that meant working throughout the night. Special Lists at times diverted me from my other tasks, though I always recognized the Director's right to ask questions. Once, working on a major espionage matter, I had four Special List requests at the same time; I asked a superior which of them I was to work on first, and was told that my humor was not appreciated and that I was to find a way to get all of them done at once.

Over the years my superiors came to believe that I was adept at writing what we called "summary briefs," which organized all the pertinent information on a case or a problem and our recommendations for major steps to be taken in the immediate future; these briefs were frequently essential in keeping the Director informed about the progress of an important case. Here my ability also threw me off track sometimes, when I was often asked to spend my weekends working with from three to a dozen supervisors writing such briefs for the Director. Part of what galled me about putting together a seventy-five-page brief over a weekend was to come in on Monday and find that the document had been derailed on the way to the Director's desk by some intermediate official who'd want unimportant changes. In most instances the Director's requests for information were well justified, but there were plenty of times when I thought his demand for briefs in espionage areas not related to my cases was a bad use of my hours and ability.

Going to see the Director personally was not something one did casually, and during my seven years at headquarters I saw Hoover infrequently, mostly at social functions, and once or twice a year in his office.

Having made an appointment with the Director—usually to thank him for such things as merit raises for high performance—you then took special care to see that your suit was well pressed, your shoes shined, your white shirt neat and your tie knotted perfectly. Sam Noisette, a black staff assistant, ushered you through the long ante-chamber from the door to Hoover's office, announced your name, and closed the door after you were inside. The Director stood up and shook your hand, then took his seat behind a desk that was on a raised platform. He'd motion you to sit in a black leather chair next to the desk. The chair was comfortable but on a lower level, so that you were always looking up to the Director.

In such situations you generally said your well-thought-out piece to him as quickly as possible, for as soon as you paused for breath the Director would take over the conversation, and from then on all you'd be able to do would be to agree with whatever he was saying. At one audience, no sooner had I spoken my thanks to him than he took off for quite a while on the subject of wives of FBI agents. In too many instances, he said, the wives knew a lot about what the Bureau was doing, and they talked about it to excess—so much so that their loose talk might compromise current investigations and hurt the Bureau's image. As I listened to the Director, I began to wonder: Was the Director really addressing his remarks to me, albeit obliquely? Because of the nature of my counterintelligence work, I'd been quite closemouthed about it at home, and I knew that my wife was not one to talk loosely about the Bureau's business. The Director's voice was staccato, and he spoke in a rapid-fire fashion with a good command of the language but given to repetition. After half an hour on this subject he thanked me for coming and ushered me out of the office. I was completely perplexed, and it wasn't until I was halfway down to my floor that I understood what the Director had been doing in our conversation. Neither my wife nor I had been the target of his monologue—but he knew that I'd be asked by my colleagues how the interview had gone, and that I'd tell them of his concern about loose talk from Bureau wives. It was part of the way he got word out on the grapevine on subjects that vexed him.

The Director had a high regard for agents who'd been with the Bureau for many years. If one of these agents requested, say, a transfer back to his home city to be close to an aged parent, such request was granted with alacrity. Moreover, when the agent arrived home, he'd find that flowers had been delivered to his sick parent and that the SAC in the office would make periodic inquiries on the Director's behalf about the parent's health. Agents did not forget such kind treatment and, in return, gave Hoover their loyalty.

He was the font from whom all things flowed in the FBI, both the good and the bad, including letters of commendation, which led to salary upgrades, and letters of censure, which stayed in an agent's file and could scotch advancement. However, when agents were censured or disciplined, they often acted as if the punishment had come solely from someone in the organization other than the Director, even though the disciplinary memorandum would have been signed by Hoover. In some instances, the censured or disciplined agent could manage to get the punishment revoked or lessened by in-person appeals to the Director—which also increased the agent's sense of gratitude to Hoover.

I hated the disciplinary system, which I felt got in my way more often than it kept me on the straight and narrow path of being a good FBI man. In any organization, people make mistakes; it was always my view that as long as the error had not been intentional, an FBI agent ought to be counseled, not disciplined—for example, that's how I treated mistakes when I supervised the actions of the field. I, personally, managed to stay pretty clear of the disciplinary system during my fourteen years in the organization, so I'm not speaking of being hampered myself—but the system was distasteful, and more important, it didn't really make for better work. For instance, when something went wrong on a case, someone had to pay; this was true even when (as we'll see later in this book) the Director had personally approved the course of action that eventually resulted in the error's being made. The rationalization was that if the Director had approved the course of action, the error must have been made in the way the instructions were transmitted down or in the way they had been carried out.

I also didn't like the obverse of the disciplinary system, the expectation at headquarters that to get ahead you had to effusively praise the Director. Although I wrote several letters to the Director in which I thanked him for raises in language that was perhaps more purple than necessary, I could never bring myself to write him congratulatory notes on his birthdays, awards or anniversaries of service. It has always bothered me that the Director didn't seem to be able to see through the flattery and to know that it was phony. Could it be that his ego was so large that on this issue it screened out his intellect and let him actually believe the flatterers? I know only that being able to discern the Director's wishes and to accommodate them was a key to advancement within the FBI. For example, Deke

DeLoach, a neighbor of mine in the Silver Spring apartment complex, was one of the FBI's first liaison men with the CIA, and in that capacity he reflected the Director's negative attitude toward the CIA by working to exacerbate the problems between the two agencies, rather than to damp them down. I much preferred the attitude of Sam Papich, who followed Deke as CIA liaison, and who believed, as I did, that both agencies were fighting a common enemy and that we should work together as best we could. Sam's stance earned him considerable criticism from Hoover, while Deke's mucking about got him promoted to the point where, during the presidency of Lyndon Johnson, he was being talked about as a future Director of the FBI.

Maybe that attitude of preferential treatment worked well in the early days of the FBI, when it was quite small. Men who'd been around the Bureau in the 1920s and 1930s told me that as the agency grew, the Director had become more distant, more of a czar in his own house. Also, too many people spent too much time telling him that he was a great man, and in many senses he lost perspective.

What Hoover never really understood was that the organization that he had created was bigger than himself—that the FBI was a fine investigative agency and that it would go on being effective and efficient even if he did not wield an iron hand over it at every moment. For instance, Hoover believed that no one in the FBI knew more about investigations than he did; this was patent nonsense, because a supervisor, or a section chief, or an assistant director almost always knew more about a particular area like Soviet espionage or a particular case than the Director could. However, there were times when Hoover was more right than any of his underlings, especially when it became a question of politics or public relations. In most instances, though, the people who were in continual and detailed touch with an investigation knew more about how to conduct it than did any higher official. This was true precisely because the FBI had become so good at what it did, so skilled in techniques and training and utilization of resources—that is to say, because the FBI had grown to become what the Director had always envisioned it to be.

Now, this was not the attitude of most of the men in the FBI, and one reason that my viewpoint was somewhat different from that of my organizational colleagues was that counterintelligence was very different from the bulk of the FBI's work, which was in criminal and security-related cases. And if the system often irked me, perhaps it was because the work that we did against the Soviets didn't fit neatly into the pigeonholes provided for the rest of the FBI's cases.

It was part of my mission at headquarters to force that system to work for us in our fight against the Soviets, and not to hinder us. And of course, we did have marvelous resources at our command. Let me just take one small example of how the system worked at its best. One of the duties that took up an enormous portion of a supervisor's time was to review the amazingly complete FBI files on each new case. When we requested a listing of all the references in the indices on a subject's name and aliases, we would generally get back a mountain of material. I didn't like burrowing through such mountains, but the system provided me with a clerk whom I was able to train to review and summarize the files, and who helped me immensely. My first clerk, Jim Almeter, was a young, intelligent high-school graduate from Minneapolis—later on he worked for the Armed Forces Security Agency and became a lawyer. In short order Jim became better at reviewing and summarizing the pertinent data in a Bureau file than I was. And that paid off.

Once I asked Jim to do a thorough file review on a KGB agent named Mikhail Chaliapin, whom Elizabeth Bentley had identified and characterized as rather stupid. Chaliapin had been one of the KGB men at the Soviet consulate in New York. In the back of his mind Jim also retained the notion that I was interested in trying to identify another of Bentley's contacts, a man whom she'd known as "Jack." She had described Jack vividly—175–180 pounds, athletic and husky build, with dark-blond kinky hair, unusually thick eyebrows, blue eyes, a slightly curved Jewish nose, dentures. Jack had dressed poorly, in gray suits and brown shoes, and walked with a slight limp in his left leg which was noticeable when he moved rapidly. He told Bentley that he'd been born in Lithuania and spoke Russian, Yiddish, Hebrew, Lithuanian and English with a "typical West Side New York accent." Bentley had liked him and found him sympathetic. We'd been unable to identify Jack in more than three years—until Jim Almeter was reviewing the Chaliapin file and came to me, all excited.

It seemed that in 1944 FBI men from the New York office had followed Chaliapin and had seen him meet an unknown man on a street corner. When the two men separated, the FBI men, using standard procedure, dropped Chaliapin and tailed the new man, who went to a brownstone in Greenwich Village, which he entered with a key. What excited Jim was that the agents had described the unknown contact as walking with a limp. Bentley's Jack limped on one leg and the agents' unknown suspect limped on the other, but when a person walks with a limp it is frequently hard for an observer to say on which leg he's limping.

Unfortunately, the file petered out there. In 1944 the field agents had tried to find the superintendent of the building in which the unknown limping man was staying, but couldn't do so right away; when they returned the next day, the super claimed not to know the man.

From headquarters I sent immediate instructions to the New York field office to go back to the Greenwich Village apartment house and try again to identify the unknown man. The trail was cold, but with the new impetus and sense of importance that my instructions conveyed, the New York office learned from people in the building that the man whom they sought was named Joseph Katz. That we were able to discover his identity was a testament to the thoroughness of the Bureau's investigative actions and files, and also to the ingenuity of an experienced and committed file clerk who was similarly a part of the system.

Unfortunately, when we went to look for Katz, we found out that he was no longer in the United States. I would continue to find his name linked with other cases for many years, and we'll meet up with him again in this narrative at several points.

Another way the system helped us was through its in-service training for field agents. After Bill Harvey joined the CIA, Emory Gregg took his place as a lecturer on Soviet espionage, and some time later I also became a lecturer on the same subject. I thought I was good and competent at lecturing, but I paled in Emory's shadow—he could tell the story of a case with such drama and excitement that our hard-boiled agents would applaud as he came to its end. In any event, in these lectures we were continually pushing the more aggressive policies we championed, and as the years went on and our "graduates" returned to the field to put them into practice, we could see that what we wanted was beginning to have an impact on actual casework.

Looking at the big picture, I think it's fair to say that we had the right ideas at the time for what needed to be done. In the late 1940s it became increasingly obvious that the Soviets were the enemy, and the Bureau responded by putting more manpower into the fight against them—both in terms of agents in the field and of supervisors at headquarters. In 1947 we were seven supervisors; later there were fifty of us. Our increased field manpower also meant that we were able to put saturation coverage on the official establishments of the Soviets and their satellite countries. By the late 1940s we were more routinely winding up dormant cases by interviewing suspects rather than by simply closing the files; in a number of these we were getting confessions that opened up new avenues of investigation. We were doing rather well with some double-agent cases—these, if they did nothing else, kept Soviet operatives occupied while enabling us to identify the Soviet agents and to learn to some degree what information they were seeking.

On a higher level, the Bureau's power was felt in the major role it played in convincing the State Department that Soviet consulates in New York and San Francisco were havens for espionage and should be closed. Both consular offices were shut.

Communist pressure in Iran, on Berlin and in Asia helped convince both the Director and Mickey Ladd that we needed to do more against Soviet spying in this country. In good cases we began to get the go-ahead to try actions that in prior years had never been approved. We used more microphones, did more black-bag jobs, interviewed more people and pushed harder to get Soviet and other Eastern European officials to defect. The Soviets didn't like our aggressive moves and saturation coverage—but I'm sure they came to respect us more because of them.

After a while there were signs that we were disrupting some Soviet espionage operations. KGB and GRU people showed by their actions that they were never quite sure whether or not we were following them. Captured Soviet handbooks carried warnings to Soviet agents that the FBI understood KGB methods and was actively countering Soviet penetrations, and directed that KGB people in the United States assume that the FBI was watching their every move. Our double agents verified for us just how cautious the Soviets had become, and how much they feared our actions.

A good chunk of this progress against the Soviets came by dint of hard work and application. Emory and I and people like us at headquarters were young men with a mission, and we pursued the fight as hard as we could on every available front. But sometimes hard work can be supplemented by a break—and in the fight against the

KGB in the Cold War era, the FBI got one enormous break, which enabled us to take very important actions to disband Soviet networks, expose longtime spies and protect the United States.

As it happened, within a short time after I arrived at FBI headquarters that break came—and it came my way.

6
THE BREAK

MY FIRST ASSIGNMENT at Bureau headquarters was to set up counterintelligence coverage on Soviet satellite countries operating within the United States. After a few months of this I longed to get back into fighting the main threat, Soviet intelligence, and I believed that in a locked safe in our espionage unit at headquarters was a means of doing so.

The safe contained several pieces of paper that had a special top-secret classification. These were the fruits of an attempt to decode intercepted KGB messages that had been sent, in code, from the Soviet consulate in New York to KGB headquarters in Moscow in 1944–45. To date, the cryptanalysts of the Army Security Agency had only been able to decipher and translate from the Russian a few words in these messages, and some of these were code names. So the pages were mostly blank and in their present form were almost meaningless. However, they were very intriguing. Several of us in the espionage section had previously met with the supervisor who had charge of the partial message translations, and had discussed them a bit. While we were all interested in them, not much had developed because there wasn't much to go on.

I went to Espionage Section Chief Pat Coyne and asked if I could take charge of the fragmentary messages and be relieved of my work on the satellite countries. Pat had no objection, and neither did the supervisor to whom the messages had originally been assigned. And so, one day in late 1947, I took over the few mostly blank pages and the task of doing something with them.

The KGB messages were to change my life. More important, they were to affect the course of history: in the coming years their revelations would lead directly to decisive actions that the FBI took against KGB operations in the United States.

Today, nearly forty years after I took charge of a few sheets of paper sparsely covered with seemingly unconnected words, I am able to tell in some detail the story of the breakthrough into the KGB's networks that was accomplished through the decipherment of these messages. The Soviets have known for many years that we cracked these messages; they learned of it from double agents within the British intelligence services, including Kim Philby, and I have now come to believe they learned of it from these sources even prior to the time Philby arrived in the United States in October 1949. In recent years there has been some publicity about the deciphered messages; the first hint came from leaks by former British intelligence men in Great Britain. Even this present version will lack many details, for the National Security Agency (successor to the Army Security Agency) does not want me to reveal certain aspects. However, I can now tell enough of the story so that anyone reading this account will comprehend the magnitude of the breakthrough that the deciphered KGB messages provided.

Every counterintelligence man's dream is to be able to secretly read the enemy's communications. If we could know what instructions were being given, how many networks were operating against us, who the agents were, what information was being sought and obtained—then a whole host of possibilities for countering and controlling enemy espionage efforts would be feasible. Methods used, recognition signs, dead-letter drops, places and times of rendezvous, courier routes—all would be open to our counterintelligence coverage. In the best possible scenario, the enemy would never know of our penetration; we would learn in advance his every move, though, and we would achieve the ultimate counterintelligence goal, complete control of the enemy's moves against us.

Since biblical times, countries have tried to conceal their communications from their enemies' prying eyes. Codes and ciphers of varying degrees of sophistication have been in use for many centuries. In the modern era, cipher systems have become quite technically refined, and use machines that allow both speed and almost perfect security.

When I took on my new assignment, I knew very little about codes and ciphers, although I had had some instruction from the FBI's cryptanalysis section and had studied a bit on the subject. Several of us had taken considerable interest in the shining example from the north, namely, what had happened when GRU code clerk Igor Gouzenko had defected to Canada and brought out with him the plain texts of many messages to and from Moscow. Most of the cables that Gouzenko provided to the RCMP covered a short period in the summer of 1945. Nonetheless, with these and with pages from the diary of his superior, the RCMP had been able to identify seventeen agents by code names, together with sixteen Soviet diplomats involved in espionage; many of the Canadian citizens in the net had been tried and convicted, and the Soviets had been expelled. While Gouzenko was GRU, he knew something of the KGB system, which was similar to his own "one-time cipher pad" system.

From Gouzenko and from other investigations we knew the basic method used by the KGB to transmit information to and from its embassies and consulates abroad to Moscow. A message to Moscow would be written out in Russian and delivered to a code clerk. To put it into the cipher the clerk would first turn to the KGB codebook; the front part of this book had (in alphabetical order) hundreds and hundreds of words, as well as the letters of the alphabet, each accompanied by a five-digit number. (The back part of the book had the obverse—that is, the five-digit number-groups, accompanied by the Russian words.) As the first step in the cipher process, the clerk would convert the words in the message into five-digit number-groups as taken from the codebook.

Next, the clerk would turn to the one-time cipher pad, a sheet with five-digit number-groups on it. This is called a one-time pad because each sheet in it is to be used only once and then destroyed. The number-groups on the sheets are produced in a completely random way. The clerk then adds the number-groups from the one-time pad to the number-groups he has already put down from the codebook. This makes a complete message, which would then be taken to the commercial cable company for transmittal to Moscow.

In order to provide a better understanding of the process, I'll invent a very short message: ALEK HAS ARRIVED.

In the cipher process for this message, the code clerk would first turn to his codebook. Let's suppose that in it there is no single five-digit number for ALEK—so that the clerk will have to look up a separate number-group for each letter of that word—but that there are number-groups for HAS and ARRIVED. The message, in five-digit numbers, would read:

A	L	E	K	HAS	ARRIVED
03152	13415	05789	12141	81324	14287

The clerk would then go to the one-time cipher pad and use the top sheet for this message, working with the first six number-groups, which will suffice for this very short message. The clerk would add these groups to the others in a special addition process that has no carry-overs from one column to the next. With this transformation, the number-groups would be:

03152	13415	05789	12141	81324	14287
74932	44734	65277	53865	00118	54968
77084	57149	60956	65906	81432	68145

This last series of number-groups is what would then be sent to Moscow. When the message arrived at Moscow KGB headquarters, a code clerk would reverse the process. He would use the one-time pad known to be keyed to the sending station and, taking the appropriate five-digit number-groups from his pad, would subtract them from the message he received. This would give him the number-groups that would then be looked up in the codebook.

As long as the numbers on the one-time pad have been produced in a completely random way, a one-time cipher pad system has always been regarded as "unbreakable," offering "perfect secrecy."

I wondered how it had been possible for the Army Security Agency to make even a few partial breaks in the supposedly impregnable system, and contemplated whether the FBI might be able to assist in widening the breakthrough. Normally, to get answers to these sorts of questions one went to the appropriate liaison representative in the Bureau, but I wanted to meet directly with the man or men of the ASA who were working on the messages. With a little difficulty, our liaison to the ASA, Wes Reynold, obtained an appointment for me with the chief of the intelligence division of the agency, Frank Rowlett. Frank, whom I later came to know well, had been a top cryptanalyst at the agency for many years; under President Lyndon B. Johnson he was awarded the National Security Medal.

Rowlett wanted to impress upon me the absolute importance of maintaining the top-secret nature of the attempt to break the Soviet code system. He wanted to make sure that if the FBI mounted any investigations based on the messages, we would never quote directly from a deciphered cable; rather, our information would be paraphrased and couched in the euphemism that it had come from a highly sensitive source of known reliability. Only persons cleared to handle this special top-secret material would be given access to the messages themselves. I had already been apprised of Rowlett's concerns by Wes Reynold, but the ASA man's demeanor in laying out the importance of protecting the source made a big impression on me.

Frank Rowlett then described to me the cryptanalyst who was working to decipher the KGB code, Meredith Gardner. Gardner, said Rowlett, was unusual and brilliant, not only as a cryptanalyst but also as a linguist. He spoke six or seven languages and was one of the few Western scholars who read Sanskrit. Until the outbreak of World War II he had taught languages at a university in the Southwest. On joining the ASA, Gardner taught himself Japanese in three months, to the amazement of his colleagues. Throughout the war he had worked on breaking the Japanese codes, and after the war was over Rowlett had put him on the KGB codes. Rowlett told me I'd find Meredith Gardner to be a shy, introverted loner, and that I'd have a hard time getting to know him.

The ASA offices were at Arlington Hall, across the Potomac from the District of Columbia, in Virginia, at what used to be a girls' school. Gardner met me in one of the brick-and-wood-frame buildings, and as we sat down to talk I soon realized that Rowlett's description of him was accurate. Gardner was tall, gangling, reserved, obviously intelligent, and extremely reluctant to discuss much about his work or whether it would progress any distance beyond the first fragments that the FBI had already received. I asked him how I could be of assistance to him; he seemed not to know. I told him I was intensely interested in what he was doing and would be willing to mount any sort of research effort to provide him with more information; he simply nodded. I offered to write up a memo about one of the message fragments because I thought the FBI might have a glimmer of understanding of the subject matter being discussed by the KGB; he was noncommittal.

From that day on, every two or three weeks I would make the pilgrimage out to Arlington Hall. Meredith Gardner was indeed not easy to know, and was extremely modest about his work, but eventually we did become friends. Neither the friendship nor the solution to the messages was achieved overnight, but steady progress was made. Little by little he chipped away at the messages, and I helped him with memoranda that described what the KGB might be referring to in some of them. The ASA's work was further aided by one of the early, rudimentary computers.

Sometimes a few words would be deciphered, but when they were translated, their meaning would be unclear because of the fragmentary nature of what was available or because of the Soviets' extensive use of code names. This use of code names for countries and things as well as people can be clearly shown from the GRU messages that Gouzenko brought out of the Soviet embassy in Ottawa. For example, the GRU had made extensive use of the Canadian Communist Party for espionage recruits, and in its communications designated the Party by the code name "corporation," and its members by the unusual but logical name "corporants." Other code names used by the GRU in its cables to Moscow included:

CODE NAME	MEANING
dubok	hiding place
roof	a front to conceal espionage operations
Gisel	the GRU
neighbors	the KGB
Lesovia	Canada
Metro	Soviet Embassy, Ottawa
sabot (shoe)	passport
shoemaker	forger of false passports
nash (ours)	he works for us
Grant	GRU Colonel Zabotin
Debouz	GRU agent Fred Rose, member of the Canadian Parliament

There is a distinction between code names and cover names. While KGB agent Elizabeth Bentley knew her own cover name— "Helen" —which she used on her contacts with other agents, she did not know her code name, which would be used in the KGB's own correspondence with Moscow.

In Canada, because Gouzenko was cooperating with the RCMP, the authorities had been able to find out who the people were that were referred to in the cables by code names. In the KGB messages that the ASA had deciphered, we had no such help. To begin with, only parts of the messages were deciphered. In addition, the KGB had a habit of assigning code names to prominent people, or to those who were targets of recruitment but who might never have been successfully recruited. At times we could discern that a message from New York to Moscow was in answer to a question from KGB head-quarters, but without knowing the question it was difficult to comprehend the meaning of the cryptic answer.

From the first I was curious as to how Gardner had gotten even as far as he had in breaking into the KGB code system. Little by little I came to understand what had happened. In his office Gardner had a copy of a partially burned KGB codebook. It was not the current edition that the KGB was using, but it was immensely helpful to him in laboriously building his own version of the correct KGB codebook. During World War II the partially charred codebook had been recovered by the Finns from a battlefield, and in November 1944 William Donovan, then head of the OSS, purchased 1500 pages of code and cipher material from the Finns. A copy was provided immediately to the ASA.

Because the United States and the Soviet Union were allies, Secretary of State Edward Stettinius objected to our having and using the Soviet code material; he took his protests to the White House, and Donovan was then forced to return to the Russians the material he had purchased.

I have always wondered at this gesture of friendship by Stettinius. It certainly did the United States no good, and in the reverse circumstances, the Soviet Union would have seen no necessity to provide us with the information that they had obtained our codes.

I was also chagrined—but not surprised—to learn that by May 1945 the KGB had changed its codes, and Meredith Gardner could not break into any messages dated after that time. It is a virtual certainty that the Soviets' change of ciphers was related to having recovered their "lost" material. They assumed that the United States had kept a copy of the charred codebook, and accordingly changed their codes.

In any event, in 1948 Meredith Gardner had a codebook that the KGB had used in Finland in 1944. It wasn't the current codebook, but it was similar and above all it provided him with a start.

The sheaf upon sheaf of undeciphered KGB messages that the ASA had were ones that had been sent over regular commercial cable wires from the Soviet consulate in New York and from the Soviet embassy in Washington, to Moscow. How had these been obtained? As James Bamford has recently revealed in *The Puzzle Palace*, during the war the Office of Censorship exercised its authority to get cable traffic, and directed cable companies to delay the transmission of messages to more than a dozen different countries—including the Soviet Union—so they could be copied and used for various intelligence purposes. This practice was continued on a regular basis throughout the war. So the cable traffic was available, albeit in cipher, and a KGB codebook was available, although it was not the right one. That gave Meredith Gardner two sets of clues.

With these Meredith had been able to make a crack into the KGB system, and by his brilliance was laboring to enlarge that crack. I wanted desperately for him to get inside that KGB communications system, and was willing to mount any kind of research effort to help him.

As he and I worked together over the first few months of 1948, and he became more comfortable with me, he began to be more willing to ask me to do things for him. One day he inquired if there was any possibility of obtaining the plain text of certain materials that had been sent to the Soviet Union in ciphered form in 1944. With the lapse of four years, I didn't hold out much hope, but told him I'd investigate the possibility. I then asked the New York field office to look into the matter; in my request I didn't go into the specifics of why I wanted the information, but at the same time I emphasized the importance of the request.

To my surprise, by return mail I received a mass of material, all in Russian except for a few translations into English—the work, I was certain, of my old translator friend, Mr. Boguslav. This material had been photographed by New York FBI agents in the course of an investigation into Soviet operations in New York in 1944.

I was still not optimistic about this when I took the stack of papers across the river to Meredith at Arlington Hall. When I returned two weeks later, I found Gardner in the most excited mood I'd ever seen him display. In his shy way he explained that we'd hit the jackpot. He now had the plain texts of some very important material.

This, then, was the beginning of an important new phase in our breakthrough, for in a short while Meredith began to give me some completely deciphered messages, and portions of others that he was deciphering at a more rapid rate than had heretofore been possible. The material I had delivered was of great assistance to him as he worked to make his own, correct KGB codebook. I remember well his slight smiles of pleasure when in his work on the messages he would stop for a moment, reach for his own version of that KGB codebook, and hand-print a word in Russian next to one of the number-groups.

Many times during the next several years I was able to give Meredith assistance in his work. We'll encounter some of these instances at greater length in later chapters, but I'll mention a few here. Once I managed to provide him with copies of telegrams from Winston Churchill to Truman; some of these, repeated with meticulous accuracy down to the identifying numbers on the cables, had been in the KGB messages. Also, I obtained a copy of a scientific report on the gaseous diffusion process for making uranium 235. The Anglo-American cables had been stolen and given to the KGB by an agent inside the British embassy in Washington, we later learned. In a similar manner, someone inside the Manhattan Project had provided the KGB with a copy of the scientific report that was summarized in an espionage cable to Moscow. For Gardner to obtain the original materials greatly enhanced his work.

From the moment of our breakthrough in 1948, each week I would receive additional deciphered messages and new fragments of messages that had earlier been partly deciphered. As the messages became readable, I could set in motion investigations based on what they said.

I stood in the vestibule of the enemy's house, having entered by stealth. I held in my hand a set of keys. Each would fit one of the doors of the place and lead us, I hoped, to matters of importance to our country. I had no idea where the corridors in the KGB's edifice would take us, or what we would find when we reached the end of a search—but the keys were ours, and we were determined to use them.

Each day was an opportunity to exploit the breakthrough. Sitting in headquarters, I directed our agents in the various field offices to explore the possibilities and connections that the information in the messages divulged—at times I'd have agents in a dozen cities looking into a dozen different matters.

Each morning I'd come into headquarters and work with the messages, which I kept locked in a safe. I had a file system for information from the messages, arranged by code names; it was an arbitrary way of dividing up the material, but it sometimes proved effective.

One group of messages which I kept under the code name of a

KGB agent had to do with White Russian émigré circles in New York. The KGB had always been interested in the émigrés, seeing in them both potential recruits and people who knew the Soviet system and hated it. We understood that émigrés were one of the many targets of Soviet espionage, and we had some contacts among them. We used these contacts to give us help in broadening our understanding of the meaning and intent of particular messages.

A few years later one particular message in this group was deciphered. It clearly had to do with a KGB agent in the White Russian community in New York City, and immediately someone came to mind who could help me with it: Elsa Bernaut. Back in 1947, Hede Massing had introduced me to her. Elsa was the widow of "Ludwig." I had interviewed her in New York several times in connection with the Eisler case. She was a small, intense woman with graying hair and a heavy Eastern European accent. She'd been somewhat cooperative with me but, despite what the Massings had told her about me, distrustful of the FBI—a result, I'd concluded, of her European suspicion of police, whatever their name. I was therefore quite surprised when, one day at headquarters, I received a call from the reception desk that Elsa Bernaut was waiting to see me. I brought her into the office and we had a nice chat about her recent trip to Europe. That was why, when this message about the White Russian colony in New York came in, I thought of her. We had already begun to suspect that the KGB agent denoted by a code name in the messages was Mark Zborowski; I told the New York field office to go and ask Elsa about him.

Elsa told the New York office that she was positive her old friend Zborowski could not be a KGB spy; they had been through too much together.

Undeterred, we continued to tail Zborowski, and a week or two later as our men followed him, Zborowski drove out of New York and toward Connecticut. On a lonely road he met a small gray-haired lady, and the two talked for a while. Of course his rendezvous was with Elsa. Unable to believe ill of a man whom she had known for more than a quarter century, she'd made contact in order to warn Zborowski of the FBI's queries.

Shortly thereafter we picked up Zborowski for questioning; unnerved by Elsa's warning, he confessed to fifteen years of service for the KGB, which dated back to his tenure in Paris in the 1930s. One of his revelations was that he had been the KGB agent within the circle around Leon Trotsky's son Sedov; in fact, Mark Zborowski had

had a hand in setting up Sedov for execution by the KGB. He also had been an important factor in the KGB's theft of Trotsky's archives and possibly in the execution of Trotsky's secretary. In a later confrontation with Elsa, Zborowski led her to believe he might also have played a small role in putting the KGB on the path of her husband, "Ludwig," when "Ludwig" was in hiding and trying to avoid being murdered by them.

Zborowski gave the FBI excellent information on the KGB's interest in Russian émigrés in the United States, which led to the shutdown of the activities of other KGB agents. For his own illegal activities, Zborowski himself was sent to prison for five years.

Not all the cases begun out of the deciphered messages were so successful. Many, in fact, could never be concluded. One of these (also from a slightly later time frame) suggests the lengths to which the FBI would go in a field investigation to try and track down the leads we obtained from the KGB message fragments.

The messages told us that in 1944 in New York the KGB had advised Moscow that it was interested in a woman and her son, both Rumanians; the son was in the U.S. Army and was stationed in Alaska, and the messages mentioned that the family had previously lived at an address in Istanbul. Looking at the message fragments, we were unable to determine if the people mentioned had been agents, possible recruits, targets of one sort or another, or what. But if the KGB had been interested in them, I would be.

I sent a teletype to the St. Louis field office asking that the nearby U.S. Army records depot be checked for soldiers who had been posted to Alaska in 1944 and who were either born in Rumania or had Rumanian-sounding names. I also asked the New York and Washington field offices to check their files for possible suspects.

Let me digress for a moment to speak of how I sent information to the field with regard to the deciphered KGB messages. Heeding the instructions from the ASA, I did not send the text of the deciphered messages. What I did was to take the information the messages divulged, rephrase it, and incorporate it into a paragraph that might show that a "confidential informant of known reliability" had told it to us. The telex or memo would say "Espionage, R" (for Russian) under the title, and I also used other designations that told the field offices that it was my interests they were trying to follow up, even though all communications to them went out in the Director's name. Most local offices and agents reacted well and promptly to my requests; they knew, in a vague way, whence the information had come to the FBI, and they were out in the field dreaming the counterintelligence man's dream along with me.

In the Rumanian-sounding-names case, after some time had gone by, I received a rather short list of names from the army records depot that had been compiled by the St. Louis office; running my finger down it, I picked out a soldier who was born in Rumania and who listed a mother in New York. "I'll bet this is the one," I told an associate.

With this information in hand, I then asked the CIA to assist us by checking out the address in Istanbul, and to try to find any families that had lived at that address and had emigrated to the United States. The CIA's effort to find out what I wanted to know took much longer than had my request to St. Louis. As it turned out, the agency had to send someone first to Switzerland and then on to Turkey. Eventually I got back a confirmation of what we already knew—the names of the mother and son who had lived at that particular address in Istanbul and who had emigrated to New York, the same ones as those on the army depot records from St. Louis.

Then, sure that we had correctly identified the people in whom the KGB had shown an interest in 1944, we began to dig into their backgrounds. Almost immediately, we came up with a surprise. The mother was currently working for the CIA. We apprised the CIA of our information, but questions still remained. Was she a KGB agent? Had she ever been one in the past? I never found out, because the investigation took so long that it was still in process when I left the FBI in 1955.

Even such inconclusive investigations could add to our store of knowledge about the information in the messages; we would increase our ability to measure their detail, their accuracy and the ways in which they reflected KGB methods.

Early on, among my colleagues, there was a difference in the level of interest in the messages. Some were avid for all developments; others believed little would come of all the work and research. For quite some time my superiors did not appreciate the worth of the work very much. Their low level of interest may well have stemmed from my own desire to conform to the ASA's wishes and to keep secret insofar as possible the fact that the cryptanalysts were solving the KGB's ciphers. I had, of course, written a memo on the subject, which went to Director Hoover and to other top officials. I don't recall now any significant reaction to my memo; probably, as was his wont, the Director merely initialed it to indicate that he had seen it.

Another deciphered KGB message advised Moscow of a meeting that was to take place between two men, identified by code names, one from New York and one from the West Coast. The recognition signal between the men was to be the two halves of a motion-picture-theater ticket, one of those that had the number printed at both ends. Even the number on the ticket was reproduced in the messages.

I recalled that some time prior to our decrypting the message, the San Francisco office had broken up a KGB operation—and so I asked San Francisco, by teletype, if any of the FBI people there could shed any light on a rendezvous the KGB had proposed in 1944–45. Here again, we were lucky. As it happened, the FBI had obtained confessions from a KGB agent in San Francisco, who had said something about a meeting he was to have had with a man in New York in which the recognition signal was a movie ticket. The KGB agent had said that the meeting had never taken place. When the San Francisco office got my request, they went back to the confessed spy and asked for more details about the meeting that hadn't been consummated. Through another stroke of luck, the man had kept his half of the movie ticket, and, sure enough, the numbers on it matched those on the KGB message we had deciphered. The confessed KGB man in San Francisco then identified the photographs of the man whom he was supposed to meet—because later, they had met: he was Joseph Katz. This meant we now had additional information about Katz's activities, and it also meant we knew the KGB's code name for him.

Of course, we never knew in advance of making an investigation based on the deciphered KGB messages whether it would lead to a dead end or to an important case. I stress this point because in the next pages I'm going to tell of three instances where deciphered KGB messages provided the initial clues that directed the FBI to people who were then unknown but who later came to be well known and associated with "the Rosenberg case." We had no idea that such a thing as the Rosenberg case would develop when, in the spring of 1948, we began these investigations based on the 1944–45 KGB messages.

In recounting these inquiries, I have supplemented my own memory with some data from FBI files that have been released to the public under the Freedom of Information Act (FOIA). Let me take a moment to speak of these released files. The impression of most people is that all of the FBI's old files can be obtained under FOIA.

This is not so. One of the exemptions that the government may cite in refusing to release certain documents or portions of documents is that they may contain data relating to cryptanalytic processes or their products. From 1948 to 1955 I wrote hundred of letters and teletypes based on the deciphered KGB messages, but in nearly every instance the references to the messages have been blanked out on documents released under FOIA. However, because I was the originator of many of these documents, and handled plenty of those which I did not originate, I am able to see in some of the partially blanked-out documents what others may have missed.

In the spring of 1948—that is, relatively soon after Meredith Gardner and I had begun to work intensively—some of the KGB messages came clear. One message from the KGB resident in the Soviet consulate in New York said that someone (designated by a code name) had approached a man named Max Elitcher and had requested that Elitcher provide information to him on his current work at the navy's Department of Ordnance.

This message contained quite a bit of information on Max Elitcher. It gave a date of the contact—June 1944. It provided a code name for Elitcher that would be used in all future messages. It said that Elitcher was married, had been known to his KGB contact for some years, and was a member of the Communist Party of the United States.

The message didn't say whether or not Elitcher had agreed to provide information, nor did it give us the name of the KGB agent who had approached him, only his code name. But when we started looking for Elitcher, we immediately discovered he was a man in a position to do the United States some damage, because he worked in 1948 for the Navy Bureau of Ordance, which dealt directly with weapons development.

We might have an active spy on our hands! The possibility immediately put a sense of urgency and importance into our investigation. We needed to know, first, whether Elitcher had ever agreed to work for the KGB; second, if he had been recruited, whether he was still active; and third, whether we could identify the person who had tried, successfully or unsuccessfully, to recruit Elitcher. This last was the most important objective because the recruiter might lead us to others in a network.

I instructed both the Washington and the New York field offices to open investigations into Max Elitcher, and almost instantly found that the Bureau was already conducting a loyalty check on him, begun at the request of the Office of Naval Intelligence. Because the loyalty check threatened to make our suspicions known to Elitcher, I moved to have it suspended. We got data from ONI about Elitcher, and it showed that he'd first come to their attention in January 1941, when he and fellow navy employee Morton Sobell had been observed using Sobell's car to take people to and from an antidraft rally sponsored by the American Peace Mobilization Committee—an organization whose membership included many known Communists. ONI had tried and failed to determine if Elitcher and Sobell were Communists, and the investigation into the two men had lapsed. Though Sobell left the navy shortly after the 1941 incident and returned to school for graduate work, Elitcher continued in his navy position through the war.

Something had tripped the ONI's special interest in Elitcher again late in 1947, and in 1948 the FBI had an additional reason to notice him. We had the post office send us photostats of the outsides of all envelopes and postcards mailed to Elitcher's residence (this was called a "mail cover"), reviewed some of his long-distance telephone calls and tailed Elitcher in an effort to find out just what he was up to. Background checks revealed that Elitcher had attended the City College of New York from 1934 to 1938, and had graduated with a degree in electrical engineering. Sobell had been Elitcher's classmate at CCNY, a fellow Communist sympathizer, and, in Washington, Elitcher's bachelor roommate.

During the early surveillance of Elitcher and his wife, Helene, the agents thought the Elitchers might become aware of the FBI's interest in them. Elitcher almost immediately began to lay plans to leave the navy, and went to New York several times in search of new employment. Morton Sobell helped Elitcher find a job alongside his own at Reeves Instrument Company, which was working on secret navy and air force projects; Sobell also steered the Elitchers to a new development in Queens and a home whose backyard bordered his own. The processs of securing new employment and shelter in New York took several months. It was not yet complete when, on July 30, 1948, Max and Helene Elitcher and their child got into their 1941 two-door Chevrolet sedan and headed for New York.

The Elitchers were tailed by several FBI surveillance teams. Shortly after the Elitchers' car passed Baltimore, it began to speed and to make erratic moves as if the occupants were trying to lose the tail. Near Philadelphia one team of FBI men in a car took over from another, and the Elitcher car's progress settled down once again; the new surveillance team followed the Chevrolet without difficulty all the way into New York City. The Elitchers drove to an apartment on upper Lexington Avenue in Manhattan, where Max's mother lived. As the later FBI report put it,

> From the time the car left the express highway on the West Side of New York until it arrived at Elitcher's family residence, both Helene and Max gave definite indications of checking for surveillance.

Noting this, the FBI agents dropped back, though only far enough so that the Elitchers wouldn't notice them so easily. They were not discreet enough, for, as the report continues,

> on the trip from Manhattan to the Sobells' home it was confirmed without a doubt that the Elitchers were "tail conscious" and, therefore, the surveillance was discontinued.

Physical surveillance was reinstituted when the Elitchers moved to New York, but was later cut back. Not only were the Elitchers conscious that they were being followed, but the investigation so far had developed nothing of significance. However, Elitcher's case remained open, assigned to an agent in the New York field office.

While the Max Elitcher investigation was still in the initial phase, other message fragments were deciphered that named Joel Barr as a potential recruit for the KGB. Here was another startling possibility, for in 1944 (the date of the messages) Barr had worked for the Western Electric Company, a major defense contractor. Furthermore, the message gave us reason to believe (as the words of a later FBI report phrased it) that Barr might "have acted as an intermediary between person or persons who were working on wartime nuclear fission research and for MGB agents (1944)."

We looked quickly for Barr, and discovered that he was in Finland. If he had been a spy in 1944, at least he was currently out of the United States. I began to search for more information about him. Again, some material on this new suspect was already in our files. Joel Barr's name had been listed, together with eight others, as having transferred from Branch 16B of the Industrial Division of the Communist Party to various small Communist community clubs in the New York area in March 1944. Another file entry on Barr noted that in 1947 he had become a project engineer at Sperry

Gyroscope, with access to "A.O. 19440 information secret and unlimited."

So in 1947 Barr had still been working on defense contracts, and in 1944 he'd been in the Communist Party. As we developed Barr's background, we found a number of interesting things. He'd been in the same CCNY undergraduate electrical engineering department as Sobell and Elitcher, and at the same time, graduating in 1938. In 1940 he'd gone to work at the Army Signal Corps Laboratory in Monmouth, New Jersey; one co-worker there became his close friend, Alfred Sarant, and another, Vivian Glassman, became his fiancée. Barr had been dismissed from the Signal Corps in 1942, when army officers learned that he had signed a Communist Party nominating petition. He had then applied for engineering work at Western Electric but had been careful not to mention the reason for his dismissal from the Signal Corps. He got a job with Western Electric working on highly classified radar systems for the B-29 bomber, and stayed with that company until the end of the war, after which he resigned and went back to school to obtain a master's degree.

He'd joined Sperry Gyroscope in 1946, but was dismissed in 1947 because he'd been denied government clearance to work with classified documents. Then, evidently believing that the Communist associations of his past would prevent him from obtaining further government work, Barr had gone to Europe. He had landed in France in early 1948, and had spent three months in Holland before going to Finland.

Knowing all this about Barr, in the summer of 1948 I wondered whether he might go over the Finnish border into Russia and disappear—because there was a strong possibility that he had been a spy. We didn't know if Barr had ever actually done espionage for the Soviet Union—but we surely wanted to find out. I asked the New York field office to see what they could learn about him from a discreet visit to his family.

An FBI agent pretended to be an old school chum who had lost touch with Barr, and prevailed upon Barr's mother to see him. He learned that Barr was supporting himself by playing the piano while traveling through Finland—but little else. We found out later that Barr crossed into Sweden and enrolled at the Royal Technical Institute in Stockholm. At this point I turned the investigation over to the CIA, which had the facilities and jurisdiction to track Barr while he was abroad. Should Barr return to the United States, we would again pick up his trail.

So far, the inquiries had been tantalizing but inconclusive. Both Elitcher and Barr might have been spies in 1944, or neither of them might ever have been a spy. What was certain was that both had been privy to military secrets at the time of the messages, and that both had ideological leanings which might have convinced a KGB resident that they were worthy targets of recruitment.

When would we find an active spy? I knew it was only a matter of time, but didn't know which of the keys in my hand would lead to his door. We continued to pursue investigations from data provided by the messages. In the same batch of messages that had named Barr and Elitcher, another person was named—a female.

Today it is hard to find out much about the early phases of that investigation because it remains buried in the FBI files. However, a few pieces of information do exist. One of these was Scotty Miller's early report referred to above, which references a June 4, 1948, letter of mine to the field. That letter has not been released, but I remember it well enough to know that it was the beginning of an investigation into someone who was then referred to as an "unknown subject," and was a woman. The Scotty Miller report paraphrased mine in saying that they had been looking for someone thought "to have acted as an intermediary between person or persons who were working on wartime nuclear fission research and for MGB agents (1944)." The Miller report is basically a report on Joel Barr, who we thought might be the person referred to as the intermediary.

But that is not the only inference of the document, because another page of the Miller report suggests that someone other than Barr could have been a suspect as the intermediary. The clue, which has been overlooked by other writers on this matter, is on the second page of the October 18 report; it is a clue that has been made public through a mistake. When the document was readied for release, one small paragraph was left legible while the rest of the page was blanked out. I believe that what happened in the releasing process was that instead of covering up the small paragraph and leaving intact and legible the rest of the page (which would have been about Joel Barr), a mistake was made that blanked out what was supposed to have been left in while printing what was supposed to have been excised. Thus the small paragraph remains intact. It reiterated my June 4, 1948, letter to the field, and reads:

Christian name, ETHEL, used her husband's last name; had been married for five years (at this time); 29 years of age; member of the

Communist Party, USA, possibly joining in 1938; probably knew about her husband's work with the Soviets.

The intent of my original letter was to suggest that either this woman or Joel Barr might have been the person who acted as an intermediary between wartime nuclear fission workers and the KGB.

This paragraph contained a considerable amount of positive information about a subject who was then otherwise unknown. We thought for a time that the woman might somehow be connected to Joel Barr, and this led to a separate investigation of Barr's women friends. We determined rather quickly that Barr was not married, and that the particulars given in the message (and reiterated in my June 4 letter) did not fit the background of Vivian Glassman, Barr's longtime girlfriend. Another lead took us to a woman named Elaine Goldfarb, who had lived with Barr for a short time. She had been referred to by someone once as Barr's wife, but we learned that the two had not seen one another since 1941.

We came to a dead end on the investigation into "Christian name, ETHEL," in 1948. As with many other situations, we kept on working, studying, and waiting for more information to develop. The matter remained less specific than those of Barr and Elitcher, because we could not yet identify the unknown subject of the message. In time, the investigation of the woman described in the paragraph would assume great importance—but in 1948, hers was simply one unsolved mystery among many. The lead had come from a deciphered KGB message, but as yet it had led us nowhere.

By the late summer of 1948 a considerable number of the KGB messages had been deciphered in whole or in part, and we had investigations reaching out in many directions. Meredith Gardner was leaping ahead in the amount of information he could decipher; instead of mostly blank pages, we now had dozens of entire messages in the clear. Sometimes we could make educated guesses and fill in some blanks. I was excited about the possibilities.

While in this mood, I once became firmly convinced that, all on my own, I had come up with a new and important clue. We were investigating what some messages showed to be the code name of an agent. It seemed to me that this code name looked phonetically close to a cover name in a previous investigation we'd conducted. Mexico was the setting for both situations; maybe the two things referred to the same man! If there was a match, new facts could be added to our description of the unknown agent. Intrigued, I took my hypothesis out to Arlington Hall and waited for Meredith's compliments. He listened carefully and then shyly explained that when correctly pronounced, the two names were not phonetically close. He was gentle, and quite embarrassed while pointing out my mistake. I was amused at my own stupidity.

Still, for me as a counterintelligence man, that second half of 1948 was a golden time. We were inside the enemy's house; men were coursing down the corridors, following the leads to which our keys had opened the doors. Already I had begun investigations of Max Elitcher, Joel Barr, Morton Sobell, the unknown "Ethel," White Russians and odd recruits. It was easy to envision that soon, very soon, there would be more keys available, more corridors to explore. I could look ahead and see us coming closer and closer, not only to Russian agents whose trails the intervening years had muddied, but also to spies who were actually still at work among us.

Thus it was that in late 1948 some newly deciphered messages struck me quite forcefully. These said that a woman who in 1944 had been working for the Department of Justice in New York had been a KGB agent; the messages further reported that as of the 1944 date of the transmission, this woman was being transferred to work for Justice in Washington.

These messages did not refer to a potential recruit but to an agent in place. I took the information right into the office of Howard Fletcher, the assistant director in charge of my section.

Fletcher was the man among my FBI superiors whom I most admired. Superbly organized, with a great understanding of the Bureau's resources, able to command the respect and loyalty of all who worked for him, Howard Fletcher was a model of excellence for many of us agents and supervisors. I needed his advice on how to proceed with Justice. Government jobs being highly valued, I thought there was a chance that the woman identified in the KGB messages might still be working for the Department of Justice in 1948. How could we find out that information and make the best use of it without alarming Justice? While it was important to know who she was, it was equally important to keep her working at her job so that she might lead us to other agents, couriers and contacts. Fletcher agreed that we had to know the identity of the spy before we could make any further decisions on what to do with her, and said he'd handle the matter with Justice on a personal basis. He excused himself and went over to the other side of the building, to the headquarters of Justice. I don't know to whom he spoke, but within a half hour he was back in his office and motioned for me to come in and sit down.

"The woman is still working there," Fletcher said. The date of her transfer to Washington had pinpointed her location and identity. "There can't be any doubt, it's her. Her name is Judith Coplon."

At last! The deciphered KGB messages had turned up the existence of a spy who was at that very moment working against the interests of the United States.

7
THE SPY NEXT DOOR

WHEN WE STARTED after Judith Coplon, the time was rife with the rising passions of revulsion over Communism and espionage. It was December 1948, just after the election of Harry S. Truman together with a Congress that was leaning toward a conservative bias. The previous summer Elizabeth Bentley and Whittaker Chambers had testified before the House Un-American Activities Committee, and the shock waves from their testimony still held the headlines. In those hearings Chambers had made allegations about Alger Hiss, and when the HUAC started looking into Hiss, one of the names that came up was Laurence Duggan, a former colleague of Hiss's at the State Department who was now president of the Institute of International Education.

That development hadn't surprised me, because I knew of Larry Duggan—Hede Massing had recruited him to spy for the KGB, and had told me (rather reluctantly) that she'd done so. When Duggan's name was mentioned prominently in 1948, other FBI agents questioned him; ten days later he apparently committed suicide by jumping out of a Manhattan hotel window. This death, coupled with the death by heart attack of Harry Dexter White, who had been named before the HUAC by both Bentley and Chambers, and who had been grilled by the committee harshly, incensed many people. I, too, was disturbed by Larry Duggan's death, but wasn't losing any sleep over it because I knew from my work with Hede Massing that he'd been a Soviet spy. I guess that's why I could hardly believe my ears when Duggan's close friend, broadcaster Edward R. Murrow, charged over the airwaves that Duggan had been hounded to his death by the FBI. Murrow made the man seem like a martyr, and acted as if there had been no basis for the FBI's ever having investigated Duggan as a spy. Then I could hardly believe my eyes as I read in the pages of the New York *Herald Tribune* a poem by Archibald MacLeish that referred in passing to Hiss and Duggan by saying: "God help that country where informers thrive! / Where slander flourishes and lies contrive."

It was ironic that while the left began to believe that people such as Duggan had been unjustly pursued by the FBI, we were uncovering the identity of another Soviet spy, Judith Coplon.

Coplon's case had to be handled with the utmost care, because her position at Justice was a difficult one for us. The FBI had always felt relatively secure from Soviet penetration, but here was Coplon, as a political analyst in the Foreign Agents Registration (FAR) section of Justice, who also worked on some "internal security" matters in which sensitive FBI reports were continually on her desk or within easy reach. That meant the agency most compromised by her was the FBI. Coplon routinely handled some Bureau materials that had to do with the Soviets. While the most sensitive stuff—such as that dealing with our breakthrough in the KGB's communications— never went near her, what she did see on a regular basis was damaging enough.

Howard Fletcher and I sat down to try to figure out what to do with Coplon, and to speculate on what, precisely, she might have compromised to date. It was possible that she might have increased the Russians' awareness of the revelations of Bentley and Chambers, and of our investigations that were being pursued on the basis of their accusations. Her penetration might mean that in late 1945 the Soviets had been able to warn the Silvermaster and Perlo groups of imminent danger. It certainly meant that through her the Soviets had become aware of FBI methods, informants, targets of investigation and capabilities for counterespionage.

We initially gave little thought to prosecuting Coplon. Our charge was to protect the country, and we needed to figure out what tactics would best serve that goal. How long could we afford to let Coplon, placed as she was in a sensitive position, continue her operation? This was both a counterintelligence decision and a political one. Among the factors we had to balance was Director Hoover's well-known antipathy to recommending to another government official that a suspect be kept in a potentially harmful position in order to facilitate an FBI investigation. In this instance we had the added difficulty that it was FBI material that was being compromised, and the fact that it was the Justice Department that had been penetrated—the top official of the department was Attorney General Tom Clark, Hoover's friend of over a dozen years, and his superior.

All of these factors notwithstanding, as a counterintelligence man I knew I needed time and opportunity to build the case and to find out Coplon's network and methods. Fletcher and I agreed to recommend to Hoover a mix of FBI actions that would keep Coplon where she was, minimize the damage she could do, and give us time to discover her contacts. In a memo we argued that although Coplon was a real and present threat, she'd been operating from her post for several years, and it was more important to discover her contacts than to remove her before those connections could be found. We recommended that William Foley, head of Coplon's section of Justice, be informed of our suspicions so that he could keep our agents aware of Coplon's plans and activities, and we suggested physical surveillance of her. We also recommended that Hoover ask Tom Clark for permission to place wiretaps on Coplon's office and apartment telephones.

Hoover agreed with all the recommendations. I was pleased, and excited about what was to come. William Foley was told what was going on—incidentally, he was astounded at the notion that Coplon was a spy—agents were sent to tail Coplon, and I prepared a memo for the Director's signature that informed Clark about the case and requested permission to install the two wiretaps. Within a few days Clark granted permission for the taps—a fateful decision, and one that would cause us no end of difficulty.

Today when we hear the word "wiretap," hackles are almost automatically raised, and the impression remains that the FBI used such taps all the time in the forties. That's just not so. In the late 1940s the FBI used wiretaps sparingly, and always after prior consultation with and authorization by the Attorney General's office. The AG's authority to order the taps was backstopped by presidential orders, opinions of high-ranking attorneys, and so on. In 1939 the U.S. Supreme Court had ruled in the case of *Nardone* v. *U.S.* that under normal circumstances the government ought *not* to wiretap because such an action was almost certain to lead to an unconstitutional invasion of privacy. But President Roosevelt made an exception for matters involving the national defense; in a letter to AG Robert Jackson on May 21, 1940, which reviewed the *Nardone* decision, Roosevelt wrote:

> I am convinced that the Supreme Court never intended dictum in the particular case which it decided to apply to grave matters involving the defense of the nation . . . You are, therefore, authorized and directed in such cases as you may approve, after investigation of the need in each case, to authorize the necessary investigating agents that they are at liberty to secure information by listening devices direct to the conversation or other communications of persons suspected of subversive activities against the Government of the United States, including suspected spies.

In 1946 Tom Clark advised President Truman to continue the FDR directive because it was "imperative" to use wiretapping "in cases vitally affecting the domestic security," and said in a letter to Truman that the two previous attorneys general had concurred in the idea that wiretapping was necessary in such matters. In the FBI's files was the opinion of a Justice Department attorney to the effect that a wiretap didn't violate the spirit of *Nardone* unless there was both an interception of the information and a dissemination of that information beyond the confines of the FBI.

So we had adequate authority to use the taps. We didn't expect that they would give us much in the way of direct evidence of espionage, but we did hope that they would provide a wealth of information on Coplon's personality, habits and contacts, and possibly give clues about impending trips or meetings.

I was simultaneously having background checks done on Coplon. She had been born in 1922 to a family that dated back in the United States to before the Civil War. The father had been a toy jobber and was now in ill health, still living in Brooklyn with Coplon's mother. She had one sibling, a brother. In 1943 Coplon had graduated with honors from Barnard College, where she'd been one of the mainstays of the campus's extracurricular activities, a "personality kid." When she had applied for a job with the Economic Warfare Section of Justice, in New York, the FBI had run a background profile on her and had told Justice that she'd been involved at school with a branch of the Young Communist League and had published pro-Soviet writings in the campus newspaper. Justice had hired her anyway, and in January 1945 allowed her to make a lateral transfer within the department, which brought her to Washington as a political analyst in the FAR section. It was this move that had been the subject of the KGB cable that had brought her to our attention in the first place.

At Justice, Coplon constantly expanded her work, and soon it included registration of agents representing the Soviet Union and satellite countries. She was rated "excellent" by her superiors and made steady progress up the civil service ladder. By 1948, because of cutbacks in personnel, she was the only political analyst left within her section and, because of her expertise in Communist matters, had taken over the job of reviewing the investigative data that the FBI supplied to Justice on internal security cases. In her off-hours Coplon attended classes at American University, working toward a master's degree in international relations and writing a thesis on economic planning in the Soviet Union.

When I had all these data in front of me, I groaned—everything about her pointed to her having been a Soviet agent, and no one at Justice had even given a second thought to her expanding horizons and "expertise" in the area of matters concerning the Soviets.

Then a new wrinkle appeared: the agents tailing Coplon reported that she was having an affair with a Justice Department attorney named Harold Shapiro. Now, there is an old adage in the FBI to the effect that there has never been an espionage case in which sex did not play a part. We wondered if Shapiro had any connection with espionage, so we watched from outside as the couple went into Coplon's or Shapiro's apartment of an evening, and turned out the lights. Agents followed them to a Baltimore hotel one weekend, where they registered as Mr. and Mrs. Shapiro. At this point, though, the agents became satisfied that the affair between Coplon and Shapiro was just that—an affair—and dropped the surveillance of Shapiro.

On the night of January 14, 1949, however, our watching and waiting game showed signs of paying off. Coplon was in the habit of going up to New York twice a month to see her parents. When we learned from William Foley that she was going to be in New York on the fourteenth, we made plans to cover her entire trip to the city.

It was quite a chase. Upon arrival in Pennsylvania Station, instead of taking a subway to Brooklyn, where her parents lived, Coplon took one in the opposite direction, to the Washington Heights section of Manhattan. FBI agents under the direction of Scotty Miller watched as Coplon waited for someone on the corner of Broadway and 193rd Street; after ten minutes a man appeared. He was rather short, with dark hair, clean-cut and conservatively dressed. The two went to an Italian restaurant and had dinner; Miller and another agent slipped into the restaurant as well, but couldn't overhear their conversation. After dinner, as Coplon and the dark-haired man walked to a subway, they seemed to be arguing, and Coplon raised her voice and poked at the man with a rolled-up newspaper. Both took the subway downtown several stops, and at 125th Street the man waited until the last second and then bolted out of the subway door, losing the agents who were tailing him.

Initially alarmed at having lost the dark-haired man, the agents the next day combed our extensive files of Soviet nationals and found him listed as Valentin Alekseevich Gubitchev.

We had one hell of an espionage case in the making.

We quickly found out what we could about Gubitchev. He was born in 1916 in the Orlovsky province, in the Ural mountains, trained as a construction engineer, and had entered the United States in 1946 as a diplomat, a secretary to the Soviet United Nations delegation. We wanted to know if he had diplomatic immunity—if so, of course, we couldn't arrest him. The answer delighted us: shortly after he had entered the country on a diplomatic passport, he'd changed jobs and become a direct employee of the United Nations Secretariat, assigned to work on the construction of the new U.N. building complex in Manhattan. Therefore he was no longer considered a diplomat and had no automatic immunity from prosecution.

I longed to be able to arrest both of them, preferably in the act of passing and receiving secret information. But on a Saturday morning within days of the moment we identified Gubitchev, the entire game was nearly lost. I was working alone in my office when Howard Fletcher walked in and sat down. He had, he said, been talking with the Director, and reported that Hoover was no longer willing to recommend that Coplon be kept on at Justice. With the Soviet national involved, it was all too hot. Further, Hoover had evidently been under pressure from Tom Clark and others at Justice to have Coplon removed.

"I can't believe it," I said. "This case has great potential. We've worked for years to penetrate a situation just like this, and now it's all going down the drain because no one is willing to take a risk?"

That was the way it was going to be, Fletcher said: Judith Coplon would be discharged from the Department of Justice under the Loyalty of Government Employees program. There'd be no fuss made about it whatsoever.

"You can't let this happen," I protested. "You've got to do something about it."

"This won't be the end of the world, Bob. Perhaps we can get her to talk."

"I don't know what I'm doing in here on a Saturday morning, working like a dog," I shot back. "I think I'll go home."

"Simmer down," Fletcher said.

I told Fletcher that he absolutely had to change the decision. More time was needed to develop the case. I pleaded for a couple of months and said that whatever damage Coplon already had done wouldn't be magnified if she were kept on a bit longer.

Fletcher didn't believe anyone could do anything to change the minds of Hoover, Clark and the Justice Department hierarchy—but he said he'd try. After he left the office, I sat there, depressed, sure that a lot of work and a precious opportunity had all come to naught.

I must have lit a fire in Fletcher, though, for later in that day he told me that I could have a little more time with the case. I thanked him profusely. But I knew that the reprieve was only temporary, and that quite soon the powers that be would again become nervous and would want to shut down Coplon's operation. Before that time, I had to do something to speed up the process and to catch Coplon and Gubitchev in the act of committing espionage.

I decided to bait a hook for Coplon and Gubitchev.

After some hours poring over our files, I prepared a memo that contained enough truth to make it seem important and enough false information to make it imperative for Coplon to grab it and quickly deliver it to her Soviet contact. The memo was supposed to go from Hoover to a division of the Department of Justice, and would carry a security classification; the subject was the Amtorg Trading Corporation, long known to us as a front for Soviet espionage. It summarized some of what we knew about Amtorg and contained the completely false statement that we had placed an informant inside Amtorg and expected that he would soon prove a valuable source for us.

Everybody up the line seemed to like the idea of the memo, including Hoover and the Justice Department officials in charge of the Coplon matter, and when it had the Director's signature, we alerted

Bill Foley that it was coming over. He was to make sure that a copy of it fell under the eyes of Judith Coplon. This took place prior to the afternoon of February 18, 1949, when Coplon was to make another trip to New York.

On the eighteenth, our watching agents in Pennsylvania Station saw Coplon come off the train with a broken ankle-strap on her shoe. Thus hobbled, she didn't reach the 193rd Street rendezvous point until 7:05 P.M. Not seeing anyone there, she wandered around for a few minutes and then stopped to get the shoe-strap fixed. Meanwhile, at the U.N., other agents saw Gubitchev come out of his office and perform a series of maneuvers designed to determine if he was being followed. We'd made the field agents aware that under such conditions they were to drop the surveillance rather than let the subject know he was being followed—and so the guys near the U.N. let Gubitchev go. Other agents watching 193rd and Broadway saw Gubitchev arrive there at 7:00 P.M. and then leave. It was standard KGB procedure for espionage people to reach a meeting precisely on time; if for some reason one or the other of them was late, both would avoid the contact and come to a "fallback" rendezvous at the same place exactly an hour later. The broken shoe-strap had made Coplon a bit late, and Gubitchev had gone into his fallback routine. At 7:58 P.M. our agents observed Coplon and Gubitchev approaching the meeting-place corner from different directions. As they passed one another, Coplon had her hand in her purse. The agents weren't close enough to be able to tell if something was exchanged—they thought there had been a transfer, but weren't sure. Coplon and Gubitchev parted, and neither did anything suspicious later in the evening. Coplon then returned to Washington.

The first hook hadn't worked, and I was under increasing pressure to obtain some concrete evidence that would show Coplon passing materials to her Soviet contact. Our wiretaps revealed that she was reaching out beyond Justice for information—on February 24, 1949, she spoke with Walter Anderson of the State Department, who told her that her request for material about a particular unnamed individual was "very complicated and very sticky and he was unable to give her the information." She said she'd try to get the data through the FBI.

I decided to rebait my hook with a stronger lure, and met with two high officials of the Atomic Energy Commission to obtain some information that would be classified and related to the national defense, but which wouldn't do too much harm if it reached the Soviets. The

AEC gave me some data on a measuring device called a geophone; countries in the process of developing atomic power would have to have such instruments, and the AEC was relatively certain that the Soviets didn't have them as yet.

I constructed another memo that would go from Hoover to Justice, about Amtorg. It said we had learned of Amtorg's interest in geophones, which was in line with other instances in which the Soviets had sought atomic-energy-related equipment. The memo listed one shipment of such equipment (though no geophones) from Cyclotron Specialties Company sent to the U.S.S.R. in August 1947 aboard the *Mikhail Kutuzov;* another that was intercepted in September 1948; and a third that had been seized at a New Jersey dock only a few days prior to the date of the memo. All this was factual. But the next section, which updated the previous memo about the supposed informant inside Amtorg, was not. In it, I said that Isidore Gibby Needleman, Amtorg's American legal representative, was our source. Now, Needleman had never been an informant for the FBI—in fact, we'd investigated him in the past—but for the purposes of the memo I said we'd been maintaining contact with him through an intermediary, but weren't entirely satisfied with this arrangement and wanted to check out his sincerity by getting him to obtain more information on a variety of matters. This business about Needleman was entirely false, but it was something no Soviet spy could afford to ignore.

We learned from Foley that Coplon was planning another trip to New York on March 4, 1949, and so on March 3 we sent the decoy memorandum, over Hoover's signature, to Deputy Attorney General Peyton Ford, and had him buck it down to Foley's section.

"Got a hot one," Bill Foley said off-handedly to Coplon, and made the memorandum sound tantalizing. She asked if she could see it— the Justice Department had already altered her job so that she no longer routinely saw such memos—and Foley told her he didn't know if she could view it. Then he left her office.

From that moment on, we didn't know for sure whether Foley had touted it highly enough so that Coplon would manage the trick of getting herself a copy of the decoy memo so she could take it to New York. We could only hope that she'd apply her ingenuity to the task —as she'd done in earlier instances.

If we were going to arrest Coplon and Gubitchev, it had to be now or never, for there was a strong possibility that they knew they were being watched and might break off contact for some time. If that happened, I was sure Hoover and Clark would have Coplon removed from her sensitive position before any further damage could be done —and we'd have no case at all.

At this point the FBI took the very clear step of asking Deputy Attorney General Peyton Ford if we could obtain a warrant to arrest the pair. Ford advised us that while we didn't have enough evidence in hand to obtain a warrant, our agents could arrest Coplon and Gubitchev without one if they saw Coplon give something resembling a document to Gubitchev, or if the agents had "probable cause" to believe they were witnessing a felony. Here, too, was a decision we could come to regret.

In New York we put a fleet of radio cars and a total of thirty field agents on the streets to cover any possible meeting place of the two spies. My old chief, Bob Granville, and Miss Sappho Manos, the chief clerk of the New York office, were pressed into the surveillance duty. Assistant Director Ed Scheidt, the man in charge of the New York office, was on the street, and Special Agent in Charge Al Belmont directed the teams. Down in Washington at FBI headquarters I sat with Howard Fletcher, and we maintained an open direct telephone line to Belmont, who was in the radio room of the New York office.

The evening hours of March 4, 1949, were among the most agonizing I have ever spent. Having baited the hook, I wanted badly to be there to reel in the fish. I still longed for the action, to be out on the pavement, and preferably to be the man on the spot to arrest the agents of the KGB in the act of making the pass. But I'd gotten beyond that stage, and as a supervisor I was privy to the big picture —that of the whole platoon of agents closing in on the quarry. The problem was that the only way I could keep close to that picture was by hanging on to Howard Fletcher and his telephone, which was relaying information from Al Belmont in the New York radio command room.

Judith Coplon arrived in Pennsylvania Station and took the subway to 190th Street. Ed Scheidt, Sappho Manos and Bob Granville were all on the train with her. Coplon was a bit confused, and when she got off the train she literally bumped into Miss Manos and then asked her for directions. Manos coolly told Coplon that she, too, was lost and was unable to help. Scheidt and Manos then walked in the direction opposite to that taken by Coplon.

The agents who had been tailing Gubitchev had once again let him go because they thought he was on the verge of detecting the surveillance. Coplon reached the presumed meeting place at 7:00 P.M., but Gubitchev didn't show up. Coplon wandered about, in an apparently aimless fashion, killing time. However, we were observing her every step: agents posted in cars on side streets called in radio reports on Coplon's location and direction of travel. Belmont relayed these to Washington.

We had to hope that the fallback rendezvous would take place, as it had on earlier occasions. As eight o'clock neared, agents spotted Coplon and Gubitchev moving separately toward the meeting place. In Washington we rooted for an exchange. The pair came together momentarily at 8:00 P.M. but immediately parted. Undoubtedly, one of them had been alerted that they were being tailed—it was probably Gubitchev—and told the other. Agents continued to tail both Gubitchev and Coplon as they went their separate ways. Gubitchev soon lost his tail because the agents had to be extra cautious. Coplon was also hard to follow, but one agent did succeed in getting on the same subway with her.

While that subway was coursing downtown, we were out of touch with the action. All might have been lost. We had to hope that our last agent might still be on Coplon, and that he might not have been noticed. We also had to hope that Coplon and Gubitchev had another fallback rendezvous in their contingency plans.

At Forty-second Street Coplon got off the subway and got into a downtown bus. At the very last second Gubitchev appeared and also got on the bus.

The agent who had managed to tail Coplon on the subway saw the pair get on the bus. He raced to the telephone and called in to the radio room. Moments later, FBI cars began to fly down the West Side Highway to try to catch up with the bus. One of our cars had a flat tire while traveling at 70 mph. Another car just barely managed to catch up with the bus at Fourteenth Street. This was fortunate, because at Fourteenth Coplon and Gubitchev got off the bus and transferred to a subway line that went crosstown. One agent got out of a car and caught the same train. Its cars were nearly empty, so the agent couldn't tail the pair too closely; in fact, he was forced to ride one stop beyond where they got off before he could telephone the radio room. Agents flooded the area where their colleague had seen Coplon and Gubitchev get off, and luckily soon caught sight of the pair.

The fact that Coplon and Gubitchev were still together led the FBI men to conclude that no exchange of material had yet taken place —for if it had, there would have been no further reason for them to stay together. Perhaps on the subway and on the bus they had behaved as if they were strangers in order not to risk someone witnessing an exchange between them. In any event, the agents believed the activities they saw constituted probable cause that a felony was being committed, and proceeded to arrest both Coplon and Gubitchev in the vicinity of Fourteenth Street and Third Avenue.

When they were arrested, Gubitchev was carrying a plain white envelope holding $125 in small bills. This could have been a payoff. Coplon's purse, however, contained a copy of my second memorandum with its false information. She had taken the bait! The paper had been folded into a square the size of a postage stamp, then sealed with Scotch tape; an arrow was inked on one corner to indicate where to start to remove the tape. Also in Coplon's purse was an important message that Coplon had written to her contact, as well as about thirty FBI data slips that contained confidential information, and finally, three biographical sketches of what seemed to be potential recruits for the KGB.

On March 5, 1949, the Soviets tried hard to claim diplomatic immunity for Gubitchev; the ambassador expressed his shock that the United States would arrest a Soviet citizen as if he were a "common criminal." The State Department retorted that under United Nations rules, Gubitchev had given up his diplomatic immunity when he signed the U.N.'s oath of employment. At a hearing before a federal judge, Gubitchev refused to speak English or to recognize the court's authority. He was clapped into jail for seven weeks until the Soviet Embassy recognized the court's jurisdiction by posting $100,000 bail.

There were two Coplon trials. The first took place in Washington, and Coplon was the sole defendant. The second and later trial was in New York, where the charge was conspiracy and both Coplon and Gubitchev were defendants.

The late-spring headlines were of the blockade of Berlin, the intensification of war in China and the first perjury trial of Alger Hiss. The Coplon trial, which would generate plenty of headlines of its own, opened on April 25, 1949—the day my pregnant wife went into the hospital; our son George was born the following morning. I really wanted to be in two places at once.

To anyone outside the FBI, the Washington trial must have seemed a circus. Spectators included many "G-girls," the female government workers of the city, intrigued to see one of their own lifted from obscurity to notoriety. In the overflow crowd of reporters was a Tass representative who we thought was taking notes for the KGB. Ray Whearty, one of the prosecutors, had formerly been Cop-

lon's boss in the FAR section of Justice, and had only recently joined
the Criminal Division. The government's case was principally handled by Assistant Attorney General John Kelley, an able man. The
chief contributor to the feeling of circus in the courtroom was Coplon's defense attorney, Archibald Palmer—a short, rotund, florid and
wily man. His previous experience was mostly with bankruptcy and
claims cases. Presiding Judge Albert L. Reeves of Kansas City, Mis-
souri, seemed never to have run into anyone to equal Archie Palmer.
Reeves was seventy-six, a friend of President Truman's, and a visiting
judge out of his circuit. *Time* described the match-up of Reeves and
Palmer thus:

> [Palmer] gauged the temper of mild, white-haired Federal Judge
> Albert L. Reeves with the eye of a mule trader sizing up a parson;
> after that he did everything but shoot off firecrackers under the
> judge's nose. He objected incessantly. He told bad jokes. He brayed,
> waved his arms, and quoted the Bible with enthusiastic piety. On
> one of those rare occasions when the judge reproved him, he re-
> plied obsequiously, "Beggars mustn't be choosers and I'm happy to
> get what you're gonna give me. . . . I subside." Then he would
> continue as before. As he ranted, he stood close behind U.S. Attor-
> ney John M. Kelley, Jr.; from time to time Kelley brushed chewed
> fragments of Palmer's Life Savers from his hair.

In fact, the press was all over the trial, and touted its twists and
turns each day. The government's case was sensational, consisting as
it did of reports of clandestine meetings between a Justice Department employee and a Soviet national—but it was presented in a
straightforward manner. It opened by calling a number of FBI agents
who'd been on the scene and were witnesses to the maneuvers of
Coplon and Gubitchev on the night of March 4. Prior to the trial,
Scotty Miller and I met with Kelley and Whearty, and we jointly
decided to have FBI graphics experts prepare a display map that
would make clear to the jury what the large number of FBI agents
who'd been on the surveillance had observed. The map was an effective exhibit, and Palmer naturally objected to its presence.

One of Archie Palmer's favorite stunts when he was cross-examining FBI agents was to administer a Soviet Union geography test. He
wanted to show, he said, that the FBI agents were too ignorant about
Russia to know a Soviet spy if they fell over one. Most other judges
would have immediately stopped this sort of shenanigan, but Judge

Reeves let Palmer get away with it; this and other Palmer tactics protracted the trial. However, in his attempt to portray FBI agents as dumb, uneducated boobs who merely happened to have a badge, Palmer's contempt for the FBI and all of the government was palpable, and in my view didn't sit well with the jurors, a handful of whom were themselves federal employees.

Coplon thought Palmer's antics were amusing. In the courtroom, she giggled. During recesses she ran or skipped down the halls, laughing and smiling. Newspaper reporters believed her to be thrilled at the chance to appear in the limelight. Because her father had passed away in the interim between her arrest and the trial, Coplon dressed in black. Her mother, also in the courtroom and also dressed in mourning, did not find the proceedings comical; rather, she appeared sorrowful and occasionally dabbed at her eyes with a small handkerchief.

The opposing attorneys' strategies were clear from the start. The government's case hinged on Coplon's having had classified material in her possession when arrested, which we believed she had been planning to pass to Gubitchev. We cited as evidence the clandestine, evasive manner in which she and Gubitchev conducted themselves during the three meetings in which they'd been observed by the FBI. The defense characterized the meetings as part of an unrequited love affair, and labeled the materials in Coplon's handbag as research data for a novel she was writing—a novel that she had destroyed rather than let it be used in court.

The prosecution's evidence contradicted Coplon's explanations at every turn. For example, she carried in her purse three slips of paper that were biographical sketches. One dealt with a former high school friend, the second with that friend's husband, and the third with a young man whom Coplon had met at American University. Very similar biographical sketches had surfaced in the Gouzenko affair, and the defector said they were routinely used by the Soviets to evaluate potential recruits. Coplon's sketches, like those that came from the Canadian cases, included information on where the writer had met the subject, his or her age, job, origins, family, education, friends, political affiliations and sensitivity to Communism, as well as the subject's personality flaws. She characterized the young man from American University as "pro-Communist, albeit a bit of a 'wishy-washy' idealist, and politically naive," and made similar judgments on the other two candidates. In a revealing note about herself within the biographical sketch of her high school chum, Coplon wrote that the woman

> remembers me as a Communist, and I think she is confused as to whether I am still a C, and if so why I continue to work for the government in Washington or if I've sold out. I think her opinion is somewhere between the two, that is, that I'm just a neurotic.

Another sheet of paper in her purse had some autobiographical data which we thought was a brief for her Soviet superiors so that she could be promoted.

Another damning piece of evidence from the handbag was a lengthy note to someone—presumably Gubitchev—about a 115-page FBI memo that summarized the Bureau's information about KGB and GRU activities and well-known Soviet agents over the past fifteen years. It said, in part:

> I have not been able (and I don't think I will) to get the top secret FBI report which I described to Michael on Soviet and Communist intelligence activities in the U.S. When the moment was favorable, I asked Foley where the report was (he'd previously remarked that he had such a report). He said that some departmental official had it and he didn't expect to get it back. Foley remarked that there was nothing "new" in it. When I saw the report for a minute, I breezed through it rapidly, remembered very little. It was about 115 pages in length; summarized first Soviet "intelligence" activities, including Martens, Lore, Poynts (sic), Altschuler, Silvermaster et al. It had a heading on Soviet U.N. delegation, but that was all I remember. The rest of the report I think was on Polish, Yugo, etc. activities and possibly some info on the C.P., U.S.A.

We thought Michael was Gubitchev or Coplon's ultimate controller in the United States. Archie Palmer said the name came from the Bible and referred to a character in Coplon's novel.

Along with my decoy memorandum, which Coplon had folded up into a small square the size of a postage stamp, this note to Gubitchev or Michael was at the heart of the government's case. Also important were the thirty-odd "data slips" which she carried. These were Coplon's summaries of FBI security investigation memos—not the reports themselves, but digests of the important information in them.

Quite soon these FBI reports themselves—rather than her summaries of them—became a center of controversy in the trial.

I had always disliked the idea that we sent such reports outside the FBI. They usually consisted of undigested data, sometimes of unconfirmed allegations which we had been given by informants, as well as the results of investigative work. I had, in particular, considered it of dubious value to send the reports to the Internal Security section at Justice. But in the intelligence community, once you've collected information the impulse is always to send it somewhere—and so Coplon's summaries of our reports ended up in her handbag.

The FBI reports on which these "data slips" were based contained some highly confidential information, and the government sought to introduce as evidence only the slips that Coplon had in her handbag—not the underlying FBI reports on which the slips were based. In fact, to release the basic file reports might not only endanger security and compromise informants, but also bring to light many unsubstantiated allegations which would do no one any good. While the trial was going on, and this issue was hot, columnist Drew Pearson gave a good picture of how these files had been made and why they shouldn't be allowed in court:

> The FBI builds its files somewhat like a newspaperman builds his files. A piece of information comes in from one source which means nothing. Then something comes in from another source, and perhaps from a third source, which taken separately mean nothing. But put together, they begin to tell a story. Therefore, the FBI is duty bound to keep unchecked rumors in its files. However, these unchecked rumors should not be made public any more than a newspaperman can afford to publish rumors without checking for accuracy.

When the slips had been found in Coplon's handbag, I'd made an analysis of their content and concluded that they amounted to identifications of persons suspected by the FBI of working for Soviet and related intelligence services. Some of these identifications were innocuous, but the files behind them could, if made public, lead to more sensitive matters. For example, one slip named a woman who'd made an application for a job with the Soviet Embassy publication *Information Bulletin.* If the Soviets knew we were interested in her, and the files were made public, the Soviets might learn something we didn't want them to know—that the FBI had the woman's job application as processed by the embassy, which was a clear indication that we must have an informant inside the embassy. In addition, the slips led to other files which contained names and allegations that we didn't want to make public and that cried out to be kept confidential.

Even though we didn't want the files themselves to go into evidence, we were willing to put in photostats of the title pages of the FBI reports, as well as copies of the particular portions from which Coplon had excerpted her data—because we wanted to show clearly that Coplon's data slips had been based on confidential and classified FBI security reports.

The legal problem, of course, was the defense's contention that if anything at all about Coplon's slips or portions of the files were introduced, the complete files would have to be brought into court. Palmer argued that the jury would not be able to tell much about what Coplon had allegedly lifted from a file unless the entire file was there to examine.

Palmer's tactic was a blatant attempt to blackmail the government. He knew we didn't want those files in the open, and believed his demand could force the prosecution to withdraw Coplon's indictment. He believed Justice would rather forgo the trial than have FBI methods, informants and targets made public.

Only the opening skirmish of this battle over the data slips had taken place when the moment came for me to take the witness stand. I was to be a witness for two purposes—first, to identify and introduce the decoy memorandum, and second, to do the same with the data slips and to testify that they had come from FBI reports on internal security matters. Howard Fletcher had previously testified that I'd told him that a "confidential informant of known reliability" had given us reason to suspect Coplon of espionage. This was technically true—we always referred to my contact at NSA and the deciphered KGB messages in this manner. Over the intervening years, this appellation has led other writers on Coplon to assume that it was someone in Coplon's department who informed on her. At the trial, I had to state that the "confidential informant" who began the investigation was not a wiretap. Also, under direct examination by Kelley, I produced the decoy memorandum and testified that it contained classified as well as false information, and that it had been designed to prove attractive to anyone working for the Soviets. I also produced photostatic copies of the title pages and pertinent paragraphs of those FBI reports from which the information in the data slips had been abstracted. Judge Reeves allowed these to be received in evidence. My direct testimony didn't take very long, but then I came under cross-examination.

I had testified at many trials, but had never experienced anything like Palmer's tactics or the absence of control from the bench. Palmer pushed his face close to mine and from time to time sprayed me with saliva and partially chewed Life Savers. He made many derogatory remarks in his questioning of me. The previous FBI agent witnesses had maintained their traditional civility while on the stand; I quickly decided not to be bullied and became as uncivil to Palmer as he was to me.

He attempted to get me to admit that I had entrapped Coplon; I refused to say that the memo had been for the purpose of entrapment, a term that had legal connotations. Then Palmer wanted to know what parts of the decoy memorandum were true and what parts were false. He somehow managed to get permission from Reeves to stand behind me peering over my shoulder as I began to read and characterize the various portions of the memo. I had just started when he screamed an objection—in my ear—that I hadn't read the letterhead, which showed this to be an FBI document.

I was so angry that I almost reached for Palmer to throw him over my shoulder and down into the courtroom. Kelley jumped up and objected to Palmer's antics—after all, he pointed out, the memo had already been introduced as evidence. Judge Reeves moved Palmer in front of me but didn't quiet him; we battled through the memo sentence by sentence. After a while I went into so much detail about geophones, Needleman, and every other item in the memo that it became obvious the memo had been worded very precisely—and Palmer gave up on this tactic.

Then he tried to derogate my background and knowledge of Soviet intelligence. In one answer, I said I'd gone to law school at the University of Idaho. Was this located in Boise? "No," I answered, "in Moscow." The entire courtroom burst into laughter, and even the judge joined in as he gaveled us back to order. Moscow, Idaho, was the location of the University of Idaho law school.

In questioning me over the contents of the data slips, Palmer started shouting his queries at me. I began angrily shouting my answers back at him. He demanded that I stop shouting and I told him I'd do so as long as he did. Finally the judge brought the situation under control.

Palmer argued that he must have the entire FBI file reports available to him so he could understand the relationship of their contents to the data slips; he said it was not appropriate for the government to be able to introduce only portions of the reports. This was the great legal battle of the trial, and I was excused from the witness stand while it was raging. As I listened to the attorneys, it became apparent to me that although Judge Reeves had previously made several rulings in the trial favorable to the government, in this instance he was going to rule in Palmer's favor and allow the introduction of the full FBI reports.

The smell of disaster was in the air. There was a noontime recess; in the afternoon, I was sure, Reeves would rule that Palmer could see the files.

I hurried back to headquarters and got hold of Howard Fletcher, and the two of us went into Mickey Ladd's office and briefed him on the situation. I pleaded that the only way to block Reeves from giving the files to Palmer was for us to ask for an immediate recess and get a ruling from the Court of Appeals that would prevent Palmer from obtaining the material. To make the files public was unthinkable. If that seemed likely to happen, we might have to withdraw the indictment of Coplon and lose the whole case. If, however, we got a favorable ruling from a higher court that would allow us *not* to give Palmer the files, we could still have a successful prosecution.

Ladd seemed in full possession of the facts when he left us to go to see the Director—but when he came back, his attitude had changed. He reported that Hoover had spoken by telephone to Attorney General Tom Clark, and that he, Ladd, had listened to the conversation on the speaker phone. Hoover had used his best machine-gun delivery, and periodically the soft-spoken Clark had tried to calm Hoover with a "Now, Edgar" line, which had only provoked another burst of talk from the Director. At the conversation's end, Ladd reported, both men had agreed that the data slips and the FBI files behind them would not be put into Palmer's hands.

A knot formed in my stomach. What, I asked, would prevent Judge Reeves from ruling in Palmer's favor this afternoon? Ladd reiterated that it just wouldn't be permitted to happen. But how was it to be prevented—by intercession with the Court of Appeals? Ladd didn't say, but it was clear to me that all the higher-ups believed that the wish of the Attorney General and of the FBI Director would prevail upon the judiciary. I couldn't believe my ears: for the first and only time in my years of working with Mickey Ladd, he had failed to comprehend the realities of the situation. *The Director had spoken,* and Ladd had been mesmerized.

I tried to convince Ladd that unless we applied for an immediate appellate ruling, the files would be made public. Even though I became quite agitated, I couldn't get through to Ladd, and Howard Fletcher had to drag me from Ladd's office.

An hour later, in the courtroom, Judge Reeves read a carefully worded opinion saying that he recognized that the materials in the FBI files might compromise some FBI investigatory methods and some confidential informants, and that some people might be embarrassed or hurt—but in the interests of a fair trial, the defense must be allowed to have the FBI files that underlay the "data slips" in Coplon's handbag.

I thought the trial was over, and asked Kelley and Whearty if they now intended to withdraw the indictment. To my surprise, they told me they did not have instructions from the Attorney General to do so, and that they were going on with the trial. So courtroom proceedings went on, and the FBI files became part of the trial record. The information thereby divulged was devoured by the press. While some of it was germane—the Washington *Post* reported, "Russia Got Atom Equipment, Court Told"—much of it was hearsay and things that should never have seen the light of day, such as the *Evening Star*'s headline story, "Fredric March Labeled Red in FBI Report." Hoover was livid, and blamed Tom Clark for the debacle, though not publicly.

Palmer had a field day. He took to reading aloud the FBI reports so they could be entered into the trial record; when he became too hoarse to read further, a substitute reader held sway for a few days in the courtroom.

As the names of March, John Garfield, Paul Muni and others surfaced, Hoover and the Bureau came under fire. Dr. Edward U. Condon of the Bureau of Standards called for a public apology from the FBI for mentioning his wife's name. President Truman was rumored to be angry that unchecked allegations had gotten into the FBI's files. Hoover did not apologize for anything, but let it be known that perhaps a dozen confidential informants, including one within the Russian embassy, had been compromised by the release of the FBI reports behind the data slips.

Finally, the defense took over, and the star witness was Judith Coplon. Her demeanor, so boisterous during the first part of the trial, changed to demure when she took the stand. Archie Palmer was respectful and solicitous as he drew from her the story of how she met "Val." Their chance meeting at the Museum of Modern Art had led to discussions of paintings and to her chaste and unrequited passion for Gubitchev. The quarrel the FBI had observed was when Gubitchev had told her he was married; their evasive actions were to avoid the private detectives they thought the jealous Mrs. Gubitchev had hired to tail them.

Coplon's love story made wonderful copy for the newspapers. When John Kelley started to cross-examine her, he quietly led Coplon over her testimony about her love for Gubitchev; he carefully reiterated her theme that it had all been done for love of Val, and asked her if it would be reasonable to assume that Gubitchev was the only man in her life. She said he was. Kelley asked again if she was sure about that, and Coplon reiterated her assurance. Then Kelley suddenly raised his voice and asked:

> If Gubitchev was the only man in your life, how is it that on January 7, 1949, you registered in a hotel in Baltimore as the wife of Mr. Harold Shapiro, and the following night in another hotel, in Philadelphia?

The demure G-girl instantly vanished, replaced by a wounded tigress who screamed at Archie Palmer, "You son of a bitch! I told you this would happen. How could you let it happen with my mother in the courtroom?"

The courtroom erupted with the spectators' excitement. Reporters leapt for doors and waiting telephones. Mrs. Coplon began to wail. When order was restored, Judge Reeves directed Judith Coplon to answer Kelley's question. She said she'd been at the hotel with Shapiro but hadn't known they were registered as man and wife, and furthermore, hadn't removed her clothes during the night. Kelley asked her if she'd had breakfast in bed at the Philadelphia hotel and produced a copy of the bill and the room service order. He asked rhetorically if the truth was that she and Val had never been in love, and that their meetings were not the assignations of lovers but rather the clandestine rendezvous of spies. Coplon screamed in disbelief, Mrs. Coplon's wails rose ever higher, and Palmer was on his feet with a welter of objections—but in essence, the trial was over.

After deliberating for twenty hours, the jury brought in verdicts of guilty on two counts—that Coplon had tried to obtain documents vital to the national defense for the benefit of a foreign nation, and that she had stolen government documents. Reeves sentenced her to serve forty months to ten years.

The second trial of Coplon, this time with Gubitchev, took place in early 1950, and in the interim between the first trial and the second, many things happened in our investigations arising from the deciphered KGB messages—the identification of Klaus Fuchs, for one—and I'll get to these in later chapters. For now, though, I want to consider the Coplon affair in its entirety.

The second trial was less spectacular than the first, because Judge Sylvester Ryan presided and kept Archie Palmer under firm control. Gubitchev was very ably represented by Abraham Pomerantz, who had worked with the government during the Nuremberg trials. Yuri Novikov of the Soviet embassy sat next to Gubitchev at all times; Novikov was known to us as a KGB man, and there were indications that he was as much in charge of Gubitchev's defense as Pomerantz.

Palmer represented Coplon in the pretrial hearings, but shortly after the trial had begun, she fired him as her attorney. Her new representatives, Leonard Boudin, Samuel Neuberger and Sidney Berman, were given one week by Judge Ryan to review trial records. After they had done so, they moved for a mistrial on the grounds that Coplon had previously been represented by incompetent counsel. Judge Ryan denied their motion, and the trial proceeded. However, because their motion was refused, Coplon's new attorneys would not actively participate in the proceedings and didn't even deliver a summation on their client's behalf. Unmoved by these antics, the jury found both Coplon and Gubitchev guilty on several counts; Coplon and Gubitchev were sentenced to fifteen years each.

Then, once again, the State Department intervened in an espionage case and recommended to Judge Ryan that Gubitchev's sentence be suspended on condition that he leave the country and never return. The reason given by State for this action was that it hoped by doing so to ameliorate the sentences of some U.S. citizens currently being held in Eastern European jails. Unrepentant to the last, at dockside Gubitchev said to reporters who asked him why he was taking a television set to the U.S.S.R., where as yet there were no broadcasts, that television had been invented in Russia. Gubitchev went home, and no Americans got out of jail or had their sentences reduced because he had left the United States.

Meanwhile, Coplon's convictions worked their way up to the Circuit Court of Appeals. While she was researching her own case, Judith Coplon met a young lawyer at the Boudin offices, married him, moved to Brooklyn, and soon became pregnant.

One of the issues raised in the second trial—by Archie Palmer in pretrial hearings before he got fired—was wiretapping. Palmer established that taps had been installed on Coplon's phones. In the trial, this became an important matter, and the *Nardone* decision was bruited about by the defense. In that case, Justice Felix Frankfurter had written that wiretap evidence could not be used in court, and neither could any evidence or leads derived from wiretaps, which were the "fruits of a poisonous tree." Frankfurter had written precise instructions on how a trial should be handled if wiretapping was involved:

> Once wiretapping is established, the trial judge must give opportunity, however closely confined, to the accused to prove that a substantial portion of the case against him was a fruit of the poisonous tree. This leaves ample opportunity to the Government to convince the trial court that its proof had an independent origin.

At the second trial, Judge Ryan had followed this procedure and made the prosecution demonstrate that none of its evidence had come from the taps or leads provided by the taps. In fact, we'd felt that Ryan had gone further than necessary to ensure that the defense was given the latitude to determine whether or not the prosecution's evidence had come from the taps. Actually, none of the evidence had come from the taps; we knew all about *Nardone* and had been careful in this regard. For example, the taps had provided facts about Coplon's affair with Shapiro, but our evidence on this came independently from agents who tailed Coplon.

Archie Palmer had also claimed in the pretrial hearings that the FBI's arrest of Coplon had been illegal, since it had been made without a warrant. This was apparently an afterthought with Palmer, who hadn't raised the issue in the first trial. (He also hadn't brought up the wiretapping then.)

And then, in a decision that was a shock to me, Judge Learned Hand of the Circuit Court of Appeals overturned Judith Coplon's conviction. In law school I had probably studied more of Learned Hand's opinions than those of any other jurist. He was regarded as one of the great legal minds—an evaluation in which I concurred—but in this case, I thought his decision was dead wrong.

He had been convinced by the issues raised by Archie Palmer, the man whom I disliked with a vengeance. Palmer was a first-class boor —but he saved Judith Coplon from a prison term. It was the pretrial raising of the wiretapping and the claim that the arrest had been improper that did it. Learned Hand ruled that Judge Ryan had erred when he'd prevented the defense counsel from seeing certain wiretap records that Ryan felt were dangerous to national security. That denial, Hand wrote, was a "refusal of a constitutional right—it is extremely unlikely that she [Coplon] suffered the slightest handicap from the Judge's refusal, but we cannot dispense with constitutional privilege." Hand also ruled that Ryan didn't allow for sufficient exploration of the identity of the "confidential informant" whose information had begun the investigation, to prove that the informant had not been a wiretap. I believed Hand went much further here than Frankfurter had gone in *Nardone,* and that he was wrong.

On this point alone, I'm convinced we could have sought a retrial and won—because we could have showed in even more detail that all of our evidence had come from sources other than wiretapping —but on the next point Hand raised, all we could do was mutter in our beer about having been caught between a rock and a hard place. Learned Hand was of the opinion that the FBI had indeed had enough time and evidence to have obtained a warrant to arrest Coplon and Gubitchev—and since we hadn't done so, Hand declared our arrest had been illegal. Therefore, any evidence obtained from that arrest was likewise illegal and inadmissible. This meant that the contents of Coplon's handbag couldn't be used against her in court —the decoy memorandum, the note to her unnamed superior about the 115-page FBI report she hadn't been able to copy, the data slips, etc. Without such evidence, we would have no case on a retrial.

I was very bitter. On the precise point about obtaining a warrant, we had sought advice from Deputy Attorney General Peyton Ford, who had specifically told us that although he didn't think we had enough evidence to swear out a warrant, we could make an arrest if our agents had "probable cause" to believe they were witnessing a felony. We had taken the advice of this high-ranking officer of the government, and now because of it our case was lost, and the FBI appeared to outsiders as if we had stupidly blundered and blown it by ourselves. It was small comfort that, one month after the reversal of the Coplon case, Congress passed a law that allowed the authorities to make arrests in such espionage-related cases without a warrant.

In the aftermath of the Hand decision, the National Lawyers Guild fastened on the wiretap issue and demanded that President Truman revamp the FBI and "curb" the excesses that the Guild felt were demonstrated through the unchecked allegations of the FBI file reports, and through the "illegal" wiretaps of the Coplon case. The NLG was a well-known Communist organization, and Director Hoover managed to quash its suggestions, though it became known that President Truman had agreed with some of the NLG's criticisms of the FBI.

Nothing that happened in the entire Coplon affair—especially in the reversal of the conviction—pleased Director Hoover. Even though the Coplon case had given us a lot of new information on, for example, how KGB people acted under surveillance and the use of the United Nations for a cover, Hoover was angered by the case. For instance, Hoover ordered the Bureau's own internal system of wiretap reporting changed. He sought reaffirmation of the 1940 and 1946 directives on wiretapping, though he obtained nothing definitive on this subject until 1954, from a new attorney general, Herbert Brownell. Hoover was furious over the mishandling of the case by Justice; he could do very little about that, but he could punish some of the FBI agents who he thought had mishandled their own courtroom testimony in the trials. Hoover believed that some of these agents had testified to things that were outside their immediate knowledge and that did not reflect well on the Bureau. Howard Fletcher came in for a lot of heat. Some critics had become alarmed that Fletcher seemed to have ordered wiretap recordings burned, an act they believed was a factor in Learned Hand's decision; the truth was that the actual vinyl records of such wiretaps were routinely recycled, and that the destruction of these materials was not a factor in the Court of Appeals decision. Hoover understood this particular fact, but his anger at Fletcher was widely based and ranged over the conduct of the entire case—and it was an anger that would last for some time.

I escaped major criticism, and for this I was considered inside the Bureau to be quite lucky or wise, depending on the sentiments of the opiner.

Judith Coplon didn't go entirely free. Learned Hand's decision had let the indictment against her stand—an indication that he thought the evidence against her was strong, even if he disagreed with the way it had been obtained. Technically Coplon was still out on bond and the threat of a new trial hung over her head, but everybody knew there would be no new trial. Coplon married, had four children, and faded into obscurity.

When the deciphered KGB messages first led us to Coplon, they also led us to two other women who had been Coplon's former classmates at Columbia. She had suggested both for recruitment in 1944–45. This, of course, was something that had never been brought up at the trials, and has never been made public before this writing. In 1949 we were unable to establish whether one of these women had ever been recruited, but we did learn a good deal about the other one, whose name was Flora Don Wovschin.

Flora Wovschin's mother and father were White Russians who had emigrated to the United States. After the father died, the mother remarried, to Enos Wicher. Both Flora and Judith Coplon were members of the Young Communist League at Barnard. After graduation, Flora went to work for the Office of War Information in Washington, D.C., and we thought it had been at that time that she had been recruited by Coplon for the KGB. In 1947 Flora resigned from government service, married a Soviet Amtorg engineer and went with him back to Russia. In her correspondence with her mother, Flora indicated that she was not happy, and by 1949 she and the engineer were divorced. We interviewed the Wichers in 1949, and they told us of these developments. Shortly thereafter, Flora wrote to her mother that she was going to the home of "old blind Minkie's parents," a veiled reference to the origin of the Wichers' old and blind Chinese poodle. During the Korean War, word reached the Wichers that Flora had died. I always had the strong suspicion that Flora had perished while working in some capacity—perhaps intelligence or propaganda—with the North Koreans.

The wry nature of the Coplon affair was finally symbolized for me by the matter of Isidore Gibby Needleman. In spite of my repeated insistence at the trials that Needleman was not and had never been an FBI informant, a cloud hung over him, at least as far as the KGB was concerned. Evidently the KGB could not decide whether I had lied about him or had told the truth, and determined not to leave any doubt about the matter—Needleman was fired from his Amtorg post.

A year later, in 1950, Needleman came under actual FBI investigation in connection with Harry Gold, a case I'll detail in another chapter in this book; while being interrogated about that matter, he asked the interviewing agent in regard to the Coplon affair, "Why did Lamphere have to name *me,* of all people?"

8
CONTAINING THE BREAKTHROUGH

AN EVENT OCCURRED in the late summer of 1949 that I hardly gave any thought to at the time. I was between the first Coplon trial and the second, and immersed in dozens of other investigations that were coming out of the deciphered KGB messages. So I didn't pay that much attention when the MI-6 representative, Peter Dwyer, dropped by my office and informed me that he'd be leaving soon to take a job in Canada, and that a new man would be replacing him as the MI-6 rep in Washington.

It was only years later that I began to reflect on that moment, and to see in it a signal of a catastrophe to come.

To tell its story properly, I have to start back a bit further, at that golden time in 1948 when we were first hitting our stride with investigations coming out of the messages. As that year wore on, it became increasingly difficult to contain the knowledge of the breakthrough to a small circle of my immediate FBI colleagues and superiors. The understanding that we were on to something big was spreading, and outsiders wanted a piece of the breakthrough. Among those most anxious to share the wealth were the British intelligence services, MI-5 and MI-6. MI-5 was considered the counterpart of the FBI in that its bailiwick was counterintelligence; MI-6 was more like the

CIA, as it dealt with espionage overseas, away from Great Britain.

Director Hoover retained suspicions about British Intelligence from the war years, when he had been forced to cooperate with Sir William Stephenson. However, the Director had continued to work with Stephenson's office even after the "emergency" was over—for instance, when Bentley first came to the FBI in 1945, Hoover immediately informed Stephenson that she had named several British subjects as sources of information. However, in the years just after the war, the Director had become more concerned with the challenge to the FBI from the just-forming CIA, and stopped looking askance at the British. In fact, with Hoover's encouragement, Assistant Director Mickey Ladd played the British off against the CIA, and he did so primarily through his close personal relationship with Peter Dwyer, a clever, witty and charming Briton who at that time served both MI-5 and MI-6 as liaison to the FBI.

There was a reciprocal arrangement. In London our legal attaché, John Cimperman, was allowed to visit freely in the offices of MI-5 and MI-6. In Washington Ladd gave Peter Dwyer permission to drop in at the various offices of the FBI's Domestic Intelligence Division, and to talk freely with supervisors such as me. No other intelligence man, even from a U.S. agency, could do so; Dwyer's privilege was unique.

Then, in early 1948, MI-5 decided that they wanted their own man in Washington, and Dwyer's fiefdom was cut back to representing just MI-6. The new MI-5 man, Dick Thistlethwaite, I personally found more likable than Dwyer.

Actually, throughout the intelligence community, MI-6 had the reputation of being a bunch of skillful horsetraders with whom you trafficked at your peril. MI-6 would give out a small piece of information and tout it highly in order to obtain a lot in return; when you gave them something, as if to appear grateful they would offer a little more of what they had held in reserve in order to gain even more on the next round. Dwyer was one of the best horsetraders, and I guess that was why I didn't trust him. In my view, we were all working against a common adversary, and to vanquish the enemy we had perforce to share all that we had. After my colleagues and I had been burned a few times by the MI-6 trading tactics, we weren't quite so willing to share. However, because Dwyer had close ties to Ladd, he could sometimes go over our heads to get what he desired.

There came a day in 1948 when Ladd told Dwyer about the deciphered KGB messages—and then called me in and told me to deal with Peter Dwyer but to be cautious about it. Ladd was FBI through and through, and even though he was friendly to Dwyer, he wouldn't stand for the Bureau's being snookered.

Forthwith Dwyer and Thistlethwaite came to see me, and citing his conversation with Ladd, Peter asked to see the messages. "Peter," I said, "I'll be glad to give you any information where there's a British interest."

"That's not the way I understand it," Dwyer said indignantly. "We would like access to all that you have. We don't really think you can tell in advance whether there's a British interest or not."

"I'll lean over backwards to give you anything that might possibly involve Soviet intelligence operations outside the United States—but not what relates solely to this country."

Dwyer angrily threatened to return to Mickey Ladd for authorization to obtain what he wanted—which was everything we had in the cupboard. I matched his anger and told him, point-blank, that if he went over my head, whatever further cooperation he got from me would be only on a forced basis. Dick Thistlethwaite understood immediately what I was implying, and tried to smooth things over by telling Peter that I'd surely be more reasonable if he played this thing my way.

Dwyer, still stubborn, said, "I know what Ladd said."

"Play it whichever way you want," I retorted, "but if you go back to Mickey, though you may get the information, I guarantee you'll lose any willing help from me."

Because Thistlethwaite insisted, Dwyer settled for letting things stand, for the present.

And so, in return for that partial victory, I shared with them one nugget of information. (We Idaho men know something of horses, too.) That information was quite relevant to "British interests," and on the face of it looked as if it could lead to sensational disclosures. Several fragments of deciphered KGB messages indicated that someone in the British embassy in Washington in 1944–45 had been providing the KGB with high-level cable traffic between the United States and Great Britain.

Both Dwyer and Thistlethwaite were startled by this revelation, as well they should have been, for it meant that the KGB had been aware of high-level negotiations carried on by cable between Washington and London in the closing phases of World War II. Communications at the highest levels of the American and British governments had been compromised, and for all we knew they might still be in jeopardy. This most serious matter called for immediate investigation. We agreed that MI-5 and MI-6 would endeavor to come up with a list of possible suspects, and then the FBI and MI-5 would conduct a joint investigation of those suspects on both sides of the Atlantic.

With this bone in their teeth, the British bulldogs should have had a field day, I thought. However, the British didn't respond to the startling information from the KGB messages as I believe we would have. Nothing happened in a week or two, or even a month. I considered that if the situation had been reversed, and the FBI had to attempt to locate a spy in an office of comparable size and importance to that of the British outpost in Washington in 1944–45, we would have had a roster of all the employees in a day or two. Working through that list, it soon would have become clear to us that the person in question would have had to be one of the small handful of people who had had access to the restricted cables. By matching names and dates against transfer and vacation lists and entry-and-exit logbooks, we would have doggedly winnowed down this small group and zeroed in on the most likely suspects to have been the KGB spy. Of course, this sort of investigation, even when conducted by the FBI, sometimes led us to dead ends, but I couldn't help wondering why the British seemed to be coming up with nothing. Every month or so, when I'd inquire about it, I'd be told that there was no new information, but that MI-5 and MI-6 were still working on finding that possible spy in the British embassy in 1944–45.

In late 1948 Dick Thistlethwaite returned to London and was replaced by Geoffrey Patterson as MI-5 rep. And then, in the late summer of 1949, the ambitious Peter Dwyer came to tell me he was moving on.

In that conversation Peter described the man who was to replace him; the replacement was very bright, rather senior in the MI-6 service, and had a good chance of one day becoming the head of the service. Peter said the man's name was H. A. R. Philby, and everyone called him "Kim."

I listened politely, but my mind leapt forward to the idea of the replacement. Perhaps I'd get along better with this new man than I had done with Dwyer. I wasn't sorry to hear that Peter was going, because I thought he'd been too much of an influence on Mickey Ladd.

In fact, in the interim between my earlier conversation with Dwyer on the messages and the present moment, the British had pulled a classic flanking maneuver to go around both Ladd and me to obtain access to the deciphered KGB messages. In accordance with an agreement between the United States and Great Britain, the British arranged for their own cryptographic service to get in touch with its counterpart, the Army Security Agency, and had made a formal request to share in the details of the breakthrough. Thus by the summer of 1949 the British had their own man working with Meredith Gardner and had access to all the deciphered KGB messages.

In that interim, also, I had been putting continual pressure on the British, first through Thistlethwaite and then through Jeff Patterson, to find and identify the spy in the British embassy in 1944–45. So far, I'd gotten nowhere. I found it hard to accept Jeff's repeated "no progress" reports, but, busy with Coplon and other matters, I didn't do much about it.

In early October 1949 Peter Dwyer came around to introduce his replacement as MI-6 representative. Removing files from some chairs, I tried to make the men comfortable. We shook hands, sat down and engaged in small talk. Immediately I began to wonder at Peter's earlier description of his successor. Kim Philby was seedy and spoke with a stutter. His clothes were loose-fitting and shabby, and his face and figure had few notable features. I could hardly believe that this unimpressive man was being spoken of as a future chief of MI-6, in line for a knighthood. When Sir Stewart Menzies, chief of MI-6, had visited Washington, I'd been introduced to him, and when Sir Percy Sillitoe of MI-5 had made a similar visit, I'd spent some time with him also. Both men had impressed me—Sir Stewart, the upper-class Etonian clubman, and Sir Percy, the tall and striking former police chief. Philby was utterly unlike either of these great men. The most disturbing aspect of Philby was his lack of friendliness; he seemed to have little interest in the conversation. Perhaps, I thought, his sterling qualities were hidden, and he'd be warmer when I got to know him better.

Peter and I did most of the talking in this session with Philby, and the conversation turned on the matter of the spy in the embassy; although MI-6 did not have direct responsibility for this, Peter had always been personally interested in the case. Philby said little, but it was clear from his comments that he had received a briefing on the deciphered KGB messages before he had left London, and that he knew of the ongoing investigation.

We didn't realize at that time that Philby knew precisely who that spy in the embassy had been—his fellow Soviet double agent Donald Maclean.

Today, of course, it is well known that Harold Adrian Russell Philby was a Soviet agent within MI-6, a traitor to his own country and a man who betrayed many of the most important secrets of the Western democracies to the Soviet Union. Now Kim Philby is a legend— a demon or an antihero, depending on one's philosophical bent. Philby himself, or a thinly disguised fictional counterpart, stalks through many modern spy novels.

At the moment of my first meeting with Philby in 1949, there was no way I could conceive of the depth of treachery reached by the seedy-looking man next to me. After that initial meeting I was glad to learn that Philby seemed content to leave relations with me to Jeff Patterson, and to concentrate on the CIA. He'd see me not every week, as Dwyer had done, but approximately once a month, and then, if possible, only in conjunction with Jeff Patterson. When Philby and I did meet one-on-one, the sessions were boring. The threesome was better. Patterson and I were friends, and we'd chat about the difficulty of covering Soviet and satellite officials whom we believed to be intelligence operatives, or about the general development of Israeli intelligence capabilities. I stayed away from discussing my present U.S. cases, still mindful of the restrictions that Mickey Ladd had earlier placed on me.

That didn't mean Philby had no access to my material, though. When we needed information from abroad on our developing cases, we'd send a memo to "STOTT," our acronym for the British intelligence office in Washington, which would give copies of our requests to both the MI-5 and MI-6 reps. We were working closely with the British because we trusted their abilities more than we did those of the fledgling CIA—but in the process, many things about our current cases came into Philby's hands, and presumably were passed by him to the KGB. In effect, then, Philby had no need to rely on me personally, or on anyone else in the FBI such as Mickey Ladd, with whom he developed a "friendship," to obtain information on what the FBI was doing in counterintelligence.

Occasionally, on the weekends, Jeff Patterson and his wife and my wife and I would all get together; usually there would be a few others from the intelligence community around. I don't remember Kim Philby at these gatherings.

9

KLAUS FUCHS

O N SEPTEMBER 23, 1949, President Harry Truman announced to the world that the Russians had exploded an atomic device.

This was stunning news: the United States nuclear monopoly was
now at an end. Because the Russians had a bomb, we would have to
seriously reassess our foreign policy, which was already reeling from
the recent triumph of Mao Tse-tung over Chiang Kai-shek's Nationalists in China.

We in the intelligence community learned of the Russian bomb
before the public announcement, but it was as much of a shock to us
as to the general public. Atomic Energy Commission and U.S. Navy
monitors had begun to detect the radioactive evidence of the blast
earlier in September, and scientists concluded that the actual bomb
test had taken place in August 1949. A most important question was
raised by the event: Had the Russian scientists actually been several
years ahead of our estimates of their progress on the bomb, or had
they been aided in their effort to build it by information stolen from
the United States?

In early September 1949, when the news of the Russian explosion
came to our attention, I was deeply embroiled in the Coplon case.
The first trial was over, and the second trial was to begin in a few

months. I was called into a meeting to discuss the implications of the Russian bomb. The meeting was chaired by Lish Whitson, who had replaced Pat Coyne as chief of the Espionage Section; Lish was on an interagency committee that was looking into the matter of the Russian explosion, and wanted to have our thoughts on whether the Russians might have stolen information from us that they could have used in constructing their device. Lish, his assistant Bill Branigan, and case supervisors Bert Turner, Emory Gregg and I were the men in the FBI who were the most knowledgeable about KGB and GRU efforts to penetrate the Manhattan Project. As we sat around a table, we were quickly able to list three major Soviet attempts at obtaining atomic secrets:

1. Vassili Zubilin's efforts, through Gregory Kheiffets and CPUSA functionary Steve Nelson, to obtain information from scientists around J. Robert Oppenheimer at Berkeley. Though the FBI had countered this operation, some material might have gotten through to the Russians.

2. Arthur Adams's recruitment of Clarence F. Hiskey, an employee of the Metallurgical Laboratory in Chicago, which resulted in some information—probably of minor value—being transmitted to the Russians.

3. Nicolai Zabotin's successful attempt, through Allan Nunn May at the Canadian National Research Council, to send back to Russia bomb research data and an actual sample of U-235. Nunn May, of course, had confessed to this crime and was now in prison in England.

We knew the degree of success of this Soviet espionage, but in early September 1949 it wasn't possible for us to assess accurately how much direct help these penetrations had been to Soviet scientists who had fashioned the Russian A-bomb.

Enmeshed as I was in the Coplon case, and in several other investigations that had been initiated on the basis of the deciphered KGB messages, I put the matter of the Russian A-bomb out of my mind for about a week. Then, in mid-September—still before the President's announcement—I found a startling bit of information in a newly deciphered 1944 KGB message.

In this cable were data and theories that seemed to have come directly from inside the Manhattan Project. The subject was the gaseous diffusion process, one of the key scientific techniques used to obtain the type of uranium needed in the manufacture of the bomb. When I read the KGB message, it became immediately obvious to me that the Russians had indeed stolen crucial research from us, and had undoubtedly used it to build their bomb.

I dropped everything and began to work intensely with the deciphered message.

Part of it summarized a detailed scientific paper, while another part referred to the identity of the agent or messenger who had provided the information. This second part showed clearly that in 1944 the KGB in New York City had had an agent within the British Mission to the Manhattan Project.

This was startling news. I grabbed Ernie Van Loon, who had recently come to work with my section, and together we asked the AEC for a copy of that scientific paper which the Russian message had summarized, and obtained all the names of those who had come over to the United States in the British Mission. In two short days we had learned that Klaus Fuchs was the author of the paper summarized in the KGB message, and that Fuchs was one of the top British scientists on the Manhattan Project. Thus by the time of President Truman's announcement, we had a prime suspect for the KGB spy who had stolen A-bomb secrets and given them to the Russians.

But Fuchs was not the only suspect at this point; we also had some reason to be suspicious of the British Mission's leader, Rudolf Peierls, and of another member of the scientific mission. I had our own files and those of the Manhattan Project combed for data on these three people.

Our files contained two derogatory pieces of information about a man by the name of Klaus Fuchs. While we couldn't be absolutely certain that this Fuchs and the scientist from the British Mission were one and the same man, the likelihood was great. The first of these items was a captured Gestapo document that had come into the hands of the FBI only after World War II. (I emphasize that, because Fuchs had been in the United States during 1944–45, before the document had been found.) The Gestapo paper said that in 1933 one Klaus Fuchs had been identified as a German Communist, to be arrested when and if the Gestapo found him. The second derogatory mention of Fuchs came from a wholly different source. Fuchs's name was listed in an address book found in the apartment of Israel Halperin, who had been one of the GRU agents in Canada found during the Gouzenko affair. This mention of Fuchs puzzled me, because the deciphered message told me that Fuchs's involvement—if it was

Fuchs—was a KGB matter, and usually there was no crossover of GRU and KGB operations.

In our files I could find nothing that cast similar doubt on the integrity of Peierls or on the other members of the British Mission —and so I became convinced that Klaus Fuchs was the prime suspect.

I sat down and prepared a top-secret letter to the British Intelligence services. I told them of the deciphered message, and of the two pieces of information in our files that referred to Fuchs. While I couldn't be certain of the identity of the Soviet agent, I wrote, Fuchs had to be considered the prime suspect. When the letter was typed, I had it delivered to the STOTT intelligence office of the British embassy in Washington, and I waited for MI-5 to act on it.

In the meantime, Ernie initiated an investigation into Fuchs's family in the United States. His sister Kristel, her husband, Robert Heinemann, and their three children lived near Boston; Kristel was confined in a mental hospital, and we had to be cautious about talking to her.

Within a few weeks we got an answer on Fuchs from MI-5. The British, too, believed Fuchs to be the prime suspect, but were as yet unsure of how to go after him. The problem was that there was no evidence that could be used in court; we couldn't reveal that the clue to his espionage and identity had come from the messages. Unless Fuchs could be forced to confess, there would be no case.

Ernie continued investigating the Fuchs connections in the United States, while I returned to my involvement with Coplon and waited for the British to do something. In December 1949 MI-5 came up with a plan to get Klaus Fuchs to confess, and much of it hinged on the persuasive power of William Skardon, who was in charge of the investigation. As I later learned, Skardon wasn't from the upper crust of British society, but rather was a friendly, low-key fellow—sort of a British *Columbo* character, complete with disheveled appearance and an intellect that was sometimes hidden until the moment came to use it to point to incongruities in a suspect's story.

Skardon's plan involved some information that the British had obtained about Fuchs's aged father, who was about to accept a post at the University of Leipzig—which was behind the Iron Curtain, in East Germany. The idea was that British security was not too happy with having a prominent scientist who worked at the Harwell Research facility on atomic energy projects while such a scientist's father was within easy reach of the Soviets; such a setup could easily be turned into one in which Fuchs might be blackmailed. In fact, Fuchs had discussed his father's new post in just these terms with a security man at Harwell.

Over a period of several weeks in December 1949, Skardon met with Fuchs and started to gain his confidence. Skardon had to be careful not to reveal to Fuchs that the FBI (and MI-5) knew of his existence through deciphered KGB cables, but he also had to let Fuchs know that the authorities had found out a lot about his possible espionage while in the United States. Fuchs at first categorically denied Skardon's charge that he had spied for the Soviets, and then, on January 22, told the head of security at Harwell that he wanted to see Skardon again. On January 24, 1950, Fuchs began to confess to Skardon his long involvement with Communism and with Soviet espionage. It turned out that Fuchs had spied in England during the war, in the United States while in the British Mission, and after the end of the war when he returned to England.

Fuchs had confessed, but the British waited two weeks to arrest him. Since there was no independent evidence, Sir Hartley Shaw-cross, the British attorney general, decided Fuchs could not be prosecuted for espionage. But he could be charged with violation of the Official Secrets Act. Fuchs was arrested and so charged on February 2, 1950. A week later, in a brief session at the old Bow Street police court in London, Fuchs pled guilty, and Skardon testified to the main elements of Fuchs's confession. On March 1, 1950, Fuchs was sentenced to the maximum penalty possible under the Official Secrets Act—fourteen years in prison.

Fuchs's confession was only one of many events in the opening months of 1950 that brought Communism to the forefront of public consciousness. President Truman announced that because the Russians now had an atomic bomb, the United States was going to build the hydrogen bomb. The President also let it be known that the United States was, for all practical purposes, conceding mainland China to the Communists by cutting back on our military aid to the Nationalists on Taiwan. Communist agent Judith Coplon was tried for the second time and was again found guilty. Alger Hiss's second trial ended in his conviction for perjury. One cumulative effect of these instances of Communist influence, historians now believe, was to spur Senator Joseph McCarthy to make his February 9, 1950, speech in Wheeling, West Virginia, in which he claimed to be in possession of a list of 205 Communists in the U.S. State Department.

Senator McCarthy's crusade, which was to last for the next several years, was always anathema to me. McCarthy's approach and tactics hurt the anti-Communist cause and turned many liberals against legitimate efforts to curtail Communist activities in the United States, particularly in regard to government employment of known Communists. While I, personally, was more interested in countering the activities of the Soviet KGB and GRU, I was well aware that the CPUSA was controlled by and subservient to Moscow. McCarthy's star chamber proceedings, his lies and overstatements hurt our counterintelligence efforts.

It was before McCarthy's speech, and in reaction to a very different event—Fuchs's confession—that all hell broke loose at Bureau headquarters. The information that Skardon got out of Fuchs turned what had been a quiet and careful investigation of Fuchs's connections in the United States into a raging monster of a quest. Its focus was the man whom Fuchs said he knew only as "Raymond." Fuchs confessed that he'd turned over to "Raymond" the atomic information he had developed in the United States. At Director Hoover's behest, we supervisors began a search to locate "Raymond" in which most of the FBI's field offices and teams of agents were mobilized.

Shortly after we began our search, word came down that the Director wanted a detailed brief on what we were calling the "FOO-CASE." I was put in charge of developing the brief, but wasn't told the purpose to which it would be put; I assumed it was only for internal consumption. What a mistake that turned out to be!

To tell the story concisely, Emory Gregg, Ernie Van Loon and another supervisor were assigned to work on the brief with me, and we split the task. The portion that later became the problem— Emory's—was a summary of everything we knew about Fuchs. In it went the Gestapo "stop" sheet, the listing in Israel Halperin's notebook, and some material about Fuchs's early background, gleaned from Skardon's interviews. It took us almost all night to complete our work and to give it to the stenographers to type.

The problem arose several days later, when the Director gave testimony to a closed-door session of the Congressional Joint Atomic Energy Committee and used our brief as the source of his information. When Hoover was asked if the security office of the Manhattan Project had run name-checks through the FBI files of people in the British Mission at the time they arrived in the United States, the Director replied that no name-checks had been made. General Leslie Groves, former head of the Manhattan Project, then contradicted Hoover by testifying that yes, indeed, a name-check had been run through the FBI on Klaus Fuchs in 1944, and it had come up empty.

To say the least, the Director was not used to being caught in an error before the members of Congress—and he was furious. He demanded to know who had "misled" him.

But our assignment had been to convey information, in summary form, on everything we knew about Fuchs. We had not anticipated the pertinence of the question as to whether or not the Manhattan District had ever asked for a name-check on Fuchs.

Nevertheless, someone had to take the heat, and we who had worked on the brief met and decided, better two than four. Emory and I agreed to be the guilty parties. I had been in charge of the overall presentation, and had we anticipated the question of the name-checks, the answer would have gone into the section Emory had written. We drafted a carefully worded memorandum of explanation and handed it to Assistant Director Howard Fletcher.

Howard said that, as he was our penultimate superior, the buck ought to stop at his desk. He said he'd take the responsibility for not having had the information on the name-check included in the brief. Emory and I both admired Fletcher and persuaded him that such a stance on his part would not serve to deflect the Director's anger from us. We didn't want Howard tarred unnecessarily by this particular brush. At last Fletcher agreed with our position, and sent our memo upstairs.

When Hoover read the memo and recognized that he had not been "misled," but rather that we had simply failed to include information on the name-checks, he became even more irate.

Now the Bureau's own internal power structure got involved. There were parts of the FBI that had very little to do with day-to-day conduct of field investigations—but that had a lot to do with the hierarchy and the management and discipline of agents, as well as with the maintenance of the Bureau's image. Assistant Director Louis B. Nichols's basic job was to be the Bureau's public relations man, but he was also in charge of the FBI files. Since the problem might have begun with information in the files, Nichols entered the fray. He discovered that at the time Fuchs had first become a suspect, Ernie Van Loon had written a memorandum that summarized each file reference to Fuchs. Nichols contended that if Van Loon hadn't summarized, but had simply copied out all the information about Fuchs in that memo, the Manhattan Project name-check would have come to light much earlier. The fact that a summary is supposed to condense information, not regurgitate it, was ignored.

Another part of the power structure joined the fray. Inspector John Mohr of the Administrative Division was assigned to determine for Director Hoover precisely who had been at fault, and why. Mohr looked into everything with 20/20 hindsight, and the result was letters of censure for Emory Gregg and me, and a recommendation for disciplinary transfer of Ernie Van Loon. We could bear the letters of censure—relatively light slaps on the wrist—but to transfer Ernie would have been truly harsh treatment. On February 24, 1950, when Ernie received word of the transfer, he went to see the Director and managed to have the punishment downgraded to probation. It was fortunate that Ernie was able to do this, because within three months he would receive a commendation for his work on the Fuchs-Gold case.

While all of us were still answering John Mohr's questions, the Director sent Espionage Section Chief Lish Whitson to London to interview Klaus Fuchs. The Director undoubtedly believed at this point that since the FBI had furnished the lead to Fuchs, we would now be able to talk to him. But Sir Hartley Shawcross ruled that no FBI interview of Fuchs could take place until Fuchs had been sentenced and all appeals had been exhausted. The Director had dispatched Lish to London without prior consultation with British Intelligence to see whether or not he would be welcome at this time, and when Lish couldn't get in to see Fuchs, the Director was furious with Lish and outraged at MI-5. Sir Percy Sillitoe of MI-5 tried in vain to intervene with Shawcross so that Lish could see Fuchs, but to no avail. The Director then became convinced that MI-5 was actually opposed to an FBI interview of Fuchs. This was a mess that would not be quickly resolved.

In Hoover's view, there had now been three major failures. The first resulted in his embarrassment before a congressional committee. The second gave rise to the insult to the FBI of Whitson being barred from seeing Fuchs. The third error was a continuing one having to do with our investigation: the Director could not understand why Fuchs's American contact, "Raymond," had not been positively identified and found. Calling Howard Fletcher into his office, the Director made these points—and Howard did something I suspect no one had done in more than a quarter-century: he told Hoover that he was dead wrong on all three counts. Hoover responded that Fletcher must be sick and in need of a rest.

Howard Fletcher was the epitome of loyalty to the Bureau and to J. Edgar Hoover personally, and he took the Director's remarks in stride and kept going. Fletcher was a strong man, but in the ensuing weeks he came under unbelievable pressure, especially from the inquiries of Inspector Mohr, which were ranging further and further afield. One day Mohr called me up to his office, where I found Fletcher, looking terrible. Lifting his head from his hands, he looked up at me and said, "Bob, tell Mohr what you told me about the start of the Fuchs investigation." I could hardly believe that at this time Mohr was unable to grasp that the lead to Fuchs had come from the deciphered KGB messages, and that it was we who had put MI-5 onto Fuchs in the first place. This, however, seemed to be the sticking point, and so I went over it in detail; by means of various markers I had put into the files, I offered proof of the way in which the investigation had proceeded.

When Mohr interrupted me during my recital with a sharp question, Howard Fletcher roared at him, "God damn it, shut up and Lamphere will prove it to you!" Cowed, Mohr shut up, and I continued with my story until I had reached its logical conclusion.

At that moment I hoped the inquisition had spent its energy and we all could get to work on the more important matter at hand, the search for "Raymond." Shortly thereafter, Howard Fletcher was removed as assistant director and was given a subordinate position in the Washington field office.

I hit the ceiling. For me, Howard Fletcher had embodied the best qualities of an FBI man; his intelligence, capacity for work, willingness to do battle for his men, and extreme loyalty to the Bureau and to Hoover personally would have recommended him to be the Bureau's director at some future date. Now his upward movement had stopped, probably forever.

For me, this was a severe crisis. Both Emory Gregg and I thought seriously about quitting the Bureau. I would have followed Howard Fletcher through fire, and could not stomach what the Bureau was doing to him. Howard sat me down and tried to persuade me not to leave—at least not then, when there were important investigations to conduct. He argued that it was unreasonable for Emory or me to take such a drastic step out of loyalty to him, when his own loyalty was to the FBI. He was taking his punishment and staying on, and he extracted a promise from both of us that we would do nothing then, and that when and if we ever wanted to quit, we would first come and talk to him about it.

In such a strained atmosphere it was difficult to conduct any investigation—let alone one that was considered, by the Director's own later admission, one of the most difficult and most important quests ever undertaken by the FBI, the search for Fuchs's American contact.

I discussed Hoover's orders—that the unknown "Raymond" had to be found, regardless of cost and manpower—with the man who replaced Howard Fletcher as assistant director of the Domestic Intelligence Division, Alan H. Belmont. Though I deeply regretted the departure of Fletcher, Belmont was a worthy successor. In New York in 1942, and again at the end of the war, I had worked under Belmont, and considered him an extremely able man perhaps even better suited than Fletcher had been to operate under Director Hoover's "one-man rule." Hardworking, intelligent and pragmatic, Belmont was respected by all the agents and supervisors. He and I agreed that Hoover's orders with regard to "Raymond" meant that we would be able to command all the Bureau's resources—but there could be no excuse for not finding him.

While I was still tied up answering questions from Inspector Mohr —he was raising my hackles by calling me "Bobby," a nickname I disliked—Ernie Van Loon was directing the investigation into "Raymond."

We were checking every conceivable lead, including interviewing those who had known or worked with Fuchs. The most promising interviews proved to be those with Fuchs's sister, Kristel Heinemann, and her husband, Robert. Mrs. Heinemann was in a mental hospital outside Boston, but she remembered a man who had come to her house in late 1944 and again in 1945, trying to get in touch with her brother. The first time she saw the man, she had told him to come back again after Christmas, when Fuchs would be visiting the family, and he had done so.

Both Heinemanns recalled the man, but the description they provided could have fit any of several million Americans: white male, age forty to forty-five, five feet eight inches tall, dark-brown hair, broad build, round face. They believed him to be a first-generation American.

We checked the Heinemanns' description with that given by Fuchs himself, and it was a match. Fuchs added one very important detail: he felt, from the questions "Raymond" had asked, that he must have known something about chemistry and engineering.

Fuchs had met "Raymond" nine times. From January to July 1944 they had kept rendezvous in New York City five times. Then Fuchs had gone to Los Alamos, and "Raymond" had gone to see Kristel to try to locate him. According to Fuchs, he met "Raymond" twice in Cambridge in early 1945—once at the Heinemann home and a second time on the banks of the Charles River. Two later meetings had been held in Santa Fe, New Mexico, in June and September 1945.

Ernie Van Loon and I believed that the most potentially helpful clue to "Raymond" was his probable background in chemistry or engineering. Combing the extensive FBI files for men who had that background, we came up with nearly a thousand men who had such training or who met the physical description given by Fuchs and the Heinemanns. We went through the tedious process of having all these photos shown to Fuchs in London, and to the Heinemanns. At first Fuchs couldn't identify any of them, but on March 13, 1950, he thought he recognized "Raymond" as a man named Joseph Regenstreich, or Robbins. However, when Robbins's picture was shown to the Heinemanns, they didn't agree that he was "Raymond." Further, our investigation quickly showed that Robbins could not have been in New York or Cambridge or Santa Fe at the times when Fuchs had met "Raymond."

We went back to square one. Still concentrating on that science background, we checked out chemical laboratories on the East Coast. To our dismay, we found that some 75,000 license permits had been issued to chemical manufacturing firms in New York City in the year 1945 alone.

My frustration at not finding "Raymond" was increased by the nagging questions I continually received from the Bureau higher-ups about the progress of the investigation. We started taking real long shots—interviewing people at bus stops and airports in New Mexico, for instance, to see if anybody remembered an unusual visitor from back in 1945.

We were getting nowhere fast—but Ernie had a hunch, and as the days went by, he began to convince me of its logic. Ernie thought there was a possible "Raymond" in the involved account that Elizabeth Bentley had first told the FBI in 1945. For example, Bentley had acted as a courier to a chemist by the name of Abraham Brothman for a short time. Brothman was connected with a number of other chemists and engineers, many of whom had leftist backgrounds and whose names had, one way or another, found their way into our files.

In 1947 the grand jury looking into Bentley's allegations had called Brothman to testify. On the stand, he readily admitted that he'd known both Bentley and her lover, Jacob Golos, and that he'd given them some information, but he said it was all harmless. Brothman said he'd met Golos through a fellow chemist named Harry Gold. The Grand Jury put Gold on the stand, and Gold said that he had thought Golos was a legitimate businessman. Neither Gold nor Brothman was indicted. We in the FBI knew both men were lying through their teeth about the innocence of their transactions with Bentley and Golos, but we couldn't prove it. And so the matter dropped for a while.

But Brothman and Gold had been among the first people we'd looked at when I first uncovered Fuchs's probable espionage, back in September 1949, and their friends and associates—Oscar Vago, Jules Korchein, Fred Heller—were in our files. We'd checked them out, and had even sent their photos to Fuchs, but he had rejected them all.

However, Ernie and I were struck by how closely the physical description of Harry Gold in our files matched the description given by the Heinemanns and Fuchs. We instructed the Philadelphia office to open a very active investigation into Harry Gold, and as the reports from Philadelphia started coming in, our interest mounted. Many of the details the agents were able to obtain about Gold's life and travels fit in with the nuggets about "Raymond" gleaned from Fuchs's confession.

But Fuchs had also rejected Gold's picture.

Ernie and I decided that the photo itself might be the cause of the difficulty. Often a witness will be unable to identify a file photo of a man, but will later readily identify a better photo, or one that had been taken closer to that time in the past when the witness had known the suspect. With this in mind, we asked the Philadelphia office to surreptitiously obtain some still and motion pictures of Gold. We hoped that a better image might result in a positive identification.

In early May 1950 we received the news that Fuchs's appeals period had been completed and that the FBI would be permitted to see him. Word came down from the Director that Supervisor Robert J. Lamphere was to go to London to handle this very important matter.

Because I was relatively junior in the hierarchy, I was a bit surprised at my selection, but there was no doubt that I knew the FOOCASE as well as anyone inside the FBI and that I maintained good relations with MI-5. Ernie Van Loon, the only other logical candidate at the supervisor level, was completely absorbed in the search for "Raymond," and also didn't have the overall understanding of the larger case which I had from my vantage point of being in charge of the message data. I guessed that the Director had probably not picked me personally for this assignment, but I was willing to bet that Al Belmont or Mickey Ladd—or both men—had told Hoover that I would do a capable job.

Preparations began immediately. I received a special government passport, and was the one-man audience for an unusual briefing on the mechanics of the atomic bomb. A top Bureau laboratory man had attended an AEC school, and he taught me the rudiments of how the bomb worked. For the first time I heard the word "implosion" and learned about critical masses, plutonium cores, and lens molds which "shaped" charges. All this information was still top secret; I was made privy to it because I absolutely had to be in a position to understand the technical side of things if Fuchs began to discuss them. I needed to have enough knowledge to ask questions about what material Fuchs had furnished to the Russians. For example, I took along with me a list of AEC and Manhattan Project documents that the various U.S. authorities believed Fuchs might have passed to the enemy.

I was all set to leave for London in a few days when, on a Friday afternoon, I received a telephone call from Hugh Clegg, the assistant director in charge of the Training and Inspection Division. Within the Bureau, Clegg was known as "trout-mouth" for the odd way he had of pursing his lips when he spoke; he was an unflagging admirer and praiser of Hoover's, and, like Lou Nichols, was one of the powers in the Bureau's internal hierarchy. Although Clegg had nothing to do with the day-to-day field investigations, his post as head of the dreaded Inspection Division did not endear him to those of us who conducted and supervised the Bureau's cases. In this phone call, Clegg asked me to send him the file on the Fuchs case. Incredulous, I asked whether he wanted the entire file, which already ran to thirty or forty volumes. Clegg then agreed that it would be better if I sent him only a copy of the comprehensive summary brief which we kept up to date for the Director.

Hanging up the phone, I went into Assistant Director Al Belmont's office and said, "Do you know why Clegg wants the Fuchs file?"

"He's going to London with you," Belmont said.

"Jesus Christ, no!" I sat down in a chair and tried to unscramble my brains. "Why didn't you tell me about this earlier?"

"I didn't want to spoil your weekend," Belmont responded. He laid out the scenario for me. It seemed that someone on Capitol Hill had suggested to Mr. Hoover that, after all the difficulties the FBI had encountered in getting to interview Fuchs, perhaps Associate Director Clyde Tolson ought to go over with Supervisor Lamphere to handle protocol with the British. While the Director had not been willing to have Tolson go to London, he thought well enough of the general idea to designate Clegg to perform the function of handling the delicate relations with the British. And undoubtedly the Director thought it would be clever to send his chief inpector along with me, so that if there were any disasters, the Inspection Division would already have a good candidate for scapegoat.

Actually, sending Clegg was a bad idea. He had been in London for the FBI in 1940, and had not endeared himself to British intelligence at that time. In fact, many of the MI-5 people disliked Clegg, and were unable to separate what he had done in 1940 on Hoover's explicit instructions from Clegg's own personality.

I was still simmering on Monday, when Mickey Ladd called me to his office. With a twinkle in his eye he sat me down and asked, "How do you feel about Hughie going with you to London?"

"Not worth a damn."

"I know," Ladd said, "and that's what I want to talk to you about."

The thrust of Ladd's instructions was for me not to worry about Clegg looking over my shoulder; my basic job was to do the best, most thorough interview of Fuchs possible. Secondarily, my mission was to protect our good relations with British Intelligence—Ladd and I shared the belief that cooperation with the British was one of the cornerstones on which our own progress in counterintelligence had been built. Ladd stressed that I was to try to make sure that Clegg didn't impair the Bureau's relations with MI-5.

Just before we got set to leave for London, on May 15–17, FBI agents in several cities fanned out to interview many people who had known Harry Gold, including Abe Brothman, Abe's mistress Miriam Moscowitz, and business partners Jules Korchein, Emil Barish, Oscar Vago and Gerhard Wollan. From these interviews came a good deal of new information about Harry Gold. For instance, Miriam Moscowitz told the FBI that he had lied to her about his background, that he had invented a wife, twin sons, and a brother dead on a Pacific battlefield; she didn't say why Gold had fashioned those lies.

At headquarters we became more and more convinced that Harry Gold was "Raymond." We pressed for those surreptitious films to be taken of Gold so that Clegg and I could have them when we went to London.

The next day Clegg and I got on the train for New York, where we were to catch the plane overseas. Before we got very far, Clegg broke his eyeglasses; we had to call Mrs. Clegg from Baltimore, get her to obtain Clegg's prescription from his doctor, and have that telephoned ahead to New York, where a new pair of glasses would be made.

At Philadelphia, Bureau agents came on board and handed us a package containing motion-picture film and blow-ups from the film of Harry Gold. The pictures had been taken on the street, through the window of a car.

In New York we picked up the new glasses and went out to the airport to begin the thirteen-hour flight that, after an intermediate stop in Labrador, would take us to London.

Thus far in the trip, I had been quite deferential to Clegg, as was expected when a supervisor was accompanying a high Bureau official. To treat Clegg with anything other than the respect due his position would have been a sure way to earn his displeasure.

On the plane, Clegg read and reread the summary brief, surfacing once in a while to ask me a question about the material. I was surprised by these queries, for they revealed a lack of knowledge about espionage and counterintelligence operations. Then, as we talked further, I was taken aback by Clegg's anxiety about the assignment. I wondered how he could let me see his fear of the Director's wrath. Later in the flight I was appalled at something else Clegg showed me: after determining that I was a Protestant, Clegg voiced his opinion that the Bureau was suffering from an overabundance of Catholic influence in the hierarchy. This display of prejudice saddened and infuriated me.

One good thing did come out of our talks on the plane. While Clegg said he'd be present at the interviews with Fuchs, he reaffirmed that I would handle the actual queries. His main job was to take care of our relations with the British. This put the pressure squarely on me, but I welcomed it. I knew my material and believed myself quite ready for my face-to-face meetings with Fuchs. In fact, I considered the chance to interrogate Klaus Fuchs one of the great opportunities of my life.

We were met at the London airport by John Cimperman, the Bureau's liaison with British Intelligence, and an experienced agent; John would sit in on some of the interviews with us.

Even five years after World War II had ended, London was still suffering. There was a great deal of bomb damage, and whole blocks had not been cleared of debris. Meat, butter, other foodstuffs and coal were rationed, along with nearly every other commodity. It was late in May, but the city was still cold, and there was no heat in our hotel room nor in many of the offices we visited during our stay.

Cimperman, Clegg and I discussed how we would proceed with MI-5. Clegg emphasized that Hoover did not want us to give MI-5 any information on the progress of our investigation into "Raymond." To me, this seemed ludicrous, and I pointed out that William Skardon was to sit in on our interviews of Fuchs, and that it would be impossible for him not to understand that Harry Gold was our prime suspect. Cimperman agreed with me, but Clegg was opposed to telling Skardon anything.

We were guarded in our initial meeting with MI-5, which, in any case, was a bit strained. Whitsun weekend was approaching; Sir Percy Sillitoe was in Canada. His deputy at MI-5 was a bit taken aback when Clegg insisted that we wanted to interview Fuchs right away, even if the next morning was a Saturday and a holiday weekend. Clegg also talked about his concern that the press would learn of our presence in England; he didn't want us bothered with reporters or photographers during our period of interviewing Fuchs. So, though Scotland Yard had assigned us a car and driver, it was agreed we'd travel back and forth to the prison where Fuchs was held in a closed and darkened police van. As it turned out, this subterfuge might have been necessary, for the British press did eventually find out about us, and some of the stories were less than complimentary and accurate. The general gist of the worst of them was that the FBI was in England to give Fuchs the "third degree." We smiled at that one.

In any event, on Saturday morning, May 20, Clegg and I went to MI-5 headquarters and, together with Skardon, climbed into the black-windowed police van and were whisked out the back exit. We rode for about twenty minutes to the outskirts of the city. Wormwood Scrubs was dreary, bare and cold—it fit my mental image of a British prison exactly. After passing through one or two exterior gates, we were taken into an unheated "solicitors' room" that was relatively near the prison building's entrance, and across the corridor from the governor's (warden's) office. The room was generally used for lawyers to meet their inmate clients. It had windows that looked out on an exercise courtyard, and small glass panels in the door to allow a guard outside the room to view what was going on inside. The main feature of the room was a large circular table, about which were a number of chairs.

Fuchs was brought in and introduced to us by Skardon, whom he knew well. We sat down and tried to begin. Skardon said very little, and Clegg took notes while I addressed Emil Julius Klaus Fuchs.

The man whom I had waited so long to confront looked much as I had expected him to: thin-faced, intelligent, and colorless. He was thirty-nine years old, of average height but a bit stoop-shouldered. His complexion was sallow, his eyes were brown and he wore glasses; his hair was receding and his scalp balding. When he pondered something, his forehead wrinkled, and there was a very noticeable vein that ran from the level of his eye across the temple and up into the hairline. His teeth were darkened from cigarette smoking, and he had a prominent Adam's apple; he swallowed hard, frequently and audibly, when under pressure. His hands were long, with wrists that were fairly wide in proportion. He blinked his eyes more than most people, and spoke English fluently, with a soft voice and a German accent.

Our conversation did not start off on a promising note. Fuchs wasn't sure that he would answer any questions from the FBI. After all, he was under no obligation to do so, and he wanted to have some guarantees that if he talked, nothing would happen to any of the people with whom he had been associated in the United States. As Fuchs went on about his concerns, I began to understand that what he was doing was setting up a bargaining situation. The person whose safety he most sought to assure was that of his sister, Kristel Heinemann.

I needed to get Fuchs to talk, but in this bargaining situation I had no chips. I told Fuchs that he obviously did not understand the function of the FBI, that our role was simply to conduct investigations and not to prosecute, and that in the case of a prosecution, only an attorney general or a judge could make a promise.

That didn't do much to push things along, and so I, too, began to talk about his sister, Kristel. She had been, I said, most cooperative with our agents, who had interviewed her on several occasions. Of course when we talked to her, it was only after consultation with her doctors. I was letting Fuchs realize that we knew where Kristel was and would continue to keep tabs on her. Fuchs's face showed no reaction. I tried again. I had no reason, I said, to believe that Kristel had any involvement with Fuchs's espionage in the United States other than the fact that she had been contacted by "Raymond" when he had sought to resume transactions with Fuchs; I did not regard that contact as significant. This time I thought I saw a glimmer of interest in Fuchs. His unspoken thoughts were coming through as

loudly as the spoken ones. I understood that he believed that the FBI
—like the Gestapo or the Soviet secret police—might act against an
innocent person such as Kristel Heinemann. We had no such action
in mind, but I was not above letting Fuchs conclude that if we were
the bastards he posited us to be, Kristel would continue to be in
jeopardy.

With that skirmish over, I turned to the real business at hand.
Fuchs had, I said, furnished information to William Skardon about
"Raymond," and the identification of "Raymond" was the prime
purpose of our visit. Since Fuchs seemed not to want to tell us everything, why not confine our conversations to the topic of "Raymond"
while we got to know each other better? Fuchs demurred; it was
clear that in his mind talking to Skardon was far different from
talking to the FBI, although he didn't want to come out and say so
directly.

At this impasse I took out a dozen photos of people who might be
"Raymond" and asked Fuchs to look at them. He could, I said, always
refuse to answer questions about any other subject, but because we
had come so far we felt it imperative to try to get him to identify
"Raymond."

Fuchs agreed to look at the photos. In the pile were three of the
blow-ups from the recent surveillance film, several old photos of
Gold, and several photos of various other suspects. One by one, Fuchs
rejected the photos of the other subjects, and then the earlier photos
of Gold. Only the three new photos of Gold remained.

"I cannot reject them," Fuchs said to me. My heart leapt. But the
identification was less than complete. Fuchs declared that the photos
were not clear enough for him to state unequivocally that they were
of "Raymond."

Later that day Clegg and I went to Cimperman's office in the
American embassy in London, where Clegg supervised the preparation of a first cable to Director Hoover. Such cables became a nightly
chore throughout our stay—not only for us, but for two secretaries
who worked far into the morning hours to encipher our reports. Our
cables actually went in code; we used a one-time cipher pad in their
preparation. Clegg was intent upon providing Hoover with the most
detailed reports imaginable, and was also insistent that we answer in
our cables all the questions that headquarters was already forwarding
to us by their own cables.

At least once a day, and sometimes more often, we would get
cables from headquarters with new information, or with questions

that we were to put to Fuchs and then relay the answers back to the Director.

During a lull in this first cable session, Clegg asked me why I had made occasional notes during the interviews when we had agreed he'd take all the notes. I explained that it was my style to jot down a word or phrase now and then to remind me of some point—but that, basically, the essentials of the interview were all in my head. During these cable sessions Clegg and I would sometimes differ on what we remembered Fuchs to have said; invariably I would press for my own understanding of Fuchs's comments, notes or no notes. Each time, Clegg would eventually choose to trust my memory over his own pencil-markings.

On Monday John Cimperman accompanied us to Wormwood Scrubs to assist in showing the films of Gold which had been taken without Gold's knowledge in Philadelphia. Prison employees placed blackout curtains over the two windows and the glass door panel in the solicitors' room, and then projected the film. In it Gold walked, stopped and moved about on an open street. At the end of the film Fuchs said, "I cannot be absolutely positive, but I think it is very likely him ["Raymond"]. There are certain mannerisms I seem to recognize, such as the too-obvious way he has of looking around and looking back." Fuchs added that there was something about the man that wasn't congruent with his memories of "Raymond," but this might be explained by the passage of time—after all, it had been five years since he had seen his American contact.

The film was shown a second time. After this viewing, Fuchs said that he thought the item that was bothering him was the man's manner. The man in the film was serious, and Fuchs remembered "Raymond" as smiling, happy and "bombastic . . . as if pleased with the importance of his assignment." For a third showing the projector was moved further away from the screen in order to enlarge the image. During this third showing I watched both Fuchs and the screen—the physicist showed no emotion as he peered intently at the images. But after this showing he again pronounced his identification as "very likely."

I was not satisfied with this, but we broke off the session. I knew from the incoming Bureau cables that Gold was being interviewed in Philadelphia, and while we believed Gold had not yet confessed to being Fuchs's American contact, we understood that the agents questioning Gold felt fairly certain that he would soon admit the connection.

Actually, the coup de grace was being administered on that same day, by Scotty Miller, my former colleague in the New York field office, and Richard Brennan. On May 22, having obtained permission from Gold to search his apartment, they were carefully going through his possessions as Gold sat and watched them. Previously Gold had denied knowing Klaus Fuchs, meeting Kristel Heinemann, or ever taking trips to Boston or west of the Mississippi River. But Scotty Miller and Brennan kept finding materials in Gold's bookcase that compromised those denials, such as a railroad timetable for Boston. At last Miller pulled out a Chamber of Commerce brochure from Santa Fe, New Mexico, which contained a detailed street map of the city. "I thought you said you'd never been out West," Scotty Miller commented to Gold. As if stunned, Gold opened his mouth wide, then slumped down into the chair Miller had just vacated, and said, "I am the man to whom Fuchs gave the information."

On May 24 a courier arrived at Wormwood Scrubs with new motion and still pictures of Harry Gold—taken, this time, under good lighting conditions. We had not told Fuchs the name of our prime suspect, nor had we allowed him to know that Gold had already confessed. While the blackened curtains were set up and the new film was threaded through the projector, I showed the new still photos to Fuchs.

Fuchs's response to the new photos was almost instanteous. "Yes," he said, "that is my American contact."

An unbelievably great weight seemed to lift from my shoulders. The essence of my mission to London was already accomplished: the FBI had located "Raymond," and now Fuchs had identified the man as well. The Director had charged us to find Fuchs's American contact, and e had fulfilled that assignment.

Despite my elation, I peered closely at Fuchs as we turned out the lights in the room and showed the new motion-picture film. Fuchs watched it, unemotional as ever, and reiterated his identification of the man on the film as "Raymond."

Two days later, for our records, Fuchs wrote on the back of each of two still photographs of Harry Gold, "I identify this photograph as the likeness of the man whom I knew under the name of Raymond —Klaus Fuchs—26th May, 1950."

The FBI public relations people announced both the arrest of Harry Gold and Klaus Fuchs's near-simultaneous identification of Gold as

"Raymond." After this the press found out our presence in London, of course, but the announcement also created another problem for us. It seemed to the public that the FBI had done in a few days what MI-5 had been unable to do in a number of months—"break" Fuchs, uncover and arrest Gold, and get both men to identify each other.

This was, strictly speaking, not true. Fuchs had told Skardon of "Raymond," and had rejected earlier photos of Gold—but the public didn't know that. Behind their polite faces Bill Skardon and the others of MI-5 were distressed about this public misapprehension. They felt as if they had been had, and I was a bit embarrassed at the misleading publicity. On the other hand, Clegg was delighted that the British government's stubbornness in not making Fuchs available to us earlier had now been rewarded with MI-5's eclipse by the FBI in the identification of Harry Gold.

However, I still had a job to do—to obtain a great deal of new detail from Fuchs on his espionage, and Clegg's gloating and the press coverage didn't make that task any easier. Over the next ten days I interviewed Fuchs many more times. These sessions were inordinately difficult because Fuchs, a brilliant man, volunteered nothing and would answer quite narrowly any question I put to him. In order to obtain full details, I would have to ask precisely the right questions, and a great many of them. Days faded into one another as I posed my myriad of questions and probed for hundreds of details that filled out the story Skardon had earlier elicited from Fuchs. As I conducted the interviews, Clegg wrote down the physicist's answers, and Skardon smoked his pipe.

At about this time, an article appeared in a London paper that contended just that—Lamphere was conducting the interviews while Assistant Director Clegg was taking notes. Clegg wasn't too happy about this but, because we weren't talking to the press, couldn't do much about it. We wondered who had told the press about this—the warden? One of the guards? Or someone in MI-5? We never found out.

After a while, spending every day and every evening with Clegg started to wear on me, and I asked John Cimperman to arrange a diversion. Dorothy Lamour, a friend of Director Hoover's, was doing a show in London, and Cimperman and I said we were going to see her. Clegg thought reporters would be there because Miss Lamour was known to be close to Hoover, and that he'd be ambushed with questions—so he went to another show, alone. Cimperman and I enjoyed Miss Lamour's performance and conveyed the Director's regards to her without ever seeing a reporter. The following night I went to see the show Clegg had seen when we were with Lamour, and we kept up this sequence of switch-offs for several evenings before Clegg and I hooked up again. During my time away from Clegg, I came to the conclusion that I had to treat him more as a colleague and less as a superior, and I think he'd seen enough of my work to respect it, regardless of my junior rank. From then on, we got along better.

As I drew out the story of Fuchs's life and his involvement in espionage, I was reminded of the stories of German Communist life I had heard from Hede Massing and had learned about Gerhart Eisler. Fuchs was born in 1911, the son of pastor Emil Fuchs. His brother and his two sisters, as well as Klaus himself, all hewed to the political left. While Fuchs was at the University of Kiel, he became an active Communist and the head of a student anti-Fascist group. Because of this open Communist Party activity, Fuchs was bound to be in trouble when Hitler came to power; when Fuchs heard the news about the Reichstag fire in early 1933, he decided not to return to his university, fearing arrest by the Nazis, who were trying to pin the fire on the Communists. Fuchs went underground for a time until the German Communist hierarchy, recognizing that the young physicist would not be the best soldier in the losing guerrilla battle against the Nazis inside Germany, instructed him to go to England to continue his education. Arriving in England, Fuchs sought contact with émigré German Communists.

The details of Fuchs's life in England suggested to me quite strongly that when it came to Communists in the 1930s, British security had been very lax. The Gestapo told the British in the mid-1930s that Fuchs was a Communist, but the warning was ignored. After the onset of war, in September 1939, Fuchs, along with many "friendly" Germans, was interned in Canada. At the Sherbrooke camp, near Quebec, Fuchs briefly came in touch with Israel Halperin. Halperin was attempting to help the Communist internees—that was how Klaus Fuchs's name got into Halperin's notebook.

Fuchs's stay in Canada was not lengthy—he was too valuable a young scientist to waste. After a short while he was allowed to return to the British Isles to do research at Edinburgh University. Within months he began work with Rudolph Peierls on the "tube alloys" project, which involved the gaseous diffusion process for separating uranium isotopes. After the Soviet Union was attacked by Nazi Germany in mid-1941, making Russia and Great Britain unofficial allies,

Fuchs decided that the research on atomic fission had to be made available to the Soviet Union. Seeking out his old contacts in the German Communist underground in England, he asked to be directed to someone who could convey his information to Moscow. He was soon obliged.

Fuchs once said, of his mental attitude in this period, that he used his Marxist philosophy to allow him to divide his life into two compartments. In one he established his friendships and lived the social life of a bachelor scientist; in the other he did his secret work of conveying information to Russian agents. "It appeared to me," he said at the time of his sentencing,

> that at the time I had become a "free man" because I had succeeded in the [second] compartment to establish myself completely independent of the surrounding forces of society. Looking back at it now the best way of expressing it seems to be to call it a controlled schizophrenia.

The underground first put Fuchs in touch with "Alexander," who was actually Simon Davidovich Kremer, secretary to the military attaché at the Soviet embassy in London. During 1941 and 1942 Fuchs delivered to Kremer copies of his own research reports, as well as write-ups in which he summarized the research conducted by his colleagues. The accuracy, completeness and quality of Fuchs's secret information brought him special cultivation by the Soviets. Kremer was later replaced as Fuchs's courier by a female—subsequently identified as Ursula Beurton—and when she learned that Fuchs was going to the United States, Beurton arranged to pass him to the KGB people in New York. Shortly after Fuchs arrived in New York as a member of the British Mission to the Manhattan Project, he had his first meeting with an American contact.

Let me digress to point out that when General Leslie Groves first received the names of the British scientists who were to take part in the Manhattan Project, he observed that no mention had been made of their reliability, and asked his British counterpart whether these scientists had been properly vetted. The answer was fuzzy, and Groves pressed for clarification; he was then told that each member of the British Mission had been thoroughly investigated and cleared. Groves accepted that at the time, but later concluded that the British had made no investigations of the scientists.

The truth is that the British had known as far back as 1934 that the

Gestapo considered Fuchs to be a Communist. However, because of the wartime alliance with Russia and the need to obtain the services of able scientists, they apparently didn't consider a scientist's Communist past to constitute a security risk. Fuchs told me, for instance, that while interned in Canada he had been classed as a German Communist; he told an aliens hearing board in Britain in 1941 that he was a Communist in order to convince the board of his anti-Nazi sentiments so that he could get a job in war-related research. The British told none of this to General Groves, and even after our investigation of Fuchs had begun in 1949, MI-5 didn't tell us about Fuchs's Communist background; by that time, of course, we had unearthed it ourselves from the captured Gestapo files.

Fuchs's meetings with Harry Gold, he told me, were full of the apparatus and techniques of clandestine meetings—odd signals carried in the hand when going to a rendezvous, chalk marks on walls, absurd answers to simple queries posed by strangers in public places. Fuchs had met with Gold five times in various boroughs of New York City in the first half of 1944, at times in public places, at times indoors in movie theaters or out-of-the-way restaurants. Since there were no maps of New York in London that had sufficient detail to locate the exact places of these rendezvous, I had American maps flown in and went over them minutely to fix the precise locations. A little thing like the wording of a street name or knowledge of a park nearby could stir Fuchs's memory and yield us additional details.

In July 1944, when Fuchs was about to be suddenly transferred to Los Alamos, he had told his sister, Kristel, that someone might try to get in touch with him through her. It was shortly thereafter that Gold had gone to the Heinemann residence and first asked for Fuchs. At that time Kristel had told Gold that Klaus would be visiting the Heinemanns near Christmastime, and that Gold would be able to get in touch with Fuchs then.

By midway in our series of interviews I had told Fuchs of Gold's confession, and let him know that I was comparing the details Gold had furnished with those he, Fuchs, was giving to me. On nearly every point, the stories of Fuchs and Gold dovetailed, down to the smallest details.

On one matter, though, the tales differed. Fuchs claimed that he had not passed information to Harry Gold while actually at the Kristel Heinemann home in Cambridge; rather, he said, the two men had met briefly at the home, and then, the next day, had a rendezvous on the banks of the Charles River. At the riverbank meeting Fuchs passed a most important report which he had written; it covered his own work, and the efforts of the entire team of scientists and technicians at Los Alamos. Gold's confession gave considerable detail on his trip to Cambridge, but said there had been only one meeting—at Kristel's house. Fuchs insisted that there were two meetings, and he held to that story even when I told him flat out that Harry Gold had remembered only one meeting in Cambridge.

Fuchs was lying, I knew, in an attempt to shield his sister from any possible prosecution as an accomplice to his espionage.

It was at our next-to-last interview session that I decided to see if I could get him to admit his lie. I took him, step by step, through the meeting at the Heinemann house. Who had opened the door? Where was he, Klaus, when Kristel opened the door and let in Gold? When did he come down from his upstairs room? What happened next? As I proceeded, it became clear to Clegg, Skardon and even Fuchs that we all knew he was lying. Nonetheless, Fuchs refused to admit that fact—the only time during our long interviews, I think, when he did not come entirely clean.

I used my newly acquired—though quite limited—technical knowledge to ask Fuchs about precisely what information he had furnished to the Soviets through Gold. In the early meetings in New York, he passed:

· Longhand drafts of the 13 out of 19 "MSN" papers on the principles of gaseous diffusion and other critical principles, which he himself had written.
· General information concerning membranes used to separate substances, and the composition of the sintered nickel powder used to keep apart portions of the fissionable material.
· General information on the scope, timing, progress and experiments of the Manhattan Project.
· Information on the identity and character of all those involved in the project whom he then knew.
· Information on the development of the plant at Oak Ridge, Tennessee.

At the meeting in Boston, Fuchs prepared a special paper to give to Gold, which dealt with:

· The principles of A-bomb detonation; which method had been chosen, and why.

- The principle of the lens mold system and the dimensions of the high explosive on which it worked.
- An extensive discussion of the principle of implosion, the central new focus developed at Los Alamos.
- Details about plutonium-240, multiple-point detonation, the time and sequence of construction of the A-bomb, and the need for an initiator to set off the device.

I asked Fuchs if this information had hastened the Russian bomb and how he knew that it had done so. He told me that he believed his information had enabled the Russians to advance their own efforts by several years. His reason for this calculation was that after he had returned to London in 1945, and renewed contact with Soviet Intelligence, the new questions he was asked revealed to him that a quantum leap had been made by the Russian scientists. During one of our late meetings, Fuchs drew for us a duplicate of a sketch he had given to Harry Gold in New Mexico in June 1945—a description of the bomb and its components, with important dimensions indicated on the drawing. Looking at this sketch years later, physicist Philip Morrison, one of those who had worked on the bomb, said that the information on the sketch would have been sufficient to convey to a knowledgeable researcher the way to construct an atomic device.

After returning to England Fuchs had continued to give to the Russians bomb-related information, including many things he learned at several United States–Great Britain conferences on the "super," or hydrogen bomb.

As our interviews were drawing to a close, I spent a day with Fuchs going back over much of what he had told us, trying to tie up some loose ends. That evening, as we worked on a cable to Washington in the American embassy, I became exasperated. Clegg wanted to send a lengthy message to the Director about the day's activities; I argued for cutting it short, saying that we had just combed over previously covered territory. I wanted to give our overworked secretaries an easy night of it. I lost that argument with Clegg.

On June 2 we had ready for Fuchs's signature a six-and-a-half-page typewritten statement that summarized his espionage activities. Fuchs read it, changed two words, and added a sentence by hand that stated that the meetings in Boston were made without the participation or understanding of his sister or her husband. Then Fuchs signed each page of the document.

At the end, I asked Fuchs if he felt that he had fully cooperated with us, and how it had affected him. He answered that he had made full disclosure to us, and that he believed in some small way this was restitution for what he had done.

In the closing days of our stay in London we took an evening to visit Parliament in session, and a weekend day to view the British Derby. I played the good American guest and brought nylons to Dick Thistlethwaite's wife. Clegg, Cimperman and I paid a courtesy call to Scotland Yard. This wasn't as pleasant as the other activities, because I was a bit put off when the chiefs there referred to Bill Skardon disparagingly as a "nice enough chap"—their euphemism, I supposed, for his not having come from an upperclass background. Skardon and I had become friends; I gave him a pipe in appreciation of his help. On almost our last day, Clegg, Cimperman and I were called into a drab conference room at MI-5 for a chat with Sir Percy Sillitoe. We expected a formal hello-and-goodbye session, a courtesy which Sir Percy would want to bestow on us because he had been out of the country when we'd first arrived in London.

It was anything but courteous. After introducing his senior people, Sir Percy, in a cultured, clipped British manner, and without raising his voice, said he and MI-5 were most unhappy with Director Hoover and the FBI's handling of the Fuchs case. He reiterated that when FBI Espionage Section chief Lish Whitson had shown up in London —uninvited—MI-5 had done everything possible to obtain permission for Whitson to see Fuchs. That Sir Percy's efforts had failed was regrettable, he said; the point, however, was that Mr. Hoover had sent messages to him that implied that MI-5 had not made a sincere attempt to get Whitson in to talk to Fuchs—and Sir Percy resented Hoover's contention that MI-5 really hadn't tried very hard on this one. Sir Percy had been further affronted by the publicity that had been generated over the arrest of Harry Gold, and the implication that the FBI had done what MI-5 could not do. Sir Percy wanted Hugh Clegg personally to convey his displeasure over these things to Mr. Hoover.

Sir Percy went through this entire sequence of grievances without showing any anger or other emotion, but there was no doubt in my mind of the firmness of his thoughts.

In response, Clegg did far better than I had imagined he might. He pointed out that the FBI had furnished to MI-5 the information that had led to Fuchs, and was, therefore, unable to understand why we had to wait many months before being allowed to interview Fuchs. He expressed regret that Sir Percy had interpreted Mr. Hoover's messages about the delay in the way he had, and promised to discuss the matter with the Director. Clegg also emphasized that we had made no statements to the press of any kind during our stay in London, and certainly had not taken the position that the FBI had succeeded where MI-5 had failed. He reminded Sir Percy that neither the FBI nor MI-5 could control the press in the United States or in England. Courteous and firm, Clegg concluded by asking Sir Percy to tell him how he felt the FBI could have handled the press stories in a different manner.

The meeting came to a close, and Sir Percy stood up and shook hands with each of us. I was last in line, and he greeted me with a "Hullo, Bob," a handshake and a twinkle in his eyes that conveyed the idea that the preceding diatribe had not been meant for me.

On the way back to Cimperman's office, Clegg began to worry. Had he been strong enough in his reply to Sir Percy? What would the Director think? Both Cimperman and I assured him that he had handled himself extremely well, had said what could have been said cleanly and firmly. In the office, though, Clegg's discomfort began to mount, and he started to think in terms of the FBI breaking off relations with MI-5 and dealing with the British only through MI-6 and the Special Branch of Scotland Yard. Clegg sent the Director a lengthy coded cable on the incident, and continued to chew it over with me as we flew back to the United States. He even drafted a memo to the Director recommending that we stop dealing with MI-5 —a memo that, incidentally, took note of the fact that I disagreed with this radical step.

As for me, I could hardly wait to get back into the office and see Mickey Ladd. Ladd listened with great interest to my stories about the interviews with Fuchs, but seemed curiously unconcerned about Clegg's memo to the Director threatening a break with MI-5. I didn't understand this lack of interest at the time, but later concluded that Ladd had already spoken to the Director and was not about to let Clegg sabotage our continued liaison with MI-5.

At headquarters Clegg and I produced a comprehensive and cohesive fifty-one-page memorandum on our interviews with Klaus Fuchs. In its time this was an important document, and it has now become an indispensable one for historians.

In the office, I was glad to see that Ernie Van Loon was to be awarded a letter of commendation for his work in uncovering and pursuing Harry Gold—fine counterbalance to the punishment he had received only a few months before. But Ernie was now quite overwhelmed with work. Cases developed from the confession of Harry Gold were breaking everywhere—dozens of them every day, and many more than Ernie could handle. As soon as I returned to Washington I was asked to take over control of all the cases springing from the Gold investigation. Since Ernie was my friend, I initially refused to do that, but after conversations with Ernie and my superiors it was agreed that I would assume administrative direction of the whole operation. Bill Branigan, now Espionage Section chief, made me supervisor in charge of a group of supervisors feverishly working on the whole array of Gold-associated cases. The crush was so great that we didn't have time to stick to normal Bureau procedures. For example, we had to ask the field to bypass the mails, and to insist that results of investigations be sent to headquarters by teletype as soon as they were obtained. Normal business hours and a five-day work week also went by the boards as we tried to keep abreast of the flood of information that was coming in from the field offices.

It was early June 1950. Within the month, the Korean War would begin—a war that many people, including some of our top military officers, believed that China and the Soviet Union and Korea would not have undertaken had the Soviet Union not been in possession of a functional atomic bomb. We had found Klaus Fuchs and Harry Gold, who had stolen the central secrets of that bomb, and they had confessed. How many more of their ilk would we now be able to uncover? The quantity of information that was coming into headquarters from the various investigations devolving from the confession of Harry Gold was enormous; as important, its factual content tended to verify our earlier notions about KGB networks inside the United States.

We were on the verge of learning, in detail, what the KGB had been doing inside our country during the war years and immediately thereafter.

10
CASES
BREAKING
EVERYWHERE

I RETURNED FROM LONDON early in June 1950 to find everyone at Bureau headquarters in a state of continual excitement. The publicity that had begun with the arrest of Harry Gold and the admission by Fuchs that Gold had been his courier had now reached mammoth proportions.

If the public now expected even bigger things of the FBI, we inside the Bureau believed we were riding the crest of a wave and that we would continue to race ahead to the point where we would be able to arrest whole KGB networks. Gold would name all his contacts, and we would find them and get them to confess and to lead us to still more Soviet agents. The break in the KGB's communications had put us head-to-head with the Soviets, and we were uncovering their agents, obtaining confessions from them and delivering them to justice. We firmly believed that solving what Director Hoover would later term "The Crime of the Century"—the Fuchs/Gold case—was only the beginning.

And in many respects, that proved entirely true. By the time we were through mining Gold's information, we had opened forty-nine separate cases. Out of these investigations eight people who worked for the KGB, either as agents or as sources, were convicted and jailed. A handful of the others—Soviet nationals—were positively identified and were never seen again in the United States. Others of the forty-nine were exposed to the point where they could no longer continue to be of use to the KGB.

Of course, not all of the forty-nine cases were opened immediately when I came back to headquarters. In fact, in Gold's first confession on May 22, 1950, he had confined his tales of the KGB solely to his liaison with Klaus Fuchs. The connection with Fuchs made Gold a major catch for the FBI—but we were convinced that Gold had other contacts he could name. However, from May 22 to June 1 Gold said little to the FBI. On June 1, 1950, the court assigned to Gold a new attorney, John D. M. Hamilton, a former national chairman of the Republican Party. Hamilton advised Gold not to limit himself in his dealings with the FBI, but rather to cooperate fully with us. Later that same day Gold began to tell his complete story and to name contacts other than Klaus Fuchs.

I returned to headquarters a few days later. Because Gold hadn't really begun to sing until June 1, some of his information was only hours old. I was instantly thrown into the maelstrom that his more complete confession engendered.

Every morning I would get to my desk to find investigative data in many different cases waiting for me, in the form of incoming teletypes that had arrived from our field offices during the night. We couldn't deal with this flood of information in the usual way. As administrative head of the supervisors on these cases, I was forced to develop a "triage" method of coping with the flow. Scanning the teletypes, I'd try to get a feel for what was being developed. Then I'd route the teletypes to the supervisors assigned to the individual cases. Each of them would analyze the teletypes for four things: (1) any investigative leads that the teletype suggested and that were not already being followed up by the originating field office; (2) new information for the summary brief, which we updated every few days; (3) significant developments, which had to be reported upstairs, to Belmont, Ladd or Hoover; (4) anything that had surfaced that we ought to transmit to another government agency, such as the AEC, the CIA, military intelligence, or the Criminal Division of Justice.

The volume was nearly overwhelming, and the work was incredibly rushed. To assist with our inundation of teletypes, I was given an experienced supervisor; I explained my system for coping with the incoming missives and gave him a stack on one of the cases. He'd never dealt with anything resembling this amount of information before; several hours later I noticed that he still had the stack in front of him and was laboriously making notes on a pad. I reviewed the procedure and stressed our real need to move on from the overnight teletypes to the ones that continued to arrive at every moment. Next morning he was still making notes on his yellow pad about the same stack of teletypes; I had to ask for him to be removed from our group and returned to his regular job, at which he was quite competent.

In the process of bringing order out of chaos, I saw that the cases developing around Harry Gold fell into three categories. The first had to do with Gold's work with Fuchs, and eventually led us to David Greenglass and to the Rosenbergs. Over the years, that is the only connection that seems to have survived in the public's consciousness. But Harry Gold was really an important espionage figure, and to point that up, I'm going to tell a bit about the people in the other two categories I devised—people who have been all but forgotten by history, but who seemed to us quite important at the time.

The second group of cases devolving from Gold touched on his associations with Abe Brothman, the chemist who had first been named to the FBI by Elizabeth Bentley. The third cluster had to do with Gold's initial recruitment into industrial espionage for the Soviets, and his early contacts.

Let's take the last group first.

Harry Gold's long espionage career spanned the years from 1935, when he was first recruited, until almost the very moment when he was arrested in May 1950. During those years Gold first conveyed to the Russians industrial secrets, then atomic secrets, and was being considered for international missions until he made a mistake that caused the KGB to drop him like a hot potato.

Gold was born in Switzerland in 1910. His Russian émigré parents moved to Philadelphia in 1913, where Harry grew up, poor and Jewish. He had a likable personality, and all who met him considered him intelligent. A frustrated athlete, he had as boyhood heroes Lefty Grove, Babe Ruth and Dizzy Dean. In politics, his mother's fascination with socialists such as Eugene Debs and Norman Thomas, and the slant of the *Jewish Daily Forward*, drew him to socialism. He never joined the Communist Party of the United States, and was opposed to many things for which the Communists stood. However, in the 1930s he believed that "progressive" Russia was the only place in the world where there was no anti-Semitism, and he gave his loyalty to Russia because of that. In the political arena the major influence of his youth had been the anti-Semitism visited on him personally in the streets and schools of Philadelphia, and on his father at the Victor Talking Machine factory.

Graduating from high school third in his 1929 class, Gold went to work as a laboratory assistant at the Pennsylvania Sugar Company, and in September 1930 entered the University of Pennsylvania, where for three semesters he majored in chemistry and chemical engineering. When his money ran out, Gold withdrew from the university and returned to work for the sugar company; soon, because of the Depression, he was laid off. In early 1933 a former colleague at the sugar company, Ferdinand Heller, asked him to go and see chemist Tom Black, who was about to leave a post with a soap-manufacturing company in Jersey City. If the men liked one another, Black would resign and see to it that Gold was hired in his place. The scheme went off as planned, and Harry Gold started work as an industrial soap chemist in Jersey City, New Jersey, at a salary of thirty dollars a week.

In this era of massive unemployment and suffering, Gold's thirty dollars a week supported him in Jersey City and the rest of his family in Philadelphia. Gold stayed close to his benefactor, Black. In return, Black, a huge bear of a man who kept unusual pets and had an overwhelming personality, pushed Gold to join the Communist Party. He took Gold to meetings and social outings; Gold didn't like the "misfits" he met at these meetings, but continued to attend because he admired Black. In 1935 Gold returned to Philadelphia to work once again for the Pennsylvania Sugar Company. At this point Black asked Gold to supply him with the company's secret industrial processes, which Black would then forward to the Soviet Union. If Gold would do this, Black said, he would no longer be under pressure to join the CPUSA. Gold agreed to his importuning in part to avoid joining the Party but also because of his deep belief that Russia was the savior of the Jews, the only country actively fighting fascism and the Nazis.

In 1950, when Gold told this story of how his lifelong friend Tom Black had recruited him, we didn't know who had induced Black himself to become a spy. Shortly thereafter, Black agreed to talk, and identified his recruiter to us. It was Gaik Ovakimian.

For as long as I had been involved in counterespionage, I had been following the shadowy trails of Ovakimian and fellow KGB spymaster Vassili Zubilin. To discover that Ovakimian had been the man who had started this particular network in action—in the 1930s—was grim but satisfactory knowledge for me. Things were coming full circle; the entire panorama of Soviet espionage in the United States over the previous twenty years was being pried open for us to understand and, hopefully, for us to learn from. To me personally, this continuity of Soviet espionage and the intensity of the Soviet effort over such a long period were of paramount interest. It was evidence of a massive and continuous attack on the United States; in the face of it, no one could reasonably hold the view that the Soviets posed no real threat to our security.

As we talked to other Gold contacts later in 1950, we learned that many KGB spymasters whom we had been attempting to track for years—Zubilin, Gregory Kheiffets, "Sam" Semenov and Joseph Katz, to cite just a few—had ties to Gold and Ovakimian. As we had suspected, the Soviet networks had overlapped extensively; with the confession of Harry Gold, we began to unravel the many intricate connections.

The particular network in which Gold had first been involved had begun in 1935, when Gold's friend Ferdinand Heller had gone to see Ovakimian at Amtorg. Heller had volunteered to go with Tom Black to Russia, to live and work as valued expert scientists. Ovakimian had turned them around; he persuaded both that they could help the U.S.S.R. far more effectively by stealing American industrial secrets. Black had nominated Gold as a new recruit to the espionage team that was being formed, and after Ovakimian had checked him out, Gold, too, started to supply information. Gold and Ovakimian never met each other.

From 1935 on, Harry Gold worked diligently as a spy, under a succession of Soviet contacts with whom he had lukewarm and sometimes even hostile relations. Among those contacts whom we were able to identify was the ubiquitous Joseph Katz. At first Gold laboriously copied by hand the sugar company's technical files, working long evening hours at the task until a friend suggested he use a commercial copier. Neither Gold nor Black had the money to pay for the copying, and they were ebullient when the Soviets said they would do so. Curiously, during Gold's long espionage career he was never paid for his information, and was only reimbursed in part for the heavy out-of-pocket expenses he incurred. After Gold had exhausted the sugar company's information, he was exhorted to obtain other secret industrial processes. Also, he was ordered to branch out into other espionage areas and given a few assignments that tied in to KGB efforts to keep tabs on the followers of Trotsky.

During the middle 1930s Gold attended the Drexel Institute in

Philadelphia and received his bachelor's degree. From 1938 to 1940 he attended Xavier University in Cincinnati. During this time, he later contended, he did no espionage work; however, his tuition was paid by the Soviets. At Xavier University he did *summa cum laude* work—in every subject except ethics.

In the early 1940s Gold came under the control of a man he knew as "Sam," who was Semen Markovich Semenov, an Amtorg engineer and KGB man closely allied with Vassili Zubilin. To Gold, Sam was an educated man with a good heart. Widely read in English and American literature, Sam was a fine drinking companion who often seemed to resent the espionage work in which both he and Gold were enmeshed. At times Sam would tell Gold not to work so hard; once he suggested that Gold quit a project on which he was engaged and go home to Philadelphia by parlor car—or, better still, find a nice girl, get married and "get out of this lousy business." In the way that Elizabeth Bentley adored and idolized Jacob Golos as the perfect Communist, and that Hede Massing gave her loyalty to Ludwig, Harry Gold respected and loved Sam Semenov. After Gold had been caught and sentenced to thirty years in jail, he composed a 123-page tract entitled "The Circumstances Surrounding My Work as a Soviet Agent." In it he described his close attachment to Semenov, wrote of his regret at having to identify Sam from FBI photos, and also contended that even though "I should want to rant and rave at those . . . who got me into this predicament," he could not bring himself to think of Semenov or Black "without sorrow."

Under Semenov's guidance, Gold's activities began to increase. He went out to the National Aeronautics Center at Wright Field in Dayton, Ohio, to see a man named Ben Smilg. Gold had been told that the KGB had helped pay for Smilg's tuition at MIT—where, incidentally, Semenov himself had studied. Repeatedly, over a two-year period, Gold met with Smilg and asked him to provide information, but Smilg refused. At last Gold told Smilg that if he didn't cooperate, he would be exposed because the KGB had receipts for three or four hundred dollars that Smilg had signed. Smilg still would have nothing to do with Gold, and Semenov told Gold to drop the matter.

In 1950, when we got in touch with Ben Smilg, the whole story came out. At MIT Smilg had tutored a Russian student and had received some money from him—it was with the receipts for the tutoring money that the KGB had been attempting to blackmail Smilg. When Gold had approached him, Smilg had not gone to the authorities primarily because he hadn't wanted to lose his job, but also because he had refused Gold's pressure. Later on, an ambitious district attorney attempted to indict Smilg for denying, under oath, that he had known Gold was a Soviet spy. The jury believed Harry Gold's contention that Smilg had known he was a spy but had given him no information, and exonerated Smilg.

Gold was more successful in his espionage connection with Alfred Dean Slack, an employee of the Eastman Kodak Company in Rochester, New York. At Semenov's behest, Gold went to Rochester in the fall of 1941 and obtained from Slack secret information on Kodachrome and other industrial processes that also had military implications. He paid Slack some money given to him by Semenov for this purpose. Although Sam usually did not like to pay Americans for their data, he told Gold he made an exception for Slack because his technical reports were so thorough, valuable and carefully written. In the fall of 1942, when Slack was transferred to an ordnance plant in Tennessee, Gold made several trips to see him and to obtain information and a sample of the new explosive, RDX. Slack was next transferred to Oak Ridge to work at the new plant there, but by Christmas of 1943 Gold was told not to keep in touch with Slack any longer.

In June 1950 we interviewed Slack, and he confessed to having passed data of military importance to the Soviets, through Gold and others, over a period of many years. Slack identified a picture of Ovakimian as one of his early Soviet superiors. He also told us of a man named Richard Briggs, with whom he had worked at Eastman Kodak in the 1920s, and who had also furnished information to Ovakimian until his own death in 1939.

When we searched the FBI files for mention of Richard Briggs, some facts came up—together with the name of then-fledgling Special Agent Robert J. Lamphere. In 1942, in New Jersey, Richard Briggs's former landlady, going through his papers, found the name "Levine" written on a scrap of paper. Believing that this might have something to do with the famous Levine kidnapping case of the 1930s, she called the FBI. In Briggs's papers there was also the name of a dentist stationed at an army chemical warfare plant then under construction in Huntsville, Alabama. An investigative lead was sent to my first field office in Birmingham, and accompanied by a young police officer, I went to interview the dentist. The man was neither friendly nor cooperative but did identify Levine as a woman known both to him and to Briggs, but who had nothing to do with the kidnapping case. On the way back, the young policeman observed that the dentist had been holding something back about Briggs; I agreed, but neither of us had a clue as to what he might have been hiding. In 1950 my headquarters associates kidded me about this old investigation; in 1942 I had been on the trail of a dead KGB spy, and hadn't even known about it.

Tom Black, Gold's longtime friend and the man who recruited him into espionage, readily confessed to the FBI that he'd been a spy for the Soviets from 1935 to 1944, but said he'd only delivered industrial processes to them and had never passed any secret or classified information. I found two things about Black that were of interest to me. The first was that at one point, on express orders from his Soviet superiors, Black had joined the Socialist Party and had infiltrated the ranks of the Trotskyites. He'd even been given money and told to go to Mexico to spy on the Trotsky household there—but, he told the FBI, he had simply not bothered to go. A few months later Trotsky was murdered, and Black's superiors never mentioned the assignment again.

The second thing of interest about Black was that he, too, had been handled by Sam Semenov and by Joseph Katz; in fact, in 1945 Katz had told him he would forthwith be handled by a woman named "Helen," but he never heard from her. In all likelihood, Helen was Elizabeth Bentley—she'd used that name with other sources; she probably never contacted Black because she herself was withdrawing from the KGB at just that time. (Incidentally, by the time of this investigation into Black, we had learned from the KGB messages some corroboration of what Bentley had originally told the FBI. For example, there was mention of her successor as a courier, a man named "Coral," whom the FBI also saw enter and leave the Nathan Gregory Silvermaster home in Washington. In other messages we found information being sent to Moscow that we were able to trace back to the various government agencies in which the members of the Silvermaster network had been situated. Still other deciphered messages revealed to us the code name for Joseph Katz himself, whom Bentley had known as "Jack.")

In 1947 Black was told that if the Soviets ever needed to get in touch with him again, he'd receive a phone call from a "Miss Watkins." For three years there were no such phone calls, but on May 22, 1950—the day Harry Gold was arrested—Black got a message at his place of employment that Miss Watkins had called. He later told us that this message was an instruction for him to go to a previously designated meeting place, where he would receive further orders. Black didn't bother making this rendezvous, and never heard from the Soviets again.

Even though Tom Black confessed, the Justice Department decided that the information about industrial processes that he'd passed had not affected the national defense, and so did not indict him for espionage. However, Al Slack was indicted, decided to plead guilty and was sentenced to fifteen years in prison. Today both men are forgotten, but they were spies, and it's important to remember that Harry Gold led us to them—as well as to other people who became more notorious and who are still remembered by history.

Harry Gold was also closely connected to Abraham Brothman. But here, things were different. The FBI had come close to both men in 1947, but hadn't been able to put them away at that time. Now the whole story came out.

It had begun, as I mentioned earlier, when Elizabeth Bentley told the FBI that she'd had ten meetings with Brothman in 1940. During those meetings Brothman and Bentley had grown to detest one another. She termed him an unreliable braggart who missed meetings, and he disliked her because she complained of his erratic behavior and couldn't comprehend the technical data he was giving, through her, to the KGB. Bentley had asked her lover, Golos, to get someone else to handle Brothman; Golos had passed that request along to Ovakimian, and Bentley never saw Brothman again.

She had told her story to the grand jury in 1947, and Brothman had been called to testify. It was at this point that Brothman had spun the story that his contacts with Golos were all innocent, and that he'd been introduced to Golos through Harry Gold. Gold had backed up Brothman's story on the stand.

Now, in 1950, the smokescreen that Brothman and Gold had put up three years earlier began to dissolve, and we found out what had really happened at the time of the grand jury hearing. In fact, it was Gold who had taken over from Bentley as Brothman's courier. When Brothman made his almost inadvertent admission to the FBI about Gold, he got in touch with Gold, told him what he'd done and apologized; he told Gold, though, that he believed the FBI would have soon connected them anyway. In return for this admission, Brothman got more than he wished, for Gold offered some details of his courier work for the KGB that astounded Brothman. Gold also informed Brothman that the yarns he had spun about his personal life —a wife, twin sons, a brother dead on a Pacific battlefield—had been wholly fabricated as a cover for his espionage and courier work. Learning this, Brothman started to panic and wanted to go to the FBI and tell them all he knew, but Gold calmed him and said they could cook up a story that would fool the government. And that's exactly what they did—Gold, Brothman, Brothman's mistress, Miriam Moscowitz, and attorney Isidore Gibby Needleman. Gold had never even met Golos, but was coached by the team so that he could recognize and identify a picture of Golos when he got to the witness stand in the grand jury room.

In 1950 Gold also told us more about his courier work with Brothman. It involved several different industrial processes, including an important one for the making of synthetic rubber, which Gold took from Brothman and delivered to the Soviets. It turned out that Gold was just as unhappy with Brothman as Bentley had been; there were the same late and missed meetings, and the information Gold received from Brothman was often less than complete. Yet both Gold and Semenov considered Brothman to be a brilliant man who could, if he set his mind to the task, supply important data to Russia.

Gold's difficulties with Brothman came to a head in 1943, and Gold brought the chemist to meet Semenov, who was billed for the meeting as a VIP from Russia. For five hours in a hotel room in Manhattan, Sam gave Brothman a pep talk. After it, an elated and inspired Brothman rushed back to his office to work through the night, supposedly obtaining military-related industrial processes for the Soviet war effort.

This burst of enthusiasm notwithstanding, Brothman still proved incapable of providing good data. Some of the information Brothman gave Gold was so worthless that Gold never gave it to Semenov; it was found in Gold's apartment when the FBI searched the place in 1950. At the time of the hotel meeting, Brothman was a partner in a medium-sized chemical firm in New York. Because of his obstreperous personality, he was ousted by his partners shortly thereafter and decided to form his own firm. Semenov objected to the idea of A. Brothman and Associates on two grounds: first, in a small firm Brothman would have less access to important government secrets; and second, Brothman wanted the Soviets to provide financial backing for the new venture. Semenov ordered Gold to drop Brothman. It was at about the same time that he told Gold to stop seeing his other source, Al Slack, and to ready himself for a new assignment and a new Soviet boss. To reward Gold for his work thus far, and to make him enthusiastic for the new challenge, Semenov conveyed to Gold the award of the Red Star; the private ceremony moved the sentimental Gold close to tears.

Then Semenov faded from Gold's life. Agents of the FBI covering Gregory Kheiffets, a KGB man, saw Kheiffets have a joyous reunion with Semenov in San Francisco in early 1944. By September 1944 Semenov had left the United States altogether.

Gold's new boss was Anatoli Yakovlev, whom he was told to call "John." Gold's new assignment, of course, was as courier to Klaus Fuchs.

In early 1950, when Fuchs first gave Skardon a description of "Raymond," we in the FBI began to reopen the files on various chemists, physicists and engineers who had come to our attention in the previous decade. Brothman and Gold were among the first people we looked at, but they were not the only suspects. Both men had partners, friends and acquaintances whose names also were in our files. Accusations of possible involvement in espionage and entanglements on the far left of the political spectrum had already been lodged against Oscar Vago, Jules Korchein, and the Joseph Robbins whom Fuchs in March mistakenly identified as "Raymond." Later on, after Gold had confessed, we continued to take hard looks at these people, as well as at others Gold had known. Ferdinand Heller, for instance, readily admitted having been recruited by Gaik Ovakimian in 1935. We talked to Vera Kane, a friend of Heller's and Black's whose associations were quite suspect.

Scotty Miller once wrote that Gold's memory was like a lemon— no matter how many times you squeezed it, there was always a little drop of information left. One of the reasons the FBI kept going back and back to Harry Gold was because those drops of information were continually leading us into potentially important territory for our investigations.

We checked out everything that Gold told us, in great detail. The confessions of Heller, Black and Slack added weight to Gold's information. When Gold told us that Sam Semenov had visited an East Coast oil company installation in 1941, we asked to look at the company's records of visits and found a notation of Semenov's excursion in a visitors' log. In a similar manner we were able to corroborate other small but significant details, such as the time and place of the meeting between Gold, Brothman and Semenov—a Manhattan hotel registration card gave us that piece of the story.

Such documentary evidence of the accuracy and extent of Gold's memory helped in the preparation of other cases. In 1947 the FBI had not been fooled by the interlocking nature of the Gold and Brothman testimony before the grand jury, but we had no witness other than Bentley to oppose this testimony. In the autumn of 1950, after his arrest, Gold became available and willing to testify against Brothman. Brothman and Miriam Moscowitz were then indicted for having lied to the 1947 grand jury. At the trial, Bentley and Gold were the main prosecution witnesses; they verified each other's versions of what had happened in 1940. Gold came under strenuous cross-examination in which he admitted that he had lied many times about his personal life in order to conceal his second life as an espionage agent. Gold was convincing enough, however, so that Judge Irving Kaufman, at the end of the trial, was able to sentence Brothman and Moscowitz to two years in jail each, plus a fine.

A last story about Gold and Brothman had to do with the breaking of ties between Gold and Yakovlev.

"John" took over as Gold's KGB controller in 1943, and for the next two years Gold worked under him. To Gold, Yakovlev was a far more demanding practitioner of the art of espionage than Semenov had been. There were more explicit instructions on meetings and fallbacks, strange recognition signals and coded conversations. Yakovlev held a tight rein on Gold, and was the initiator of every clandestine piece of business that Gold and Fuchs went through in their meetings; he also received the information Gold had obtained from Fuchs. As soon as Fuchs left for England, Yakovlev, the cool professional, cut his ties to Gold and did not see him for fifteen months.

During that interim period Gold committed a major blunder: he became a business associate of Abe Brothman's. This was a fundamental breach of the rules of espionage security. Agents and couriers were supposed to have only the most minimal contact with one another, so that if the authorities found one, they would be unable to uncover the other. As Gold soon found out, working with Brothman was also bad for financial reasons: after a year of their association Brothman owed Gold many months of salary.

In late 1946 Gold received word through the usual clandestine channels—phone calls with coded instructions—that Yakovlev wanted to see him. The two men met for dinner at a Manhattan restaurant, and after a few questions about Fuchs, Yakovlev suggested that Gold might soon be ordered to go to Paris to do some new KGB work. Gold brightened and said that a trip to Paris might even be made to look like a legitimate business journey, because he would visit some French chemists with whom he had been corresponding for his new company. And what company was that? Gold told Yakovlev that he was in business with Abe Brothman. Hearing this, Yakovlev jumped to his feet, threw money on the table and started to dash out of the restaurant. "You fool," he said heatedly to Gold, "you have spoiled eleven years of preparation!"

Trying to recover, Gold followed Yakovlev out into the night. Yakovlev angrily reminded him that the last time they had met, he had informed Gold that the FBI had learned of Brothman from Bentley. Any investigation into Brothman would quickly yield the name of Gold. After brusquely telling Gold that they would never see one another again, Yakovlev strode off into the night, and shortly thereafter returned to Russia.

Gold's business dealings with Brothman had turned so sour that he finally quit the New York firm and obtained a post closer to his father and brother, as a biochemist in the heart laboratory of the Philadelphia General Hospital. He was working at that job at the time of the grand jury inquiry in 1947, and in 1950, when the FBI began to question him about Klaus Fuchs.

Gold's June 1 confession had led us in three directions. I've just covered the first two—into the distant past with Tom Black, and then into the imbroglio with Brothman. In that interview Gold also told the agents about a third contact, but said he couldn't remember the man's name. He could, however, remember a lot about the circumstances under which they had met.

It began during May 1945, when just before a trip Gold was to take to New Mexico to obtain information from Fuchs, he met Yakovlev in a New York City bar to go over specific tasks. Yakovlev instructed Gold that in addition to picking up data from Fuchs, he would have to go to Albuquerque and meet a second source. Gold objected strongly to the notion of a side trip. He told Yakovlev frankly that Fuchs was too important a scientist and that Fuchs's information was too valuable for Gold to risk endangering him by having a courier hanging around New Mexico for an extra day or two. Yakovlev said Gold could take an excursion from Santa Fe into Texas and then come back to Albuquerque if he didn't want to attract attention by staying in one area too long. Gold again objected, but Yakovlev overruled him; a woman had been supposed to make the trip, but she couldn't go and see the second man, and so Gold would have to do so. Gold's task was to locate an address in Albuquerque, visit it, and see either the man who lived there or the man's wife. Gold was to identify himself by means of a piece of torn cardboard (which Yakovlev then gave to him and which Gold put in his wallet) and a password (which Yakovlev wrote out on a slip of paper, together with the contact's name and address). The couple in Albuquerque would have the other half of the torn cardboard, and would recognize the password. Should the couple express a need for money, Gold was to give them five hundred dollars, which Yakovlev provided; in return, Gold was to collect some information, which he was to bring back to New York and give to Yakovlev.

Gold got to Santa Fe and saw Fuchs before he traveled to Albuquerque. He arrived at the appointed address on a Saturday, and was told by a woman that the man was not home and that he should return the next day, Sunday. Terrified that he'd be discovered, Gold spent the night on the floor of a rooming house. Early Sunday he returned to the house, met the man, matched the cardboard pieces, said the password and was invited inside.

The young man was Jewish, sturdily built, spoke with a New York accent, and was obviously in the U.S. Army. After inviting Gold in, though, the young man apologized and said he didn't have his information ready yet—could Gold come back in the afternoon? Exhausted, Gold left and checked into the Hilton Hotel for a few hours of sleep. Back at the house in the afternoon, Gold was handed several handwritten pages and a sketch, scientific in nature, and he guessed that the young man must be a technician or have some scientific background. He chatted with the young man and his wife. They accepted the five hundred dollars Gold handed them, and they talked of a further exchange to be made in New York at a later date; the young man gave Gold his father-in-law's number so that they'd be able to set up the later rendezvous.

Gold then returned to New York and gave the young soldier's information to Yakovlev, along with what he'd picked up from Fuchs. Yakovlev forbade any further meetings with the man from Albuquerque.

In his June 1 go-around with Scotty Miller and Dick Brennan, Gold gave fairly precise descriptions of the young couple, but drew a blank on their names, although he thought the wife's first name might have been Ruth. He couldn't dredge up the street address, though he was certain they'd occupied an apartment on the second or third floor of a residential house. Gold suggested to the FBI agents that if he could look at a map, he might be able to pinpoint more exactly the location of the house. An Albuquerque map was quickly obtained, and Gold zeroed in on one particular block of North High Street.

Scotty Miller sent out investigative leads that suggested Albuquerque pursue the matter of the street address, but told headquarters that he thought he already knew the identity of the soldier whose name Gold couldn't remember—a man named Theodore Hall, who was a suspect in another espionage investigation, and who had once worked at Los Alamos.

Miller was wrong, of course, because Gold was referring to David Greenglass—but the tale of the investigation into an "unknown subject" ("unsub") that we'd been conducting since February 1950, which had thrown up Hall's name, shows that we had been looking for a spy in the Los Alamos woods for some time before Harry Gold confessed, before we'd known of David Greenglass, and before we'd ever caught sight of Julius Rosenberg.

The story of that "unsub" investigation has remained a secret since 1950—because its source was a deciphered KGB cable.

In February 1950 a newly deciphered cable from 1944 gave me reason to believe that someone in a lower-level position at Los Alamos, who had had furlough plans in late 1944 and early 1945, was a KGB agent. On February 21, 1950, I sent a Bureau letter to several of our offices, which reiterated the substance of the deciphered KGB message and specifically requested the Albuquerque and St. Louis field offices to look into the matter. Albuquerque was highlighted, of course, because Los Alamos was nearby, and the army records were stored near St. Louis. Those field offices got to work, but many of the other field offices responded to my initial letter with suggestions. One, made by the Boston office, was that this "unsub" might be Fuchs! I sent a sharp rejoinder to Boston telling them that their suggestion was wrong, and that the suspected man was one who was to have been on furlough in November 1944 and to have left New York in January 1945.

In this investigation, a number of names did surface. One of those, a soldier whom Albuquerque referred to as an "excellent suspect," was a man whose parents and in-laws were currently in Budapest, Hungary. We asked the CIA to check out the relatives, but that lead fizzled.

While the "unsub" investigation was being conducted, another—and relatively minor—inquiry was under way into people who were suspected of having pilfered uranium samples from the Los Alamos laboratory. In connection with this inquiry, David Greenglass was interviewed by New York field agents on March 31, 1950. Greenglass denied having taken any of the samples, and the agents went away empty-handed. It is important to note that the agents did not then suspect Greenglass of having had anything to do with the "unsub" investigation, which had been proceeding apace for more than a month.

In April 1950 memos flew back and forth between headquarters and Albuquerque urging speed on the "unsub" matter. Albuquerque and St. Louis had been telling me that the furlough records—our best clue—were rather messed up, and that some of them had apparently been routinely destroyed. On May 8 I sent strongly worded memos to the field offices which warned them to get into high gear on the case—instantly.

In early June, when Gold came up with the good description of the Albuquerque address of his contact, the Albuquerque field office, by looking into the list of those who had been interviewed in connection with the theft of uranium hemispheres, suggested the name of a very logical suspect who had lived at 209 High Street with his wife, Ruth, in 1945. He was David Greenglass.

We wired New York and immediately had field agents take some surveillance photos of Greenglass. They also did some research and came up with a 1940 graduation picture. Both photos were sent to Philadelphia, where on June 3 Miller and Brennan showed them to Harry Gold. Gold didn't recognize the man in the surveillance photo, but thought that the 1940 picture more closely resembled the man he had met in 1945. On June 7 Gold was shown motion pictures of the houses in the North High Street area and picked out 209 North High Street as the place that looked the most like the one he had visited in 1945; Gold remarked that the house seemed to have been substantially remodeled—which was true.

By June 15, it was obvious to me that the "unsub" whom we had been looking for since February of 1950 was the same man Gold had contacted in Albuquerque, and that he was probably David Greenglass. Although the deciphered KGB message had told us to look for a man who had been on furlough in November 1944 and had traveled in January 1945, and the army records showed that Greenglass had taken his furlough in late December 1944 and traveled to New York in January 1945, the match-up was pretty close. On the strength of this, we moved. On that day the New York field office began to question Greenglass.

In the course of their questioning, the agents asked Greenglass if they could search his apartment, and he gave permission. In that sweep they picked up several photos of David and Ruth. Later on

that same day, June 15, a group of photos including those just obtained from the Greenglasses were shown to Harry Gold in Philadelphia. He immediately fastened on one that showed David and Ruth
on the steps of 209 High Street, and which featured on the back the
camera shop date stamp November 8, 1945. In longhand, Gold wrote
alongside this date stamp,

> This is the man I contacted in Albuquerque, N.M. in June, 1945 on
> instructions from my Soviet Espionage Superior, "JOHN." The man
> in the picture gave me information relative to his work at Los
> Alamos, New Mexico, which information I later gave to JOHN.

The circle was complete, and we couldn't wait until morning. Late
on the evening of June 15 David Greenglass was brought into the
Foley Square office for questioning. He quickly admitted that, as
Gold had charged, he had passed information from Los Alamos to the
Soviet courier. He also implicated in this first confession his wife,
Ruth, and his brother-in-law, Julius Rosenberg, in espionage activi-
ties.

For me, June 15, 1950, was quite a day. Harry Gold and David
Greenglass identified each other and Greenglass confessed—while
on another front, Alfred Dean Slack, one of Gold's other contacts,
also confessed to espionage for the U.S.S.R. Indeed, cases were breaking everywhere.

11

THE ROSENBERG NETWORK

THE VERY SAME NIGHT that David Greenglass confessed—actually, at 1:40 in the morning on June 16, 1950—Dick Whelan, assistant special agent in charge of the New York field office, read David's signed statement over the telephone to headquarters. This first brief confession admitted his Los Alamos espionage and implicated his wife, Ruth, and his brother-in-law, Julius Rosenberg. Greenglass said he would have fled the country after learning of Harry Gold's arrest in May, because he feared the FBI would soon find him out, but he hadn't gone away because his wife was in the hospital, recovering from burns, and his first child was only a few days old.

Greenglass had told the interviewing agents that under no circumstances would he testify against Julius Rosenberg. He didn't mention his sister, Ethel Rosenberg, in connection with espionage at all.

ASAC Whelan was worried that Julius Rosenberg might try to flee the country when he learned David Greenglass had been picked up. A surveillance might do no good because no one in the New York field office knew what Rosenberg looked like, and he might easily evade watchers in the large complex of buildings that made up Knickerbocker Village, in Manhattan, where he lived. Our New York files had only a few mentions of Rosenberg, Whelan said, mainly a report on his having been fired by the Signal Corps for Communist associations. Whelan recommended that his men take Julius Rosenberg by surprise that very morning.

A few hours later FBI agents knocked at Julius Rosenberg's door and woke him up. He refused the agents permission to search the apartment without a warrant, but did accompany them voluntarily to Foley Square for questioning. There he denied all the accusations against him.

While Rosenberg was being questioned, David Greenglass was still sleeping in the nurse's station at Foley Square—nearby, but out of sight. At the same time, we who were most concerned with these two men were holding a meeting in the offices of my old friend, the head of the Criminal Division of the Justice Department, Jim McInerney. In attendance were McInerney, Ray Whearty—whom I had come to know in the Coplon case—Mickey Ladd, Al Belmont and me. On the basis of what Greenglass had said, Justice now authorized his prosecution, charging him with conspiracy to violate Section 32a of Title 50 of the U.S. Code—that is, with conspiracy to convey to another country information vital to the national defense of the United States.

Whearty thought Greenglass should be prosecuted in New Mexico, where he had given his data to Gold. During our conference we were informed by telephone that O. John Rogge, former head of the Anti-Trust Division of Justice and a lawyer well known for championing left-wing causes, would now be representing Greenglass, and was sending a man from his office to Foley Square to interview David.

None of us in Washington wanted to allow Greenglass to walk out on a possible writ. Whearty called the United States Attorney for the Southern District of New York, Irving Saypol, and asked him to take Greenglass into custody on the strength of a warrant about to be issued in New Mexico.

Meanwhile, in New York, Julius Rosenberg put off the agents interviewing him by insisting he be allowed to talk to a lawyer. Over the telephone, the attorney Rosenberg called told him to ask the FBI if he was under arrest. When he was informed that he was not under arrest, Rosenberg bowed to the agents and walked out of the Foley Square office.

At this point the FBI did not know whether Julius Rosenberg was an important espionage figure or a minor one. What we did know was that we had a confessed agent, David Greenglass, in hand, and we wanted to make sure that everything about his apprehension was handled correctly so that no appeals court judge could ever overturn a conviction based on the idea that Greenglass might have been arrested in some manner that wasn't strictly by the book.

We were still in conference in McInerney's office when word arrived that David Greenglass had been arraigned and was being held in jail. Bail was set at $100,000. We chortled a bit at the reported reaction of O. John Rogge to this high bail: he claimed that "hysteria" was "gripping the country," and that the $100,000 figure was, in effect, denying Greenglass his constitutional rights.

From this time forward, every slip of paper that had to do with David Greenglass passed across my desk.

The Greenglass case was of tremendous concern to me—but I was also involved with many other cases that we were still pursuing, based on Harry Gold's confession. For instance, Al Slack had just confessed, and plans were being made to indict Abe Brothman and Miriam Moscowitz. We were actively interviewing Tom Black, Ferdinand Heller, Ben Smilg and others who had been named by Gold.

I asked one of the people at headquarters who readied exhibits for trials to help me prepare an extensive chart that outlined the various espionage networks which we had learned about in the past few years. In its final form it showed the lines leading from Gaik Ovakimian and other spymasters to people as diverse as Gold, Rosenberg, Bentley, Briggs, Fuchs and others. The Director thought the chart of such importance that he sent copies of it to the National Security Council and to military aides of the president. (The chart is reprinted below.)

Even as this chart was being drawn and sent up the line, Harry Gold continued to come up with nuggets that related to the Greenglass case. Interviewed again in Philadelphia on June 26, he recalled —in the words of the FBI teletype that reported the interview—"the relative of Greenglass whom Gold was to contact in Dec. fortyfive was named Julius and not Philip as Gold had previously stated." Gold said he neither knew nor could remember the last name of Greenglass's relative in New York; shown a list of fourteen last names, including "Rosenberg," he said none of them rang a bell.

(Later critics have claimed that Gold was "coached" as a witness for the Rosenberg trial, and point to his early FBI interview as "proof" that Gold had not said anything about anybody named Julius to Greenglass. This discrepancy between early and late Gold testimony, the critics say, means Gold was lying. In fact, the FBI files show that while Gold did not remember the name Julius right away,

That's me at about age ten, and at nineteen, in front of a mine entrance. The first summer in the mines, my father made sure I got every dirty job imaginable, so he wouldn't be accused of showing any favoritism.

Above: Much of the KGB's espionage in the United States in the 1930s and 1940s could be traced to these two "residents," Gaik Ovakimian, *right*, and Vassili Zubilin.

Below: We were aggressive young supervisors at FBI headquarters who had a lot of ideas for actions the Bureau ought to take against the KGB. Here we are at a farewell party for Jack Ward, seated in front. *Left to right:* espionage specialists Jim Lee, Tony Litrento, Ernie Van Loon, Emory Gregg, Don Roney, me and Bill Welte.

Above: Gerhart Eisler, his wife Brunhilde and attorney Carol Weiss King. Eisler was my first big case. He'd been called "the Number One Communist in the U.S.," the man who gave theoretical direction to the Party.

Below: Klaus Fuchs identified the man in this photograph, Harry Gold, as his American contact in May 1950. The reverse side confirms this identification in Fuch's handwriting and with his signature.

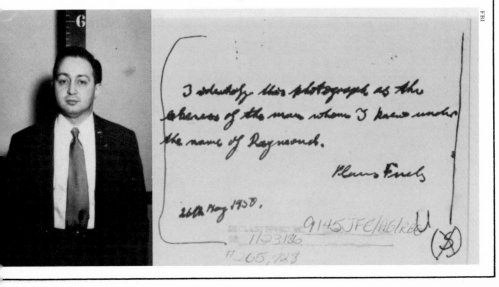

Howard Fletcher and his family chat with Director
J. Edgar Hoover at an FBI gathering. Howard, one of
my heroes, was the very model of loyalty to the Bureau;
he was demoted by Hoover for "mistakes" during
the Coplon and Fuchs cases.

The deciphered KGB messages led us directly to Judith Coplon,
shown here with her lawyer, Archibald Palmer.

The identity of Klaus Fuchs (*left*) was divulged by the deciphered KGB messages. When Hugh Clegg and I interviewed him in an English jail, he identified for us a photo of Harry Gold as his American courier. We said nothing about this as we got off the plane from London (*below*).

Left to right: Morton Sobell and Julius and Ethel Rosenberg during jury deliberations in their trial.

Deciphered KGB messages also led us into what we later discovered to be the Rosenberg network of spies. David Greenglass's confession allowed the FBI to piece together the extent and nature of that network.

David Greenglass after being arrested.

Guy Burgess and Donald Maclean.

D. Milton (Mickey) Ladd.

When British diplomats and KGB spies Burgess and Maclean fled to Moscow in 1951, intelligence outfits on both sides of the Atlantic were aghast. Kim Philby, who used to sit at a desk opposite me, was called home but, to my surprise, was cleared by the government in 1955. You can see his reaction in this photo. Both Assistant Director Mickey Ladd, who fostered close relations with the British, and I were disparaged in Philby's memoir.

H.A.A. (Kim) Philby.

UPI/BETTMANN NEWSPHOTOS

UPI/BETTMANN NEWSPHOTOS

After being convicted and jumping bail, Gerhart Eisler became a member of the East German government. Here he is, speaking at a "Save the Rosenbergs" rally in 1953—part of a worldwide KGB-inspired campaign that exploited humanitarian sentiment against the execution of the Rosenbergs.

Helen Sobell, the wife of Morton, was mentioned by code name in a KGB cable found in Colonel Rudolph Abel's wallet. This enabled me to prove the relationship between the Abel and the Rosenberg cases.

INTERCONNECTIONS OF SOVIET AGENTS IN UNITED STATES

M.G.B. MOSCOW

RESIDENT CHIEF M.G.B.
U.S.S.R. CONSULATE N.Y.C.

ANATOLI YAKOVLEV
CONSULATE N.Y.C.

UNIDENTIFIED RUSSIAN

(PROBABLY IDENTICAL)

JULIUS ROSENBERG

BEN SMILG

RUTH GREENGLASS

DAVID GREENGLASS

KLAUS FUCHS

SEMEN SEMENOV
AMTORG N.Y.C.

"GEORGE"

(PROBABLY IDENTICAL)

GREGORI RABINOVITCH

"JOHN"

HARRY GOLD

FERDINAND HELLER

VERA KANE

HOWARD GOCHENOUR

"FRED"

JOSEPH KATZ

THOMAS L. BLACK

WILLIAM STAPLER
DIED 1947

A.D. SLACK

PAUL SMITH
A.K.A. PAUL PETERSEN

STANLEY GLASS

GAIK OVAKIMIAN
AMTORG N.Y.C. (1934–41)

MIKHAIL CHALIAPIN
CONSULATE N.Y.C.

ELIZABETH BENTLEY

1944–45
(SILVERMASTER GROUP)

JACOB GOLOS
DIED 1943

ABE BROTHMAN

RICHARD BRIGGS
DIED 1939

MLT 1938–40

1944–45

1939–40

1941–44

1941

1935–37

1938–40

1936–39

1937 –38

1933 –34

1934–35

1939–40

1936–39

1938

1944

1940

1940–44

1939–40

1939–42

1941–44

1941

1944–45

1945

1944–45

1945

1933–34

1939–45(?)

1938–41

by June 26 his recollections were already becoming more precise.)

During this June 26 interview Gold also maintained that he had been authorized to deal with Ruth Greenglass if David was not present in Albuquerque, and he said that Ruth had been either in the room with him and David, or in the next room within earshot, when the men had discussed passing the information.

From her hospital bed, Ruth Greenglass initially told FBI agents that she remembered nothing of any visit by Harry Gold, and that David had probably made a mistake about the whole thing; she would believe the story, she said, only when she heard it directly from David's lips. This, however, was before she had talked to David, or to attorney Rogge.

While David Greenglass remained in custody and Ruth was getting ready to come home from the hospital, Julius Rosenberg kept to his usual daily routine in Manhattan. We tailed him loosely; the surveillance was so loose that the top FBI men in New York were worried that he might slip away from them.

On June 26, 1950, people in the United States learned that early on the previous morning a force of 90,000 North Koreans, armed with Soviet tanks and artillery, had struck south on a broad front across the neck of the Korean peninsula. This attack began the Korean War— a war which, in the minds of many people that summer, held out the possibility of rapidly escalating into World War III.

That day attorney Rogge came to Washington to keep an appointment with Mickey Ladd. Perhaps with the recent opening of hostilities fresh in his mind, Rogge told Ladd that although in the past he had been a frequent critic of the government, he currently believed that it was in the national interest, and in the interest of his clients the Greenglasses, for David and Ruth to talk freely to the FBI. He hadn't yet secured their definite cooperation, but was testing the waters. In return for Ruth's cooperation he wanted to have the case against her shelved. Such understandings, Ladd told him, would have to come from the Justice officials, and Rogge was soon repeating his offer to Ray Whearty.

Two days later, in New York, Rogge told men from the field office in Foley Square that David and Ruth had now actually agreed to be interviewed, and dropped hints about what their cooperation might reveal: that the recognition signal between Gold and Greenglass had been the two torn halves of a "box-top" which had originated with Julius Rosenberg, and that Harry Gold had replaced another courier who was at first supposed to have to come to Albuquerque to receive the information from Greenglass.

Initially, David had insisted he would not testify against Julius, and Ruth had denied all allegations of espionage. Why were they now willing to talk? In retrospect, the change of heart can be well understood. Rogge and his law associates had pointed out to the Greenglasses that David had already implicated Julius, Ruth and himself in a conspiracy, and that Harry Gold could corroborate David's own statement about himself and Ruth. David hadn't wanted to testify against his in-laws, the Rosenbergs, but it was now obvious that it would be impossible and impractical for the Greenglasses to prevent Julius and Ethel from being brought into the story. Rogge or others must have pointed out to them that if the Rosenbergs had been the instigators of the espionage, for the Greenglasses to bring out that fact might aid the Greenglasses in their own defense.

On July 10, security officer Art Rolander of the AEC called me, quite concerned with the wording of the indictment against Greenglass, which said that David had passed to Harry Gold a sketch of a high-explosive lens mold. In effect, the wording of the indictment declassified the term "lens mold"; Rolander's inquiry was a first indication of how dangerous the AEC considered David Greenglass's testimony in a trial might be.

The Greenglasses didn't want David tried in New Mexico because of a perceived backlash against the people who had "invaded" Los Alamos during the war. On July 12 jurisdiction over the case was transferred to New York. Two days later, David and Ruth began to talk in earnest to the FBI. In separate interviews, both firmly implicated Julius and Ethel Rosenberg in the recruitment and handling of David as an espionage agent. Ruth recalled that the Rosenbergs had told her the true subject of the top-secret Los Alamos project on which David was employed. She said the Rosenbergs had insisted she convey to David their request that he turn over Los Alamos data to Julius, for the Russians. David provided more detail on what he'd passed to Harry Gold, and said Gold was actually a replacement courier for Anne Sidorovich, who was to have come to New Mexico to carry back David's information.

Both Greenglasses revealed that Julius had made plans for them to escape from the United States, through Mexico, to Russia. At each step of the game—when Klaus Fuchs was arrested in February, and when Harry Gold confessed in May—Julius became quite agitated and demanded that the Greenglasses ready themselves for flight. In early June Julius gave David first one thousand dollars and then an additional four thousand so that David could take his family away. At that point David himself was in enough of a panic that, forgetting for a moment that Ruth was in the hospital and the baby had just been born, he made a feint toward an escape. He went by bus to the Catskills to look for a quiet place to hide, but realized that men in unmarked cars had followed him every inch of the way, and came home determined to stay in New York. He then turned over most of the money Julius had given them to Ruth's sister and her husband, and asked them to hide it. Later that money had been given to the Rogge firm for use in the Greenglasses' defense.

In an electrifying section of David's interview, he described how Julius had boasted many times of a network of his "boys," who were all over the United States, and who were in the business of supplying information through Julius to the Soviet Union. David said some of these people were students at colleges around the country whose tuitions were being paid by the Russians, as Julius had once offered to pay David's tuition if he would study atomic physics at MIT. David knew the name of only one of the agents—Joel Barr, who Rosenberg had said was currently living in Paris. But there were others. Julius had dropped hints that some of his people had obtained secret data on interesting projects such as an "atomic plane," a "sky platform" that was to be used in outer space, and the building of an "Aswan dam."

In a last recollection, David said that data from this whole network of spies were often microfilmed at two apartments in Lower Manhattan, which Rosenberg had told him he kept expressly for that purpose.

On July 17, 1950, with David Greenglass's new statement in hand —but with Ruth's not yet available—Al Belmont and I went back to see Jim McInerney. Much had happened in a month. When we three first met, in mid-June, McInerney had opposed arresting Julius Rosenberg because David Greenglass would not then testify against his brother-in-law. But now, on reading David Greenglass's detailed statement, Jim authorized prosecution of Julius Rosenberg. He would be arrested and charged with conspiring with Greenglass and others to violate the Espionage Act. Jim said our office in New York should get in touch with Saypol and have a complaint sworn out and a warrant issued for Julius Rosenberg's arrest.

There had been no mention in our June meeting of Ethel Rosenberg's involvement in espionage. Now David had put her into the picture, but without Ruth's statement in hand, Jim McInerney felt there was insufficient evidence to proceed against Ethel Rosenberg.

Ruth Greenglass was another possible conspirator, and we discussed her next. Jim felt, as we did, that since Ruth was consenting to extended interviews and was potentially a very valuable witness, she should probably not be prosecuted; however, Jim wanted to continue to hold over her head the threat of indicting her so she would be inclined to cooperate fully with the government. Hearing this, we told Jim that we understood that Irving Saypol might already have concluded an arrangement with Greenglass attorney Rogge not to prosecute Ruth. McInerney agreed that Saypol had probably gone too far in giving such assurances to Rogge.

Later in the day, McInerney called Belmont to suggest that in the event our New York agents witnessed Julius Rosenberg attempting to flee, they could arrest him without a warrant. Belmont didn't want to have that done because an arrest without a warrant would preclude the possibility of a search of Rosenberg's apartment—a place that might contain incriminating evidence. McInerney conceded that it would be best to have a warrant in hand. Our New York agents then went before Federal Judge John F. X. McGohey and swore out the complaint and the warrant. In the early evening Rosenberg was taken into custody, arraigned and held in jail until receipt of a $100,-000 bond. The Rosenberg apartment in Knickerbocker Village was thoroughly searched, but no important evidence was found.

The next days were incredibly hectic for me. David Greenglass had raised the possibility that many other people associated with Rosenberg were deeply involved in espionage. I looked once more at the Joel Barr investigation; there had been entries as recently as February, but nothing since. From Barr I naturally jumped to Max Elitcher, whose name had also surfaced in 1948 in connection with the deciphered KGB messages of 1944–45.

Now many things that we had struggled for several years to understand in the deciphered KGB messages became clear. It was Julius Rosenberg, referred to by a code name in the messages, who had contacted Max Elitcher and tried to recruit him. It was also Rosenberg who performed a similar function with Joel Barr; and it was most likely Ethel Rosenberg who was referred to in the message about a female, Christian name Ethel, who knew about her husband's work with the Soviets—the details in that message fit Ethel Rosenberg's background precisely. On another front, recalling Elizabeth Bentley's confession of 1945, we now believed that Julius Rosenberg was the "Julius" of the cell of engineers developed by Jacob Golos.

The men around Julius Rosenberg did seem like a cell, and all had many interconnections. Morton Sobell, for example, had been a classmate of Rosenberg's, Elitcher's and Barr's at CCNY. Barr and Rosenberg were two of the names on a 1944 CPUSA sheet that detailed the transfers of members from the Industrial Division (Branch 16-B) to smaller party units; also on the same list was Al Sarant. Sarant's name had popped up earlier in 1950 as we checked to see if he could have been the man who initially recruited Barr for the KGB—this because Barr had once put Sarant down as a reference for some government contracting work, and because we'd found out that they had worked together back in 1941. Sarant's name had also surfaced in a separate investigation of another of the CCNY classmates, William Perl; in 1949, at the request of the National Advisory Committee on Aeronautics (NACA), we had looked into Perl's background. Sarant and Perl had been roommates while both men studied for graduate degrees at Columbia University—Perl was a former colleague of Max Elitcher's and a longtime friend of Morton Sobell's, as well as a classmate of Julius Rosenberg's. In short, the FBI had been taking various glances into the lives of these men for several years, but had never put together the fact that they were all interrelated, and that the linchpin had been Julius Rosenberg.

But now, in the immediate aftermath of Greenglass's full confession and the arrest of Julius Rosenberg, we began to close in on all of these men—simultaneously. In the next days and weeks all of them were subjected to intense scrutiny, and the dimensions of the Rosenberg network became clear.

Some of these details were harder to nail down than others. For example, I was personally incredulous at aspects of what David Greenglass had told the FBI about Rosenberg's sources. I had never heard of anything like a "sky platform"—remember, this was seven years before Sputnik, and military hardware in space was a concept most people would have considered impossible. Greenglass had also said that Julius had boasted that one of his "boys" was a two-hundred-dollar-a-day consultant on an "Aswan dam" project. I didn't know what that project might be, either. I took both these intriguing ideas as my personal province and determined to understand them. Both frustrated me for a long time, but neither was as farfetched as I initially believed. A check with the Air Force revealed that, yes, there were preliminary studies being done for a space satellite that could act as a "sky platform" for military purposes. And inquiries to other government agencies told us that there was indeed a dam being contemplated for the lower reaches of the Nile River in Egypt, even though the project was unknown to the general public at the time. It was astounding to me that David Greenglass had mentioned these seemingly outlandish and certainly esoteric ideas as things being worked on by Rosenberg's "boys," and that when we checked them out, we found that they were real and important projects. To me it showed the breadth and depth of the Rosenberg network's reach—a reach far greater than we had initially imagined.

While the facts about the sky platform and the Aswan dam were being developed, we worked closer to the other members of the network: Joel Barr, Al Sarant, Max Elitcher, Morton Sobell and William Perl. Our offices in Paris, Albany, Cleveland, New York and Washington were moving in concert on these suspects. At that time we were pursuing all these investigations at once; here, however, for purposes of clarity, I'll go into them one at a time.

Within a few days after July 17, I got a report from Paris that Joel Barr had vanished. The indications were that his departure from his Paris apartment had been precipitous, and, from what we could piece together, he had flown the coop around June 16—the date on which newspapers reported the arrest of David Greenglass. Sam Perl, brother of William Perl, had last seen Joel Barr in Paris on June 2, at which time Barr spoke mysteriously about leaving the city and suggested that it would be better if Sam "did not know his intended destination." He also told Sam Perl he'd sell his motorcycle before he went, but the cycle, along with many of Barr's personal belongings, was discovered in the small apartment after Barr had gone. Barr's sudden drop out of sight squared with what David Greenglass had told the FBI: stories from Rosenberg that had cited Barr as an example of an agent who had left the United States because he was too "hot," and who would soon go behind the Iron Curtain.

Though Barr was nowhere to be found, his file contained many important leads, and now we could take the wraps off what in the past had been a discreetly conducted security investigation. For instance, we could and did check out more thoroughly his known friends and co-workers at the defense contractors where he had been employed prior to going to Europe. We could scrutinize his personal contacts, and we could look into the places where he'd lived in the United States to see if any of them tied into other aspects of the

Rosenberg network. One of the more important names in Barr's file was that of Vivian Glassman, the girlfriend who had been with him for a number of years—up until the very moment he sailed for Europe, in fact. We already knew a bit about her because in 1948 we had considered the possibility that she might be the "Ethel" of the deciphered KGB message that had seemed to us at that time to be connected to Barr.

Vivian Glassman was intriguing because she had links to other people who knew Rosenberg. For instance, her sister Eleanor had dated William Perl. Another item cropped up quickly: Vivian lived in an apartment that sounded much like one of those that David Greenglass said had been used by Rosenberg for microfilming. Agents in New York had been canvassing the streets of the Lower East Side near Avenue B, showing people photographs of Rosenberg and some of those who we suspected were involved with him. I was very pleased when this aggressive tactic paid off, and Mr. and Mrs. Frank Tusky, superintendents at 131 East Seventh Street, identified Julius as the man who had lived in an apartment in that building in about 1946; that apartment was now rented by Vivian Glassman.

The information on Glassman and 131 East Seventh Street took some time to develop, and in the meantime, we examined the records of an apartment Joel Barr had apparently shared with Alfred Sarant, at 65 Morton Street in Greenwich Village. That address interested me intensely because it sounded as if it might be the other microfilming apartment that Greenglass had described.

We soon found out that the leaseholder on the apartment, up until February 1, 1950, had been Alfred Sarant. On July 19, agents from the Albany office interviewed Sarant at his home in Ithaca, New York. Though nervous, Sarant was willing to talk, and appeared cooperative with the agents. He actually signed a paper that allowed them to search the premises.

Alfred Sarant had graduated from Cooper Union College in New York in 1941, with a degree in electrical engineering, and then went to work for the Signal Corps at Fort Monmouth, where he had first met Joel Barr. After the Signal Corps he worked for Bell Laboratories, then did graduate work at Columbia, and in 1948 moved up to the Cornell nuclear physics laboratory. He was a modest expert in radar, the first American computers and the electronic equipment needed to run a cyclotron.

During his first interview with the Albany FBI agents, Sarant admitted that he'd met both Julius and Ethel Rosenberg through Joel

Barr, and that he had held the lease on the 65 Morton Street apartment from 1943 to February 1, 1950, and when not in residence he had sublet the place to Barr and to others of his acquaintance. He and Barr had been in business together as "Sarant Laboratories," but the enterprise was hardly a business because he used it more as a setting in which to pursue his hobbies. He said he had had a fair amount of photographic equipment and high-intensity lights at 65 Morton, but that this had not been used to photograph documents. Sarant denied knowing Vivian Glassman, although he was close to Joel Barr for many years. He guessed that he had met Julius Rosenberg eight or ten times, probably most often as fellow members at meetings of the Federation of Architects, Engineers, Chemists and Technicians (FAECT). Once, as they both took a walk through the woods, Sarant thought Julius was propositioning him to supply information to the Russians, though he couldn't be sure of the intent and in any case he didn't "bite." He had not seen either of the Rosenbergs since 1946, and he certainly had never engaged in any espionage activities.

Some of the items found in the search of the Sarant home contradicted parts of Sarant's initial story—pictures of Barr and Glassman together with Al and "Puss" Sarant; letters from the Barr-Sarant firm soliciting navy contracts; a canceled check showing that Glassman had paid the rent on the 65 Morton Street apartment for a few months. Confronted with these new items, Sarant admitted that he had just been trying to keep Glassman's name out of the imbroglio, but he still denied ever having anything to do with government contracts when associated with Barr—the letters had not turned into actual work—and emphatically reiterated that he had never been a spy.

After a few more go-arounds with the agents, Sarant clammed up. He was placed under a loose surveillance and was asked to notify the FBI if he was going to leave Ithaca. On July 26 he advised the Albany office that he was going on vacation, to his father's home on Long Island; he was instructed to maintain touch through the New York FBI field office. A teletype from the Albany SAC to the New York SAC gives a hint about the difficulty of keeping tabs on a man who is not under arrest:

> Due to fact subject is probably under impression he will be surveilled in New York and since he has been instructed to maintain contact with the NY office, it is suggested that NY only confirm his arrival and spot check his activities during weeks [sic] stay.

New York did more than that, but it didn't prove to be enough. The field office did bring Sarant into New York for a few questions on July 28—principally so that he could be discreetly observed by superintendents from 65 Morton and from another building in which we suspected Rosenberg had an apartment. The man from 65 Morton recognized Sarant, the other man did not. Sarant was sent back to his vacation, and was tailed—though not intensively. A week later he vanished.

The story of Sarant's escape, as we were later able to reconstruct it from interviews with family members, was as follows: For some time, Sarant had been having an affair with a neighbor, Carol Dayton, the wife of a close friend. In fact, Weldon Bruce Dayton, Carol's husband, may well have been involved with the bunch of people around Rosenberg. In any event, when Sarant left Cornell and came to New York, he went to his sister's home on Long Island, and Carol Dayton soon joined him there. Sarant and Carol Dayton then confessed their marital problems to Sarant's relatives, and asked their help in getting away from the FBI—in all likelihood without admitting to the relatives why the FBI was following them. The relatives agreed to help out and, on the night of August 4, took the pair to Roosevelt Raceway, where the sister and brother-in-law kept horses. While FBI agents watched the main exits, Sarant and Dayton escaped through the paddock in a borrowed automobile. On a wild drive across the country they eluded the authorities, and then, in the Southwest, were aided by other relatives in entering Mexico. I'm sure it was all very romantic to them, but if Sarant and Dayton had gone in full daylight to the nearest international airport and boarded a plane for Moscow, we could have done very little about it. We might have asked a U.S. Attorney to issue a subpoena for Sarant to appear at a grand jury, and thus stopped Sarant's escape, but at that point we had no evidence against him that we could have used to obtain a warrant for his arrest. Sarant was actually free to go; this was America, not Russia.

In any event, our check of border records soon showed us that Sarant and Dayton had set foot in Mexico on August 9, and further inquiries showed us that they had forsaken Mexico for parts unknown by the middle of August. Abandoned in Ithaca were their respective spouses and children—and a lot of unanswered questions.

Barr was gone. Sarant had escaped on us. And, as we learned to our chagrin, Morton Sobell had also flown the coop.

Back on July 20, our agents had gone to Max Elitcher's office at

Reeves Instrument Company, where they found Elitcher quite upset; actually, he had been awaiting with dread the arrival of the FBI for a few weeks, ever since his neighbor Sobell had dropped from sight. Elitcher started talking freely in his own office, but said he believed he could cooperate further if he were allowed to check with his wife, Helene. The agents drove him out to his Queens home, where other agents already were interviewing Helene; after a conference, both Elitchers agreed to answer our questions, to allow a search of their house and, after the interviews, to sign short statements.

On July 20 and 21, Max Elitcher told us that he'd met Julius Rosenberg when they were classmates at CCNY, but that he hadn't seen him at all from 1938 until the early summer of 1944, when Rosenberg had been in Washington and had called him up for a surprise visit. At their reunion, Rosenberg had attempted to recruit Elitcher to "help the Russians" in their war effort by obtaining classified data from the navy. Flattered, Elitcher hadn't turned Julius down cold—he was, after all, an old classmate—but he had put Rosenberg off. On a handful of occasions in the next few years Rosenberg had continued to pressure him to supply information, but Elitcher said he had never given him anything.

On July 20, Elitcher didn't even mention to us the name Morton Sobell in connection with Rosenberg—but on July 21, in an attempt to make the agents believe his story, he included Sobell as a major participant. Sobell had arranged the first reunion meeting with Rosenberg in 1944, and had also been the intermediary in many of their later meetings. When Rosenberg had been frustrated over Elitcher's refusals to supply information, Julius had capped his arguments by telling Elitcher that Morty was already supplying reports to the Russians. Later, when Elitcher told Sobell what Rosenberg had said, Sobell had vehemently replied, "Julie shouldn't have said that." Even so, Elitcher knew that Sobell was in the espionage network and had given Rosenberg classified data.

As I sifted through these first two days of interviews with Elitcher, I experienced a sense of closure and completeness. Without knowing that he had done so, Elitcher had now verified as accurate the information we had obtained in 1948 from the 1944 KGB message. The KGB man who had tried to recruit Elitcher while on a short visit to Washington in the summer of 1944 was identified by the potential recruit as Julius Rosenberg. A thought then crossed my mind: If we had gone ahead and picked up Elitcher and questioned him closely after our surveillance in 1948, would he have been as willing to confess to his involvement with Rosenberg? And would we have broken the whole network in 1948—two years before we were actually able to do so?

In another item of interest in these first interviews, Elitcher recalled that on several occasions in 1945 and 1946, at various places— 65 Morton Street, the Rosenberg apartment in Knickerbocker Village, and the Blue Mill restaurant—there had been social gatherings at which he and his wife, Julius and Ethel Rosenberg, the Sobells, Joel Barr, William Perl, Al Sarant and various girlfriends were all present. Sometimes they held musicales at which Barr would display his talents or his record collection; sometimes they just had pleasant dinners. At such events Elitcher gained the distinct impression that all of the people in attendance—himself and Helene excepted, of course —were "cooperating" with Rosenberg to furnish information to the Soviets, though nothing about such matters was mentioned on these social outings.

Elitcher also told the interviewing agents that sometime during the week of June 18 Sobell had asked him to bring home Sobell's weekly paycheck from Reeves Instruments. As Sobell was on some kind of sick leave, Elitcher did as he was requested. Shortly thereafter the entire Sobell family had left their home (which abutted Elitcher's) in the family car, and the Elitchers had not heard from them since.

Greenglass had said Rosenberg had been trying to get him out of the country and into Mexico, as a first stop en route to the U.S.S.R., and so we now began to look into the possibility that Morton Sobell had fled south of the border. A check of airline offices told us that Sobell, his wife and two children had flown to Mexico City on June 22. We took steps to find them.

David Greenglass had also told us that Rosenberg had someone working in the Cleveland area, possibly on that "atomic plane" research project. Nuclear propulsion of airplanes was being researched at NACA, outside Cleveland. On July 19 our agents first approached William Perl in that city. Perl, born Mutterperl, had been with Rosenberg, Sobell, Elitcher and Barr at CCNY, and had roomed with Al Sarant while NACA paid for him to get a Ph.D. from Columbia. Perl was an up-and-coming scientist, a brilliant young man who had been a top assistant to Theodore von Karman, the former chairman of the Air Force's scientific advisory panel and a leading force in American aeronautics. Currently Perl supervised fifteen NACA employees in research on the problems associated with jet propulsion and supersonic flight. Such research was immediately applicable to our most advanced jet fighter planes.

In his first interview with the FBI, Perl said that he knew Alfred Sarant rather casually, having met him through Joel Barr. He had lived at 65 Morton Street off and on from 1946 through 1948, using the apartment, he estimated, about a quarter of the time.

He denied knowing Sarant's wife, Louise ("Puss"). He denied knowing Julius Rosenberg. He said he'd never had anything to do with microphotography or espionage.

There were so many obvious lies here that the agents just had to be suspicious of him. They knew, for instance, that he had been Rosenberg's classmate. In the apartment they picked up snapshots of the Sarant children and asked about them. Perl then admitted that he knew the Sarants fairly well, but wouldn't say much more.

Checking further with NACA, we soon found out that even though Perl didn't work on the "atomic plane" project, he would have had access to data about it.

Then an event occurred that, in all likelihood, we would never have known about if Perl hadn't told us directly. A few days after that first interview, on July 24, Perl telephoned the Cleveland FBI office and accused us of running an *agent provocateur* at him. When Special Agent in Charge Ray Abbaticchio had calmed Perl down (I later thought Perl might have been putting on an act), the scientist reported what had happened to him that weekend.

It began when a woman whom he said he knew only marginally —Vivian Glassman, the former girlfriend of Joel Barr—had knocked on his door, wanting to see him. Indicating by hand signals that she didn't wish to speak because the apartment might be bugged, she wrote out a note to him. It said she'd been instructed by a stranger to fly to Cleveland to see an "aeronautical engineer" and give him two thousand dollars and instructions on how to flee the country through Mexico. There had been something in the note about Julius Rosenberg—Perl couldn't recall the precise wording because, after telling Glassman that "she didn't know what she was talking about" and throwing her out of the apartment, he had torn up the missive and flushed it down the toilet. Then, probably fearing that the FBI had bugged him, and that if he denied the story he might be caught in a lie, Perl had approached Abbaticchio.

Perl insisted that he really didn't know Vivian Glassman very well and couldn't fathom the reason for her visit—this in clear contradiction to the facts we knew, which were that he'd met Glassman many times when she was with his close friend Joel Barr, and that he had dated Vivian's sister Eleanor.

It took a few days of phone calls and interviews for Perl to tell the whole story of Glassman's visit, and of some strange postcards that he said he'd just received from his brother in France. As the Cleveland office listened to Perl's story, the agents also cross-checked his previous statement with what Alfred Sarant was concurrently saying. Then, on August 3, we decided that our agents in New York were finally ready to confront Vivian Glassman.

At her apartment on East Seventh Street—the one we suspected Rosenberg had used for microfilming—Glassman told the agents a fantastic story that was as full of holes as it was of information. On the night of July 21 an unknown man had come to her apartment and asked her if she knew "John." When she had said no, the man said he had helped Joel Barr get to Europe. Because of this connection, Glassman said, she had let the stranger into her home. It was he who had given her the two thousand dollars and instructions to go to Cleveland. Glassman claimed not to know what the whole affair was about, and said she had done as the stranger requested because he was a friend of Joel Barr's. Although she made the trip to Cleveland under an assumed name, she had paid for it herself. (This was unlikely, as she made only a small salary.) On July 27 the stranger again appeared at her door—in fact, watching FBI agents had not been able to discern his visit—and Glassman had told him of Perl's refusal to take the money and had handed him back the two thousand dollars. Vivian Glassman gave the FBI a description of the unknown stranger: late thirties, five foot seven, dark hair, clean-shaven face, medium build, spoke English well and with no trace of an accent. She offered to come to Foley Square at another time to try and identify this man from FBI photos.

Glassman also said that she knew Julius and Ethel Rosenberg; that Julius had escorted her home after evenings they'd all spent canvassing for the American Labor Party in 1945; that she had been friendly with Ethel and had seen her on several social occasions, but had not talked to her since Julius's arrest. She denied that her apartment had ever been used for photography, or that she had ever done any work for Julius Rosenberg or had ever been involved in any aspect of espionage. If this was a cock-and-bull story, we had no way at present of controverting it. A few days later, under the guise of cooperating with the FBI, Glassman came down to the Foley Square field office but was unable to identify any of our photos as being the "stranger" who had come to her door.

As all these interviews and leads were being followed up, I tried to understand this group of people now emerging from the shadows, the group who all seemed to know Julius Rosenberg and to be suspected of espionage. We didn't have hard evidence on each one, but we had good reasons to believe that all might be guilty of passing secrets to the Soviet Union. Rosenberg, Barr, Sarant, Elitcher, Sobell and Perl were engineers or physical scientists of approximately the same age and from strikingly similar backgrounds. Five were the children of Russian Jewish immigrants, and Sarant was of Greek parentage. They came from poor families and had grown up in New York in the 1920s and 1930s, had gone to city schools—five to CCNY, and Sarant to Cooper Union—and graduated with marketable degrees. They had not served in the war but rather had taken draft-exempt jobs with the Signal Corps, the navy and defense contractors. In college they had publicly espoused left-wing beliefs, and most had become card-carrying Communists. Later on, their Communist activities and associations had gotten them into trouble and had brought them to the notice of the authorities long before 1950.

In 1942 Elizabeth Bentley had caught a glimpse of the leader of a group of engineers whom her lover and espionage controller Jacob Golos had been developing. He was known to her as "Julius," and she had described him to the FBI as "tall, thin, and wore hornrimmed glasses." She'd seen him in the vicinity of Knickerbocker Village. At odd evening hours he sometimes called her at home and asked her to have Golos contact him. One of these phone calls, Bentley remembered, was to ask Golos to get in touch with him because he, Julius, had lost contact with his own Soviet controller and wanted to reestablish the connection.

Bentley had originally thought that this group of engineers had something to do with Norfolk, Virginia, and submarines. From 1945 to 1950 we had checked out leads in that direction, and had come up with very little. But now, in the summer of 1950, we began to find some evidence that Bentley's guess about the engineers was a good one. Morton Sobell had made several visits to Norfolk, and William Perl had worked near Norfolk, in Hampton, Virginia. Also, the entire group of men around Rosenberg could well have been a young "cell" of engineers back in 1942 and 1943.

Actual corroboration of the Bentley-Rosenberg connection came from new interviews with Max Elitcher. The U.S. Attorney's office thought that Elitcher had been too vague in earlier statements about dates and places on which Sobell and Rosenberg could be charged with conspiratorial acts. So we went back to Elitcher for more detail —and he told us of an important 1948 incident.

It had happened when we were following Elitcher on the house-hunting trip to New York. Max and Helene had become "tail-conscious." When they arrived at Morton Sobell's house in Queens to spend the night, Max told Morton about his suspicions, and his own belief that they had now shaken the tail. Initially Sobell was furious that they had come to his home when the possibility still existed that the FBI might have followed them without their knowing it; soon he calmed down. Later in the evening of July 30, 1948, Sobell let Elitcher know that he had some material for Rosenberg that was "too good to throw away" yet too dangerous to be kept around the house in the event the FBI swooped down on them. At Sobell's request, Elitcher drove both of them to a deserted Manhattan waterfront street called Catherine Slip; there Max waited in the car while Sobell took a can of 35-millimeter film and walked off. He presumed Sobell was delivering it to the Rosenberg apartment, which was not far away.

When Sobell returned, Elitcher asked what Rosenberg thought about the possibility of the Elitchers having been tailed. "Julie says there's nothing to worry about," Sobell reported. Elitcher asked if Rosenberg had had anything to do with Elizabeth Bentley, who would make her spectacular appearance at the HUAC hearings in Washington the next day, and whose story had already been in the papers. Sobell said Julius had told him that he had talked to Bentley on the telephone, but Rosenberg was pretty sure that she "didn't know who he was and therefore everything was all right."

During the second week in August 1950, a grand jury in New York began to hear evidence in regard to the Greenglasses, the Rosenbergs and people associated with them. In her interviews with the FBI and in the grand jury room, Ruth Greenglass began to offer more detail which added evidentiary weight to the notion that Ethel Rosenberg was involved in the conspiracy.

In November 1944, when Julius and Ethel had first informed Ruth of the nature of the Los Alamos project and that they wished David to give information on it to the Russians, Ruth recalled that she had been reluctant to tell David to do as they asked. Ethel had brusquely said that cooperating in supplying data was something David would want to do, so Ruth should just deliver the message and "let David decide."

In early 1945, when the Greenglasses had returned on furlough to New York and were at the Rosenberg apartment, the recognition sign between David and the courier had to be constructed. Ruth remembered that Ethel was present in the kitchen when Julius prepared the two halves of the Jell-O box identification signal.

Later in 1945 Ruth had written to tell Ethel of her recent miscarriage; in return Ruth received a letter from Ethel (later destroyed) which said that "a member of the family" would come to visit the Greenglasses on the third or fourth Saturday in May. Ruth took this to mean that, as previously arranged, Anne Sidorovich would meet her in the parking lot of an Albuquerque store to obtain David's information—and for the next two Saturdays waited fruitlessly outside the store for Anne. Even though Anne didn't show up—Gold came on a succeeding Saturday—in Ruth's mind there could have been no other interpretation of the sentence in Ethel's letter. To her, it was obviously a thinly veiled reference made purposely obscure because both women knew the letter might well be opened due to military censorship.

Anne Sidorovich was questioned closely by the grand jury. She denied ever having been a courier for Rosenberg. However, she did say that she and her husband had been neighbors of the Rosenbergs before they moved to Cleveland, and that while on a visit to New York they had spent part of an evening with the Rosenbergs. During that evening the Sidoroviches had met the Greenglasses. It had been a brief exchange of pleasantries, and in fact, Michael Sidorovich hadn't really remembered knowing David Greenglass at Brooklyn Polytech, where they had been classmates for a few months. (Ruth Greenglass later acknowledged that Anne Sidorovich had not been present in the apartment when arrangements had been made for passing information in Albuquerque.)

On August 11, as the Grand Jury was hearing witnesses, Vivian Glassman was called before the panel and refused to answer any questions, on the grounds that her answers might tend to incriminate her. In all likelihood, Glassman was taking the Fifth because she feared an indictment for perjury. She had told the FBI that she knew the Rosenbergs, and that she'd gone to Cleveland. But there were a lot of holes in her story. If she got on the stand and answered questions similar to those we posed to her, and then took the Fifth when things got rougher, her use of the Fifth Amendment would be compromised, and she might end up indicted for lying.

Glassman's actions on the stand were enough to make Irving Saypol ask for a halt in the grand jury proceedings so he could confer in private with her. He knew that she had told the FBI that she had been to see Perl, and that she had spent some time down at Foley Square, looking at mug shots in a halfhearted and ultimately unsuccessful attempt to identify the "stranger" who had given her the money—but in the grand jury room she had refused to answer *all* questions about this or about the Rosenbergs. Saypol left Glassman in a conference room while he told FBI agents just outside the room that she was going to refuse to respond to further questions unless she was granted immunity from prosecution. Saypol said he was willing to grant her immunity, but if he did so, her later testimony might be weakened by public knowledge of her protection from prosecution. At this impasse, Saypol thought it best simply to excuse Glassman for a few days until some arrangement for her testimony could be worked out.

The few days became months, and no successful arrangement for Glassman's testimony was ever made. Today the question still troubles me: What would Glassman have told us in 1950 if she had spoken freely? In all likelihood, we would have learned something more about Joel Barr, Alfred Sarant, William Perl and the other men in the Rosenberg network. It is also possible that we would have gained additional evidence against Ethel Rosenberg.

This last conclusion is suggested by a curious incident that took place on August 11, and which was witnessed and noted by an FBI agent who was watching the corridors outside the grand jury hearing room. While sitting on a bench, waiting to testify, Vivian Glassman came face to face with Ethel Rosenberg, who had also been called to answer questions that day. Vivian had told the FBI, only a week earlier, that she and Ethel were friends; but for more than an hour, the two women sat directly across from one another, and acted as if they were complete strangers.

Vivian Glassman left the courthouse on August 11, and was never indicted. Ethel Rosenberg testified before the grand jury that day, and was arrested later on that same day and charged with being part of the conspiracy. She, too, was held in custody and the same $100,000 bail figure was imposed that had also been placed on her husband and on David Greenglass.

The grand jury also handed down an indictment of Morton Sobell for having taken part in the conspiracy, but this action was not made public until August 17. The reason for the delay in the Sobell indictment was that until that date, we didn't have Sobell in our custody.

When I had first sent instructions to Mexico to find Sobell, on July 21, 1950, I had thought the task was almost impossible. But through some imaginative investigative work, our men in Mexico City had discovered that the Sobell family was living in Apartment 5, 153 Cordova Street. Observation revealed that Morton Sobell was not there at that moment, but that his family was in residence. Our agents looked up a neighbor, Manuel de los Ríos, who told them that Sobell had asked him how to get to Vera Cruz, and what travel documents would be necessary for the family to be able to leave Mexico. Sobell had confided to de los Ríos that he was in flight from the United States because he was dodging military service. In the past few weeks Sobell had sent several letters to de los Ríos, which the Mexican had delivered, unopened, to Sobell's wife, Helen. We also learned that Sobell had cashed in all his return airline tickets except that of his stepdaughter, who usually resided part of the year with her natural father. As we later found out, Sobell had spent the end of July and the first part of August doggedly working the port cities of Vera Cruz and Tampico, looking for a freighter that would take a family, even without proper travel documents, toward Eastern Europe.

On August 16, Sobell returned to his apartment in Mexico City. In the late evening, he was picked up as an undesirable alien by men from the Mexican security police. When he protested, he was hit over the head and dumped in the back seat of a car. The police came back and put the rest of the family into a second car, together with armfuls of the family's possessions and papers. These two cars were joined by a half-dozen others, and drove the eight hundred miles to the International Bridge at Laredo, Texas, where on August 18 Sobell was handed over into the custody of the FBI; the rest of the family was set free on the U.S. side of the border.

In the papers that were found in Sobell's apartment, and from records the FBI later was able to obtain from various shipping and airline offices, hotels and other places of business, there was a history of Sobell's attempts to flee. He had used numerous aliases, such as M. Sand, N. Sand, Morris Sand and Marvin Saltig. He had tried to leave Mexico for Cuba, South America, several different countries in Europe and more in Eastern Europe. We later discovered from William Danziger—like Elitcher, a friend of Sobell's since childhood, who also had been in the electrical engineering department at CCNY—that through Danziger Sobell had sent letters to his relatives in the United States. Such actions gave the lie to Sobell's attempt to characterize his sojourn in Mexico as a family vacation.

On August 17, 1950, the grand jury had its full complement of people and returned an indictment. This was later amended on October 10. The main charge, contained in the first part, read:

> On or about June 6, 1944, up to and including June 16th, 1950, at the Southern District of New York and elsewhere, Julius Rosenberg, Ethel Rosenberg, Anatoli Yakovlev a/k/a "John", David Greenglass and Morton Sobell, the defendants herein, did, the United States of America then and there being at war, conspire, combine, confederate and agree with each other and with Harry Gold and Ruth Greenglass, named as co-conspirators but not as defendants, and with divers others presently to the Grand Jury unknown, to violate sub-section (a) of Section 32, Title 50, U.S. Code, in that they did conspire, combine, confederate and agree, with intent and reason to believe that it would be used to the advantage of a foreign nation, to wit, the U.S.S.R., to communicate, deliver and transmit to a foreign government, to wit, the U.S.S.R., and representatives and agents thereof, directly and indirectly documents, writings, sketches, notes and information relating to the National Defense of the United States of America.

In the second part of the charge there were the particulars of a dozen meetings and overt acts engaged in by the conspiracy, such as the making of the Jell-O box signal. Although some critics have later charged that the word "espionage" itself was not in the indictment, the acts that would constitute espionage, and the details, were clearly stated.

When defendants are charged with being part of a conspiracy, each one is responsible for all the acts of any of the others. This means that if a group of people is charged with conspiring to commit a bank robbery, and that group includes a getaway-car driver who did nothing but drive the group away from the bank, that driver as well as everyone else in the conspiracy can be held accountable if, in the course of the robbery, one of the members murders a bank guard. Further, the getaway driver need not actually have been present when the murder was committed to be charged also with that crime, because he had previously become part of the conspiracy. Translated to the Rosenberg case, this meant that Sobell could be held accountable for the actions of people he might never have met, such as Yakovlev or Greenglass, as long as the actions taken by these people were in furtherance of the objective of the conspiracy.

This understanding of the legal term "conspiracy" is central to comprehending the indictments of the Rosenbergs, Sobell, Yakovlev and David Greenglass. It is also imperative to recognize that all these people did not have to meet in the same place at one time in order to form a conspiracy—but that after the conspiracy had been formed, each was legally responsible for the actions of the others.

As the indictment of the Rosenbergs and the others was being handed down and then amended in the summer and early fall of 1950, the newspapers were full of the doings of Senator Joseph McCarthy. He was charging that the State Department and other branches of the Executive closely tied to the Truman White House were riddled with Communists and beset by Communist influence. Legislators' attitudes toward Communism became a major issue in the 1950 congressional elections. And, of course, the Korean War was in process.

I have always regarded it as unfortunate that the arrests, trial and appeals of the Rosenbergs and Sobell took place during the era of the McCarthy probes and the Korean conflict. This enabled supporters of the Rosenbergs to claim that the disappearances of Barr, Sarant, and especially Morton Sobell were the result of the climate of fear engendered by McCarthy's tactics. Their belief was that these "innocent" men, knowing they might be linked to the Rosenbergs, fled the United States rather than face what they considered would be trumped-up charges. I, of course, knew that these people had taken flight because of their involvement in the KGB-controlled network.

In the months following the indictments, we in the FBI concentrated on consolidating the government's case against the conspirators. We knew far more than the public could about the conspiracy, and we continued to hope and to work for confessions from one of the accused. We felt several times that Sobell was on the verge of confession. We also thought that if Vivian Glassman, William Danziger, or Anne or Michael Sidorovich would talk freely, we could broaden our knowledge of the Rosenberg network and possibly augment the existing indictments. We continued to believe, for example, that Max Elitcher and William Perl had been involved in espionage, though we couldn't prove it.

In the interim between the indictments and the trial, three of the other cases in which I had been involved were settled. Brothman and

Moscowitz were found guilty, and Harry Gold and Al Slack, who pled guilty, were sentenced.

Harry Gold was at the center of all three judicial processes. Abe Brothman and Miriam Moscowitz, Gold's two former business associates, were charged with having obstructed justice by lying to the grand jury in 1947 in regard to Gold, Jacob Golos, Elizabeth Bentley and the passing of industrial secrets to the Russians. When this trial was held, Gold had not yet been sentenced. He came in for heavy cross-examination, and was portrayed as a habitual liar, a man who was pointing a finger at others in order to save his own skin. Though his credibility was questioned, Gold was evidently believed by the court, for Brothman and Moscowitz were convicted. Both received relatively short sentences.

The case of Alfred Dean Slack did not get much publicity at the time. He pled guilty one day, and was sentenced a few days later. Slack, who had been paid by the Russians for giving them information on the secret explosive RDX, and other things, and who had conveyed his information through Harry Gold, was convicted of espionage and given a fifteen-year sentence. The maximum he could have received was death, or thirty years.

Gold came before Judge McGranery in December 1950 and was given thirty years in jail. Though Gold had been extremely cooperative with the government since the time of his arrest, the judge, citing the seriousness of the crime, had given him five years more than the amount requested by the prosecution.

In late December 1950 Harry Gold and David Greenglass were brought together by the FBI, inside prison walls, to attempt to reconcile minor differences in their stories. The men were remembering what had happened, very briefly, five years previous, in Albuquerque, and in almost every respect their stories were congruent. Both recalled the date and substance of the meeting, what was passed between them, the type of recognition signal, the plans for a future meeting in New York, and other details. However, Greenglass remembered the Jell-O box top more precisely, believed that Gold had brought greetings from someone and that Gold had identified himself as "Dave from Pittsburgh." Gold couldn't recall what sort of cardboard had been used. He agreed that he would have brought greetings—a usual procedure in such situations—but couldn't come up with the exact name he had used; he thought perhaps he had identified himself as Frank Kessler, an alias he had employed in similar clandestine meetings for many years. Gold also thought that the person whom he was to contact in New York in order to reestablish himself with Greenglass was David's father-in-law, whose name Gold had first remembered as "Philip," but had later amended to "Julius."

During the course of the meeting in prison, Greenglass said that Gold would have had to have brought greetings from Julius in order for the phrase to have any meaning for him, and Gold agreed that this was the logical possibility, although he still thought it could have been "greetings from Ben." Gold more readily conceded that the person whom he was to contact in New York was David's brother-in-law, Julius Rosenberg. Gold had disregarded David's plans for a second round almost as soon as David had suggested them, knowing full well that Yakovlev himself would reject the idea.

After the conference, the FBI reports show, the two men went back to their respective cells, the differences in their stories considerably narrowed—but not eliminated. In later years it was often charged that the FBI had coached Gold and Greenglass and had pushed them to neatly dovetail their remembrances. This was not so. Had it been so, would either man have been allowed to leave this unpublicized prison meeting with any remnants of doubt about the particulars they were supposed to recall?

At this time Julius Rosenberg was incarcerated in the Manhattan Federal House of Detention, where he awaited trial. To pass the days he sometimes played chess with a young man serving time for auto theft, Jerome Tartakow. In early December Tartakow made contact with the FBI and volunteered to tell us what Julius Rosenberg was saying and doing while in prison.

I was extremely skeptical about Tartakow. Repeatedly I told everyone involved in the Rosenberg case that he was not to be trusted. Tartakow wanted the FBI to help him get an early parole. We said we'd make no promises whatsoever.

Both Tartakow and Rosenberg had come from working-class backgrounds and had been militant leftists in their youth. Tartakow also had become friendly in prison with the general secretary of the Communist Party, Eugene Dennis, who was serving a sentence for contempt of Congress, Tartakow seems to have acted as a liaison between Dennis and Rosenberg at a time when the official CPUSA line was to have nothing to do with the Rosenbergs.

In January 1951 Tartakow was brought out of the prison and to the

Foley Square office, where he talked for hours about Rosenberg. In this session Tartakow said that Rosenberg felt he had "played the game and lost," and that he had not let the FBI search his apartment on June 16 because he had concealed a camera and seven thousand dollars in it; further, that if Rosenberg had had another week, he would have been able to escape to Mexico. Rosenberg had also told Tartakow that a second spy ring had been operating in New York, headed by a man who was now in Europe—a man whose mother had recently been interviewed by the FBI.

This last information was something Tartakow could not have known independently, as the investigation of Joel Barr had not yet been made public. But it referred so convincingly to Barr, and to our recent questioning of his mother, that it began to blunt my skepticism of Tartakow as an informer. How could Rosenberg have known the information in the first place? We found out that some members of Joel Barr's family had had dinner with Vivian Glassman, and must have told her about the FBI's inquiry—information Glassman had almost certainly passed along to Emanuel Bloch, attorney for the Rosenbergs. Bloch had told Julius, who had then confided in Tartakow.

Tartakow refused to testify in open court to anything he had heard from Rosenberg, and I continued to be wary of him. In my view he was a con man, and a single scrap of evidence from him was not enough to make us trust him. However, we couldn't afford to ignore Tartakow or any other source that would further confirm Rosenberg's espionage, and so we regularly kept in touch with Tartakow in prison.

In late February 1951, about ten days before the trial of the Rosenbergs, Sobell and Greenglass was about to begin, we reinterviewed first Ruth Greenglass and then David himself. In these later interviews, with the trial approaching, Ruth came forth with additional details on the involvement of Ethel Rosenberg in the conspiracy, and subsequently David confirmed these details.

In January 1945, when Ruth had asked Ethel why she was looking so tired, Ethel replied that she had been up late the night before typing the material that David had given to Julius—and that she occasionally had to do the same with other material obtained by Julius. In September 1945, David now said, he had given Julius his sketches of the plutonium bomb and other handwritten material right there in the Knickerbocker Village apartment's living room, in the presence of Ethel. (This contradicted his earlier statement that the pass had been made on the street.) After Julius had gone into the bathroom, read the material and pronounced it important, Ethel had gotten out her typewriter, put it on a bridge table and typed up the information for transmittal to the Russians.

Why had the Greenglasses waited so long before coming up with these additional details? The "last-minute" nature of the changes has caused skepticism for many years, but the explanation is simple rather than sinister. As the trial approached, and with their memories refreshed by the work of concentrating on the past, both Greenglasses found more details in their minds than had previously surfaced. The picture that they had first recalled in outline had now become filled in. Although David had initially and ineffectively tried to keep his sister out of the espionage story, Ruth Greenglass had put her into it since July 17. David's corroboration of Ruth's details was the last step in the crumbling of his impractical plan to refuse to implicate his sister and brother-in-law in the plot.

Since early June, when we had first informed the AEC that Greenglass was suspected of passing secrets from Los Alamos, a major problem had been brewing in regard to the technical testimony David was to give at the trial. Now the AEC had to decide what David could say about matters that were still top secret.

As the Bureau supervisor who had been on top of the Greenglass case, and as one of the few in the FBI who had been briefed on some technical aspects of the atomic bomb, I was sympathetic but anxious about the AEC's decisions on what Greenglass might be allowed to say on the witness stand. The prosecution, headed at this point by Assistant U.S. Attorney Myles Lane, was adamant that Greenglass had to give substantial detail on what he had passed to the Russians in order for any jury to be completely convinced of the guilt of the Rosenbergs; furthermore, that testimony would have to be corroborated by expert witnesses such as scientists from the Manhattan Project or the AEC.

In 1950, five years after the espionage, some of what Greenglass had told the Russians was now public, such as the size and scope of Los Alamos and the names of the top scientists associated with the project. Other material was so sensitive that the AEC wanted to prevent it from coming out at the trial; some of it, in fact, is still classified into the 1980s.

Greenglass had passed to the Russians four items that troubled the AEC. First, the sketches of the "lens molds": Though technically these were the least valuable, they had been "top secret" in 1944 and

1945. Second, the description of the implosion experiments: The Hiroshima bomb, an early model, had not used the principle of implosion, but the Nagasaki bomb had been an implosion device. The AEC had learned that the 1949 Russian device was an implosion bomb, and it was likely that the Russians had designed that, rather than the other kind, because of knowledge of the implosion experiments here. Third, a general description (in words) of how the Nagasaki implosion bomb worked: Though Greenglass's understanding of that bomb was not 100 percent correct, it was near enough to be considered dangerous. Fourth, the faulty and incomplete description of certain experiments called "levitation": These latter experiments were a major secret of the postwar era, and are still classified today.

On February 2, 1951, a high AEC official guided prosecutor Myles Lane through a six-hour debriefing of David Greenglass. Dr. James G. Beckerly concluded that Greenglass had pieced together his information from casual conversations with fellow workers at Los Alamos, and from scientific deduction; Beckerly also decided that Greenglass was telling the truth as he knew it, and there were no inconsistencies in Greenglass's story.

After this, the AEC decided that Greenglass could be allowed to reveal, in open court, everything except the levitation experiments; in particular, he could give his slightly wrong description of the Nagasaki bomb—and the AEC would make no attempt to correct it. This course of action was also agreed to by the congressional committee that oversaw the AEC, the Joint Committee on Atomic Energy. There was another safeguard: If cross-examination of Greenglass began to reveal anything new, an AEC advisor in the courtroom would notify the judge and possibly stop the proceedings, or enable them to be held out of earshot of the jury and reporters. The congressmen were worried that cross-examination of the expert witnesses called by the prosecution to verify Greenglass's importance—or those called by the defense to try to debunk what Greenglass had given the Russians—might also reveal some new data that ought not to be made public. However, the Joint Committee and the AEC seemed satisfied by Deputy Attorney General Peyton Ford's promise that the prosecution would work within the cautionary guidelines that the AEC was establishing for the trial. Everyone on the government side wanted the Rosenbergs prosecuted; it was a question of how best to go about it without further damaging the national security.

On March 2, just four days before the trial was scheduled to begin, the AEC learned that Irving Saypol, rather than Myles Lane (with whom they had been dealing), was going to be the actual prosecutor of the Rosenbergs. In conversations with Saypol over the next few days, AEC employees found to their dismay that Saypol and his team wished to conduct far-ranging interrogations of Greenglass and the two government experts. In reaction, Chairman Gordon Dean of the AEC made many last-minute calls to Attorney General Howard McGrath before he was able to obtain an agreement from Justice and from Saypol to ask the experts only questions that had been vetted in advance by the AEC.

As the conspiracy trial of the Rosenbergs, Sobell and David Greenglass opened, I was both a bit frustrated and quite pleased at what we had been able to accomplish thus far against this particular KGB network. My frustrations were that we had not yet obtained evidence that would definitely tie into the network such people as William Perl, Vivian Glassman, Al Sarant and Joel Barr, who we felt certain were involved; also, we had not even come close to others who were more peripheral but whom we suspected, such as William Danziger and the Sidoroviches. There were still tantalizing leads that had not yet been run to earth—I didn't know the identity of the "Aswan dam" consultant nor who might have worked on that "sky platform."

On the whole, though, I was pleased with our progress. Four deciphered KGB messages had led us toward members of the Rosenberg family and network—pieces of information that we had been following up since the summer of 1948 were now fulfilled. Despite the fact that we could not cite those deciphered KGB messages in court, we still had an overwhelming case against the conspirators based on the overlapping confessions of David and Ruth Greenglass, Max Elitcher, Harry Gold and Elizabeth Bentley, and a fair number of corroborating witnesses and some ancillary evidence. We had broken into the Rosenberg network and managed to disband it—at least in part.

12

THE CONSPIRACY TRIAL

ALL THROUGH THE SECOND HALF OF 1950 we at FBI headquarters had assumed that Assistant U.S. Attorney Myles Lane was going to prosecute the Rosenbergs; we were confident that the quiet and competent Lane would do a good job. However, in the early months of 1951 we learned that Irving Saypol himself was going to handle the prosecution. We'd put a lot of work into building this case, and we didn't want anything to go wrong. Al Belmont had been in charge of our New York field office before coming down to Washington, and he knew Saypol well and didn't trust him. Belmont told me he was convinced that Saypol was going to prosecute the Rosenbergs because a good deal of publicity would attend the trial. Saypol had been associated with the prosecution of eleven prominent domestic Communists for violations of the Smith Act, and he'd obtained a perjury conviction of William Remington (who had been named as a source by Elizabeth Bentley). Saypol had also had a hand in the conviction of Alger Hiss.

We already knew that Saypol wasn't going to honor the arrangements Myles Lane had made to protect data the Atomic Energy Commission considered top secret. The FBI had stayed out of that fight and had let the AEC handle it directly with Justice. Now Belmont issued instructions to all of us that while we should cooperate with Saypol's office, we should carefully consider all of the U.S. Attorney's requests before acceding to any of them.

We were also disturbed by the increasing prominence of the very young and inexperienced Roy Cohn, as Saypol's chief assistant. Obviously bright, ambitious and aggressive, Cohn seemed to care little about the careful preparation of the case we had been building for nine months. Just days before the Rosenberg trial was to open, Cohn angered many of us in the FBI by interrogating William Perl, on his own, and in the course of the conversation strongly suggesting Perl might be indicted. Perl, who had been somewhat cooperative with the FBI prior to this time, then hired a lawyer, who advised him to remain silent thereafter. I was particularly upset over this episode, and others at headquarters also felt that an arrest of Perl under other circumstances might well have resulted in a confession. This opportunity was now lost. From that time forward, the FBI viewed all of Roy Cohn's actions in the Rosenberg case with some suspicion.

The trial of the Rosenbergs and Sobell opened on March 6, 1951, in New York City. David Greenglass was technically on the indictment, but he had already pled guilty and was awaiting sentencing. I remained in Washington, but as the supervisor in charge of the men who had gathered the prosecution's evidence, I followed the proceedings closely. I envisioned the trial as an ordeal that would be long and bitterly fought. Although we thought our case against an espionage conspiracy to furnish information to the Soviet Union was very strong, it was the strongest against Julius Rosenberg. The evidence for the involvement of Ethel Rosenberg was less weighty, and the case against Morton Sobell relied principally on the testimony that would be given by Max Elitcher. On balance, we were relatively certain that the government's case would result in convictions of all the defendants.

The prosecution was represented by Irving Saypol, assisted by Roy Cohn, Myles Lane, James B. Kilsheimer III, and James E. Branigan, Jr. The Rosenberg attorneys were Emanuel Bloch and his father, Alexander Bloch, who was then seventy-four. The elder Bloch's practice had been primarily business-oriented, while Emanuel Bloch's reputation had been made in civil rights cases. Sobell was represented by Harold M. Phillips and Edward Kuntz, the latter an experienced and aggressive criminal lawyer; these two often disagreed in the courtroom. The Greenglasses had retained the O. John Rogge firm to counsel them, but were not directly represented in the courtroom.

The selection of the jury took two very long days, and an unusually high number of prospective jurors were excused either by Judge Irving Kaufman, who took a very active part in the *voir dire,* or on peremptory challenges from the prosecution and defense.

In later years there was much criticism of the jury in the Rosenberg trial. The basic complaint, which first surfaced after the trial was ended and which was loudly supported by the Communist parties in both Italy and France, was that there were no Jews on the jury; this situation was emphasized to show that the trial was anti-Semitic, and that the Rosenbergs were convicted because they were Jewish. This charge ignores the fact that the judge, the chief prosecution and defense attorneys, and many of the witnesses against the Rosenbergs were Jewish. It also does not take into account the makeup of the pool of veniremen from which the jurors were chosen. The trial took place in the Southern District of New York, which does not, as many people assume, encompass all five boroughs of New York City, where 2.5 million Jews lived in 1951. The Southern District draws from the boroughs of Manhattan and the Bronx, but not the bedroom boroughs of Brooklyn and Queens, where many Jews resided. Rather, the Southern District's territory includes the counties alongside the Hudson River north of New York City, almost up to Albany—places that were then largely rural, and not inhabited by many Jews.

Then, too, the trial record shows that the defense actually raised more peremptory challenges to people with Jewish-sounding names than did the prosecution. Gloria Agrin, at the time an assistant to the Blochs, and Roy Cohn agreed in a recent interview that neither side had actively sought or rejected Jews for the jury on the basis of their supposed religion, because neither side could be sure which way they might vote. Some might be sympathetic, while others might wish to convict Jewish "black sheep." What the defense tried to keep was people who had no connections, however remote, to military contractors or to the armed services. For its part, the government sought to excuse on peremptory challenges those who were in the arts or who appeared to be on the left of the political spectrum. As Agrin told journalist Ted Morgan:

> In a sense we were looking for iconoclasts, people who could stand up to the influence of the times. When a black juror got on, we thought, well, a black might be helpful, but a black alone, against eleven whites, it could go either way. We thought that with a woman on the jury, there might be sympathy there.

Almost three hundred veniremen were questioned and excused before the panel and alternates were seated. The jury included ten white males, a black male and a white housewife. None were Jewish —but I don't think anyone knew that for certain at the time of the trial.

At forty, Judge Irving R. Kaufman was one of the youngest men on the federal bench, and was considered among the most able. He had come up through the ranks of Justice, having been a U.S. Attorney's assistant and then a special assistant to Attorney General Tom Clark before Clark was appointed to the Supreme Court. In Washington we had some concern about Kaufman, who had the reputation of being pro-government. A pro-government judge might make rulings or take some actions during the trial that could result in the overturning of the conviction by an appeals court. But in the opening days of the trial, Kaufman's conduct was scrupulously fair; over and over again he admonished the jury to avoid the mistake of considering alleged Communist sympathies or Party membership as direct evidence that those charged were guilty. Kaufman was tough with the Blochs, but also kept a tight rein on the flamboyant Saypol.

In their opening remarks, both Saypol and the Blochs made some astounding statements. The U.S. Attorney went a bit overboard in calling the acts of the defendants "treasonable"—they were on trial for conspiracy to commit espionage, not for treason—and also suggested that they had delivered to the U.S.S.R. "the information and the weapons the Soviet Union could use to destroy us."

In his opening on behalf of Julius Rosenberg, Manny Bloch made the first of a series of tactical blunders whose cumulative effect all but vitiated the possibility of a vigorous defense. Bloch accepted the notion that David Greenglass and Ruth Greenglass had been spies, but rejected as shocking the idea that the Greenglasses could implicate their relatives, the Rosenbergs, in the espionage. In effect, Bloch told the jury to believe a major contention of the government's, that David Greenglass had been a spy. Speaking on behalf of Ethel Rosenberg, Alexander Bloch aggravated the error by saying that the jury should not condemn Ethel because her brother was a self-confessed spy.

The first prosecution witness was Max Elitcher, who was helping the government because of earlier fears that he might be prosecuted. Elitcher provided considerable detail about his long association with Morton Sobell; he told of the many occasions when Sobell had arranged for him to meet Rosenberg, and his conclusion that Sobell was providing classified data to Rosenberg. Elitcher's testimony tied both Sobell and Rosenberg to a conspiracy to commit espionage, and dated that conspiracy as having begun while the war was still on. Max Elitcher was subjected to some tough cross-examination both by Manny Bloch and by Sobell's team of attorneys, but they did not shake his testimony. Elitcher admitted that he had not told the FBI everything he knew in his July interviews, but rather had added to his story in October; when the defense tried to make it seem as if Elitcher had simply made up the details and stories that were most damaging to Sobell and Rosenberg, Judge Kaufman ordered the FBI's pretrial interviews with Elitcher to be given to the defense. Kuntz and Phillips, Sobell's attorneys, wanted to determine whether what Elitcher said on the stand differed markedly from what he'd initially told the FBI. They searched the transcripts during a long lunch recess, but could find nothing in the pretrial interviews that would add to their contention that Elitcher had changed his story as the trial had neared. Elitcher was dismissed from the stand.

The next witness was David Greenglass, and he was guided through a first set of questions by Roy Cohn. David answered Cohn's queries about his work at Los Alamos, his recruitment into espionage by Julius and Ethel (through a request transmitted by Ruth Greenglass) and his meeting with Harry Gold. In his brief testimony, newspaper reports said, David Greenglass presented a picture of a young man recruited into espionage by a brother-in-law whom he respected; that testimony also placed Ethel Rosenberg into the conspiracy, since she, with Julius, had made the request to David to provide information to the Russians.

After David had told the court what he had given to Harry Gold —some written information and a sketch—the prosecution asked if Greenglass could be temporarily excused from the stand, so an expert witness could corroborate part of what he had said. This was an unusual but effective move, for Dr. Walter Koski of Johns Hopkins and the Brookhaven Laboratory proved to be a good witness, one whom the jury could believe as having no personal stake in the outcome of the trial. Irving Saypol himself questioned Koski, and to the relief of the AEC and of us at Bureau headquarters, he stuck to a preset line of inquiry. Koski testified that at Los Alamos he would design a "lens mold" and would bring his designs to the Theta machine shop, where David Greenglass was the foreman, so that they could be made into actual molds under his supervision. The lens mold had nothing to do with glass, but was a metal device that "shaped" explosive charges so that their force was directed along a particular path and in a manner that could be mathematically described and understood. Koski said the entire lens-mold concept and its use at Los Alamos was classified; the AEC had allowed the term and the idea to be declassified for the purposes of the trial, after which it would be reclassified.

This idea of declassifying and reclassifying was so bizarre that Judge Kaufman asked the defense if it had any objections to the procedure. Manny Bloch said he'd read about the classification maneuver in the newspapers, and had no objections to it. (Other lawyers have later said they would have jumped on this point and attempted to ridicule the government's case with it.)

Koski's testimony emphasized that Greenglass had conveyed important secrets to the Russians—that is, he buttressed the idea that the secret of the bomb itself had been stolen. This was a significant contention, but the defense did not object strenuously to it, and did not present any witnesses who would say anything to the contrary— for example (as was later suggested), that Greenglass hadn't stolen anything useful because the Russians already knew how to make the bomb. (In fact Klaus Fuchs, who was, of course, a theoretical physicist, had told me in May 1950 that it would have been valuable to the Russians to obtain engineering details of the bomb to fill out the broad principles which he himself had supplied. Having more detail, Fuchs said, would enable the Russians to avoid the tedious job of duplicating our research.)

Koski was excused and Greenglass retook the stand. Shortly thereafter, the defense made another incredible goof. David was describing how he had written twelve pages of material on the Nagasaki bomb; he said he'd made a sketch of it that he'd given to Julius Rosenberg in September 1945. The prosecution then asked to introduce as an exhibit a duplicate sketch which David had made for the FBI in 1950. Manny Bloch got to his feet and demanded that this Greenglass sketch be impounded, "so that it remains secret from the Court, the jury and counsel."

Saypol dubbed this a strange request. Judge Kaufman noted that if such a request had come from the prosecution—to sequester evidence so that no one could see it—it might have become an issue in an appeal, but since the defense was making the request, that was rather unusual, but all right, and he granted the request. Moments later, Bloch interrupted the questioning of Greenglass, which was still on technical matters, to clarify his actions. He observed that he "was not at all sure in my own mind whether or not even at this late date, this information [which Greenglass was giving on the stand, and in the duplicate sketch] might not be used to the advantage of a foreign power." Now he wanted the courtroom cleared, and the testimony taken *in camera.* The courtroom was then closed off to the press and to spectators.

Why had Bloch made these requests? In retrospect, they seem to have been grandstand gestures designed to convince the jurors—and perhaps the press—of the patriotism of the defense. Bloch even said he was prepared to agree to the idea that Greenglass had passed important classified data so that the court wouldn't waste time and money establishing that. At this, Sobell's lawyer Harold Phillips finally had to object, "For the reason that I do not feel that an attorney in a criminal case should make concessions which will save the People from the necessity of proving things, which in the course of the proof we may be able to refute." The other defense lawyers also objected to the absence of the press, and Kaufman then let the reporters back in, but admonished them to use discretion when re-counting technical testimony.

But the damage had been done. Some jurors later admitted that Bloch's puzzling moves convinced them more than anything else that what Greenglass had stolen was of vital importance. By having had the sketch impounded, Bloch conceded the government's con-tention that secrets affecting the national defense were at stake, and added great credibility to what Greenglass said—and would say from this moment on, in regard to any subject whatsoever.

On the stand, after the uproar, David Greenglass filled in many details about the extent of the Rosenberg network. He recounted that Julius had told him that the Russians were paying for the tuition of a number of young scientists in this country who would later be used as spies. He described the payments Julius had given him after Harry Gold had been arrested, the aborted plans to go to Mexico, and his sister Ethel's presence at important discussions and her typing up of the reports he gave to Julius.

David came under cross-examination by Manny Bloch, and I was pleased to read in the Washington newspapers that David had stood up well under this strain. Rereading the trial transcript, I find some telling examples. In answer to Bloch's query as to precisely when he had told interviewing FBI agents certain incriminating parts of his story, David said, "Well, what I wanted to say is all these little details was something I remembered as time went on. It was just a few hours

I was there [at Foley Square, June 15–16, 1950] and I put down what I remembered without trying to conceal a thing." In response to a question about having taken money from Julius earlier that June, David told the court, "About that thousand dollars, I felt I was giving nothing [not providing any information] for this thousand dollars, I had plenty of headaches and I felt the thousand dollars was not coming out of Julius Rosenberg's pocket, it was coming out of the Russians' pocket and it didn't bother me to take it or the four thousand dollars either." In their directness, such answers were devastating, and helped shore up the government's case, rather than, as the defense had hoped, raise uncomfortable questions about it.

Next on the stand was Ruth Greenglass, who, according to the newspapers, looked cool and composed, well recovered from her burns. Her stories of the involvement of both Rosenbergs in the inception of the espionage were more detailed than her husband's, because she had dealt directly with Julius and Ethel during the recruitment. Also, Ruth's memory was sharper than David's; she remembered quite clearly episodes during which Ethel Rosenberg had typed up espionage data, or had told Ruth that she did so on a regular basis. In cross-examination, both Blochs tried to paint Ruth as a well-rehearsed parrot who was only spouting lines she had memorized—but they were unable to get her to stumble or to change her story from one recitation to the next.

On March 15, as the Blochs were cross-examining Ruth, newspapers announced the arrest of William Perl on perjury charges—that he had lied to the grand jury in August by denying that he knew the Rosenbergs and Sobell. The headlines noted Perl's connection with the Rosenbergs, and the New York *Times* quoted Irving Saypol, who said he expected to put Perl on the stand in the Rosenberg trial, to corroborate testimony from other witnesses; Saypol refused to identify those other witnesses.

From my point of view, the Perl arrest was a prosecution ploy of Saypol's which neither was well executed nor resulted in any reward for the government's case. Perl never took the stand in the Rosenberg trial. Having been warned earlier by Cohn, Perl had hired a lawyer who convinced him not to talk further to the FBI or to say anything if called as a witness in the Rosenberg trial.

Perl's continued silence made my own work more difficult. We were on the verge of tying Perl more closely to the theft of data about the "atomic airplane," and were concurrently meeting with the AEC and NACA on that subject. We were also exploring the possibility that Perl, while an assistant to von Karman, had removed secret files from von Karman's office, copied them and turned the copies over to Rosenberg. The warning to Perl and his arrest during the Rosenberg trial stopped us from dealing with Perl directly, as the FBI had done since the summer of 1950, and it also had the effect of stymieing further investigation into the Rosenberg network.

At the trial, Dorothy and Louis Abel, Ruth's sister and brother-in-law, briefly took the stand. Dorothy confirmed Ruth's story that in 1945 Julius had come to the Greenglass apartment and asked Dorothy to go into another room while he spoke to Ruth about what she later found out to be espionage matters. Louis said he'd received the four thousand dollars from the Greenglasses, had hidden it in a sofa, and then turned it over—still in its brown wrapper—to the Greenglasses' attorney, O. John Rogge.

When Harry Gold was sworn in, he first informed the jury that he had already been sentenced to thirty years in jail for Soviet espionage. Gold's testimony was cold, dispassionate and very convincing, as he spoke of Anatoli Yakovlev and the clandestine procedures he had been taught over the years. He described how he had been told by Yakovlev to initiate conversation with Greenglass in Albuquerque —by saying "I come from Julius," and presenting his half of the Jell-O box-top. Gold told the story of how David had asked him to come back in the afternoon, and how he had checked into the Hilton hotel for a few hours' sleep.

Later in the trial the prosecution did something so usual and ordinary that no one gave it a second thought at the time: the government wanted to introduce as evidence a photostatic copy of the Hilton Hotel registry card that Gold had signed. The date noted on the front was June 3, 1945—but the mechanical date stamp on the back read June 4. The prosecution asked the defense for a stipulation that would save a little time and effort. The government said it was prepared to bring the manager of the hotel, Fletcher Brumit, from Albuquerque to testify to the authenticity of the card; however, the defense allowed the government to introduce the photostat of the registration card as evidence without having Brumit testify. This procedure of introducing documentary evidence by stipulation is common in many criminal trials. But in later years, critics of the Rosenberg trial hit upon this hotel card and the stipulation as the crux of a complicated "forgery" which presumes an FBI "frame-up" of the Rosenbergs.

The key, the critics say, is in the disparity in the dates on the front and back of the card; to them, this is evidence of a clumsy FBI forgery.

If there had been a frame-up perpetrated by the FBI, I would have had to be at the center of it.

Let's look at what such a conspiracy would have required. First, we would have had to start out to "get" the Rosenbergs (whom we did not yet know) in 1948, when I first came across evidence that said that Joel Barr and Max Elitcher were both being recruited by the KGB. From that point on, any conspiracy against the Rosenbergs would have had to include almost every office of the FBI and every top Bureau official, and it would have had to do so for many years—especially during the crucial spring and summer of 1950, when thousands of pages of reports and memoranda were being produced—right down to the present day.

An FBI conspiracy would mean, for instance, that in 1950 we supervisors would have had to look into a crystal ball and see that 25 years later, in 1975, Congress would pass legislation that would enable the public to obtain copies of secret FBI files. It would mean that we would have had to "doctor" the evidence in dozens of matters, such as this small one of the hotel registration card, that are contained in the nearly 250,000 pages of Rosenberg case files thus far released to the public. Of course we didn't doctor this evidence, nor did we make a conspiracy of our own to frame innocent idealists in the persons of the Rosenbergs—the sheer, overwhelming bulk and sprawl of the files, as well as the occasional instances of FBI wrong-headedness revealed in them, make this point clear to any who take the time to sift through the evidence. If the FBI had been intent on making a forgery of the Hilton Hotel card, would we affix different dates to both sides, thus raising questions that might echo thirty-five years later?

The simple explanation of the difference in dates on the card is human error—and it bothered the Albuquerque agents and us in Bureau headquarters at the time, as released files now show. We sent agents back to the hotel to comb over old records until we found other registration cards from June 3 that also had the machine-stamped date of June 4 on the back; then we were satisfied as to why there had been a disparity in dates on our piece of evidence.

Not only did Manny Bloch not object to the matter of the Hilton card during the trial, but, in regard to Harry Gold's overall testimony, he did something that to us in the Bureau—and to any lawyer —was quite astounding: he refused to cross-examine Harry Gold at all.

"I didn't ask [Gold] one question," Manny Bloch later explained to the jury, "because there is no doubt in my mind that he impressed you as well as he impressed everybody that he was telling the absolute truth." The point was, Bloch said to the jury, that Gold had never seen Rosenberg—Gold had dealt exclusively with Greenglass and Yakovlev—and so really hadn't tied Rosenberg to the case. However, this tactic of Bloch's—granting validity and weight to the government's case while quarreling with a fraction of it—was a high-risk maneuver. As later writers, such as celebrated trial lawyer Louis Nizer, have pointed out, the refusal to cross-examine Gold is incomprehensible, because you never know how you might shake a witness with strong questions. Personally, I don't think Bloch could have changed a jury's impressions of Gold in cross-examination, but it certainly seems to have been a mistake not to try.

Some minor witnesses followed. Dr. George Bernhardt, the Rosenberg family physician, said Julius had called his office to inquire about vaccinations needed to go to Mexico. This corroborated David Greenglass's earlier testimony that Julius had insisted that the Greenglasses flee to Mexico. William Danziger and Manuel de los Ríos then added some details to the picture of Sobell-the-conspirator, by telling something of Sobell's behavior while in Mexico. Danziger reluctantly gave out the story of how he had forwarded mail to Sobell's relatives after receiving it himself. He also said he'd visited Rosenberg in the machine shop during the time Sobell was away—thus shoring up the idea that Sobell and Rosenberg were connected, and that Sobell's disappearance had something to do with the charges that at that time had already been lodged against Rosenberg's brother-in-law, Greenglass. Manuel de los Ríos told the court how Sobell had said he was hiding from the army in Mexico, and how he had solicited advice on the best way to leave Mexico without proper travel documents. These witnesses did not tie Sobell specifically to the conspiracy, but served to characterize his actions in Mexico as those of someone fleeing arrest.

There were also two expert government witnesses, both of whom had been at Los Alamos. Colonel John Lonsdale, Jr., testified that during the war the Manhattan Project was so secret that the government even wanted to keep people from knowing the name of the scientists there—Greenglass had given some of these names to Gold.

Lonsdale reiterated that the work on the lens mold was "top secret." Next, John Derry, a liaison officer to General Groves during his time at Los Alamos, pronounced Greenglass's sketch of the implosion bomb as "substantially accurate." Both of these witnesses, assumed to be neutral, backed up Greenglass's testimony and made quite an impact on the jury.

The last prosecution witness was well known to the press: Elizabeth Bentley. Basically, Bentley reiterated on the stand what she had told the FBI in 1945 about the group of engineers developed by Jacob Golos earlier in the 1940s. Bentley said that she had received phone calls from a man who called himself "Julius," and whom Golos described as the leader of this group of engineers. She recounted her earlier description of this man as tall, thin and wearing horn-rimmed glasses.

Bentley's testimony echoed that of the first prosecution witness, Max Elitcher, who had told the court that Julius had admitted to Sobell that Bentley might know him and that he had spoken to her on the telephone. It also supported remarks by David Greenglass, who had said that Rosenberg had mentioned that Bentley was a potential threat to him.

The original plan for the prosecution had been to call many more witnesses—such people as Dr. George Kistiakowski, the distinguished scientist in whose lab Greenglass had worked, and such probable Rosenberg networks members as Perl, Glassman and the Sidoroviches, together with neighbors and those who might testify about Rosenberg's difficulties with the Signal Corps. Now, however, Irving Saypol agreed with his assistant Roy Cohn that enough evidence against the conspirators had already been presented, and he rested the government's case.

Sitting in Washington, we wondered whether curtailing the prosecution's side of the case was a mistake. In most instances, shortening a case obviates the possibilities of making errors that can be reversed on appeal. The evidence already presented was quite substantial enough to prove the defendants' guilt—but a few things had been left out, primarily the stories about the extent of the Rosenberg network. When, later on in the trial, Saypol asked Julius Rosenberg about Sarant and Barr, the jury, not knowing these names because they had never been introduced into the evidence by the prosecution, was confused. Still later, in the aftermath of the trial, its shortness became an issue with critics, who saw its brief duration as an indication that there had been something wrong with it.

In any event, the Blochs got to present the defense's side of the case sooner than they expected, and did very little with it.

Were the Blochs just incompetent, as some later critics have charged, or were they severely hampered by what was available to them? As later documentation shows, the Rosenbergs themselves were the stumbling block for the defense. They didn't want their friends called as character witnesses, for example, and the defense attorneys had to rely entirely on their clients' versions of events and had no documentation to back up their claims of innocence. Also, no scientists would come forward to shore up the defense's contention that what Greenglass had stolen was not important information. Eventually, the defense had to rely on the tactic of putting Julius and Ethel Rosenberg on the stand and leading them through lengthy denials of the stories told by the prosecution's witnesses. For example, under questioning by Manny Bloch, Julius characterized the payments to David (one thousand dollars, and then an additional four thousand dollars) as partial compensation for David's share in their business partnership; similarly, Ethel put entirely innocent interpretations on her meetings with Ruth and her letters to Albuquerque. Julius denied that he had been engaged in espionage or that he knew Yakovlev. Manny Bloch buttressed testimony of this sort by asking Julius questions that elicited the details of the Rosenbergs' poverty —as if to show that someone who paid only fifty-one dollars per month for an apartment could not possibly be a spy.

Irving Saypol's cross-examination of Julius Rosenberg brought forth many instances in which Julius took the Fifth Amendment. When questioned as to whether he had ever belonged to any group that discussed the economic system of Russia, Julius refused to answer. Such refusals to answer questions were somewhat damaging to Rosenberg's credibility. More problematical for Rosenberg were his partial answers to questions from Saypol about his dealings with David Greenglass. Julius could not say why, really, David had wanted the five thousand dollars he had provided; similarly, though Julius had said he had asked Dr. Bernhardt about inoculations for Mexico on David's behalf, he could not venture an explanation as to why David would want to go to Mexico. Rosenberg also said that Greenglass had threatened to "blackmail" him if he didn't give him the money—which didn't square with Julius's protestations of his own innocence.

In his cross-examination of Ethel Rosenberg, Saypol used another tactic. He read to the jury portions of Ethel's grand jury testimony from the previous August, and asked her why she was now able to answer questions that she had previously taken the Fifth Amendment to avoid answering before the grand jury.

"I can't recall right now what my reasons were at that time for using that right against self-incrimination," Ethel said.

Saypol retorted, "Well, the right, as you expressed it, was that it might incriminate you. You said, 'It might incriminate me.' Those were your words, weren't they."

Emanuel Bloch hastened to inform the jury that there was a difference between a grand jury hearing—where a witness's lawyer is not present and the witness is compelled to testify by a subpoena—and a regular trial, where a witness testifies voluntarily, but the damage to Ethel's credibility was considerable.

One of the last questions that Saypol put to Julius Rosenberg during the cross was an apparently random inquiry as to whether Rosenberg had had any pictures of himself or Ethel taken prior to their arrest in the summer of 1950. Ethel Rosenberg also denied having had any passport photos taken. In the courtroom, no particular notice was taken of these questions—but it was a deliberate plant of an issue by Saypol, in response to some new evidence that had just been given to the FBI by jailhouse informer Jerome Tartakow.

All through the first months of 1951, in conversations with Tartakow over chessboards or on walks together in the prison exercise yard, Julius had been divulging details about his life to the younger man, which Tartakow dutifully passed on to the FBI. For example, Rosenberg was concerned because a woman had traveled (as Tartakow put it in a report) to "a distant city to bring funds to a man who was hiding there, but for some reason the funds were returned." This was a detail about Vivian Glassman's trip to see Perl that Tartakow could not otherwise have learned. Similarly, there was a Rosenberg story that he'd given money to a couple to open a business in the Midwest; the man was a former school companion and member of the Abraham Lincoln Brigade, who was now a courier for the Soviets. Tartakow could not have known that this background information fit well with the information we had about Anne and Michael Sidorovich. Tartakow also told the FBI that Rosenberg had said that, if convicted, he might be swapped for an American spy held in the Soviet Union.

On March 23, as the Rosenbergs were on the stand, testifying and being cross-examined, Tartakow sent a letter to the New York field office that said Rosenberg was afraid that the FBI would find a Manhattan photographer who had taken passport photos of the entire Rosenberg family just prior to the arrest of David Greenglass. This galvanized a large effort by the FBI. Agents fanned out over lower Manhattan in a search for a photographer who might remember having taken photos of the Rosenbergs in the spring of 1950. This search turned up a Lower East Side photographer by the name of Ben Schneider.

Schneider was located just as the defense was finishing the presentation of its side of the case. That came rather suddenly, for when the Rosenbergs' attorneys concluded, Morton Sobell's attorneys told the court that Sobell would not take the stand in his own defense. Sobell was, of course, fully within his right to do this, but as we later learned, his refusal to deny the charges against him on the stand didn't sit well with the jury. The Sobell team had no other presentation to make, and now both sides had finished the initial stages of the case. The government announced that it had two further witnesses who would rebut testimony heard earlier, the Rosenbergs' part-time maid, Mrs. Evelyn Cox, and Ben Schneider.

First on the stand was Mrs. Cox. Both Greenglasses had testified about an unusual console table in the Rosenbergs' apartment. It had been labeled to them as a gift from the Russians which Julius boasted was a platform for his microphotography, and which Ethel also used as a base on which she could place the typewriter to redo handwritten espionage reports. As a witness, Ethel had testified that the table was simply a regular piece of furniture purchased from Macy's department store. Now, in rebuttal, Mrs. Cox, a black woman, testified that she had noticed the unusual console table because it was far and away the best piece of furniture in the apartment. Mrs. Rosenberg (whom she liked) had told her it was the gift of a friend—which caused Mrs. Cox to wonder, one day when she saw it in a closet, why it had been put away.

Next, photographer Ben Schneider took the stand. He said he remembered the Rosenbergs because they'd come by his Foley Square area shop on a Saturday—a less busy time than during the work week—and because they'd ordered three dozen passport photos, a purchase of unusual size. (We speculated that Rosenberg had wanted such a large quantity of photos for obtaining visas to several countries and so that copies could be given to the KGB for recognition purposes in those countries.) Julius Rosenberg had told Schneider that he was going abroad to settle an estate in France. Schneider's testimony directly refuted Rosenberg's answer on cross-examination that he hadn't visited a photographer near the time of Greenglass's arrest. It also echoed the testimony of David Greenglass, who had earlier said Julius had told him to use excuses such as needing travel documents in order to settle an estate in France.

Members of the jury later said that the testimony of Mrs. Cox and Ben Schneider were quite devastating to the Rosenbergs, for the jurors perceived that neither of the two witnesses had any reason to lie. Their answers provided important, independent corroboration to what the Greenglasses had said—and refuted the Rosenbergs' claims to innocence.

In his closing summation, Manny Bloch effusively thanked both Kaufman and Saypol for "many courtesies" and a fair trial—this despite Kaufman's dozens of interruptions of Bloch's questioning of witnesses, and having taken over the querying of witnesses himself, and in the face of continual belittlement of the defense counselors by Saypol. Later on, when the defense sought to overturn the convictions on appeal by charging that Kaufman had been biased toward the prosecution, these blandishments proved important. To the jury Bloch said, emotionally, that only lower forms of life would do as the Greenglasses had done, and testify against relatives; he contended that the prosecution's case, based as it was on the Greenglasses, was simply an instance of relatives trying to drag down others in the family to save themselves.

Sobell's attorneys maintained that their client was innocent, and that his behavior while in Mexico was not tantamount to an admission of guilt, no matter how quirky it might seem to the jury. They painted the testimony of Max Elitcher as flimsy, and contended that it was not believable—and, therefore, Sobell must be found not guilty.

In his summation for the prosecution, Irving Saypol pointed out that conspirators are most often brought to justice because of the testimony of former associates who have, willingly or not, come over to the government's side. He said that in addition to the testimony of the Greenglasses, the jury also could consider as very damaging the corroborative testimony of Harry Gold, Dr. Bernhardt, Mrs. Cox, Ben Schneider, and the documentary evidence such as the Hilton Hotel registration card and the four thousand dollars that had been turned over to Rogge. Saypol told the jury that the defendants were guilty of a "terrible disloyalty, proof which transcends any emotional consideration and must eliminate any consideration of sympathy."

In his charge to the jury, Judge Kaufman admonished them not to draw any inference from his own behavior in the courtroom, and to determine guilt or innocence based on what they had heard. This instruction later proved to be of great importance during the appeal. Kaufman also cautioned the jury that he alone could impose the sentence; their task was to weigh the evidence, and they must not let consideration of his possible sentence affect their evaluation of whether or not the defendants were guilty or innocent of the charges.

The jury then retired for its deliberations.

In Washington, I reflected on a trial that had been neither very long nor very bitterly fought. It had taken a scant three weeks, and the rather inept defense attorneys had not really refuted one iota of the prosecution's contention that the Rosenbergs, Sobell, Greenglass and Yakovlev were guilty of conspiring to steal secrets relating to the U.S. national defense.

We didn't know what was going on in the jury room at that time. But twenty-five years later, some of the surviving jurors told journalist Ted Morgan about the deliberations. Vincent Lebonitte, the foreman, recalled that the first poll showed all twelve jurors willing to convict Julius Rosenberg and Morton Sobell, and eleven ready to convict Ethel Rosenberg. Wanting some clarification, the jury sent several requests to Judge Kaufman to view exhibits and to have the testimony of Ruth Greenglass read back to them by the court reporter. The lone dissenter on the jury wanted to have the panel recommend leniency for Ethel, but when the jury sent a query on this subject to Kaufman, the judge had the section of his charge that dealt with punishment read back to them. This part said that the sentencing was solely the responsibility of the judge.

The jury retired for the night, but after its return in the morning came in with guilty verdicts against all the defendants, including Julius and Ethel Rosenberg, and Morton Sobell. Judge Kaufman put off the sentencing for a week in order, he said, to give himself time to prepare.

I had been giving the matter of sentencing considerable thought myself. I wanted all three defendants to receive sentences that would bring them to the FBI, prepared to tell us everything they knew— which would enable me to get on with my job of uncovering the full extent of the Rosenberg espionage network. If the defendants talked, I believed we might be able to arrest and convict ten or fifteen more people. We had reason to believe the Rosenbergs and Sobell might talk after sentencing: in February Rosenberg had told Tartakow he would consider bargaining if heavy penalties were imposed; evidence from other, similar sources suggested Morton Sobell might confess if faced with the certainty of a long prison term. I had come to the conclusion that the correct sentence for Julius Rosenberg might be the death penalty, but only if in announcing it Judge Kaufman made it clear that this would be reduced if Rosenberg cooperated fully with the FBI.

I had also arrived at the belief, shared by others in the FBI, that no purpose would be achieved by sentencing Ethel Rosenberg to death. I had no doubt about her involvement in the conspiracy, but felt she had been acting under her husband's direction; further, I believed that because she was the mother of two boys who would be orphaned, and would become the focus of public sympathy, she ought to receive a lesser sentence.

It was FBI policy that special agents were not to make recommendations to the length or severity of sentences in individual cases, even though the agents worked closely with the various U.S. Attorneys' offices and had ways to get such recommendations into the courtrooms. However, Director Hoover did not always follow this "hands off" policy himself, especially in cases where he felt that a proposed sentence might be too light.

On April 2, 1951, just prior to the sentencing, Deputy Attorney General Peyton Ford called Hoover and asked for his recommendation on sentencing the Rosenbergs and Sobell. Ford told the Director that both he and the Attorney General felt that Julius Rosenberg and Morton Sobell should receive death sentences, but that Ethel might cooperate with the government if she received a lesser sentence. In a memorandum to Ladd and others, Hoover said he'd told Ford that his information suggested that Ethel would not cooperate, but that he was concerned about the "psychological reaction" of the public to giving a death sentence to a woman and a mother. Hoover told Ford he'd get back to him with the FBI's recommendations.

This generated a flurry of activity within the Bureau, most of it concentrated in my unit, which prepared a memorandum for Ladd to give to the Director on April 2, and another on April 3; in addition, the New York field office submitted its recommendations. All of these memoranda suggested the death sentence for Julius Rosenberg (as the leader of the conspiracy), and thirty years for Ethel Rosenberg, who, in the language of our unit's memo, was "presumed to be acting under the influence of her husband." The memorandum also said that Morton Sobell, who was not as centrally involved in the conspiracy as Julius Rosenberg, ought to receive thirty years. The memorandum gave some background for the severity of these sentences by recalling that Fuchs had received fourteen years, Alfred Dean Slack, fifteen years, and Harry Gold, thirty years.

The Director's final recommendation to Peyton Ford was for death sentences of Julius Rosenberg and Morton Sobell, a thirty-year sentence for Ethel Rosenberg, and fifteen years for David Greenglass. From a study of the extant FBI documents on the recommendations for sentencing, it is clear that no one in the hierarchy of the FBI who was at all connected with the Rosenberg case wanted a death sentence for Ethel Rosenberg.

Later evidence shows that the FBI's recommendations were conveyed by Peyton Ford to Irving Saypol, who, in turn, communicated them to Judge Kaufman. The actions of Kaufman in seeking recommendations and of Saypol in offering them have been criticized in recent years as possibly being improper, but such seeking and offering of sentencing recommendations were considered usual and completely legal occurrences in federal courts at that time.

However, it appears that Saypol's recommendation of a lesser penalty for Ethel, and of the death penalty for Julius Rosenberg and Morton Sobell, did not accord with Judge Kaufman's own views; at any rate, Kaufman then asked Saypol not to make his sentencing request in open court, so there would not seem to be disagreement between judge and prosecutor on the matter. Saypol agreed to this maneuver.

In the courtroom on April 5, 1951, Judge Kaufman described the crimes of the convicted defendants as "worse than murder." He said that the conspirators had put the A-bomb into the hands of the Russians "years before our best scientists predicted Russia would perfect the bomb." This had already "caused" the Communist aggression in Korea, with its 50,000 American casualties. "By your betrayal," Kaufman concluded as he addressed the defendants, "you undoubtedly have altered the course of history to the disadvantage of our country." Kaufman then sentenced both Julius and Ethel Rosenberg to die in the electric chair during the week of May 21, 1951, and sentenced Morton Sobell to thirty years in prison with a recommendation of no parole. The next morning Kaufman sentenced David Greenglass, who had pled guilty before the trial, to fifteen years in prison.

When I heard that both Julius and Ethel Rosenberg had been sentenced to death, I was surprised and shocked. Over the years I'd been responsible for a number of people being sent to prison. It was sobering to realize that two people might now be executed as a result of an investigation in which I had played a major part. I continued to believe, however, that one or the other of the Rosenbergs would save both of them by confessing to their involvement in espionage, and helping us bring to justice the other members of the network.

13

PHILBY

IN THE SPRING OF 1951, around the time of the Rosenberg trial, developments began that shook the Western intelligence and counterintelligence services to their cores—and which had a tremendous impact on me and my work. Out of these matters would come the sure and unsettling knowledge that the KGB had become aware of our once-in-a-lifetime breakthrough of their messages, and had taken steps to counter our efforts to roll up their networks—that is to say, that our great break was compromised. The treachery involved in all of this was monumental, and even after thirty-five years have passed, it continues to bother me.

The whole matter really began with the investigation into the spy inside the British embassy in 1944–45 which I'd initiated on the basis of a deciphered KGB message in 1949. As you'll recall, I was unable to get any action from the British on this affair for some time. In late 1950 or early 1951 some additional information from the messages came clear: it seemed that the spy, whose code name was "Homer," had met weekly in 1944–45 with his Soviet contact in New York.

Now, this was a clue that could not be ignored. "Homer," the KGB source, had to be a fairly highly placed person in the British embassy because he'd had access to top-level cables between our government and the British; when this new information about "Homer's" visits to

New York was added to his access to the cables, the result should have been to narrow the list of possible suspects drastically. Yet when I pressed Jeff Patterson of MI-5 to come up with such a list, he'd report back that London said there was "nothing new" on the investigation.

In this period I was seeing Patterson at least twice a week, and I saw Kim Philby, the MI-6 rep, perhaps once a month. I knew by now that Philby was concentrating primarily on the CIA, but my general impression and that of some of my CIA contacts was that Philby was quite lazy.

Philby, his wife, Aileen, and their four children lived in a big house on Wisconsin Avenue, not far from Mickey Ladd's home. One evening during the spring of 1951 the Philbys invited a number of people to their house for cocktails and dinner. It was, I believe, the first time Philby had given a sizable party since coming to Washington in 1949. There were twenty-five to thirty people in all. From the FBI I remember Mickey and Catherine Ladd, Emory and Molly Gregg, and my wife and me. The CIA group included Jim and Cicely Angleton, and Bill and Libby Harvey. Jeff Patterson and his wife, and Bobby Mackenzie represented British Intelligence.

I had never met James Jesus Angleton in person, though I'd heard a lot about him. To many people he was the epitome of the CIA, with many contacts in intelligence services throughout the world. We talked a bit. He was tall, spare, acerbic, intelligent and very reserved, but charming. I remember sitting next to Cicely Angleton, who had a cigarette in her hand, and having her ask me, "What Freudian impulse causes you not to smoke?" Nonplussed, I explained that I had a pipe in my coat pocket in the hall.

Generally, at the party, the FBI and CIA groups tended not to mingle, and chatted apart from each other. During cocktails I listened to a discussion among several of the CIA people which concerned intelligence priorities—blue-sky stuff. I found it too far out for me, not oriented enough toward reality.

I was more comfortable speaking with Bill Harvey, an old friend who had been with the FBI before going to the CIA. He described Angleton as very bright, out of Yale and the OSS, a real comer; there was something about Bill's portrait of Angleton, though, that wasn't entirely complimentary. Libby Harvey joined us. She'd already had a lot to drink, and wanted to share her disgust at the entire array of dinner guests and the party itself with anyone who'd listen. Somehow she became my dinner partner, and I spent most of the meal attempting to quiet her. She hated the typically British cold roast beef, and loudly said, "Isn't this God-awful?" about every detail of the food and service. The end of dinner came none too quickly for me, and as soon thereafter as we could politely manage, the Greggs and my wife and I left the party.

We should've stayed, for, as I later learned, things got more interesting as the night wore on. Guy Burgess, a British embassy employee who was living with the Philbys, came wandering home quite drunk and evidently intent on causing a scene. A flamboyant homosexual as well as a big drinker, Burgess evidently liked baiting people. He got into an insulting debate with Mickey Ladd—which Ladd probably enjoyed, because he was the sort of man who'd take part in the sparring while at the same time storing up his impressions for later use. But then Burgess turned to Libby Harvey. He said to her, "How extraordinary to see the face I've been doodling all my life." She invited him to sketch her portrait; Burgess executed a caricature so lewd and savage that Libby demanded to be taken home immediately. Bill Harvey had to be restrained from physically attacking Burgess, and was walked around the block by Angleton until he calmed down. After that, the party broke up.

Not too many days later, Burgess drove a car so wildly as to be slapped with several speeding tickets; he then claimed loudly, to arresting officers, that he could ignore the summonses on the grounds of diplomatic immunity. Burgess's actions precipitated angry protests from the Virginia governor to the State Department, which passed them on to the British embassy. Burgess's previous exploits in Washington had also raised eyebrows, and this was the last straw; he was called home to England in disgrace.

Then, on May 25, 1951, newspapers throughout the world printed the sensational news that Burgess and fellow Foreign Office employee Donald Maclean had disappeared and were presumed to have gone behind the Iron Curtain.

As soon as I learned that Donald Maclean had been in the British embassy in Washington in 1944–45, and had made frequent visits to his American wife at her mother's home near New York City, it was apparent to me that Maclean was the spy I had been trying to identify since the fall of 1948.

In a number of telephone calls back and forth between those of us in the FBI and the CIA who had been at the now-infamous Philby cocktail party, we speculated on the link between Burgess and Maclean, and worried about the more sinister implications of Burgess's having lived in Philby's home in Washington.

The day after the disappearance of the two diplomats was announced in the press, both Kim Philby and Jeff Patterson came to see me. To say the least, it was a rather uncomfortable meeting. I had already learned about the incidents that caused Burgess to be called back to London, and was trying to sort out the implications of the disappearance. My discussion with Philby and Patterson went nowhere; each of us was busy with his own thoughts, I expect. Mine were disconcerting: Had Philby deliberately, or even inadvertently, tipped off Burgess about our inquiry into the embassy spy? Was it possible that Philby was a spy? Had Patterson lied to me, and if so, why?

I must admit that I initially doubted that Philby was an *active* Soviet spy. I reasoned that a real Soviet agent would have worked harder at establishing closer relations with me and with the other key people; I understood that Philby had concentrated on the CIA, which was certainly a KGB target, but why hadn't he taken the opportunity to penetrate the FBI as well? Since Philby hadn't spent much time on us, I temporarily concluded that he must not have been an active spy.

My first reactions were clouded by anger—at MI-5, and at my friend Jeff Patterson, who I was sure had lied to me for some time. I conveyed my impression about Patterson's role to Al Belmont and Mickey Ladd when I sat down with them. We later found out that MI-5 had indeed held out on us. All during those months when Jeff had been reporting to me that MI-5 didn't have a good suspect in the British embassy matter, the British had, in fact, narrowed their investigation down to one man, Donald Maclean. But we still didn't know Philby's connection to Burgess and Maclean, although we concluded he had somehow been involved in their disappearance.

In June 1951 two high officials from MI-5 came over from London to see us: Sir Percy Sillitoe, the head of MI-5, and case officer Arthur Martin, who was then my counterpart. Al Belmont instructed me to push Martin for the whole truth of why MI-5 had kept the FBI in the dark so long about the Maclean investigation.

In our conversation Martin was so open with me, and so upset about having to admit MI-5's bad faith, that I was almost sorry for him. He explained that Donald Maclean's high position in the Foreign Office (head of the American section) had made the situation very sensitive, and that the F.O. had not allowed MI-5's investigation to proceed unhampered as the intelligence service might have wished it to. In fact, Martin said, the F.O. had insisted that the FBI not be told of the possible identification of Maclean as the embassy spy.

"I don't buy that explanation," I retorted. "You wouldn't have run any risk if you'd told us that Maclean was your prime suspect. We would have understood the sensitivity of the situation."

"I'm sure that's true," Martin said, embarrassed, "and we are very much aware, Bob, of your personal cooperation with us over the years. That makes it doubly hard for me to admit all this. However, I have for you now several memoranda which go into the background of Burgess and Maclean."

"Where does Philby fit in? Burgess was living with him."

Somewhat relieved, Martin replied, "Most of what I have to tell you relates to Philby. We now have the gravest suspicions about him."

The memoranda that Martin gave to me outlined the lives of all three men as they were then known to MI-5. Over the years since 1951, many details have been added to the portraits of Burgess, Maclean and Philby, but the basic facts of their lives remain substantially the same as when I first learned the details that June.

All three were born in the years just prior to World War I, to families that were essentially members of the upper class. Maclean's father was a member of Parliament and a sub-cabinet minister. Philby's father, St. John Philby, was a well-known and controversial Arabist whose exploits in the Middle East read like echoes of those of his contemporary T. E. Lawrence. Burgess was the least well born of the three; his father was a career naval officer. All of them entered Trinity College at Cambridge, with scholarships, in the early 1930s. There they became closely allied with the political left.

Burgess, already a practicing homosexual, carefully cultivated an outrageous personality. One of his close friends, another homosexual, was Anthony Blunt, who was also a very bright student of art history. Maclean and Philby were less conspicuous at Trinity College, though Maclean drew attention for an article in a socialist review that predicted the imminent disappearance of capitalism.

In 1933 Maclean suddenly appeared to have reversed his leftist sentiments; in an examination for the Foreign Office he did well on the written test, and also managed to field quite easily the interviewers' queries about his change of political heart. He entered the F.O.

Upon graduating, Kim Philby traveled across Europe by motorbike to Vienna, where he fell in with a militant Communist, Litzi Friedman. Together they helped a handful of Jews, socialists and Communists flee a 1934 government-inspired attack on flats occupied by socialist workers; after this, Philby and Friedman were married. Burgess learned, to his chagrin, that he was too old to take the Foreign Office exam, but landed a job as investment adviser to a wealthy friend's mother. Burgess and Blunt visited Moscow together in 1934. By 1936 Burgess was the host of a weekly BBC radio show on which his guests were primarily members of Parliament. Because of his extensive contacts—among them, the homosexual secretary of Edouard Daladier, the man who later became premier of France—Burgess formed a link to MI-5; he was a useful source of information.

Maclean received a posting to the Paris embassy and soon became its third secretary. Burgess was a success on the radio. Philby was slower at finding a niche; for a time he worked with the pro-Nazi Anglo-German Fellowship (another unexpected turn to the right) and then finagled press credentials and went to report on Franco's forces in the Spanish Civil War. He was wounded and decorated for bravery by Franco himself. Philby finished the Spanish conflict as a full-fledged foreign correspondent for the prestigious London *Times*.

In 1939, if the British Intelligence services had been more on their toes, at least two of the three men might have been uncovered as Soviet spies. This was because Walter Krivitsky, the recent defector, had been extensively interviewed by the British Foreign Office and by the intelligence services, and had given some particulars about people he knew to be Soviet agents. As you'll recall, Krivitsky had worked for the GRU and the KGB; he was the lifelong friend of Ignace Poretsky (whose murder had caused Krivitsky to flee the Soviets), and was the acquaintance of Hede Massing and the employer of Noel Field. Krivitsky established his *bona fides* with the British by identifying Captain John Henry King of the coding department of the F.O. as a spy; the British were able to catch King red-handed, and he was sentenced to ten years in prison in October 1939. Krivitsky also told the British that there were two other Soviet agents in the F.O.; one of them, he said, was a Scotsman of good family who had been educated at Oxford and Eton. He mentioned, as well, a third important Soviet agent who was a journalist, a man who had been with the Franco forces during the recent Civil War.

Now, Krivitsky's details were slightly wrong—Maclean had gone to

Cambridge, not to Oxford—but most of his information was correct enough to have identified both Maclean and Philby. However, neither Maclean nor Philby came under suspicion, despite Krivitsky's warnings. And two years later, in 1941, Krivitsky was found dead in a Washington hotel room, an apparent suicide.

At the beginning of the war, in 1939, Burgess, Blunt and some other friends from Cambridge all went to work formally for MI-5. Burgess kept this association when he returned to the BBC to continue his talk shows. In June 1940, Philby the war correspondent came home to London just ahead of the retreating troops at Dunkirk; Burgess helped him land a job at MI-6. One of the top men in that service, Colonel Valentine Vivian, had served with Philby's father in India, and evidently overlooked or did not know of Kim's pro-Franco writings and Communist associations; Philby was put in a special branch of MI-6 responsible for operations in the Iberian peninsula. Donald Maclean also returned to England after the fall of France, newly married to American heiress Melinda Marling. In London he frequented Guy Burgess's flat and often drank himself into unconsciousness. In October 1941 Maclean was shocked by the arrest of Communist Douglas Springhall on espionage charges; to keep Maclean in line, Burgess got him drunk and photographed him nude in another man's arms, then blackmailed him so that Maclean would remain in the Soviet employ.

Despite his bouts of drunkenness, Maclean won a coveted post in early 1944: first secretary to Lord Halifax, the British ambassador to Washington, D.C. He and Melinda moved across the Atlantic, and Maclean got into that position at the British embassy in Washington from which he did such an inordinate amount of damage to all of the Western democracies.

When we considered what information was flowing through the embassy in those crucial months near the end of World War II, we were staggered at the implications of Maclean's treachery. For instance, through him the Russians could have known ahead of time of the Anglo-American plan to have our troops in Europe halt their advance to the east at the Elbe River, which would have given the Russians a free hand in breaking through to Berlin and occupying the eastern half of Germany, unopposed. The Soviets would have been able to read all the cable traffic between Roosevelt and Churchill, and later, between Truman and Churchill; these cables set up the parameters of the postwar world. Especially of interest to Stalin would have been cables that discussed the configuration of the Balkans; the dictator would have known in advance what his Western counterparts' negotiating positions were at Yalta and at Potsdam.

Maclean continued on in his position at the British embassy in Washington until September 1948. He probably fed the Russians many details on the plans for the formation of the North Atlantic Treaty Organization, which was being discussed back and forth across the Atlantic. We learned that Maclean had been the U.K. secretary to the Combined Policy Committee, which shared information on atomic research and development among the English-speaking nations. From this post Maclean probably passed to the Soviets data on the quantity of uranium being mined in Canada and purchased in the Belgian Congo, which would have allowed Soviet scientists to estimate the number of bombs that the United States could fashion at a time.

Back in June 1944, when Maclean was in the United States and Philby was working with MI-6 on matters involving Spain and Portugal, Burgess took a job with the press department of the F.O. When the war ended, the Labour Party returned to power, and Burgess's friend Hector McNeill became the number two man in the Foreign Secretary's office—and chose Burgess to be his personal assistant. From this post, far more than in his others, Burgess was able to pass to the Soviet Union secret information affecting the national security of Great Britain and of the Western allies.

In August 1945 an incident occurred that might have blown the covers of all three traitors. Konstantin Volkov, the recently appointed Soviet consul in Istanbul, walked into the British consulate in that city, gave out a little information as a free sample, asked for £27,500 and a promise of asylum, and said that if his requests were met, he could expose as Soviet spies two men in the British Foreign Service and an officer in counterintelligence. He demanded an answer in three weeks, and insisted that Istanbul not send his information to London by cable because, he said, the Soviets were reading some of the British cipher system traffic. Volkov's demands, sent to London by diplomatic courier, were given to Sir Stewart Menzies, head of MI-6. Unfortunately, Menzies handed the assignment of bringing in and debriefing this important prospective defector to none other than Kim Philby.

Recognizing the threat to Burgess and Maclean as well as to himself, Philby decided that it was Volkov's head or their own. He managed to delay his arrival in Istanbul until the twenty-one days were almost up. By the time he got there, witnesses had seen a

Soviet military aircraft land at the Istanbul airport, take on board a heavily bandaged figure carried on a stretcher, and hastily depart. The prostrate passenger was most probably Volkov, going to his death at the hands of the KGB. Philby reported to London that the would-be defector could not be found, and the incident was soon forgotten.

Returning to headquarters, Philby told Colonel Vivian that he wished to marry Aileen—who was pregnant with their fourth child —but he was having difficulty obtaining a divorce from Litzi Friedman. Vivian asked MI-5 to run a check on Litzi; she was reported back as being a Soviet agent living with another man in East Berlin. This information did not dismay Colonel Vivian; he helped Philby get the divorce and marry Aileen and then gave Philby his first overseas intelligence command, in Turkey. One of Philby's tasks there was to infiltrate back into Russia two Georgian émigrés; one was shot while crossing the border, and the other crossed successfully but was never heard from again.

In the late 1940s Burgess traveled to Tangier and Gibraltar; his behavior was so provocative—unpaid bills, barroom brawls—that complaints about him were submitted to MI-5. Once again his mentor, McNeill, reprimanded him but shielded him from being fired. In Turkey Burgess stayed with Philby and Aileen; shortly after Burgess's arrival, Aileen suffered a nervous breakdown.

Meanwhile, Donald Maclean was going to pieces in Cairo, where he was appointed counselor to the embassy in September of 1948. As his marriage to Melinda deteriorated, he drank heavily and engaged in homosexual practices. One drunken escapade caused such a scandal that he was sent back to England, to a sanatorium, in May 1950. However, after he recovered. Maclean was awarded the sensitive position of head of the American section of the Foreign Office. At nearly the same moment, August 1950, Burgess was appointed first secretary to the embassy in Washington, and went to the United States to take up residence with the Philbys, who had arrived in October 1949.

The whole long story was incredible to me. All three men had acted so wildly, and on so many occasions, that it was difficult for me to comprehend how any competent intelligence service could overlook the danger they posed to their country's security. But for many years they had been promoted through the ranks until they reached high positions, and no one seemed to have been worried about them.

Arthur Martin also handed me another memo—a shorter one—in

which the evidence pointing to Philby as having been a Soviet agent was summarized. It listed the following facts and suspicions:

1. Philby, Burgess and Maclean had all been Communists or left-wing Socialists at Cambridge.

2. After graduating, Philby had switched to being pro-German; this was regarded as the sort of action taken while building a cover story.

3. Philby had married Litzi Friedman, an Austrian Communist and a known Soviet agent.

4. Krivitsky had pointed to a British journalist serving with the Franco forces as a KGB agent.

5. The Volkov affair.

6. The affair of the two Georgian émigrés.

7. Philby was suspected of playing a part in the disappearance of Burgess and Maclean.

I would have liked to interrogate Philby about all of these matters, and more, but he'd been recalled to England. In the United States, he would have had diplomatic immunity anyway. But from the moment I learned the details of his life and how they intertwined with the lives of Burgess and Maclean, I had little doubt left in my mind that Philby had been a KGB man for many years.

The ramifications of his treachery began to concern all of us. For example, we had a handful of sensitive cases on which we had specifically asked MI-5 and MI-6 for help. Fairly recently, we had instructed John Cimperman, our liaison man in London, to ask MI-5 to oversee meetings in London between one of our own double agents and a high Soviet intelligence officer. I wasn't sure whether Philby knew of these meetings. If he had known of them, had he compromised them? Counterintelligence always worries about the safety of double agents, especially when they go abroad; in this instance, we had to think of the worst possibility—that the Soviets might have turned the men back against us.

I'd never liked Philby, and now I began to hate him. The worst thing was that I believed he had compromised a lot of the intelligence advantage the FBI had as a result of deciphering the 1944–45 KGB messages. For years I had had the optimistic feeling that, based on the breakthrough that the messages provided, we would go on and on uncovering and rolling up KGB networks in the United

States. Now I understood that the KGB had to have known of our decipherment of the messages, and that our advantage was gone.

On a personal level, it occurred to me that the KGB must know about my work, and, in fact, about me personally. In a sense, I had been violated because they had penetrated my office in the person of Philby. Heretofore I'd thought that the KGB probably had a few facts about me tucked away in a dossier, perhaps as a result of the Eisler and Coplon trials and the publicity attendant on my interviews with Fuchs in London—but this was different. Now they probably knew my idiosyncrasies, and looked for ways to counter my every move.

I sat at my desk and tried to recollect precisely how much Philby had been told about the FBI's counterintelligence operations, and how much he might have deduced from conversations with Peter Dwyer (his predecessor as MI-6 rep) and Jeff Patterson. What about the techniques we were perfecting, the direction and training of our agents, our relations with the British, the French and the Canadian intelligence services? Philby had been in a position to know so much!

The reaction of the people at the CIA must have been one of even greater horror, since Philby had worked more closely with the CIA —but they wouldn't admit it. All I heard in my conversations with the agency officials and with our liaison man to the CIA were attempts to minimize Philby's access to sensitive operations. That didn't fool me: the FBI knew Philby had dealt directly with CIA chief Bedell Smith, with Bill Harvey and Jim Angleton, and with such men as Frank Wisner, head of the CIA's Office of Policy Coordination. Later I learned that Philby and Wisner had co-directed a joint Anglo-American operation that was to infiltrate into Albania bands of armed émigrés to overthrow the Communist regime. Over a period of two years, three hundred men went to their deaths in this tragedy. All the groups that attempted oceanfront landings were captured. Once a radio operator apprehended by the Albanians was instructed to send an "all clear" signal to his base in Cyprus, and was prevented by his captors from including in it a prearranged "fail-safe" signal; they knew all about the way he was to warn the next wave of émigrés. The result was another dozen men shot to death as they parachuted into the country.

Another possible instance of treachery was much discussed at the time, and might well be attributed to actions by Philby or Burgess. Douglas MacArthur and his intelligence chief, General Charles Willoughby, came to believe that the early success achieved by the

Chinese troops in Korea was due to their having secret information about the war plans of the United Nations troops. Both men were certain that the Chinese had learned of a U.S. military policy decision to hold American troops to the area south of the Yalu River. A State Department official later revealed that people in his department had had contact with Philby and especially with Burgess, and that one of the two men, probably Burgess, could well have passed to the Soviets the policy decisions and the American insistence on containing the war within the Korean peninsula so that it would not involve our major enemy, the U.S.S.R. Certainly, knowledge of these policies would have enabled our adversaries in Korea to allocate their military resources in the most effective manner against the United Nations troops.

By the summer of 1951, in my in-service lectures to FBI field agents, I was discussing Philby as a major spy; simultaneously, over at the CIA, Bill Harvey and Jim Angleton had no doubts about Philby's perfidy. In London, MI-5 also was convinced that Philby was a spy, though they couldn't prove it. Philby was interrogated by barrister Helmus Milmo and by my old friend Bill Skardon—but neither man could get Philby to admit his guilt, and without a confession, MI-5 had no positive evidence with which to prosecute Philby. The inability to prosecute was understandable, but MI-6's reaction to it was incredible: the agency pronounced Philby innocent because he hadn't been proven guilty, and did not cut off his connection with MI-6 right away. They supposedly eased him out of the service.

It was astounding to me that MI-6 would not concede that Philby had been a traitor. I guess they couldn't believe ill of a man who had been well bred and who was a favorite of Colonel Vivian and of Sir Stewart Menzies.

Today many popular books on espionage pin every dirty deed done by the Russians in the Cold War era on Kim Philby. I dislike Philby as much as anyone, but he's not the chief villain on every matter. For a very important example, in the possible KGB warnings to all agents associated with Yakovlev during the time when the FBI was closing in on Fuchs, Gold and the Rosenberg network, I think the culprit is not one man, Philby, but several.

The story is fascinating. In the summer of 1951, as we were trying to figure out the warnings, we knew two things: one, that the British had had access to our deciphered KGB material since 1949; and two, that Russian counterspies had been working inside British Intelligence at that time. From this we reached the inevitable conclusion that the Russians had known about our breakthrough on their 1944–45 cables perhaps as early as the spring of 1949.

The very idea was terribly disconcerting to me. I looked back and shuddered. I visualized KGB officers in New York and Moscow going back into their own files, combing over the messages that had gone between the consulates and Moscow at the end of the war. Of course the Russians would be able to read their own messages in the clear, to know the people whom code names designated, to understand which of them would be in danger of being discovered, and to warn their people of our actions.

Now I looked at the situations in time sequence. As we learned from Harry Gold, in July 1949 he'd received a typewritten envelope with the words "St. George Hotel" and a Brooklyn postmark on the outside. Inside the envelope was a handwritten signature, "John," which Gold recognized as a previously arranged signal for him to meet Yakovlev in a New York City bar in late July. Even though he hadn't heard from Yakovlev in three years, Gold went to the rendezvous, but no one showed up. (Yakovlev had actually left the country in 1946.) Most probably the KGB watched the bar to see if Gold would still follow instructions, and to discover if the FBI had tailed Gold. On Saturday, September 24, 1949, Gold was visited in Philadelphia by a Soviet whose photograph he later identified as Filipp Sarytchev. During this meeting Sarytchev asked him about his grand jury testimony, and returned to the subject at a subsequent meeting held in early October in New York. The Soviet wanted to know if any of Gold's friends had been interviewed about Gold since the time of the grand jury. Sarytchev warned that if any of Gold's associates were asked about him, Gold must make immediate plans to leave the country. Sarytchev set up another rendezvous for October 23, 1949 —but didn't show up at that one.

By October 1949 Ernie Van Loon and I had deduced from a deciphered KGB message that the spy at the British Mission to the Manhattan Project had been Klaus Fuchs. In my first memo to STOTT about this I mentioned, along with my suspicions of Fuchs, Abraham Brothman. I did this because of some clue within the deciphered message, which I have now forgotten—but the same point in the message may well have been noticed by the Russians. The KGB would have read the entire old message in the clear, months before NSA and I were able to do so, and the point about Brothman might have been the genesis of the Soviet inquiry to Gold in the summer of 1949 about the 1947 grand jury testimony, which featured Broth-man.

But who was it that told the Russians that we had deciphered the 1944–45 cables, allowing them to warn Gold?

In his book, *My Silent War,* Philby says that he received a briefing about the deciphered KGB cables just before he came to the United States in September 1949. If Philby's book can be believed on this point, that would put his knowledge of the cables *after* Gold had been sent a note by "John"; in turn, that would exonerate Philby from having been the source of the Russians' knowledge about the breakthrough. Of course, Philby could have lied in his book, but as I'll explain below, I think not. There was another, more logical sus-pect to be the person who first alerted the KGB about our break-through—but we didn't find that out until years later.

In 1951, recalling my conversations with Philby in the latter part of 1949, I was certain that he had told his KGB contact in the United States about our breakthrough on the messages. In addition to gath-ering some information from the FBI, Philby would also have spoken with the British cryptanalyst who was working directly with Mere-dith Gardner, and would have learned more from him about how the messages had been broken. Further, Philby's own background—his handling of cryptanalytic successes against the Nazis in World War II—would have given him an understanding of the messages' impor-tance.

Next in the chronological sequence of the warnings came a star-tling revelation to David Greenglass at Christmastime in 1949—be-fore Klaus Fuchs had confessed, and months in advance of the time that we identified Harry Gold as Fuch's courier. David was out of money, and he went to Julius Rosenberg to ask if the Greenglass shares in the machine-shop business could be bought from him. Rosenberg said the shares might be purchased because David was "hot," and might soon have to leave for Paris. Upset by this news, David wanted to know what Julius meant by his being termed "hot." Julius said "something is happening" which would eventually make it necessary for Greenglass to flee, and added that he himself might have to give up the place where he did the microfilming (later iden-tified as 65 Morton Street) in the near future. He urged David to get passports and travel visas to Paris for himself and the pregnant Ruth; when the time came, contacts in Europe and money for their escape would be provided, Rosenberg said.

Again, look at the timing: the KGB has anticipated that Fuchs may confess, that Gold can be identified from Fuchs's knowledge of him, and that Gold may confess and give the authorities a lead to Greenglass. And all of this before Fuchs has confessed anything to Bill Skardon.

Fuchs's arrest on February 2, 1950, made headlines, and immediately afterwards Rosenberg told Greenglass that the man (unnamed) who had served as Fuchs's courier in the United States was the same man to whom David had given his own information in Albuquerque. This revelation so startled David that Julius took him outside the apartment to discuss it further.

The forty-five-minute conversation between Julius Rosenberg and David Greenglass on the street in February 1950 was full of warnings and information which we later found highly significant. Several times during the conversation, Julius urged David to get away, and soon. Should the FBI find Fuchs's courier, Julius said again, Greenglass would next come under suspicion; Julius explained that the Russians always tried to stay six months ahead of the FBI, but if the Bureau was successful in locating Fuchs's contact, the FBI might move too swiftly for that much advance notice. David then suggested that the courier ought to stay out of sight for a while, and was not convinced of the necessity of fleeing instantly. David's resistance exasperated Rosenberg. At another point in the conversation—or perhaps in another one a month or so later (David wasn't certain about the date)—Julius mentioned Joel Barr, who was in Paris, and who had gone there because he was hot.

Thinking about Barr, I concluded that the Russians could have learned about my 1948 investigation of him after the British became aware of our information in 1949.

At about the same time as this long conversation between David Greenglass and Julius Rosenberg, on the first Sunday of February 1950, Harry Gold went to a small park near the Ninetieth Street station of the Flushing subway line in Elmhurst, Queens. The signals had previously been arranged by Sarytchev in early October, and as he'd been told, Gold was smoking a pipe and was looking to be met by a man smoking a cigar. A man with a cigar did come and passed by Gold and peered closely at his face—but no real contact was made. When we later showed Gold a photograph of Julius Rosenberg, he said Rosenberg closely resembled the man who had peered at him in February. So convinced was Gold of this impression that he tried to persuade the prosecution team to let him first appear in the courtroom with his pipe in mouth; thus arrayed, Gold believed, he might startle Rosenberg into making an inadvertent recognition of Gold and so give evidence of his own guilt. This strategy was not used, but Gold's contention adds weight to his belief that the stranger who eyed him carefully in February 1950, was Julius Rosenberg.

There are no known warnings between February 1950 and late May; I'll come back to the probable reason in a moment, but will continue on in sequence here. In May 1950, as I've indicated in an earlier chapter, on the day Gold was arrested, Gold's friend and mentor Tom Black received a message which he understood to mean that he was to make a rendezvous that would have something to do with escape. Black didn't go, but he was warned nonetheless.

Just after Gold's arrest became public, on May 24, 1950, Julius Rosenberg appeared at the Greenglass apartment, quite excited, and waved a copy of the *Herald Tribune* in David's face. It featured a photo of Harry Gold on its front page. David, of course, recognized the photo. Julius told David and Ruth that they had to flee immediately, and it was at this time that he issued elaborate instructions on how to get to Mexico City and to make contact there for subsequent escape to Europe and Russia; he also gave David the thousand dollars in cash. After consultation among themselves, the Greenglasses decided not to flee, but in the next days there were more frantic appeals from Rosenberg and additional money (four thousand dollars) to speed their journey.

Why, in February 1950, was Rosenberg doubtful that the Russians still maintained six months' lead time on the FBI—and why was he so sure that the Russians had had such sure information in the past? And why were there no warnings between February and late May 1950? As you'll recall, when Lish Whitson was denied permission to interview Fuchs in 1950, Director Hoover became irate. One of the actions he took was to order us, the supervisors, not to give any information about our own investigations to British Intelligence until the situation with Fuchs was resolved—and so, for a period of several months between February and May 1950, neither MI-5 nor MI-6 knew that we had developed Harry Gold as the prime suspect for "Raymond," Fuchs's courier. And if British Intelligence didn't know, then the double agent—or agents—inside those organizations had no information to pass on to their Russian controllers. After May 20, when Clegg and I arrived in London, the FBI again took British Intelligence into its confidence; this renewed contact may account for the warning to Tom Black.

If it wasn't Philby who first warned the Russians about the deciphered KGB messages, then who was it? In the 1950s, although we'd concluded that Philby had told the Russians about our work after he came to the United States, we didn't know who had given them the initial tip-off about our breakthrough. It has only been in recent years that the evidence has been put together to point to the most likely suspect. Here's a short summary of it: In 1945 Gouzenko had told his interviewers that there was a top Russian spy inside MI-5 (Philby was in MI-6). In the same year Volkov, the would-be Istanbul defector, had said to the man at the British consulate in that city that a Soviet agent was actually the "acting head of a department of British Counter-Intelligence directorate," which would also have meant MI-5. More recently, on the basis of evidence presented to secret tribunals and having to do with other instances of investigations gone astray and stymied, British journalist Chapman Pincher has published a strong case that the Russian spy in MI-5 was Roger Hollis, who in 1945 was the acting head of that section of MI-5 responsible for counterintelligence against the Soviet Union. Hollis actually became chief of MI-5 in 1952 and served in that capacity until 1956; he has since passed away. To me, there now remains little doubt that it was Hollis who provided the earliest information to the KGB that the FBI was reading their 1944–45 cables. Philby probably added to that knowledge after his arrival in the United States, but the prime culprit in this affair was Hollis.

Burgess and Maclean fled in 1951, and Philby supposedly continued on in Britain, free, but under suspicion. In 1955, in Australia, Vladimir Petrov defected from the Soviet Union. He knew a few tidbits about Burgess and Maclean, and on the basis of his information and the inquiries to date, a "White Paper" was issued by the Foreign Office. Member of Parliament Marcus Lipton then criticized this paper for its failure to cover the activities of the "third man," Philby. Lipton's source for the mention of Philby was Bill Harvey, the CIA man who had been so angered by Philby at the infamous party in 1951. Lipton's remark and press criticism provoked a lengthy statement by Prime Minister Harold Macmillan to Parliament on November 7, 1955; in it was one sentence that shocked counterintelligence men on both sides of the Atlantic: "I have no reason to conclude that Mr. Philby has at any time betrayed the interests of this country." After this,

Philby challenged Lipton to repeat his remarks in a setting where he would be outside the protection of Parliament and subject to a libel suit; Lipton was forced to apologize and retract what he'd said. Philby took this public exoneration as an opportunity to press MI-6 to take him back officially; he was accepted back and given a cover job as a stringer for the London *Observer* and for *The Economist,* in Beirut. In that city he found a new love and married her a year or two later, after Aileen's death.

But Philby's past was at last catching up to him. Dick White of MI-5, who had participated in the initial inquiry into the disappearance of Burgess and Maclean, was made the chief of the MI-6 service. When he found out that Philby was on the payroll, he couldn't believe it, and moved to have him severed. In 1961 White's efforts were given fuel by the revelations of a new defector, Anatoli Golitsyn, who came right out and named Philby as a Russian agent. In 1963 Philby sat through an interrogation by MI-6 which must have convinced him that he could hide no longer; shortly afterwards he disappeared from Beirut and surfaced in Moscow.

Thus by 1963 all three men were in Moscow. Burgess died there, of heart disease, shortly after Philby's arrival. Philby brought the wife he'd met in Lebanon to Moscow, but she left after he had an affair with Melinda Maclean; later Philby married a young Russian translator.

In 1967, under supervision by the KGB, Philby wrote *My Silent War.* There is a lot of disinformation in it, but it is so cleverly concealed that even as astute a man as Graham Greene, who worked with Philby in MI-6 during the war, wrote in a preface, "We were told to expect a lot of propaganda, but it contains none, unless a dignified statement of [Philby's] beliefs and motives can be called propaganda." The disinformation is an attempt to shape public opinion toward a Communist viewpoint on many events, not only those in which Philby was personally involved. For example, Philby includes a brief treatment of the Coplon case to demonstrate that the FBI was in a "sorry state" when he reached Washington in 1949; he doesn't mention that Coplon was caught red-handed in possession of secret information which she was about to pass to her KGB controller, but adds the spurious conclusion that the overturn of Coplon's conviction on appeal was "the triumph of a brave woman."

For another example, in a gratuitous comment on the Rosenberg case, Philby contends that the FBI had nothing to do with the tracking down of Klaus Fuchs.

In his chapter entitled "The Lion's Den," Philby disparages Director Hoover, Mickey Ladd and me, but admits there was a great danger to himself in our inquiry into the spy in the British embassy in the 1944–45 period. Perhaps Philby's stutter and coldness of manner in our initial meetings in 1949 masked his fear, and perhaps this fear kept him from being more active in his liaison with the FBI. In the book, Philby says his dilemma came to a head when Burgess arrived; he resolved part of it by deciding that Burgess might behave better in Philby's household than he would in a bachelor flat.

Philby also tries to make the reader believe it was he who managed to steer the embassy spy investigation so that Burgess would be called back to London and be in position to warn Maclean. I believe that is a deliberate lie. In 1950 and 1951, as far as the KGB was concerned, Philby was the perfectly placed spy with access to MI-5, MI-6, the CIA and the FBI; his value was so great that, in my view, the Soviets would never have allowed him to jeopardize his own position by becoming involved in the flight of Burgess and Maclean. In fact, in his book Philby writes that he was surprised and disturbed by the pair's escape, because their action so clearly aimed a finger of suspicion at him, Burgess's last host in the United States. Actually, it was "fourth man" Anthony Blunt who warned Burgess of the imminent danger to himself and Maclean.

One matter on which Philby did not need to give any disinformation was the laxness of British security checks. Philby was amazed (as was I) that he had been allowed to enter and to continue in British Intelligence despite a questionable background which included many switches in allegiance as well as a marriage to a known Communist.

I have always been struck by the lack of any sense of outrage in Britain at the treachery of Burgess, Maclean, Blunt and Philby. There have been very few expressions of disgust at the failure of the intelligence services to find them out. The reluctance to criticize has to do, I fear, with the inability of the British upper classes to believe ill of one of their own. For example, much of what Philby, Burgess, Maclean and Blunt did is chalked up to the deep disillusionment with the West and concurrent infatuation with Marxism that was common in their university set in the early 1930s. Crocodile tears have been shed over the notion that homosexuals were forced to remain "in the closet," as if that social stigma were reason to excuse treason. Even after Anthony Blunt's 1964 confession, he was allowed to keep his title and position as curator to the Queen's art collection, and many cabinet ministers were never informed of his perfidy. Blunt was, in fact, only stripped of his honors in 1979, when his role in espionage was finally made public. And Philby, the man who sat across the desk from me in the FBI's espionage section, lives in retirement in Moscow. I recall his treachery often, with disgust.

14
EXECUTION: AFTERMATH OF THE ROSENBERG TRIAL

IN THE SUMMER OF 1951 a new KGB message from 1944–45 was deciphered. It concerned a courier who had taken information from New York to Mexico City; the message gave the date of one particular trip over the border, and a few other clues that provided leads to the courier's identity. By reviewing border-crossing records together with some data already in our files, we were rather quickly able to come up with a prime suspect, a young New Yorker who spoke fluent Spanish.

For a few weeks our New York field agents tailed this man, but uncovered nothing unusual. We decided to bring him in for questioning, and to our astonishment, as soon as the man was interviewed, he confessed that he'd been a courier and named a close friend as the person who had recruited him for the KGB. We picked up the second man, who also quickly admitted his espionage work. We wondered why they had confessed so readily.

According to both men, the explanation for their panic had to do with the severity of the sentences recently given to the Rosenbergs. They had had nothing to do with the Rosenberg network, but when the first man discovered he was being followed, he'd told his recruiter about it, and they'd both decided that if interrogated by the FBI, they'd confess, in order to avoid heavy punishment.

In any event, these couriers were minor figures who never knew what information they carried to and from Mexico. From clues provided by other investigations, we were rather certain that the two men had been bit players in a failed attempt to free Frank Jackson, the killer of Leon Trotsky, from a Mexican prison.

Although both men had worked for the KGB, there was no evidence that either had violated the espionage statutes, which covered only the transmittal of information relating to national defense. We could possibly have prosecuted them for being in violation of the Foreign Agents Registration statute, but the Justice Department decided against it. We'd gotten the confessions, though, and we would never have done so if it hadn't been for the impact of the Rosenbergs' sentence.

The scheduled execution of the Rosenbergs, and the all-out effort the FBI continued to make on underground networks, was also inhibiting the KGB's recruiting efforts. Ultimately, in the 1950s the KGB was not able to find as many people as it had earlier to work for the Soviet Union's espionage apparatus against the United States.

After the Rosenberg trial, we continued to try to track down Joel Barr and Al Sarant, and I pieced together various odds and ends having to do with William Perl. He was under indictment for perjury, but we still hoped to find a basis to upgrade that to a charge of espionage.

Jerome Tartakow, the jailhouse informer, told the FBI earlier that Rosenberg had described Perl to him as a Russian agent, and said that the men who sent Glassman to see Perl in 1950 were actually Russians. We'd asked Tartakow if he could get more detail from his fellow prisoner about Perl, and he soon reported, through the clandestine channel we'd set up, Julius Rosenberg's boast to him that Perl had furnished information about "the use of nuclear fission to propel airplane engines." We'd been trying to connect Perl to the "atomic plane" ever since David Greenglass had first mentioned what I'd thought to be a fantastic idea to the FBI in the summer of 1950. Tartakow's corroborative story helped prove Perl's involvement in that "atomic plane" to me, although there was nothing about it that we could use in court, because Tartakow would not agree to testify about anything he'd heard from Rosenberg.

Another Tartakow story from Rosenberg was about a July Fourth weekend of microfilming. According to Rosenberg, Perl had come to New York from Cleveland, gone up to Columbia University and removed some files containing secret data from a safe; then, together with Rosenberg and two other men, Perl had gone to one of the apartments Rosenberg kept specifically for microfilming, and had photographed the secret data. Tartakow guessed that the four men were Rosenberg, Perl, Michael Sidorovich (whose name he had heard Rosenberg use several times) and a fourth man whose name Rosenberg wouldn't reveal because it was not known to the FBI.

As we checked out this tale, our excitement grew. Perl and Sidorovich had both come to New York from Cleveland over the July Fourth weekend in 1949. Records showed that Perl had visited the Columbia laboratory and office of his former boss, Theodore von Karman, and von Karman told us that Perl knew the combination to his locked safe and could well have removed documents from it. We discovered that after the weekend, both Perl and Sidorovich had extra money—Perl made an unusual deposit to his bank account, and Sidorovich purchased a car for cash.

We also discovered that Perl was known to have access to work done all over the NACA laboratory in Cleveland, and top officials there thought he might well have copied research reports on projects other than his own, which would have been of interest to the Russians. Later, in 1953, when a new MiG fighter appeared in the skies over Korea, the Air Force was chagrined to note that its unusual tail design was similar to an American design developed out of NACA antiturbulence research, and let the newspapers know that such research had been carried out during the time Perl had access to the data.

We were also able to identify Perl as the person David Greenglass had referred to when he said that one of Rosenberg's "boys" was an "Aswan dam consultant." Perl had worked for a consulting firm in New York on the aerodynamic calculations that went into the design of the Egyptian dam project. On all of these, however—the "atomic plane," the theft of fighter-plane tail designs, and the stolen research from Columbia—we had only circumstantial evidence, not enough to stand up in court to prove Perl had been a spy. So in 1953 Perl was tried and convicted of perjury—having lied to the grand jury about knowing Rosenberg and Sobell—and was sentenced to serve five years.

As for the fourth man in the marathon microfilming session, Tartakow believed he was also linked to Rosenberg's travels to Ithaca to obtain material from Al Sarant.

Now, this was an intriguing notion, one I was eager to follow up because it might give us something or someone who would more closely connect Sarant to Rosenberg and enable us to show the public the full extent of the Rosenberg network. Tartakow said that he had understood from Rosenberg that this unknown fourth man lived with another young man who was (1) the son of a wealthy family, (2) a former law student who did not practice law, (3) an acquaintance of O. John Rogge, and (4) the owner of a late model black Buick convertible with a white top, which had been used to take Rosenberg back and forth to Ithaca. The young man had driven the car because Rosenberg didn't know how to drive.

Rosenberg had also told Tartakow that Sarant's contacts at Ithaca were "Bedda" and "Morris." This was quite startling, because "Bedda" was probably Hans Bethe and "Morris," Philip Morrison, two of the United States' most distinguished nuclear physicists, who had both been deeply involved in the research on the bomb.

Klaus Fuchs had categorically denied to me that either Bethe or Morrison had engaged in his espionage efforts, but we knew Fuchs had been in touch with both men in the postwar period, and that David Greenglass had mentioned their names to Gold as potential recruits. After intensive investigations, we concluded that neither Bethe nor Morrison had been spies, but had probably been targets for Sarant—targets that Sarant was still trying to develop when the FBI entered the picture.

A black Buick convertible surfaced again when someone remembered that during the hectic summer of 1950 it had been mentioned by a man named Gary Pickard, who had once lived in the 65 Morton Street apartment that Rosenberg used for microfilming (and in which Sarant and Barr had once lived). Pickard had mentioned the car in connection with the day he'd moved out, when a man named Max Finestone had come to help him with his furniture. There had been two other helpers, as well, called "Bill" and "Bruce."

Bells began to ring all over the place as we thought about Pickard's interview. "Bill" was probably William Perl, and "Bruce" could have been Weldon Bruce Dayton, husband of Carol Dayton, who had run off with Sarant—and Finestone was also known to us. In the summer of 1950 we'd identified him as a man who had dinner one night with Vivian Glassman, and we'd interviewed him in connection with 65 Morton Street. Now, taking another look at his life, we quickly discovered that his roommate, James Weinstein, fit the particulars of the fourth man given us by Tartakow—the inherited wealth, the law degree not in use, the friendship with Rogge, and the ownership of the Buick convertible.

That's as far as we got in 1951, because neither Weinstein nor Finestone would admit to having been involved in espionage, either to the FBI or to grand juries that called them to testify. But thirty years later, Weinstein told his longtime friend author Ronald Radosh that he had, indeed, driven Rosenberg from Ithaca to New York once, and—more important—that his roommate Max Finestone had been fairly deeply involved with Rosenberg. Finestone, he said, had told him once that he'd dropped out of the CPUSA to do "secret work" connected with Rosenberg. Radosh confronted Finestone with this accusation, and Finestone denied it. "Even if I knew anything you didn't know," he told Radosh, "I certainly wouldn't say anything."

Many American Communists, and indeed, all of the Communist press in this country, hardly mentioned the Rosenbergs in this period, just as they had ignored the entire conspiracy-to-commit-espionage trial. The *Daily Worker* had never even mentioned the Rosenbergs until April 6, 1951, the day after their sentences had been meted out, when the paper protested the severity of the death penalties and maintained that the Rosenbergs were scapegoats for the United States' involvement in the Korean War.

This posture on the Rosenbergs was consistent with that taken by Communist organs in England, Canada and in the United States when Alan Nunn May, various others in the Zabotin GRU network exposed by Gouzenko and Klaus Fuchs were arrested and convicted of espionage. The Communist press in England took note of Alan Nunn May only after his trial, and then merely in an attempt to lessen the severity of his sentence. Around this time a Russian diplomat told Rebecca West that the Communist press of the Western countries virtually ignored the espionage cases because the hierarchy knew full well that the accused people were guilty, and allowed the cases to go without comment so that the furor over the actual espionage would quickly die down.

As we later learned, the CPUSA's stance after the Rosenberg trial was that the Rosenbergs were innocent of the charges, but that the Party would not come to their aid. Even after repeated pleading by Manny Bloch, the *Daily Worker* would not take up the Rosenbergs' cause. Party Secretary Eugene Dennis had recently emerged from prison, and spoke of fellow inmate Julius Rosenberg with awe and admiration for Rosenberg's espionage and his courage in not revealing what he knew. Cultural chief V. J. Jerome told Central Committee member John Gates at the time that the Rosenbergs were "heroes" who would go to their deaths and not say a word. "It was taken for granted," Gates said recently, "that [the Rosenbergs] were guilty. We had this kind of double thinking. They were framed. Because anyone who was indicted by the capitalists was *ipso facto* framed."

Sometime during the summer of 1951, Manny Bloch met with James Aronson, the editor of the *National Guardian*. Aronson and co-editor Cedric Belfrage say in their memoir about the *Guardian* that they became convinced that the Rosenbergs had been railroaded, and engaged investigative reporter William A. Reuben to write a series of articles to show (in the words of an opening paragraph) there were "strong grounds for suspecting the Rosenbergs are victims of an out-and-out political frame-up."

It was these articles by Reuben, printed in the *National Guardian* in the fall of 1951 and expanded into a book entitled *The Atom Spy Hoax,* that stirred up many people on the left. These provided the ideological ground for those who came to believe that there was "something wrong" with the conviction of the Rosenbergs and Sobell. Looked at in the clear light of today, the articles themselves are laughable. Their basic contention was that the Russians hadn't needed any information on atomic weapons from the United States because the U.S.S.R. was quite far advanced in the production of such weapons in 1944–45, and had simply delayed the test of the first Russian bomb until 1949, for humanitarian reasons.

A major focus of the Reuben attack on the trial itself had to do with the testimony of Elizabeth Bentley. The articles suggested that the "Julius" of Bentley's late-night phone calls was not Julius Rosenberg, but rather Emil Julius Klaus Fuchs, who was known to some intimates as Julius. This disregarded the fact that Fuchs did not arrive in the United States until December 1943, a month after the death of Jacob Golos, the man whom "Julius" was trying to reach through Bentley.

To me, the articles' concentration on the Bentley testimony revealed the bias with which the editors of the *National Guardian* proceeded in their series: the fact was that co-editor Cedric Belfrage had been described by Bentley, in her 1945 statement to the FBI, as one of Jacob Golos's espionage sources.

Bentley had been careful to point out that she had never met the source and wasn't sure of his name; at one point she had been instructed to get in touch with him, but the contact hadn't come off. However, she knew the man was British, that his first name was

Cedric or Cecil and that his last name began with a "B," that his wife had written a cookbook, that he worked for the British Information Service in New York and lived in the Bronx. Bentley believed that Belfrage had been recruited by V. J. Jerome, the editor of *Public Affairs,* the official publication of the CPUSA, and that he was a close friend of Earl Browder; she also charged that Belfrage had given material to Golos from the British Information Services' files, including a Scotland Yard secret instruction manual on the training of British Intelligence agents. As a result of Bentley's allegations, Belfrage came under scrutiny by both the FBI and Sir William Stephenson's British Intelligence office in New York, in 1945 and 1946.

The important thing was that the Reuben articles provided the fodder for a concerted campaign to make the public believe not only that the Rosenbergs were framed but also that the United States government was guilty of murdering innocent Jewish idealists. This campaign was ultimately of great benefit to the Soviet Union, and I'll discuss its probable instigation and flowering in detail a few pages further on.

First, however, and to continue chronologically, I want to deal with the opening step in the appeals process for the Rosenberg case, which took place in the early part of 1952, just after the Reuben articles had finished running in the *National Guardian.*

In January 1952 the appeal of the Rosenberg trial was heard by judges Jerome Frank, Thomas W. Swan and Harrie B. Chase of the Second Circuit of the United States Court of Appeals. The Second Circuit court was a bastion of liberalism, and Judge Frank was a highly regarded legal scholar, the leading authority on the law of evidence and the author of *Courts on Trial,* an analysis of judicial tyranny. The counsel for the Rosenbergs and Sobell had high hopes then that a panel chaired by such a liberal jurist would reverse the lower court's conviction of their clients. However, on February 25, 1952, the panel sustained the conviction and the sentences of all three defendants.

When I heard about the Second Circuit's decision, I was pleased; when I read Judge Frank's twenty-four-page opinion, which considered and refuted every one of the main legal objections to the trial, I felt that my work and that of my colleagues in the FBI were well vindicated.

To begin, Judge Frank quickly demolished the Rosenbergs' claim that even if U.S. secrets had been conveyed out of the country, it had been to our wartime ally, Russia, an action that was not covered by the espionage statute. Frank wrote that the statute did cover such an act, that it did not distinguish between ally and enemy in its language, that the words "National Defense" in the statute were precise and defined in such a way as to cover the actions alleged to have been taken by the defendants, and that communicating information to a foreign government was not a privilege protected by the First Amendment.

The Blochs' appeal contended that the government's case had been based on the testimony of witnesses who traded light treatment for accusations against his clients; they pointed out that David Greenglass had received "only" fifteen years, and that Ruth had not been prosecuted at all. Judge Frank dismissed this claim, holding that it was the jury's province to consider the credibility of the witnesses, not the appellate court's, and he cited numerous occasions on which Judge Kaufman had cautioned the jury to scrutinize the answers given by the Greenglasses and Harry Gold because those witnesses were admitted spies.

The defense charged that Kaufman himself had acted improperly, in such a manner as to deprive the Rosenbergs of a fair and impartial trial. The Blochs cited over a hundred instances in which Kaufman either had taken over the questioning of witnesses from counsel, or had said something to the jury that they considered prejudicial. Going over these incidents one by one, Frank concluded that Kaufman had "stayed well inside the discretion allowed him," and found no other purpose in the judge's questioning except that of "clarification." Frank also pointed out that Kaufman had charged the jury to disregard any supposed prejudice on his part and to decide the case only on the facts.

Frank tackled the notion that the issue of Communism had been wrongfully and prejudicially inserted into the trial. He noted that the introduction of evidence of Communist beliefs had not been irrelevant, because it addressed the defendants' possible motives for espionage. Further, Frank commented on Judge Kaufman's oft-repeated warnings to the jury that a defendant's alleged beliefs or membership in the CPUSA did not automatically mean that he had been a spy. These comments by Kaufman, as well as his excellent charge to the jury, Frank ruled, were enough to balance the mention of Communism in the trial.

The panel of three judges was agreed on the disposition of the Rosenbergs' appeal, but was split in regard to Sobell. Frank himself thought Sobell ought to receive a new trial. He agreed with the point raised by Sobell's lawyers—that there had been two conspiracies, the first involving Sobell and the possible stealing of navy documents, and the second (the more serious) involving Rosenberg, Greenglass, Gold and atomic secrets, but which did *not* involve Sobell. They said there should have been two trials, not one. Frank thought the jury should have been asked to decide whether Elitcher's testimony painted Sobell into the larger conspiracy or only into the smaller one. Judges Chase and Swan outvoted him, 2 to 1, and ruled that there had been only one conspiracy.

A less potent point brought up by the Sobell team was that their client deserved a new trial because he'd been kidnapped from Mexico and brought to the dock against his will. They had not raised this issue during the proceedings until after all the testimony had been taken, and Judge Frank ruled that in deliberately holding back on making this point until that late moment, the defense had taken a gamble and lost. The idea of the kidnapping could not be raised now. Judge Frank ruled further that even if the point had been brought up at the proper time, it would not have been significant. Sobell's conviction was also upheld.

The matter of sentencing presented legal scholar Frank with a quagmire, and he did his best to suggest that the Supreme Court would have to provide a way out because the appellate court could not. Writing for the majority, Frank cited the long-standing rule that if the sentencing judge had not exceeded his authority, and if the sentence given had been within the parameters approved by law, the appellate division did not possess the power to review or reduce the penalty. Actually, Frank's views on this point differed from those of Chase and Swan, and he cited some civil case exceptions to the rule of nonreview—but his written argument for the majority was nonetheless persuasive. Frank suggested that the Supreme Court resolve the matter of the appellate court's power to alter sentences, and even included law citations on which the defendants' appeal to the Supreme Court could be based, the most important of which was a reliance upon the Eighth Amendment's provision against "cruel and unusual punishment."

However, in another section the opinion had already countered the proposed citation of the Eighth Amendment's protections. The defense had argued that the death penalty was cruel and unjust because it was excessive, and had only been imposed because the defendants had really been tried for treason when they were charged with espionage. In rejecting this contention, Judge Frank in effect disposed of any Eighth Amendment arguments as well.

In sum, the twenty-four pages showed a Judge Frank who was disquieted by the death sentences even as he ruled the trial that had led to the issuance of those sentences to be quite proper. He had uncovered few instances of error, all minor, and nothing on which the lower court's conclusions (or sentences) could be overturned.

The very respected and liberal judge had not found anything that smacked of tainted evidence, nor any prejudicial instances of prosecutorial or judicial excess that were not later balanced. The trial, in the opinion of the appeals panel, had been just and fair. Taken on balance, the Second Circuit's ruling demolished on nearly every legal ground the appeal of the defendants, and held out only the slim hope that the Supreme Court might find a way around its conclusions.

In late 1951, before the Frank ruling, a small group of people, including some neighbors of the Rosenbergs, formed a "National Committee to Secure Justice in the Rosenberg Case." Some were swayed by the rhetoric of the *National Guardian* articles—even when confronted by the appeals court decision, they continued to believe that the Rosenbergs were innocent, that they had been convicted on the basis of bad evidence, and that they might soon be wrongfully executed. Soon, others long identified with Communist-front activities joined the committee.

One of the committee's principal speakers was Helen Sobell, wife of defendant Morton Sobell. At an April 1952 rally in Far Rockaway, New York, Mrs. Sobell first made the astonishing statement that the Rosenbergs could save themselves by informing on their friends but wouldn't do so, and then went on to contend that the sentences given to her husband and the Rosenbergs were warnings to "innocent" people not to espouse causes unpopular with the majority. Rabbi S. Andhill Fineberg of the American Jewish Committee tried to ask Helen Sobell why, if her husband was innocent, he wouldn't take the stand in his own defense. Mrs. Sobell fainted, and the discussion was ended.

Fineberg attended that meeting and many others because he felt that in it the issue of anti-Semitism at the trial was being raised— wrongfully, in his view. In fact, all over the world, the idea that there was an anti-Semitic cast to the Rosenberg trial was beginning to surface in publications and in public opinion.

It is significant to me that such allegations of anti-Semitism became common at the same time when actual and virulent anti-Semitism in the U.S.S.R. and its Eastern European satellite countries was at flood tide, in mid-1952.

The wave had first begun in 1948, when the aging Stalin took umbrage at the tumultuous reception given Mrs. Golda Meir by Soviet Jews on her visit to Moscow. Shortly thereafter, press campaigns were initiated against Jewish intellectuals, Jewish army marshals and what were termed the remnants of former Trotskyite groups. Stalin told his daughter Svetlana that the thread of treason led from America through Zionism to the many Jews still residing in the Soviet Union; Svetlana also overheard Stalin discuss on the phone the execution of at least one important Jewish figure in the arts. A "Jewish Anti-Fascist Committee of the U.S.S.R.," which had served Stalin in good stead during the war, was then dissolved and its leaders imprisoned; *Pravda* said the organization had been established by American intelligence. Foreign minister Molotov's Jewish wife was arrested and he himself was demoted, an action that began a purge of many influential older party members.

The strain of anti-Semitism was at first paralleled by and then intertwined in a series of bloody Eastern European purges of men who would not adhere to the Stalinist line, and who seemed to Stalin to be following Marshal Tito, who successfully broke away from him in 1948. There were systematic decimations of regimes in Albania, Hungary, Bulgaria and Czechoslovakia. In each country there were arrests, show trials, forced confessions and the execution of a few dozen people in public; thousands more simply disappeared.

In Washington we watched the headlines with grim fascination. In mid-1949, Albanian Vice-Premier Koci Xoxe was accused of collaborating with Tito, and was shot to death. Next, in Hungary, the Jewish foreign minister, Laszlo Rajk, was arrested. I was startled to learn that one of the witnesses against him was Noel Field—once recruited by Hede Massing—who charged that Rajk had worked for him in the OSS; Rajk and three other high-ranking officials were hanged. Similarly, in Bulgaria, a handful of men were publicly executed.

In November 1951 fourteen officials of the Czechoslovakian Communist Party were arrested, including the Party's secretary-general, Rudolph Slansky; eleven of the accused were Jewish. As these men were held incommunicado, there were mass resignations of Jewish members from the Communist Parties of Western Europe and the United States, in response to this and other obvious instances of anti-Semitism in the purges. This surge of defections reportedly worried Stalin and those in charge of the international Communist movement, for Jews had been among the most important Party members in the Western countries during the entire decade of the 1940s.

I believe that the KGB then began a disinformation campaign in an attempt to head off further loss of Communist Party membership among Jews, and to deflect attention from the anti-Semitic purges. This program used the Rosenberg case to divert the world's focus from the purges in the Communist countries.

There was already sentiment among some sections of the public that held that the Rosenbergs were innocent, or that even if guilty they did not deserve to die in the electric chair. What the KGB did, I believe, was to provoke, embellish and aggravate the idea of the Rosenbergs' innocence, to fan a few smoldering coals into a conflagration of protest.

Strong likelihood of KGB involvement in the hue and cry over the Rosenbergs comes in the timing of events in the latter part of 1952. All during the spring, summer and fall of the year, the CPUSA was silent about the case, even as it reached the Supreme Court for review and was rejected, and even as it was refused several other reviews by the lower courts. In November, however, things began to change, in regard both to CPUSA involvement and to the stance of Communist organs abroad.

It was in this period, scholar Adam B. Ulam writes, that anti-Semitism reached its height in the Soviet Union, with the imprisonment of Jewish intellectuals, former high party members, and "conspirators" from Stalin's home state of Georgia. In November the dying, near-paranoid dictator issued orders to arrest and torture fifteen Jewish doctors who practiced in the Kremlin—they were accused of plotting his murder and that of leading members of the Politburo and the Red Army. They were called "cat's-paws" for a powerful but unidentified international clique that had Zionist connections. Then, on November 20, 1952, the trial of Slansky and thirteen other Czechoslovakian Party stalwarts began. The Prague prosecutor summed up the charges by saying, "If we realize the true meaning of Jewish bourgeois nationalism from which the international Zionist organizations (develop) . . . we understand why Rudolph Slansky finds himself a prisoner in court." In case anyone failed to get the point, the prosecution said that the fourteen defendants were traitors, Trotskyites, Titoists, Zionists and agents of American imperialism. On December 3, 1952, eleven of the defendants, including Slansky and all the other Jews, were hanged.

At the same time that the trial was being reported in the Western press, and that the Rosenberg case was looking more and more hopeless for the defenders because of rejections by the Supreme Court, branches of the National Committee to Secure Justice suddenly began to spring up in many cities in the United States, and in other parts of the world. Before the calendar year was out, committees were formed in twenty-four countries, including Austria, Belgium, Denmark, England, France, Germany, Ireland, Israel, Italy, Sweden and Switzerland, as well as in all the Eastern European satellite countries. Jacques Duclos, chairman of the Communist Party in France, voiced the Party position by observing, "The conviction of the U.S. atom spies Julius and Ethel Rosenberg was an example of anti-Semitism, but the execution of eight Jews in Czechoslovakia last week was not." In France and Italy, where there were large Communist voting blocs, the greatest outcries were heard; articles in Communist newspapers had strong undertones of anti-Americanism—a line that echoed the Kremlin's other efforts to separate those countries from the NATO alliance.

As later evidence has shown, the main thrust of KGB disinformation campaigns at this time was to undermine the relationship between the United States and its partners in NATO. Soviet disinformation specialists Richard N. Shultz and Roy Godson, in a recent book, explain that one of those campaigns was an attempt to convince people that the United States had used chemical and biological weapons in Korea. Another had to do with the front group called the World Peace Organization, which claimed to have 500 million signatures on the "Stockholm Pledge," whose ostensible purpose was to ban the bomb but whose covert goal (the authors document) was the embarrassment of the United States, the only nation to have used the bomb in actual warfare. All these campaigns involved telegrams signed by European intellectuals protesting American actions, mass meetings organized by Soviet front groups, some well-placed forgeries and careful direction and timing from Moscow.

Those last aspects were also characteristic of the campaign to exonerate or to spare the lives of the Rosenbergs which seemed to spring into high gear, overnight, in the last months of 1952. In retrospect, it seems even more clear to me now than it did at the time that the signal had come from Moscow. The CPUSA and other organizations that had held back on their support for the Rosenbergs for so long then took the leadership positions in the fight to champion their innocence. In the winter of 1952–53 there were demonstrations in twenty-four different countries; these included candlelight vigils, scattered incidents of violence and objects thrown at American targets, mass meetings and parades.

Characterizing KGB disinformation campaigns, Richard Pipes, director of the Russian Research Center at Harvard, said recently,

> Public demonstrations are particularly useful. These are never spontaneous, but they appear as such and always receive public notice. A well-organized campaign can create a completely false impression of the actual state of opinion in a given country and sway fence-sitters.

Swaying fence-sitters certainly was the objective of the campaign to "Save the Rosenbergs." As time went on, and even as the Supreme Court again refused to hear an appeal, the demonstrations grew in size and furor.

Many of those in sympathy with the Rosenbergs had come around to the *National Guardian*'s view that the couple had been "framed." Most had not carefully followed the progress of the trial itself in the daily newspapers, but were willing to accept that there had been some foul play in it, despite the continued reviews by the courts that found the trial itself to have been fair and impartial. Other people were not so convinced about the Rosenbergs' innocence, but were adamant that they should not be executed.

Of course, not all of these people were "dupes" of the KGB, but the campaign to "Save the Rosenbergs" swept them along toward an objective that meshed well with the aims of the KGB. Let me jump ahead in time for a moment to bring in the views on disinformation of some highly placed Russians. Dissident Andrei Sakharov recently pointed out that the West is filled with people whom the Soviet state routinely uses to spread its views, including people who merely want to seem progressive, those who are poorly informed, as well as journalists and politicians who can be led down the garden path by their infatuation with finding and working a "good" angle on a story. Sakharov suggests that "diplomacy, information and disinformation services inside and outside the country . . . and all kinds of clandestine activities—all these are coordinated from a single center." His views are buttressed by those of the highest-ranking defector ever to come from the U.S.S.R. to the West, Arkady Schevchenko (a United Nations official), who said recently that journalists and public opinion are always the prime targets of KGB campaigns. The swaying of public opinion through disinformation has also been documented by defectors who worked directly for the KGB or for satellite country intelligence services in the 1950s and down to the present, such as Ladislav Bittman, Stanislav Levchenko, and Alexander Kaznacheev.

By the time Dwight Eisenhower took office in late January 1953, there were picketing vigils around the White House on behalf of the Rosenbergs. The war in Korea was still in progress, and I believe that the KGB or anyone else could well have anticipated that the liberator of Europe and former General of the Armies would be inclined to reject an appeal for clemency.

Not everyone wanted the Rosenbergs freed. The majority of people still agreed that they had been fairly convicted. Columnist Dorothy Thompson wrote that the Rosenberg case was being used to deflect attention from the anti-Semitic trials in Eastern Europe; she also predicted that the Rosenbergs "will die because the Communist Party under whose discipline they stood wants them to die rather than open their mouths. . . . They are indeed victims," Thompson concluded, "but they are not victims of American justice but of the monstrous organization they elected to serve."

On February 11, 1953, Eisenhower refused clemency—a matter that had been left for him by President Harry Truman—and said in a printed statement that the Rosenbergs had been tried by jury and their appeal rejected many times; his statement concluded, "The nature of the crime for which [the Rosenbergs] have been found guilty . . . involves the betrayal of the whole nation. . . . By their act these two individuals have in fact betrayed the cause of freedom for which free men are fighting and dying at this very hour."

Those were my sentiments as well, and I was very glad to have the President state them in so forthright a manner.

In mid-April of 1953 two "new" pieces of evidence suddenly surfaced which, the defense claimed, strengthened their contention that the Rosenbergs had been wrongfully convicted. The first item was the console table: government witnesses had said it was a gift from the Russians used for microfilming; the defense insisted it was an innocuous purchase from Macy's. As the story became known to the public, the table was supposedly found by the *National Guardian*'s reporters in the home of Julius's mother, who didn't read English and so hadn't known the table was an important piece of evidence. Since the table had some markings that could have come from Macy's, and since it wasn't hollowed out as Ruth Greenglass had testified, the defense claimed the table showed the Rosenbergs' innocence. The second evidence was several memoranda stolen from the office files of Greenglass attorney O. John Rogge and printed in the French Communist paper *Le Combat;* according to the defense, these showed that (1) Greenglass said he wasn't certain, the morning after his arrest, that what he'd told the FBI was the truth, and (2) that the Rogge firm had made a deal that allowed Ruth Greenglass to testify falsely about the Rosenbergs in exchange for being allowed to remain free.

In the left-wing press there was a great furor over these "new" pieces of evidence, a furor that has lasted to the present day, when both are still cited by critics as supporting charges of frame-up. At the time, we in the FBI were convinced that this "so-called" new evidence was a sham, and time has since proved that we were correct. (The later examination showed that the console table had three minuscule holes in it—a detail that matched the description of a table Rosenberg had told informer Tartakow he hoped the FBI wouldn't find. Similarly, whoever stole the Rogge memos and gave them to *Le Combat* had removed the second page of a three-page memo; when that page was restored and the memo read in its entirety, it showed that David Greenglass had merely been expressing his doubts about the *technical* accuracy of what he'd told the FBI in regard to his dealings with Harry Gold, five years previous—not that he'd lied to the FBI.) In 1953 Judge Kaufman ruled on June 8 that the two items did not raise substantial questions about the defendants' guilt, and would not have been enough to alter the verdict of the trial; he denied the request for a new trial.

Two days after Judge Kaufman's ruling, on June 10, 1953, the appeals court confirmed Kaufman's decision and refused to hear motions for dismissal or to stay the execution date, then planned for June 18.

Between the June 10 and 18 there were hundreds of demonstrations of support for the Rosenbergs around the world. In Paris a teenager was shot and 386 people were arrested as tens of thousands took to the streets. Two Molotov cocktails were hurled through a window of the U.S. Information Service office in Dublin. In London a thousand protesters blocked traffic. In Turin, Italy, and throughout that country there was a fifteen-minute nationwide strike; police and firemen battled mobs with clubs and hoses. In East Berlin my old adversary Gerhart Eisler publicly addressed a save-the-Rosenbergs rally; he dubbed the case a clear example of American anti-Semitism and compared it to the Dreyfus affair in turn-of-the-century France. There were enormous demonstrations in Poland, the Scandinavian countries, and as far away as Australia.

Were all of these demonstrations KGB-led? I can't prove that, but I do believe the KGB had a hand in exacerbating public sentiment and in orchestrating the protests. On the issue of the Rosenbergs, as with so many others, people who held moderate positions kept getting swept up into the furor raised by those with more extreme views. Many perfectly reasonable people felt then that the real issue was no longer the possible innocence of the Rosenbergs, but rather that they should not be executed. One of these was Albert Einstein. He had written a public letter stating that the United States' moral stance would be well served if the Rosenbergs were allowed to live —but that spring of 1953, when the Committee to Secure Justice pressured him for an affidavit that would say that Greenglass's sketch of the bomb had been nonsense, Einstein refused, saying he thought that the cause had become "Communist-inspired."

Just before the executions were to take place, two new lawyers for the Rosenbergs got into the act, and their efforts resulted in a stay of execution issued by Justice William O. Douglas of the Supreme Court on June 17, 1953.

Behind-the-scenes maneuvering among the Court's justices had been going on for some time; in fact, Douglas had previously voted against hearing arguments presented by the Blochs on five separate occasions. This time, however, Douglas was apparently convinced of the worth of a new argument: that the Rosenbergs might have been tried under the wrong statute. The lawyers now argued that the Rosenbergs' crimes should have been subsumed under the Atomic Energy Act of 1946, which did not then carry the death penalty. Thus, on June 17, acting alone and without consultation with the full Court, Douglas granted the stay.

The Court was actually in recess, and Douglas's action would have meant a reprieve for the Rosenbergs until the fall. Justices Frankfurter and Jackson were outraged by Douglas's ruling, which they regarded as a grandstand play aimed at Douglas's liberal constituency. Chief Justice Fred Vinson, in an unprecedented action of his own, called all the justices back for a special session on June 18. Douglas barely made it, and another justice got out of a hospital bed to attend.

The full Court considered whether the Rosenbergs had been tried correctly under the Espionage Act, or incorrectly. After hearing arguments, the justices voted, six to three, to vacate the stay granted by Douglas, and by so doing, to reimpose the death sentence. In chambers, Justice Burton had originally favored continuing the stay (so as to hear more arguments), but had switched his vote to go with the majority. The three remaining minority votes (Frankfurter, Black, Douglas) were not necessarily convinced of the merits of the argument; some also wished for more time to study the matter. Writing for the majority, Justice Jackson pointed out that the main overt acts of the conspiracy took place prior to the 1946 Atomic Energy Act; had the Rosenbergs been prosecuted under the 1946 law, it would in fact have violated the constitutional prohibition against *ex post facto* laws.

The decision of the Supreme Court was made public on Friday morning, June 19, and since President Eisenhower had already expressed in advance his views on clemency, the Rosenbergs' execution was scheduled for early that same evening.

The case had now been reviewed, at least in part, seven times by the Supreme Court, and sixteen other times by applications to various lower courts. More than two years had elapsed between the time that the Rosenbergs had been convicted and the time they were to die.

Al Belmont had gone up to Sing Sing to be available if either or both of the Rosenbergs should decide to save themselves by confessing, and to be on hand as the expert if the question should arise whether or not a last-minute confession was actually furnishing substantial information on espionage. I was sitting in Mickey Ladd's office, with several other people; we had an open telephone line to Belmont in Sing Sing, and as the final minutes came closer, the tension mounted. I wanted very much for the Rosenbergs to confess —we all did—but I was fairly well convinced by this time that they wished to become martyrs, and that the KGB knew damned well that the U.S.S.R. would be better off if their lips were sealed tight. Belmont telephoned us to say that the Rosenbergs had refused for the last time to save themselves by confession. Julius was reported dead to us at 8:05 P.M., and Ethel at 8:15 P.M.

As we got up to leave the office, one of my associates, a man who hadn't been directly involved in the case, made a gross remark in a grisly attempt at humor. I whirled on him in anger, but Ladd raised his hand at me, a sign that said I should let it go. I turned and walked out the door. I felt, not satisfaction, but defeat. I knew the Rosenbergs were guilty, but that did not lessen my sense of grim responsibility at their deaths.

The ugly fact remains that the Rosenberg case was not closed by the deaths of Julius and Ethel. For into the popular mind had been inserted the belief that there had been something wrong with the case, that the Rosenbergs had been "framed" by the witch-hunting FBI, that the vindictive United States had "murdered" two innocent Jewish idealists and made a mockery of freedom and justice in America. That these abominable and untruthful ideas have survived through the 1950s and down to the present day, despite repeated attempts to reveal and to document the facts of the case and the evidence of the Rosenbergs' espionage, is verification of the magnitude of the propaganda victory for the KGB.

15

THREE STRIKES

BY MID-1953 and the end of the string of cases that had begun with Klaus Fuchs and ended with the Rosenbergs, I was known within the FBI and to the intelligence community as an experienced counterintelligence specialist. However, under the system Director Hoover ran, a specialist was not highly regarded; rather, he was sometimes looked upon as a man who had been in the same job too long. The Director believed in generalists, men who could deal equally well with a criminal case one minute and a security case the next; we were supposed to be interchangeable and able to handle any assignment.

I'd been at headquarters for six years, most recently as head of a group of supervisors on major cases, and I was getting a bit restive about my overall future within the Bureau. I discussed the possibilities of being advanced in the hierarchy with Assistant Director Al Belmont, the head of my division. Belmont made it clear that he regarded my chief value to the FBI as a counterintelligence specialist, and that I should continue as such. While I agreed with him in principle—it took a lot of training and experience to handle these cases, which were unlike any of the others the Bureau saw—at times I was somewhat chagrined to have stayed behind in headquarters

while a number of men who'd worked under me received promotions in rank and good assignments in the field.

The Bureau ladder of promotions was well established. After being
a supervisor, you became the ASAC of a small field office. The next
rung took you back to headquarters as an inspector in the Inspection
Division. Then you were evaluated and, if deemed good enough, sent
to the field again as the SAC of a small office. From there you worked
up to the direction of larger and more important field offices. The
criterion for advancement was managerial ability. I thought I'd
proved my worth as a manager by three years of supervising a group
of other supervisors! What had happened was that I'd become too
valuable where I was, and there was no place for me to go.

Staying where I was had also brought me into more and more
brushes with the FBI's disciplinary system. Two of my closest friends
had just left the FBI for other government jobs because they no
longer wished to fight the Bureau's strictures. At headquarters, far
more easily than in the field, you could get into trouble, even over
matters that weren't your fault. I'd watched unhappily as Howard
Fletcher, one of the best men I knew, had received an undeserved
reduction in grade and a punitive transfer. More recently, I'd been
through a divisional inspection in which Director Hoover had given
orders in advance that things were to be found wanting, so he could
justify a shake-up.

Actually, I had been fairly lucky in my run-ins with the disciplinary
system thus far. After a dozen years in the Bureau I only had a few
letters of censure in my personal file—that was considered equiva-
lent to a spotless record.

As described earlier, one letter of censure had come out of my
work on the Fuchs case summary brief. The second and third were
more recent and no less characteristic of the system. In the divisional
shake-up, the inspectors discovered that one of my memos had been
composed of information from two related cases. Nobody had any
problems with the memo. But the man reviewing the file believed
I'd breached Bureau procedure by having written the memo and not
having also sent a letter of criticism to the field agent who'd originally
handled one of the cases and who, in his report, hadn't included data
from the companion case. I told the inspector's aide that I was certain
the field agent would correct this in a subsequent report, and so
hadn't criticized him. For not having raked the field agent over the
coals, I received my second letter of censure.

I was due to get a raise within a few months, and the letter of censure would have precluded that. I went in to Al Belmont and started shouting. The Administrative Division had reduced my efficiency rating from Excellent to Very Good on the strength of this stupid censure, and I told Belmont that I was going to resign and go to work for the CIA if I didn't get my raise. Harvey, Angleton and some of my other friends at the CIA would appreciate my ability and experience even if the Bureau didn't. Belmont let me blow off steam that day, but on the next lectured me about losing my temper and threatening to desert the FBI for the much-disliked CIA. I quietly told him that if the raise didn't come through, I was walking. Belmont then worked some sort of bureaucratic miracle, and I got my raise; a few months later I received two more raises, one awarded on merit by the Director himself, and the second, a grade increase.

I was very lucky to get what I wanted after spouting off, but I knew better than to ever try that ploy again.

I then ran into Helen Gandy, the much-feared secretary to Director Hoover. Somehow the Director's office had misplaced his copy of a Bureau memorandum to the attorney general, and Al Belmont told me to take our best carbon to Hoover's office. The carbon wasn't very legible, and I told Miss Gandy that I could have a clean copy typed in about twenty minutes; she sweetly asked me if I was aware of the rule that all copies had to be legible. I told her I was aware of that, but the original memo to the AG had required many carbons—for Justice, Hoover, Tolson, Ladd, Belmont, the file and myself—and that the best I could find was this one. Miss Gandy asked me for a solution to the bad-copy problem on this memo. I told her again that I'd have a new one typed. She then said, "Well, Mr. Lamphere, I have a solution." The following week I received my third letter of censure.

Al Belmont wasn't very happy about that letter, since he felt he'd unwittingly gotten me in trouble—but it was my censure, not his; and it irritated me no end. I was pretty good at rolling with the punches, and I loved counterintelligence work, but incidents such as these created an atmosphere at headquarters that was difficult to bear; many of my colleagues and I came to feel that good investigative results were beginning to take second place to the bureaucratic strictures that had slowly been accumulating during the Director's long reign.

Starting in 1953, three episodes highlighted the problems I faced inside the organization.

The first of these involved a man whose name I didn't encounter until several years after I had finally left the Bureau—Colonel Rudolph Abel.

Because of my work with the deciphered KGB messages, I had become the Bureau man who was supposed to know what could be known about Russian ciphers. It was on the basis of that reputation, I guess, that in the summer of 1953 a fascinating package arrived on my desk. It contained a print of a microfilmed message full of five-digit number-groups, and some photographs of a hollowed-out nickel, together with a description of how and where these had been found. It seemed that a few weeks earlier a Brooklyn newsboy had received the nickel in change, had accidentally dropped it on a stairway and had been amazed when the microfilm fell out. He gave it to the police, who gave it to the FBI in New York, who sent it to headquarters.

After some preliminary checking and help from our laboratory, I dismissed the idea that this might be a hoax. The microfilm with the five-digit number-groups had been typed on a Cyrillic (Russian) typewriter. The hollowed-out nickel was very professionally made. I felt certain that the newsboy had delivered to us something of considerable importance.

I sent memoranda in various directions. I asked the FBI laboratories to evaluate for me the origin of the nickel and the typewriter that had been used. I directed our cryptanalytic experts to see if they could crack the code, and made a similar request of the National Security Agency. I sent letters to the other U.S. intelligence agencies, to British Intelligence and to the Royal Canadian Mounted Police, describing what had been found and soliciting their advice. Their answers solidified my belief that the nickel and cipher were part of a Soviet intelligence operation that involved a code apparently fashioned with a one-time cipher pad—a code that could not be read by our experts.

We had the hollowed-out nickel shown to people who made somewhat similar novelty items for the United States market, and all agreed that it hadn't been manufactured in this country. The FBI laboratory agreed with my initial guess that the nickel was a very professionally made item.

The RCMP sent two men down from Ottawa to see me. They advised me that the coin and cipher were important, but they didn't say how they knew—and it was obvious to me that they were under instructions to be helpful but not to let me in on certain details of their own work against the KGB. They wouldn't give me anything in writing, but were willing to chat. Finally, they suggested that I strongly consider the possibility that the KGB might have an "illegal" agent in New York—illegal meaning one who did not work from the embassy or from one of the offices connected with the Soviets (such as Tass), and who was essentially outside the embassy's control. They also put forth the idea that the nickel and microfilm might be somehow connected to the "Allo" broadcasts.

The "Allo" broadcasts were known to originate in Russia. On different frequencies and at various times during the week, an announcer would come on the air, say, in accented English, "Allo, allo," and then recite, in English, groups of five-digit numbers. These broadcasts had been monitored by the NSA and other communications intelligence people for some time; the number-groups had never been deciphered.

By mid-1953, the game of counterintelligence had changed markedly from what it had been at the end of World War II. In the United States we had succeeded in breaking up a number of KGB networks; in addition, the Soviet consulates in New York and San Francisco had been closed, our agents were closely watching the offices of Amtorg, the Soviet U.N. delegation, the Soviet embassy in Washington and other places connected with Soviet intelligence in the past—and we knew from double agents that we were badly disrupting Soviet intelligence operations.

It seemed logical to me to conclude that the Soviets had indeed changed their operations to include an "illegal" agent in New York. Legal agents had the advantage of a guaranteed secure communications system through both coded cable traffic and the diplomatic pouch—but illegals might be able to operate for years without ever becoming known to the FBI.

Drawing on what I had learned in the past ten years, I constructed a memo about this unknown illegal agent. It was unlikely, I wrote, that the man would have extensive contact with official Soviet personnel in the United States—the whole point was to keep him away from the embassy, which the KGB knew that the FBI would be watching. But he'd have to have communications, somehow, and this was the purpose of the "Allo" broadcasts, I postulated. He would also require some embassy for the purpose of communicating back to Moscow; I didn't think an agent in New York would work through London or Ottawa, because the British and Canadians were covering those embassies tightly, but I thought it probable that Paris or Mexico

City would serve as the communications outpost. Couriers for the agent and embassy might well include Communist sympathizers who were employees of Air France or one of the other airlines (or shipping lines) that regularly went between Paris or Mexico City and New York. It was a virtual certainty that our man in New York had entered the country on a false U.S. passport, possibly one issued abroad at an American embassy or consulate; once inside the United States, he had probably switched to another identity.

My memo would go from Al Belmont to Mickey Ladd, and then up the line. In it I listed eight points to support my contention that an illegal agent was operating in New York. I cited the "Allo" broadcasts, the hollowed-out nickel, and the five-digit groups on the microfilm as evidence of a sophisticated communications system. Then I outlined the Canadian hints, and my guesses as to the embassy base of the agent, the use of couriers from the airlines or freight lines, a possible flurry of false passports, and little or no contact with Soviet representatives in the United States.

I recommended that we redeploy some of our manpower currently being used to cover official Soviet establishments, to concentrate on suspected couriers who worked for airlines or foreign-based shipping companies and who regularly went from France to New York or from Mexico to New York. I also suggested that we work more closely with Customs, the Immigration and Naturalization Service (INS), and the State Department in reviewing the documents of people who were entering the United States on passports issued by U.S. outposts abroad.

Belmont called me in after reading the memo, told me it was interesting, and asked me what else I had to support my conclusions.

"Not a thing, Al. That's all I have."

"Well," Belmont answered, "it's not enough. I can't send the memo forward unless you have more to support it."

We sat down and talked. The memorandum would obviously entail more work for the Bureau; it would mean a dramatic shift in emphasis, as well as the redirecting of personnel from one task to another. I told Al I understood that this would be unpalatable to the hierarchy, but that time would prove that I was right about the illegal agent in New York. Belmont agreed that there might well be such an agent operating in the United States, but that my suggestions for a major manpower shift, made on the basis of such scanty evidence, would not now receive the proper attention upstairs, and so there was no point in sending the memo forward.

Several years after I had left the FBI, in 1957, Colonel Rudolph Abel was identified and then caught in New York City. I later learned that when Abel was first located, the Director asked whether the FBI had had any previous indication of his having been in the United States, or how he was operating. At that point someone reviewed my memorandum and found that I'd been proved correct on six of the eight points I'd made.

I followed the Abel case with great interest, and will recount it briefly now, not only because of the memo I'd written, but also because it touched on KGB messages and on one of the major cases in which I had played a part.

Aside from the clue of the hollowed-out nickel, the first hint that there was such a man as Colonel Abel in the United States came in late April 1957. A drunken and incompetent KGB officer, Reino Hayhanen, fearful that his superior (Abel) was having him called back to Moscow to be disciplined for botching an assignment, defected to the United States while in Europe. He told the authorities about his New York superior and where he thought they might find him. After some difficulty, FBI agents found a photographic studio in Brooklyn and watched it, around the clock, for weeks; once they actually saw Abel, then followed and lost him in the vicinity of Fifth Avenue and Twenty-eighth Street. (I'll bet there was hell to pay on that one.) Three weeks later Abel showed up at his studio again, and this time the agents succeeded in tailing him to the Hotel Latham in Manhattan.

The Bureau was then presented with a quandary. It seemed likely that the KGB was not yet absolutely certain of Hayhanen's defection, and so there existed the possibility that the FBI could apprehend Abel and turn him around—that is, make him a double agent against the U.S.S.R. If, however, Abel was arrested on a warrant that charged him with espionage or with failure to register as the agent of a foreign power, he would have to be immediately arraigned before a U.S. commissioner, and would be entitled to a hearing; the publicity generated would alert the Soviets and blow the opportunity of making Abel into a double agent. But if the INS arrested Abel as an illegal alien and whisked him to Texas to await a deportation hearing, the proceedings would be relatively secret, and the FBI could then try to turn him.

Abel was arrested by the INS and the FBI at 7:00 A.M. on June 21, 1957, in the Hotel Latham, where he was registered as Martin Collins, one of his aliases. Many compromising articles were found in the room. In a wallet there were three slips of paper; the first two contained what were obviously directions and signals for clandestine meetings. One read:

> Balmora, Avenida Oberon. 3 P.M. Display left of entrance. I. "Is this an interesting picture?" L. "Yes. Do you wish to see it, Mr. Brandt?" L. smokes a pipe and has a red book in his left hand.

The second read:

> In Mex: Signal "T" on pole opposite #191 Chihnaavha St/ (Fonolia Roma), using side of pole towards roadway. Sat. or Sun, Tues, Thur. Met on Mon, Wed, Fri at 3 P.M. movie Balmora.

The third slip had two addresses on it:

> Mr. Vladinec, P.O. Box 348, M-w. K-9, USSR. Sign "Arthur."
> W. Merkulow, Poste Restante, M-a USSR (Russia). Sign "Jack."

In a hollowed-out tip of a pencil were eighteen microfilms. One of these had the transmission schedule for 1957 with each month listing "Basic Sessions" and "Alternate Reserve Sessions"; there were also the dates and times and kilocycles of the transmissions. (This confirmed that Abel had been the recipient of the "Allo" broadcasts.) In a block of wood was a small booklet of 250 pages, in red and black, which turned out to be a one-time cipher pad. A tie clip that Abel tried to dispose of, and several others found in the apartment and later in Abel's studio, had compartments for storing microfilm. The studio also held books on cryptanalysis, as well as hollowed-out nails, nuts, bolts and other items. No more hollowed-out nickels were found, but the cipher pad and other materials, together with ciphers supplied by Hayhanen, allowed the FBI to decode the message that had been in the original nickel. It was addressed to Hayhanen, and he had probably lost it when drunk. It read:

> We congratulate you on a safe arrival. We confirm receipt of your letter to the address "V" repeat "V" and the reading of letter Number 1.
> For organization of cover, we gave instructions to transmit to you three thousand in local [currency]. Consult with us prior to investing it in any kind of business, advising the character of this business.

According to your request, we will transmit the formula for the preparation of soft film and news separately, together with [your] mother's letter.

It is too early to send you the Gammas. . . . [The FBI never found out what this meant; literally translated, gammas are "musical exercises."]

Encipher short letters, but the longer ones make with insertions. All the data about yourself, place of work, address, etc., must not be transmitted in one cipher message. Transmit insertions separately.

The packages were delivered to your wife personally. Everything is all right with the family. We wish you success. Greetings from the comrades. Number 1, 3rd of December.

The FBI found out that Hayhanen had entered the United States on a false passport in late October 1952, and that this message predated his first meeting with Abel, whom he did not get to see until 1954.

In Texas, Abel refused to cooperate with the FBI. Because of the amount and scope of the evidence found on Abel and in his various apartments and studios, and the information from Hayhanen, it was decided he should be charged with conspiracy to commit espionage, along with Hayhanen and some other Soviets who were no longer in New York.

The specifics—all brought out at the trial—included the attempted recruitment and blackmailing of several people in the United States, including an army sergeant who had worked for the Soviets while in Europe.

One of the things that riveted my attention was that Hayhanen told the FBI he had been given money and instructed by Abel to get it to Helen Sobell, the wife of Rosenberg case co-defendant Morton Sobell. She was known to Abel and Hayhanen as the "wife of Stone," because Stone was Sobell's code name. According to Hayhanen, Mrs. Sobell was a KGB agent herself. Hayhanen, in fact, absconded with the money intended for Mrs. Sobell.

I've always found this link between the Rosenberg and Abel cases tremendously important. The idea that Mrs. Sobell could be involved with the Soviets was debunked by Rosenberg case critics at the time, but was later confirmed by a fortuitous find of microfilm in an old wallet of Abel's. After Abel's trial and conviction, when Abel's lawyer asked FBI agents to go over his possessions prior to sending them overseas for his client, an agent found a one-inch square of microfilm in an old wallet. When deciphered, it read:

Comrade Vik [Hayhanen]. We have been worried by your long silence. What is your situation and health at the present time? We will receive your letter in the nearest future. You are granted leave with a trip to the homeland. We request to think through all the details of the trip: [including] explanations of your absence to associates. We communicated to you our ideas on the itinerary. We are awaiting your opinion. At the end of August we will send conditions for communication in Europe. We request to advise before departure: A. possibility of obtaining Finnish foreign passport according to our letter May 11, of this year. B. Would you be able to deliver money to wife of Stone? Relay to T.M. [Tovarisch, or Comrade, Mark, the name by which Hayhanen knew Abel] conditions for communications with ASKO [code name for Finnish sailor/courier], so that he will be able to use this channel through drops. Family is well, but worried by absence of letters. Regards from comrades. August 22.

When lawyer James Donovan told Abel in prison that the microfilm had been found, Abel's face flushed and he became silent for a few seconds, then said to Donovan, "You have shaken me up. I don't remember leaving any such paper in that particular wallet." According to Donovan's book, though, Abel clearly remembered the old billfold.

The significance of the deciphered message would not have been lost by Abel: it provided documentary proof that the KGB had been interested in providing Helen Sobell with money. Mrs. Sobell had made it her life's work to keep the Rosenberg case alive even after Julius and Ethel had been electrocuted. This late message, discovered in the wallet of an illegal KGB agent, provides the evidentiary link between the Rosenberg and Sobell matters.

Long after Abel went home to Russia, people wondered why, if he had been such an important agent in the United States, he hadn't done more. Judging from the materials found with him, and the elaborate precautions surrounding his arrival and the extensive training given to Hayhanen before he was to join Abel in the United States, I believe Abel did quite a bit in the United States—and that his principal mission may have been connected with the Rosenberg case.

Another clue about this comes from the contents of a safe-deposit box in Brooklyn that had been used by Abel. In this box were pictures of a man and wife named Morris and Lona Cohen. Morris Cohen, a local New York high school football star, had fought with the

Abraham Lincoln Brigade in Spain and worked as a guard at the Soviet pavilion at the New York World's Fair in 1939. (The FBI had learned, as far back as my time in the Bureau, that many young Soviets attached to the fair had been in training for missions in the United States by the KGB.) Morris met Lona at the fair and married her in 1941. A witness later told the FBI that the Cohens had given a dinner party in the spring of 1950 at which the featured guest was Abel, introduced under his cover identity. That summer, when we were arresting members of the Rosenberg network, the Cohens disappeared from the United States. If Abel knew the Cohens, why would their photo be in his safe-deposit box inside an envelope with $15,000 in twenty-dollar bills? I think the answer is that while Abel didn't need the photo to identify them, someone else might. That's why the photo is labeled on the back "Shirley and Morris," and bears the cryptic notation "Who are Joan's murderers." This latter phrase is undoubtedly a "parole," a verbal recognition line, part of the identification system involved in a first clandestine meeting between two KGB agents.

In 1957, having established the identities of the Cohens, the FBI obtained their fingerprints from its own files—Morris had been in the U.S. Army, and Lona had worked in a defense plant—and copies were sent to intelligence services all over the world.

Those fingerprints provided the key identification in another seemingly unrelated case in 1961, in England. The Portland Naval Secrets case in England was a major KGB operation. In it a spy named Gordon Lonsdale was arrested, together with a couple named Helen and Peter Kroger. In the Krogers' home were sophisticated shortwave transmission equipment, hollowed-out objects, microdot reading machinery, radio broadcasting schedules, one-time cipher pads and false passports. The Krogers initially objected to their fingerprints being taken, and Scotland Yard obtained a court order allowing them to print the Krogers. Comparison with the prints of the Cohens revealed them to be the same people.

One more intriguing fact about the Cohens: they were ultimately returned to Russia, along with Gordon Lonsdale, in exchange for imprisoned British businessman Greville Wynne. This was the first known instance of spies who were not Russian-born being exchanged by the Soviet Union.

One of the reasons the Soviets might have been so eager to get the Cohens back behind the Iron Curtain is that the KGB did not want them to spend too much time in a British prison, where they might be inclined to tell a few tales in an effort to obtain reduced sentences. I believe some of those tales might have been about the Rosenbergs, because I think it's highly probable that the connection between the Rosenbergs and the Cohens goes beyond the fact that the Cohens disappeared from the United States near the time of the Greenglass arrest. Yakovlev, Rosenberg's controller, left in 1946 from the United States, but I knew that Rosenberg had reported to other men during the next few years. Abel arrived in New York in 1948, and there was a strong possibility that Rosenberg was controlled by Abel—and that the Cohens had been used as "cut-outs" so that Julius Rosenberg would never be able to identify the man who was directing his network's activities.

That scenario fits well with the new, more sophisticated approach to espionage which "illegal" agents like Abel personified.

Abel was eventually exchanged for U-2 pilot Francis Gary Powers, in 1962, after long negotiation by attorney Donovan.

The colonel received rather unusual treatment when he returned to the U.S.S.R. Generally, spies who had been caught by a foreign government and later exchanged were treated as if they had failed in their assignment, and were either disposed of or kept quiet in a backwater. But Abel was lionized as a hero, given decorations, and allowed to speak in public, where he averred that he had duped the FBI and managed to dump his codes when he was being arrested. (Of course, he had not dumped the codes.) It was said that his father had been a comrade of Lenin's in revolutionary days, that Abel had worked for the KGB since 1927, that during the war he had penetrated the German Abwehr and done fancy exploits, and that while in the United States he had trained Gordon Lonsdale.

Much of the written praise of Abel came in a book supposedly written by Lonsdale, one that American intelligence sources later concluded had been ghosted by Kim Philby. Most of the interesting tidbits about Abel, including his vaunted background, were later revealed as lies. For instance, it was eventually established that he had been born William Fisher in England, and taken to the Soviet Union by his parents when he was young. I guess Abel had been so much in the public eye in the West that his usefulness as an operating espionage agent was through, and so the KGB decided to use him for public relations and training purposes; only when he was finished as a spy could he be retroactively upgraded to espionage superstar.

As I've described in a previous chapter, early on in my work with the deciphered KGB messages I found in them considerable corroboration for the data provided to the FBI by Elizabeth Bentley—for example, messages that verified that a man named Coral had taken over as courier to the Silvermaster network when Bentley had been eased out of the KGB. By 1953 I had inherited the entire Bentley case —175 volumes of material, or somewhere between four and five hundred thousand pages of investigative reports, letters, memoranda, teletypes and other bits and pieces. Since Bentley had named eighty people to the FBI, and all had been investigated, the number of volumes was not considered excessive.

Aspects of the Bentley case still rankled many of those in the Bureau, including Director Hoover. Of all the people she had named, only William Remington had been successfully prosecuted (for perjury), though Abe Brothman, Miriam Moscowitz and the Rosenbergs had also been convicted partially on the basis of Bentley's testimony. But many others had evidently betrayed the country while working in sensitive government positions—and that was what bothered us. I began to consider the possibilities of using the Bentley files and the new knowledge we had gained in recent years to try to develop some of these cases for prosecution. Since the espionage Bentley had described took place during World War II, and violation of the wartime espionage statutes was a capital offense, that meant the statute of limitations did not apply, and if we could build a good case, we might still be able to convict some of these people.

Bentley could personally testify against people such as Nathan Gregory Silvermaster, his wife, Helen, Ludwig Ullman of the Treasury Department, Victor Perlo of the War Production Board, and a number of others.

What I needed was someone who could back up Bentley's testimony in court, and perhaps even provide leads for further investigation. I thought I had a candidate in the man Bentley had known only as her Soviet superior, "Jack," but whom we had later identified as Joseph Katz, a Russian agent of long standing. Bentley had been impressed by Katz's humanitarian manner and concern; for example, he had admitted to her that he was nearly as dissatisfied with the espionage work as she was. Katz was in touch with the extensive American KGB network which Bentley knew, apparently through Anatoli Gromov (the KGB chieftain from the U.S.S.R.'s Washington embassy). In 1950 Katz had been reidentified to us by both Harry Gold and Tom Black, both of whom had worked as agents under his direction. We also had other evidence against him. On the basis of this testimony, plus Bentley's, we now had enough ammunition to be able to prosecute Joseph Katz—and possibly to make a deal with Katz or otherwise convince him to be a government witness against the Silvermasters and others named by Bentley.

The problem was that by 1953 Katz had long since disappeared. We knew, however, that his brother Morris was a poet who spent most of his time drinking coffee and talking with cronies in Brooklyn cafeterias. Putting a mail cover on Morris, we soon learned that he was receiving letters from Paris. We then asked our legal attaché in Paris to request the French counterintelligence agency, SDECE, to identify who lived at the address from which Morris was receiving mail; we sent SDECE a photo of Joseph Katz to help them along. Soon SDECE sent word back that Joseph Katz was indeed at that address, but that a preliminary investigation turned up nothing of significance. Katz appeared to be living a quiet life.

Our extradition treaty with France did not cover what the French termed "political" crimes like espionage, and the Department of Justice said we couldn't arrest Katz in France even if he were inside the American embassy. How would we get him back? I was considering the possibilities of tricking him into getting aboard an American airplane or an American ship so that when the carrier reached international waters we could arrest him—when Katz suddenly disappeared again. SDECE had no idea where he had gone or if anything had alerted him.

Refusing to give up, we went back to our mail cover on Morris the poet, and within a few months learned that he was now receiving mail from Haifa, Israel.

This time our liaison man to the CIA, Sam Papich, and I went to Jim Angleton, whose connections with the Israeli intelligence services were quite strong. Angleton asked his contacts to assist us, and they quickly determined that Joseph Katz was in Haifa, but could find nothing to support the idea that he was still active in espionage. I began to consider the probability that Katz had broken with the KGB; if, in fact, this had happened, then he might be a more willing witness against those named by Bentley. But first I had to get Katz back to the United States.

Little by little, in our conversations, Sam Papich, Jim Angleton and I began to formulate a joint FBI-CIA operation to return Katz to the United States. The key would be luring Katz onto a U.S.-registered boat, outside Israel's territorial waters, where I could make a legal arrest. This was not something that we wanted done by others; I hoped to get Katz by myself.

I wrote a memorandum for the Director that outlined the plan, and one to Justice that detailed the legal evidence of Katz's violation of the Foreign Agents Registration Act, and what we believed we could accomplish with Katz in our hands. Director Hoover gave us the go-ahead on the preliminary aspects of what I had in mind. He didn't like the idea of a joint FBI-CIA operation, but had been made to understand that the FBI did not have the resources or contacts in Israel to pull off this one, whereas the CIA did.

I had a rendezvous in a hotel with Angleton and a man who was introduced to me by a false name; he would be my contact in Israel. We were going to hire a yacht registered to a U.S. owner, in Haifa, and take certain friends of Katz's out on pleasure trips. I'd pose as the yacht owner. After several of these trips, the friends would be asked to bring Katz along on the next one. We'd leisurely go out past the three-mile limit, and then I'd arrest Katz. Later he and I would transfer to a U.S. Navy vessel for a slow trip back to the United States. On the journey I hoped I'd be able to convince Katz to cooperate with us.

An FBI cryptographic expert taught me a special secure cipher system which I'd use to communicate with headquarters through CIA channels while on this assignment. It was a complex and unfamiliar cipher, and I didn't like it much; my teacher said I'd get used to it.

The whole cloak-and-dagger idea was full of risk, especially for me. If the scheme came apart once I had gotten overseas, there would be no way for me to avoid taking complete responsibility for the failure. If I succeeded, I might be a hero; if the operation failed for any reason—whether because of my efforts or because of something completely unknown—I'd be a goat.

I had my new passport and visas in hand and was ready to go to Israel when disaster struck. Director Hoover had a conversation with a deputy attorney general, and got the distinct impression that Jim Angleton had talked to Justice about the plan. Feeling that this was primarily an FBI operation and that the CIA had overstepped its bounds by talking to Justice, Hoover called the whole thing off.

Jim Angleton always maintained to me that he'd never had any such conversation with Justice, but the facts became immaterial once Hoover had concluded that the operation was suspect, and there was no resuscitating the mission. I was chagrined on two counts. One, both Sam Papich and I had wanted this joint operation to improve relations between the FBI and the CIA—and the result had been just the opposite, a further rupture between the agencies. Two, I was disappointed that my one best hope to reopen the Bentley case and prosecute some of the key figures was now gone.

Subsequently I arranged for Katz to be interviewed in Israel; he denied ever having been a Soviet agent. I wondered: if I had gone to Israel, would the plan have succeeded or would I have botched the effort? I don't know. But in counterintelligence, one sometimes plays for important breaks, and I would have liked to have taken this high-stakes gamble, no matter which way the affair would have come out.

I have earlier said that Director Hoover had a long memory, and that it was this memory that was part of his unique way of wielding power. In the early months of the Eisenhower Administration, in 1953, I became embroiled in one matter that typified the Director's memory and tactics. Because I was in charge of the Bentley files, I was instructed to draft a memorandum for the new attorney general, Herbert Brownell, about Harry Dexter White, the man named as a KGB source by Elizabeth Bentley but whom President Harry Truman had nominated in 1946 to be executive director for the United States on the International Monetary Fund. The memo, which went out over the Director's signature, showed that the FBI had informed the White House three times before the nomination that White was under suspicion of being a Soviet agent, and was under intensive investigation.

A bit later in 1953 I was asked for a second memo on the subject; mystified as to the purpose of the document, I merely reworded the first memo and sent it upstairs.

Then, on November 6, 1953, I was as surprised as anyone when the press reported that Brownell had made a speech to the Executive Club in Chicago in which he charged that Truman had appointed Harry Dexter White to "the most sensitive post [White] ever held in government service," in the face of information the FBI had supplied that showed that "Harry Dexter White was a Russian spy."

Now, of course, I understood the whole business. In 1946 Truman had ignored or purposely distrusted Director Hoover's warnings about a suspected spy-in-government. Hoover could do nothing about it at the time, but he waited seven long years, until the administration had changed, before exacting his revenge.

Former President Truman, replying to the charges from his home, said he knew nothing of the 1945 FBI reports on White, and maintained that in 1947, as soon as he had learned White was disloyal, he had fired him. Thus, the battle was joined.

As the news story developed, we learned that Brownell had discussed his speech beforehand with Sherman Adams and James Hagerty of the White House, as well as briefly with Eisenhower himself, and had been given the green light to make these charges. When Truman gave his response, Hagerty jumped in and reiterated the contention that Truman had known in advance of White's disloyalty, citing a February 4, 1946, Hoover memo to the President which had been written after the FBI had discovered that White was about to be nominated to the IMF position. That memo had been a strong one, citing charges against White supported by the contentions of Bentley together with some information from other sources including Gouzenko. There was no doubt that this memo had been received by the White House, and that, despite it, Harry Dexter White's nomination had been given to the Senate Banking Committee, where it was quickly approved and sent to the Senate floor for speedy confirmation.

I soon became completely embroiled in the political battle between present and past administrations, and for me the period was the most nerve-wracking I ever experienced in the FBI. In the ensuing time I worked without a day off for six weeks, and averaged about eighteen hours a day, feverishly writing memoranda about White. I hated it. I wasn't developing a new spy case—Harry Dexter White had been dead for five years—and I didn't like being in the midst of a political controversy which I believed could do the Bureau no good. The only things that kept me going were my responsibilities to my job and the belief that I knew Brownell's charges about Truman and White were true.

Bentley had told us that White, whom she'd never actually met, was one of the most important of the group that operated through Nathan Gregory Silvermaster. As chief assistant to Secretary of the Treasury Henry Morgenthau, White had access to information in his own department and to top-secret data from other agencies. Bentley said that White had pulled strings to help members of the network when they were in trouble—for example, when Silvermaster was being forced out of the Board of Economic Warfare in 1942—and had hired many people in the network into secure jobs with the Treasury. Bentley contended that White had given the Russians printing plates for marks to be issued in Germany after the war, and that he was the real author of the draconian "Morgenthau plan" whose aim was to reduce Germany to a fifth-rate economic power—both things that were of advantage to the U.S.S.R.

For instance, Bentley reported that Silvermaster had told her that White had provided information to a Soviet network during the 1930s, but had ceased doing so when his contact turned sour in 1938. She also recounted that the Silvermasters had visited the Whites and had seen a magnificent Russian rug on the living-room floor; they asked White if it had come from the Amtorg Trading Corporation, and he turned pale, insisted the rug was Persian and later hid it in an attic. Confirmation on these two particular points later came from another old espionage courier, Whittaker Chambers. (It didn't surface in 1945–46 because, as I've indicated earlier, Chambers did not actively begin cooperating with the FBI until late 1948.) Chambers had first told Adolph Berle of Harry Dexter White's espionage in 1942, and repeated his charges to a Treasury investigator in 1945, about six months before Bentley came to the FBI. Chambers had actually been White's courier in the 1930s, had given him the Russian rug and was the man who had defected in 1938.

In 1948, when Bentley made her appearance before the House Un-American Activities Committee and named White, Chambers was called three days later, primarily to back up Bentley's allegations about White. It was at this time that Chambers named both White and Alger Hiss; he later commented that, in these men, the Soviets had sat close to the heart of the U.S. government, "not yet in the Cabinet room, but it was not far outside the door." At that time the country was in the midst of the 1948 presidential campaign, and third-party candidate Henry Wallace had pledged that, if elected, he would appoint Harry Dexter White as his secretary of the Treasury. A few days later, White was called before the HUAC, categorically denied the allegations of Bentley and Chambers, and complained of being ill. Committee members scoffed at this complaint, though it was known that he'd suffered a heart attack a year earlier; within a week of his appearance before the HUAC, White died of another heart attack. Later in 1948, when Alger Hiss decided to fight Chambers's accusations, Chambers was forced into court and needed to come up with evidence against Hiss. In Chambers's "pumpkin papers" were documents allegedly typed by Hiss, and one very long memo, on yellow foolscap, in the distinctive handwriting of Harry Dexter White.

So by 1953 there was no doubt in our minds that White had operated as a Soviet spy while in a high position within the Treasury Department. But the uproar was about whether President Truman had been told about White by the FBI in enough time for him to have prevented White's nomination to the IMF, and had let that nomination go through anyway.

Whereas the opening salvos in the war between the Eisenhower and Truman administrations seemed to please Director Hoover and Assistant Director Lou Nichols, who was in charge of publicity for the FBI, what came next displeased them. Former Truman Administration Justice officials charged that the reason Truman had not withdrawn White's nomination to the IMF was that the FBI had requested that no actions be taken that might alert the suspects in the Bentley investigation to the notion that they were being investigated. Now the fat was in the fire; both Hoover and Nichols felt that the integrity of the Bureau itself was being attacked. This impression grew as Truman made an appearance on radio and television and said that as best he could determine from his records, he had first learned of the accusations against White in early February 1946, and that he'd let the White nomination go forward then because its effect was to remove White from a sensitive position in the U.S. Treasury —without alerting him that an FBI investigation was in progress. Truman suggested that no other action on his part could have served both these purposes.

Plunged into the voluminous Bentley files, together with other supervisors whom I was given to assist me, I thought that Truman's new statement was unfortunate. Already he had gone back on his first statement that he hadn't known anything about White until 1947. But the curve ball he had thrown in asserting that the actions he took were in the interests of both the FBI and the country were going to take a lot more spadework to refute. There was, however, a bonus for us in the files of the FBI. In the era in question, every contact made by the FBI had to be written down, somewhere— every phone call, every interview, every letter. And it was all filed, indexed and cross-indexed for easy reference. The FBI files, then, alone among the records of the governmental bodies, contained a complete story of our memoranda to the President about White, our discussions with Justice, and everything else.

My review of the files showed me we had alerted the White House on November 8 and then on December 4, 1945, that the FBI had very good reasons to suspect H. D. White of having worked for the Russians. Truman nominated White to the IMF on January 26, 1946. There was no question that Truman knew of our suspicions, at the very latest, in February, after a special report on White was prepared for the White House. Evidence in other files clearly showed that after careful consideration with close advisers including Secretary of State Byrnes and Secretary of the Treasury Vinson, Truman had decided to let the nomination go forward—and that this had nothing to do with protecting the FBI's investigations.

I was trying to walk a tightrope. Lou Nichols was preparing a statement for the Director to make, and he wanted my services—but I was under strict instructions from my actual superior, Al Belmont, not to get myself tied up in working directly for Nichols. One Sunday night I was called to Nichols's office and found Mickey Ladd, Belmont and some other people reading the prepared statement, which was to go out to Director Hoover's home in a half-hour. Nichols was dictating a cover memorandum to a secretary, which named each of us and stated that we'd all read it and agreed with it—with the exception of Belmont, who felt one paragraph was not completely accurate. As I read through it, scanning as quickly as I could, I came to a key page in which I felt the facts had been unduly slanted. I tried to say so, but Nichols said that everyone else agreed with it, and cut me off. Ladd demurred, saying that he wanted to hear me, and I spoke my piece; then Belmont said my objection was to the same page with which he too disagreed. Nichols was furious because he had to change his cover memorandum to say that Lamphere also objected to this particular page. After all, the Director was waiting. I later learned that the Director had agreed with my objections.

I think it was no more than a day or two after this incident that Belmont called me and said I should go to Ladd's office at noon, together with all the pertinent files on Harry Dexter White. Befuddled from lack of sleep, I simply gathered the summary brief and one or two other important files, and went to the elevator.

As I entered his office Ladd smiled, asked if the files contained all the right information, and told me to go and eat lunch and be back in his office at one, when the Director was to testify before the Senate Internal Security Subcommittee. Returning after that lunch, I found a TV set and additional chairs in the office. Ladd asked if I could see the set from where I was. So did Belmont, when he came in, and so did some other officials. Unable to contain myself any longer, I asked why everyone wanted to know if I could see the TV set.

Ladd said, "Didn't Belmont tell you? The Director is testifying, and the hearing is being televised. If, after his prepared statement, he's asked a question and doesn't know the answer, he'll roll one hand over the other. That'll be a signal for you to tell me the answer. I'll relay it to Nichols, who's on the telephone in the hearing room, and he'll pass it on to the Director. Now—are you sure you can find things quickly in the files?"

"If I don't know the answer," I said, "there'll be no time to look in the files, because I won't know where to look."

As I spoke, perspiration started running down my body, inside my shirt. I sat down and watched the TV screen with trepidation. As things turned out, after his prepared statement, the Director was asked an obviously planted question, and gave a very complete answer in his usual machine-gun delivery. The gist of what he said was that the FBI at no time had been party to an agreement to promote White in order to remove him from a sensitive position in the Treasury Department; we had, in fact, done everything prudent to alert the Truman Administration to the dangers we thought White represented.

The whole testimony took about thirty minutes. There were no hostile questions, and no hand roll-overs. To say that I was relieved is an understatement. I was also wringing wet.

The Director's words that day, and a very full discussion by Attorney General Herbert Brownell, also based on our files, quieted the controversy and ended my agony. While I didn't get into trouble at headquarters because of H. D. White, my work on the case—and my tightrope-walking—had not really pleased Lou Nichols, who was a powerful man in the hierarchy. That had been unavoidable; the problem was that he was one more person of whom I needed to be wary in the future.

Sometime in 1954 two supervisors in the New York field office were fired for having counseled agents working under them to slant a memorandum of explanation about having followed and been identified by two men from the Yugoslavian delegation to the United Nations, an incident that resulted in the filing of a protest with the State Department. One of those who'd been severed wrote a long and desperate letter to the Director, appealing his dismissal. He tried to show that it was common knowledge that discreetly following Eastern European diplomats was a difficult and hopeless task, that our agents were inadequately trained in this regard, that we lacked secure lookouts and proper equipment—anything that might mitigate his offense.

To me, headquarters' response to this letter was unbelievable. The official stance was that it contained thirty-seven separate charges of malfeasance which had to be reviewed. The Administrative Division (money and equipment), Training and Inspection Division (training) and our Domestic Intelligence Division (espionage matters) all had to respond, and I was called in on a Saturday to formulate the DI answer to these accusations. In fact, the letter had mentioned me by name. Along with several other supervisors, I had put on a seminar in the New York office; the letter said we'd indicated we knew it wasn't feasible to follow satellite and Soviet personnel closely without their becoming aware of the surveillance. This was true, but it wasn't the issue at hand.

I answered the charges in as factual and honest a way as I could, and gave my memo to Carl Hennrich, Belmont's assistant; after reading it, he passed the memo on to the man in the Administrative Division who was coordinating headquarters' response to the letter. That man called and told me my answer wasn't strong enough and had to be redone. I told him I didn't propose to change it. Next, Hennrich put pressure on me to shore up my defense of the Bureau's regular procedures; Hennrich argued that the letter writer had already been fired and wasn't going to be reinstated, and so I should do as I was told. I stormed out of his office with the memo, then sat down and stared out the window for a long time before I began to rewrite it. In the next draft I didn't exactly change my stance, but rather met the criticism from about halfway. I hated myself for doing so; my integrity was badly bruised.

Rewriting that memo made me understand that I could no longer remain in the FBI. Several months later, in July 1955, I resigned. Having been part of the fight against what I knew intimately to be the evil of Soviet espionage for more than a decade, I was reluctant to quit the front lines. My task had been an important one, and I had enjoyed it thoroughly. I was still proud of the FBI as an organization —but I did not regret my decision to leave the Bureau.

16
KNOTTING LOOSE ENDS

AFTER SERVING IN THE FBI for fourteen years, from 1941 through 1955, I took a post in the Veterans Administration dealing with investigations, security and internal auditing. Within five years I had risen through the executive ranks to deputy administrator, the number two position in the agency. In 1961, with the change in Presidents, I resigned from the VA and became an officer of one of the country's largest insurance companies, and worked with that company until recently, when I retired from the post of senior vice-president.

In the period just after I'd left the FBI, I continued to stay in touch with many of those with whom I'd worked. Some years prior to my leaving, one of my two closest friends in the Bureau, Emory Gregg, developed a retina infection in one eye; within a few years it had spread to both eyes and Emory became legally blind. However, Emory was one of the FBI's outstanding lecturers to in-service agents, and after his blindness he functioned primarily as a Bureau instructor, although he handled other assignments. As a resident expert on Soviet intelligence, he could hold an audience spellbound. Emory continued with the FBI until his retirement; he died a few years afterward, on his farm in the upper Shenandoah Valley of Virginia.

Ernie Van Loon, who had worked closely with me on the whole string of cases from Klaus Fuchs through the Rosenbergs, became the ASAC of a small office, and was on the ladder for higher promotion. However, Ernie decided that he didn't want a life of being moved around from office to office, and took a position as the supervisor in charge of all criminal investigations in Phoenix, until his retirement. To me, this was something of a waste of a top counterintelligence man.

Howard Fletcher, the man whom I had thought well qualified to become Hoover's successor, but who had been busted in the brouhaha over the Fuchs case, continued for some years as ASAC of the very large Washington, D.C., field office. Guy Hottel, who was the SAC of that office, was one of those very few in the Bureau who were companions of Director Hoover, and spent a fair amount of time accompanying the Director to the racetrack—with the result that Howard Fletcher did a good deal of the administrative work of the office. I saw Fletcher a few times in the ensuing years, and it was then that I really discovered his expertise in management, which consisted of working with the physical layout of the field office, supervising the attention paid to the files and the index system. Still later, Howard took a position with the International Chiefs of Police organization, which at that time was headed by Quinn Tamm, a former high-ranking FBI official.

Mickey Ladd, the number three man in the Bureau, the assistant director in charge of all investigative operations, took an early retirement, at age fifty, in 1954. His decision to leave was in some ways a precursor to and reinforcement of my own. It signaled the passing of an era, a time when his presence near the top helped to encourage the more active and aggressive counterintelligence policies we had tried to pursue against the Soviets. I was sorry to see Ladd go.

Al Belmont, who stepped up into Ladd's slot as number three man, stayed in that position until he retired. During the time I was in the V.A., I had some contact with Belmont, but not much, even though we were friends. There was little fraternizing when one was out of the FBI.

I also kept up with the cases in which I'd been involved, reading the newspapers, learning small bits of information from the friends who were still working in intelligence. From time to time, for example, I'd note that Gerhart Eisler continued to be the spokesman for the Kremlin in East Germany—in 1962 he was appointed chief of the information office for that country. The tiger hadn't changed his stripes.

Hede Massing—whom I'd interviewed extensively in the winter of 1946–47 because she was Eisler's first wife—called me when she came down to Washington to testify before a congressional committee. I liked Hede, and invited her to come to my apartment; I asked some of the other Bureau people who'd known her to join us for cocktails. I didn't hear much of her afterward. In March 1981 she passed away, at age eighty-one, and I was annoyed to note that the New York *Times*, which claims to be both accurate and the newspaper of record, printed, instead of a photo of Hede, a 1949 photo of Brunhilda Eisler, Gerhart's third wife.

I followed with grim interest the troubles of Noel Field, whom Hede had recruited as a Soviet agent. In 1949 Field disappeared in Europe, and was held in a Hungarian prison. He was forced to testify at the rigged trial of Prime Minister Rajk, a Jew—Field supposedly said Rajk had been his agent while Field was working for the OSS. Field had worked for Donovan and the OSS, but we knew he had also been an agent of the KGB, and had spied for Walter Krivitsky. Apparently the Soviets became suspicious of Field. He had worked under Krivitsky, who had defected, and it has been suggested that the CIA added to KGB suspicions in a rather clever way.

Of Judith Coplon I heard little over the years, except that she was a housewife and mother of four, living in Brooklyn. However, in a Senate hearing in 1956 a Soviet defector, Yuri Rastorov, named Coplon's control, Valentin Gubitchev, as a man personally known to him, and said that Gubitchev was an officer of the GRU. This raised my eyebrows, because the lead to Coplon had come from a deciphered KGB message. Did this mean that she had been recruited by the KGB and then dropped, and re-recruited by the GRU? I never found out. Rastorov claimed that Gubitchev was in serious trouble in Moscow for his unsuccessful operations with Coplon; the secret services there never again trusted him, because he had been briefly imprisoned in the United States. Gubitchev was later arrested in Russia.

From time to time, the name of Klaus Fuchs would pop into the news. After his release from prison, he took a post in East Germany involved with atomic research. At one point Marshall Perlin, an attorney who has tried to get the Rosenberg case reopened, claimed that he'd had an interview with Fuchs in which the physicist told him he'd never identified a photo of Harry Gold as his American contact.

This was, of course, a lie, since the photo of Gold which Fuchs had identified for me by writing on the back is in the FBI files. I often wondered why Perlin, an experienced lawyer, didn't manage to get Fuchs to sign an affidavit to back his claim of not having identified Gold.

When Harry Gold was released from prison on May 18, 1966, I saw a newspaper photo of him. He seemed then a tired old man; he had served half of his thirty-year sentence—a sentence that I had always believed to be excessive, given the great help he had provided to the U.S. government in pursuing other agents of the KGB in this country. Gold died six years later.

I continue to follow with interest what material emerges about Philby, Burgess and Maclean; almost every new piece of evidence serves to confirm their treachery and the laxness of the British security services in the era before Philby's departure. Not too long ago I heard that Philby had been in Cuba; I wondered what his assignment could have been. Recently there has been disclosed a connection between the Philby circle and the Abel case. The "fourth man," Anthony Blunt, named as a possible spy a former Trinity college cohort, New Zealander Paddy Costello; when he was attached to the New Zealand consulate in Paris, Costello issued false New Zealand passports to Morris and Lona Cohen, in the name of Kroger.

A Philby-network man issued passports for the Cohens, who were involved with Colonel Abel, Gordon Lonsdale and possibly with the Rosenbergs! Such intertwinings, collected both in the United States and in Great Britain in the past decades, have certified for me that the operations we traced during my time in the FBI were not isolated incidents or the work of individuals, but rather were all part of one interconnected web of espionage. In this country the thread of KGB-controlled spying led from Gaik Ovakimian in the early 1930s down through the 1940s and 1950s, and even on into the 1960s, when the Kroger/Cohens, having fled the United States, were arrested in England.

Although the public's understanding of these cases was less than complete—and, in some instances, it was unduly and falsely influenced by the twists on the facts of the cases given out by the Communists—for almost twenty years after leaving the FBI I said nothing in public about the Rosenbergs, Fuchs, Gold, Coplon or even Gerhart Eisler. This was in accordance with my training and my inclination to keep secrets that had been entrusted to me.

I believed, in particular, that the fact that the leads to many of the

KGB's agents came from deciphered KGB cables had no chance of ever being revealed, and I determined to willingly take that secret with me to my grave, as would any good soldier.

But in 1973, people from the National Public Affairs Center for Television (NPACT), in the course of researching a documentary on the Rosenberg case, called and asked me for an interview—initially, on the subject of my sessions with Klaus Fuchs. I hesitated about appearing in such a film, but producer Alvin H. Goldstein promised me faithfully that the film he was making would be an honest portrayal of the Rosenberg case. He said that his reputation, and that of public television, would allow no other stance but impartiality.

I sat for an interview in which I went over some of the facts of the case in considerable detail. I omitted, of course, any mention of the deciphered KGB messages.

When the film appeared on public television stations in 1974, I was astounded. For ninety minutes producer Goldstein arranged his interviews (and his "facts") to take, as one reviewer said, "an unmistakable stand that the Rosenbergs were given a raw deal." The charges of anti-Semitism, no Jews on the jury, the "forged" hotel registration card and all the other old canards were brought up and portrayed as evidence of frame-up. After interviewing producer Goldstein, Benjamin Stein wrote in the *Wall Street Journal* of February 8, 1974, that the film was a "veritable parody of impartiality," and said that the producer had made the Rosenbergs "not only innocent, but heroic." According to Stein, Goldstein told him, "Guilt or innocence of the charge is not the real issue. The real guts of the matter is that the Rosenbergs were being tried for their political views."

My own interview had been chopped up beyond recognition, and in my view the most important parts were left out. It was trivialized into mere denials rather than explanations of fact.

I felt I'd been had. The idea that the public's money had been used to produce this garbage irked me. I became angrier still when the text of the documentary was released as a book, and again in 1978, when Goldstein and public television released an "updated" version of the film in conjunction with a committee that included the Rosenbergs' sons and their attorney, on the twenty-fifth anniversary of the execution. The new version completely ignored the evidence from the recently released FBI files in the Rosenberg case, and made even stronger the producer's contention that there had been a miscarriage of justice.

In this continued manipulation of American public opinion

twenty-five years after the death of the Rosenbergs, I read the ultimate triumph of the KGB in the case. The enemy had managed to insert into the memories of a new generation of Americans a lie in the place of truth.

My anger at that film's inaccuracies, mixed with my determination to set the record straight, became the genesis of this memoir. Since I began this book in the 1970s, leaks from other sources about the deciphered KGB messages have been published, making it possible for me to set down information about these messages in more detail than I initially believed would be possible.

Also, in the years since I began this work, there have been some important developments in cases presented in the previous chapters. Among the most meaningful is the material gathered by Dr. Mark M. Kuchment, a Soviet science historian who emigrated here in 1975 and became a fellow of the Russian Research Institute at Harvard. Recently Kuchment and I traded details about Joel Barr and Al Sarant. Kuchment's research has proved beyond a doubt that both men did go behind the Iron Curtain when they vanished during the summer of 1950, and that both eventually became pillars of the Soviet scientific establishment. For me, this remarkable new evidence further confirms that Barr and Sarant were part of the Rosenberg network. Their modes of escape, their progress toward Moscow, and their subsequent success in the Soviet Union are all consistent with that conclusion.

Kuchment paints the following picture of the two scientists, based on official publications and interviews with many who worked for the men or who knew Sarant's wife, Carol Dayton.

After leaving the United States for Mexico, Sarant and Dayton went to Poland and thence to Czechoslovakia, where they met Barr. Sarant and Barr worked in tandem as engineers in Czechoslovakia until late 1955 or early 1956, when a meeting with a high Soviet official—some say Khrushchev himself—got both transfers to the U.S.S.R.

In the Soviet Union, Sarant changed his name to Filipp Georgievich Staros, and Barr (now married to a Czech wife) altered his to Joseph Veniaminovich Berg. They became, respectively, chief designer and chief engineer of an important Leningrad design bureau which operated under the aegis of the Soviet military establishment all through the late 1950s, the 1960s and on into the 1970s. Staros/Sarant won important state prizes and helped advance the Soviet work in computers and microelectronics, principally for military purposes. People who worked under Staros/Sarant identified Sarant's picture as that of their "Director," and details of Staros's official biography also confirm the identification. Sarant's father's name was George; Staros called himself Georgievich, which in Russian means "son of George." Both men claimed to be of Greek origin, to have four brothers, and to have worked on the development of an American cyclotron.

In Russia Joseph Berg/Joel Barr and his Czech-born wife had four children, among them a girl named Vivian—shades of Vivian Glassman, Barr's longtime American girlfriend. Vivian Berg and her three siblings are all talented musicians; Joel Barr had been known for his musicales in the United States. Emigrés who worked under Staros and Berg—there were eight hundred employees at the research institute at one time, of which twenty-two have since emigrated to the United States—led Kuchment to the conclusion that Staros and Berg's success in the U.S.S.R. was due to the support of the Soviet military under whose tutelage they labored, and to Staros's friendship with Khrushchev and with former defense minister Dmitri Ustinov. When Khrushchev faded from power, problems with the Soviet bureaucracy caused Staros/Sarant's day in the sun to wane, and he ended his career in semi-exile in a smaller research institute in Vladivostok.

Staros died in 1979, but Berg/Barr still lives in the U.S.S.R. In 1976 an American computer scientist and his wife visited the Soviet Union, and the man attended a scientific conference in Tashkent, a provincial capital. There he met Berg, who seemed quite interested in him and who spoke perfect English. Berg suggested that the two get together when the scientist reached Leningrad. In Leningrad, the scientist found that his room had been changed and didn't think that Berg would be able to reach him—but Berg found him and arranged a meeting. The scientist and his wife were picked up in a black Volga, a car much too expensive for the average Russian, and were driven to an apartment with six rooms, an unheard-of luxury for anyone in Russia. During the small talk, Berg allowed that his salary was seven hundred rubles a month, more than that earned by a deputy minister. Later, Berg tried to recruit the young computer scientist, who turned him down flat. The scientist soon found that his travel plans had been altered without his knowledge by the Soviet government, and that he no longer had invitations to visit important installations. He was told to return to Moscow, to join his wife in a bit of sightseeing, and then to go home to the United States. This he did, and later told his story to Kuchment.

To me, this tale is clear evidence that, twenty-five years after his involvement in the Rosenberg network, Joel Barr was still working closely with the KGB.

Kuchment told me that the impression he'd gained from interviews with those who had known Staros/Sarant, and from what he could find out about his life, was that despite his considerable success in the U.S.S.R., the transplanted American was not content in his later years, and died an unhappy man. It's certainly possible that Berg/Barr might share those sentiments as he shared so much else with his old friend. If so, maybe he ought to come home—I'd like to talk with him, for there are a few gaps I'd like to fill in.

It was in that same spirit that, in recent years, I made a phone call to Long Island. I had learned from a friend still in the intelligence community that another old adversary whom I'd never met—Joseph Katz—was in New York, visiting his brother. Joseph Katz was the man whom Elizabeth Terrill Bentley had known as "Jack"; Harry Gold and Tom Black had also worked under Katz. He was the man whom I had planned to lure out of Israeli territorial waters in 1953 so I could bring him back to the United States, where he might testify in a few trials and help us wrap up some old cases. Katz had probably been KGB since the early 1930s. I found his brother's telephone number quite easily, and called and asked for Joseph.

His sister-in-law was a bit surprised, but put Katz on the line. His voice was more guttural than I expected—given Bentley's description of it as being typically Brooklyn-accented—but he said he was Joseph Katz. I identified myself as a former FBI agent, long since out of the Bureau, and said I was writing a book and that he was in it.

Katz was a bit taken aback at the idea.

I told him that I knew that he'd been connected in the past with such people as Mikhail Chaliapin, Elizabeth Bentley, Harry Gold and Tom Black, and that all of them were in the book, and that I'd like to meet him and talk with him about it.

"I should write a book," he said.

I agreed with that idea, and told him that it would be a sure best-seller. Nonetheless, I said, I'd like to talk with him soon. Katz asked how he could be sure that I was who I said I was, a former FBI agent.

"You can look up my biography in Who's Who," I said.

"Why are you listed in *Who's Who*?"

"I don't know, I just am. Now, can we make a meeting?"

He said he wasn't sure. I told him to look me up, and call me. He didn't call, and when I tried to phone him again, twice, his sister-in-law told me not to bother him any more. Subsequently, he left the United States again, going back to England, where he had been living.

It's too bad he's gone; we might have had a lot to talk over regarding the long war between the KGB and the FBI.

Notes

Most of this book is drawn from memory. I have also used a number of published sources and some recently released FBI files to buttress what I recall of the era. In the notes, below, I've cited the more accessible of these published sources and FBI documents, for the reader who wishes further information. I wish to thank Ronald Radosh and Joyce Milton, authors of *The Rosenberg File*, for helping me by loaning me copies of key documents they had uncovered in their own research.

Not all citations are noted, but the reader will readily understand, for example, that quotations in the chapter on the Rosenberg trial are from the voluminous trial transcript, which itself is cited.

Often my knowledge of events differs sharply from published versions of history. Where these differences are relevant, I have gone into them in the text. In the notes I've tackled other controversies or gone into sidelights which I thought would have been out of place in the body of the text, but which may interest some readers.

PAGE   **CHAPTER ONE**

4   *Gimpel and Colepaugh:* For more details, see David Kahn, *Hitler's Spies*, New York: Macmillan, 1978, and Erich Gimpel with Will Berthold, *Spy for Germany*, London: Robert Hall, 1957.

12   *jurisdiction over all espionage matters:* Directives of June 26 and September 6, 1939. See Frank J. Donner, *The Age of Surveillance,* New York: Knopf, 1980.

12   *The FBI was known as an elite outfit:* For details on the FBI and training of new agents in this era, see Quentin Reynolds, *The FBI,* New York: Random House, 1954; and Richard Harrison, *The CID and the FBI,* London: Muller, 1956.

21   *"walking archive of the identities,":* Whittaker Chambers, *Witness,* New York: Random House, 1952.

22   *Arthur Alexandrovich Adams:* For more details, see David J. Dallin, *Soviet Espionage,* New Haven: Yale University Press, 1955.

22   *Andrei Shevchenko:* See Dallin, *op. cit.* Shevchenko is not to be confused with Arkady Schevchenko, a more recent Soviet defector.

23   *Victor Kravchenko:* A captain in the Soviet Army as well as an official of the Purchasing Commission, Kravchenko defected in 1944 and was a witness before the House Un-American Activities Committee in 1947. See his book, *I Chose Freedom,* New York: Scribners, 1946.

24   *Robert Switz:* For more details, see Dallin, *op. cit.*

24   *structure, intent and threat of the KGB:* Although the organization has been known by many names in various eras, and we called it by different initials in the 1940s and 1950s, I will refer to it throughout this book, for clarity's sake, as the KGB. The most comprehensive treatment of the KGB in this era is John Barron, *KGB: The Secret Work of Soviet Agents,* New York: Reader's Digest, 1974.

25   *KGB rings operating inside Germany, Switzerland:* For details, Louis Hagen, *The Secret War For Europe,* MacDonald, 1968; Ronald Seth, *Unmasked! The Story of Soviet Espionage,* New York: Hawthorn, 1965; and J. Bernard Hutton, *Struggle in the Dark,* London: Harrap, 1969.

25   *five KGB networks [in Sweden]:* Hutton, *op. cit.*

25   *Vassili Zubilin and Gaik Ovakimian:* Some information is taken from a summary report on Ovakimian which I recently obtained from the FBI, and which is now public; it is heavily censored, but intelligible. More details on the two men are in the Dallin and Barronbooks, *op. cit.*

29   *recognizable . . . by his full head of hair:* Compare the description of Yakovlev given by Harry Gold in "The Circumstances Surrounding My Work As a Soviet Agent," FBI file # 65–58805.

CHAPTER THREE

32   *Igor Gouzenko:* The major source remains *The Report of the Royal Commission,* June 27, 1946, Ottawa. See also Gouzenko, *Iron Curtain,* New York: Dutton, 1948. William Stevenson's recent book on

PAGE

the Gouzenko affair, *Intrepid's Last Case,* New York: Villard Books, 1983, is unreliable.

33 *diary entry . . . Mackenzie King:* From the diaries of the P.M. in the Canadian National Archives, quoted in H. Montgomery Hyde, *The Atom Bomb Spies,* London: Hamish Hamilton, 1980.

33 *the papers in his shirt:* Some of these have been printed in *The Report of the Royal Commission.*

34 *"Ignacy Witczak,":* For more details, see House Un-American Activities Committee, *The Shameful Years,* Washington, D.C., 1952.

36 *Elizabeth Terrill Bentley:* Best source, her signed statement of November 30, 1945, sent as a memo from SA Spencer to FBI headquarters, December 5, 1945, FBI # 65–56402–220. Also see Bentley, *Out of Bondage,* New York: Devin-Adair, 1951.

37 *"a small stocky man":* Bentley, *Out of Bondage.*

37 *Harry Dexter White:* See later chapters of this book, and David Rees, *Harry Dexter White: A Study in Paradox,* New York: Coward, McCann & Geoghegan, 1973.

38 *"I recall that on one occasion":* Bentley signed statement.

41 *later sworn testimony corroborated:* See Allen Weinstein, *Perjury, the Hiss-Chambers Case,* New York: Knopf, 1978; and Ronald Radosh and Joyce Milton, *The Rosenberg File,* New York: Holt, Rinehart & Winston, 1983, for more details. In some of the released FBI files on Bentley is corroboration for previously disputed areas of her testimony; see, e.g., receipt of the $2,000 given her by Gromov, acknowledged in NY 65–14603, p. 7, and 65–56402, pp. 270–292 (vol. 17).

CHAPTER FOUR

42 *Gerhart Eisler:* I have recently obtained the release of the Eisler Summary Report, which I wrote, and from which many of the details in this chapter are taken. It is file # 100-32520, serial 452X.

42 *The Comintern:* See Kermit E. McKenzie, *Comintern and World Revolution,* New York: Columbia University Press, 1964.

43 *Steve Nelson:* Nelson was convicted on contempt of Congress charges in 1952 and served a prison term. For more details, see Anthony Cave Brown and Charles B. MacDonald, *On a Field of Red,* New York: Putnam's, 1981. Nelson continues to deny involvement with Oppenheimer or with Soviet espionage; see Nelson, James R. Barrett and Robert Ruch, *Steve Nelson, American Radical,* Pittsburgh: University of Pittsburgh Press, 1981.

43 *Joint Anti-Fascist Refugee Committee:* For more details, see Walter Goodman, *The Committee,* New York: Farrar, Straus & Giroux, 1968.

PAGE

45   *"Hans Berger":* "Kremlin's Chief Agent in U.S. Identified as Ex-German Red," by Frederick Woltman, New York *World-Tele-gram*, October 1946. By reporting that "Berger" had been pointed out to him at a Communist rally in 1945, Woltman independently confirmed Budenz's identification. For a list of "Hans Berger" articles, see Eisler Summary Report.

45   *Louis Budenz:* See Budenz, *This Is My Story*, New York: McGraw-Hill, 1947.

46   *HUAC was in the midst of a probe:* Goodman, *The Committee*.

47   *Chambers had . . . known Eisler:* See *Witness*, New York: Random House, 1952.

48   *"bookish, athletic, gay":* Fischer quoted in *Life*, February 17, 1947, vol. 22.

48   *Ruth Fischer:* See Fischer, *Stalin and German Communism*, Cambridge, Mass.: Harvard University Press, 1948. Fischer was the maiden name of Eisler's mother.

48   *"Hitler presented nationalism": Ibid.*

48   *"a sneerer and a snarler": Time*, September 27, 1948, vol. 52, quoting what is probably an earlier file report.

49   *"Sink into the mud":* Quoted in Fischer, *op. cit.*

49   *"Germany is through for a while":* Fischer quoted in *Life*, February 17, 1947, vol. 22.

49   *Hede Massing:* See *This Deception*, New York: Duell, Sloan, Pearce, 1951. When I first saw a copy of this book, I had the uneasy feeling that I had actually written it. An FBI associate explained that that was nearly true, for Hede had obtained from the FBI a copy of my interviews with her and used that as the basis of her autobiography.

50   *"You don't need to be so delicate": This Deception.*

52   *Ignace Reiss:* For more details, see the book by his widow Elsa Bernaut (Poretsky), *Our Own People*, Ann Arbor, Mich.: University of Michigan Press, 1969.

53   *Noel Field:* See Flora Lewis's excellent study, *The Man Who Disappeared*, London: Arthur Barker, Ltd., 1965.

53   *Jozef Peters:* Some of the extensive information on Peters in the FBI files is cited in Weinstein, *Perjury*.

53   *"did not yield or peach.":* From Lincoln Steffens's introduction to *Fatherland*, by "Karl Billinger" (Paul Massing), New York: Farrar & Rinehart, 1935.

54   *Elsa saw Gerhart:* Poretsky, *Our Own People*.

54   *Krivitsky, ordered to take a hand:* See Walter Krivitsky, in *Stalin's Secret Service*, New York: Harper & Bros., 1959.

54   *"The letter which I am addressing":* As quoted in Massing, *op. cit.* But compare the version in Poretsky, *op. cit.*

56   *Krivitsky was found dead:* Anti-Communist writer Isaac Don Levine, associated with both Krivitsky and Chambers in his time, has

PAGE

suggested that Krivitsky was going to name Eisler to the HUAC the next morning, and postulates a link between the "killing" of Krivitsky and that possible testimony. I rather doubt that Krivitsky would have named Eisler, who was not an espionage agent.

58   *Hanns Eisler: The Committee.*

58   *"When the time comes":* Quoted in *Life,* February 17, 1947.

59   *Eisler's inflammatory activities here in the 1930s:* A report that was unavailable to the FBI in 1947, on these activities, has been cited by the authors of *On a Field of Red.* They label it the Weinkoop Report, by Joseph Weinkoop, and say it is part of the files of OSS/CIA Chief William Donovan, which are not open to the public.

62   *"This has been more than a trial":* Daily Worker, August 3, 1947. Starobin's own book, *American Communism in Crisis, 1943–1957,* Cambridge, Mass.: Harvard University Press, 1972, makes almost no comments on Eisler or on the Eisler trial. However, it does quote former New York subway union chief and ex-Communist Mike Quill as having consulted Eisler for guidance when Quill wanted to leave the Party in 1946; Quill's action would be commensurate with knowing Eisler as the Comintern rep to the CPUSA.

63   *"clean-cut . . . calm . . . mellow":* Virginia Gardner, "A Mistake, Mr. Meyer?" *New Masses,* August 19, 1947.

63   *"There are plenty of FBI men":* "How FBI Frame-Ups Work," by Joseph Starobin, *Daily Worker,* August 10, 1947.

64   *Carol King almost exploded: Time,* May 23, 1949.

64   *In later years he was seen teaching:* William E. Griffith, *Communism in Europe,* vol. 2, Cambridge, Mass.: MIT Press, 1966.

CHAPTER FIVE

67   *Bill Harvey . . . was gone from the FBI:* For more details, see David Martin, *Wilderness of Mirrors,* New York: Harper & Row, 1980.

68   *D. M. (Mickey) Ladd:* For a disparaging and unfair portrait of Ladd, dubbed Johnny Boyd, see Kim Philby, *My Silent War,* London: MacGibbon & Kee, 1968. Philby gives Lish Whitson the name of Lishman in his book, but for some reason calls me by my right name.

74   *Bentley . . . had described Jack:* Bentley signed statement.

CHAPTER SIX

79   *Soviets . . . learned of it through double agents:* For details, see Patrick Seale and Maureen McConville, *Philby,* New York: Simon & Schuster, 1973.

79   *leaks by former British Intelligence men: Newsweek,* May 19, 1980,
      p. 32, which uses a source other than myself, and Martin, *Wilder-
      ness of Mirrors.* Also see Chapman Pincher, *Their Trade Is Treach-
      ery,* New York: Bantam Books, 1982.

80   *the "one-time cipher pad" system:* See the similar examples in David
      Kahn, *The Codebreakers,* New York: Macmillan, 1967, and in
      Henry Beker and Fred Piper, *Cipher Systems,* New York: John
      Wiley & Sons, 1982.

81   *"unbreakable . . . perfect secrecy":* Beker and Piper, *op. cit.*

81   *Frank Rowlett:* See James Bamford, *The Puzzle Palace,* Boston:
      Houghton Mifflin, 1982.

82   *Meredith Gardner:* I had believed that even Gardner's name was
      secret, but it has been mentioned in print by Pincher, *Their Trade
      Is Treachery.*

83   *from the GRU messages that Gouzenko: The Report of the Royal
      Commission.*

84   *"partially burned KGB code book:* See Bradley F. Smith, *The
      Shadow Warriors,* New York: Basic Books, 1983, and Martin, *op.
      cit.*

87   *Mark Zborowski:* See *Our Own People,* for a much different account
      of this incident, which conceals Elsa Bernaut's mistrust of the FBI
      and her attempt to warn Zborowski.

91   *Max Elitcher:* The Elitcher files are FBI #65-14873. See also Radosh
      and Milton, *op. cit.*

91   *Bureau was already conducting a loyalty check:* The check, begun
      in April 1948, was suspended at my request on May 8, 1948. See
      summary memo, Wall to Howard Fletcher, September 7, 1948.

93   *"From the time the car left":* quoted in Radosh and Milton, *op.
      cit.*

93   *Joel Barr:* The Barr files are FBI #65-59453, with some listed as
      65-15392. This latter number contains the report of June 8, 1944,
      about transfers within the CPUSA. A 1947 report on Barr has yet
      another file number, 100-29040, May 13, 1947.

95   *"have acted as an intermediary":* This passage is quoted from SA
      T. Scott Miller, Jr.'s, Report of October 18, 1948, to file, entitled
      "Unknown subject, was./Espionage—R." It references my Bureau
      letter of June 4, 1948, which has not been released. The quoted
      passage substantially reiterates a similar one in that Bureau letter.

95   *"Christian name, ETHEL": Ibid.*

96   *Elaine Goldfarb:* See Barr files, 65-59453, vols. 1–5.

CHAPTER SEVEN

100   *broadcaster Edward R. Murrow charged:* Alexander Kendrick,
      Prime Time: The Life of Edward R. Murrow, Boston: Little,
      Brown, 1969.

PAGE

100   *"God help that country":* Quoted in *ibid.*

101   *Nardone v. U.S.:* 308 U.S. 338 60 Supreme Court 266, December 11, 1939, opinion by Felix Frankfurter.

102   *"I am convinced that":* FDR to Jackson, memo; from the Stephen Spingarn Papers on "National Defense—Internal Security" in the Harry S. Truman Library.

102   *"in cases vitally affecting":* Clark to Truman, July 17, 1946, Spingarn Papers. The contention that Clark's letter came at Hoover's instigation is contained in an interview with Clark conducted by Ovid Demaris for his book, *The Director,* New York: Harper's Magazine Press, 1975.

102   *Coplon . . . had been born in 1922:* Most of the information on Coplon is contained in the Washington Coplon trial, on reels 19–26 of the "Collection of Trials Involving Allegiance to the Communist Party," microfilmed for the Fund for the Republic. Other sources: Dallin, *op. cit.;* Sanche de Gramont, *The Secret War,* New York: Putnam's, 1962; and Pierre J. Huss and George Carpozi, Jr., *Red Spies in the U.N.,* New York: Coward-McCann, 1965.

106   *"very complicated and very sticky":* The Justice Department wiretap logs are quoted in Allan Weinstein, *Perjury.* There was some belief that the individual referred to in this conversation might be Alger Hiss.

107   *memo listed one shipment:* See my testimony in the trial transcript.

107   *"Got a hot one":* Testimony of William Foley, *ibid.*

111   *"gauged the temper of mild":* *Time,* May 9, 1949.

112   *"pro-Communist, albeit a bit of a 'wishy-washy' ":* See trial transcript, or daily papers that printed the memos and excerpts.

113   *"I have not been able":* Ibid.

114   *"The FBI builds its files":* "Hoover-Clark Feud Basis Denied," Washington *Daily News* and other papers, June 15, 1949. See also "Justice Department's Coplon Decision Will Hamper FBI's Work Against Spies," David Lawrence, *Evening Star,* same date. Both articles are in response to a lengthy statement issued by AG Clark at the end of the Washington Coplon trial.

118   *"Russia Got Atom Equipment"* and other headline: June 8, 1949.

119   *"If Gubitchev was the only man":* Trial transcript.

121   *"Once wiretapping is established":* *Nardone* decision.

123   *National Lawyers Guild fastened on:* Documents and commentary on this matter in Athan G. Theoharis, ed., *The Truman Presidency,* New York: E. M. Coleman, 1979.

123   *Learned Hand's decision:* See Reel 26 of the trial transcript.

CHAPTER EIGHT

127   *Hoover immediately informed Stephenson:* Letter of November 16, 1945, in Bentley file, 65-56402-8.

128   *someone in the British Embassy:* Over the years, the legend has
grown up that this spy was eventually identified through British
work alone, and that the United States had nothing to do with it;
this is, of course, incorrect, as it was our deciphering of the KGB
messages that provided the lead in this case.

CHAPTER NINE

132   *intelligence community learned of the Russian bomb:* See Gregg
Herken, *The Winning Weapon: The Atomic Bomb in the Cold
War,* 1945–1950, New York: Knopf, 1980. Herken, however, reiter-
ates the mistake of saying that the Russians learned nothing of
interest to them from the espionage of Fuchs, Greenglass and
others.

134   *asked the AEC for a copy of that scientific paper:* See an AEC memo
to files by Art Rolander, September 13, 1949, re Klaus Fuchs.

134   *two derogatory pieces of information:* Memo, Whitson to Fletcher,
September 26, 1949, re Emil Julius Klaus Fuchs. This memo, which
I wrote, also mentions Abe Brothman—see Chapter Thirteen.
Much of the memo has been withheld for security reasons.

136   *charged on February 2, 1950:* See memo to files from AD Lou Nichols, February 2, 1950, #65-58805. It recounts a conversation
between Nichols and AEC Chairman Gordon Dean. "He noted
that . . . what little they had been able to dig up so far was frighten-
ing as to the amount of information [Fuchs] has, as he was in this
matter up to his neck."

140   *by the Director's own later admission:* See "The Crime of the Century," by J. Edgar Hoover, *Reader's Digest,* April 1951.

142   *Fuchs . . . thought he recognized . . . Robbins:* The Gold and Fuchs
files, released together with the Rosenberg case files, contain numerous documents on these false leads.

143   *Lamphere was to go to London:* Details in this section drawn from
memo to Director, June 4, 1950, from Hugh H. Clegg and Robert
J. Lamphere, entitled "FOOCASE—Espionage—R/ Interviews in
England with Fuchs."

145   *fanned out to interview many people who had known Harry Gold:*
On May 15–16, many of these people were interviewed; see a
summary memo, with a "possible ID" of Gold, in Ladd to Director,
May 18, 1950, Gold file.

148   *The man whom I had waited so long to confront:* See Clegg-Lamphere report.

151   *being administered on that same day:* Some confusion still remains
on the precise timing of the Fuchs and Gold identifications of one
another. Radosh and Milton, *op. cit.,* suggest that Gold confessed
first and that Clegg and I, in London, must have told Fuchs of
Gold's action before Fuchs himself made the identification. A close

reading of the Clegg-Lamphere report, and an understanding of standard FBI operating procedure (which would have precluded telling Fuchs of Gold's confession) support the actual time sequence of events as I have depicted them in this section of the book.

151 *Fuchs wrote on the back:* The pictures of Gold with Fuchs's handwritten identification line on the back are appended to the Clegg-Lamphere report.

154 *"It appeared to me . . . that at the time":* Fuchs's statement at his sentencing is quoted by Rebecca West in *The New Meaning of Treason,* New York: Viking, 1964.

154 *General Leslie Groves:* See his book, *Now It Can Be Told,* New York: Harper, 1962.

CHAPTER TEN

161 *mining Gold's information:* This chapter is based on the multitude of materials in the Harry Gold files, 65-58805 series. See, e.g., the 104-page report of SA Robert G. Jensen of July 31, 1950, re Gold.

163 *Gold was born in Switzerland:* Facts and characterizations in this section are taken from Gold's opus, "The Circumstances Surrounding My Work as a Soviet Agent," which Gold compiled in his cell between May 22, 1950, and April 26, 1951. The document is included in a report from the SAC, NY, to Director of May 10, 1951.

164 *Black agreed to talk.* Black files, 65-59181. An extensive report is SA Jensen's, of 8/10/51. It is #313 in the Black file.

175 *Theodore Hall:* Ladd to Director, June 2, 1950, Gold file.

175 *investigation into an "unknown subject":* I have only been able to find this investigation referred to in a few of the released documents in the Greenglass files, 65-59028. These include: letter to Boston, March 8, 1950, and Bureau letter, March 29, 1950, to Boston, which reference a Bureau memo of February 21, 1950 (probably the initial date and memo of the investigation); an Albuquerque top-secret memo of April 23, 1950, and a Bureau letter of mine to Albuquerque of May 8, 1950. These materials have never before been understood correctly. Walter and Miriam Schneir, *Invitation to an Inquest,* revised edition, New York: Pantheon Books, 1983, make reference to FBI documents of April 18 and April 28, 1950, in the "unsub" investigation, but fail to correctly comprehend the information they have found. The Schneirs wonder in their book why the Greenglass file that covers the period February to May 1950, lists 212 pages of material, but only 41 highly censored sheets have been released. It is apparent to me that the unreleased materials are those that make reference to information that had originally come from the deciphered KGB cables.

177   *on the evening of June 15 David Greenglass was brought in:* See teletype, New York to Director, June 16, 1950, Greenglass file.

CHAPTER ELEVEN

178   *at 1:40 in the morning:* Memo, Belmont to Ladd, subject "Unknown American No. 5/Harry Gold, informant." This is dated June 15, 1950, probably in error, since it had to have been sent on June 16, 1950. Greenglass file.

179   *we who were most concerned:* Memo, Belmont to Ladd, June 16, 1950, subject, "David Greenglass/Espionage—R."

180   *chart that outlined . . . espionage networks:* Contained in Belmont to Ladd, July 11, 1950, and replicated in letter, Hoover to James S. Lay, Jr., executive secretary of the National Security Council, July 14, 1950, Gold file.

180   *"the relative of Greenglass":* Teletype, June 26, 1950, Philadelphia to Director and SAC, NY, Greenglass file.

182   *Rogge told Ladd:* Memo, Ladd to Director, subject, "David Greenglass," June 26, 1950, Greenglass file.

182   *Rogge told . . . Foley Square:* Memo, Director to McInerney, June 30, 1950, subject, "David Greenglass, was/Espionage—R."

183   *Rogge . . . had pointed out to the Greenglasses:* Radosh and Milton, *op. cit.,* reference files from the Rogge firm as evidence for this view.

183   *Rolander of the AEC:* Belmont to Ladd, July 10, 1950, subject, "David Greenglass/Espionage—R."

184   *Belmont and I went back:* Belmont to Ladd, July 17, 1950.

185   *as recently as February . . . Barr:* Report of SA Richard E. Brennan, February 14, 1950, covering the period December 22, 1949, to February 2, 1950. Barr files, 65-59453.

185   *Max Elitcher:* Belmont to Ladd, July 18, 1950, "Julius Rosenberg/Espionage—R." This memo discusses the desirability of immediately interviewing Elitcher, Sarant, Perl and Barr as probable Rosenberg associates.

186   *1944 CPUSA sheet:* Barr file, June 8, 1944, memo.

186   *personally incredulous at . . . "sky platform":* Belmont to Ladd, July 21, 1950, subject, "Julius Rosenberg, Espionage—R," which I drafted.

187   *Joel Barr had vanished:* See comprehensive report of SA Frederick C. Bauckham, NY, August 11, 1950. Barr file, #60.

188   *Vivian Glassman:* See comprehensive memo, SAC, NY, to Director, September 7, 1950, "Vivian Glassman, was/Espionage—R." This incorporates SA Richard T. Hradsky's lengthy report on Glassman. File 65-59334-54.

188   *Alfred Sarant:* See Director to McInerney, August 3, 1950, "Alfred Sarant/Espionage—R." File #65-59242-71.

189   *"Due to fact subject is probably"*: Teletype, Albany SAC to NY SAC, July 26, 1950. Sarant file, #24.

190   *Morton Sobell:* The initial Elitcher interview is in A. J. Nordstrom to Belmont, July 21, 1950, subject "Julius Rosenberg." Identification of Sobell in "signed statement" incorporated in teletype, Scheidt to Director, July 23, 1950, "Julius Rosenberg/Espionage— R." See also report of SA Vincent J. Cahill, February 27, 1951, "Max Elitcher/Helene Elitcher," which is a pretrial summary of their information.

192   *William Perl:* See report of SA John B. O'Donoghue, Cleveland, August 8, 1950, "Vivian Glassman/Espionage—R." This includes a statement made to the FBI by Perl, which he corrected in his own handwriting but later refused to sign. File 65-59334-3.

194   *Glassman told . . . a fantastic story:* See Hradsky report.

195   *"tall, thin and wore hornrimmed glasses":* Bentley signed statement.

195   *new interviews with Max Elitcher:* See report of SA Vincent J. Cahill, NY, October 18, 1950, "Max Elitcher/Helene Elitcher/Espionage —R." File #65–14873-218.

196   *Ruth Greenglass began to offer more detail:* Teletype, Scheidt to Director, July 17, 1950. Greenglass file.

198   *Glassman's actions:* See Hradsky report.

198   *curious incident: Ibid.*

199   *Sobell family was living:* Details in the Rosenberg trial transcript, microfilmed for the Fund for the Republic. Two volumes, 1715 pages. Also see Sobell file, e.g., Scheidt to Hoover, August 5, 1950, and report of SA Rex I. Shroder, September 21, 1950, Sobell file.

199   *William Danziger:* See reports of SAs Charles P. Silverthorn and James T. O'Brien, August 28, 1950. Sobell file.

200   *"On or about June 6, 1944":* In trial transcript.

202   *Harry Gold and David Greenglass were brought together:* Memo of SA Joseph C. Walsh, Philadelphia, December 28, 1950. Gold file.

203   *Jerome Tartakow:* See report of SA William F. Norton, Jr., NY, March 16, 1951, which covers the period December 12, 1950, to February 23, 1951, subject, "Julius Rosenberg; Ethel Rosenberg, was; Morton Sobell, was/Espionage—R." NY file #65-15348.

204   *reinterviewed . . . Ruth Greenglass and . . . David:* See two memos, Scheidt to Director, of February 1951 (exact dates illegible). One deals with Ruth's interview, the other with David's. These are summaries, not transcripts.

205   *AEC had to decide:* Brilliantly researched and documented by AEC historian Roger M. Anders, as "The Rosenberg Case Revisited: The Greenglass Testimony and the Protection of Atomic Secrets," *American Historical Review,* vol. 83, #2, April 1978.

209 *Cohn, angered many of us in the FBI:* Belmont to Ladd, March 13, 1951. Perl file.

210 *selection of the jury:* Comments upon the jury come from Ted Morgan, "The Rosenberg Jury," *Esquire,* May 1975.

210 *Agrin . . . and . . . Cohn agreed:* Interviews with Radosh and Milton, *op. cit.*

210 *"In a sense we were looking":* Morgan, *op. cit.*

213 *Klaus Fuchs . . . had told me in May 1950:* Clegg-Lamphere report.

213 *"so that it remains secret":* and other quotes, trial transcript.

215 *meeting with the AEC and NACA:* See an AEC memo to file, by C. A. Palazzolo, March 20, 1951, *in re:* Julius Rosenberg, was/William Perl et al.

217 *human error:* Key documents about the disparity in the dates on the Hilton Hotel card are Albuquerque teletypes of June 6, 1950, and June 7, 1950 (Gold file), and June 10, 1950 (Greenglass file), as well as summary report of SA Finis I. Parrish, June 21, 1950 (Greenglass file), all of which deal with and attempt to resolve the apparent disparity in the dates of the registration card.

219 *Saypol agreed with . . . Cohn that enough evidence:* Radosh and Milton, *op. cit.*

220 *the Rosenbergs themselves were the stumbling block: Ibid.*

220 *"blackmail" him:* Judge Kaufman was so interested in Rosenberg's use of this term that he questioned him about it in some detail, from the bench.

221 *Tartakow . . . passed on to the FBI:* Report of SA William F. Norton, Jr., March 16, 1951, in re Julius Rosenberg/Ethel Rosenberg, was/ Morton Sobell, was. This report of thirty-nine single-spaced pages shows the detail of Tartakow's many conversations with Julius Rosenberg before and during the trial.

221 *Tartakow sent a letter:* Scheidt to Hoover, March 24, 1951.

223 *the jurors perceived that neither of the two witnesses:* Morgan, *op. cit.*

224 *Vincent Lebonitte, the foreman, recalled that the first poll:* Morgan, *op. cit.* Lebonitte and I later worked for the John Hancock Insurance Company, in different locations and in different capacities; occasionally, at company gatherings, we would chat, although we never discussed the Rosenberg case except very briefly.

225 *Deputy Attorney General Peyton Ford called Hoover:* Hoover to Tolson et al., April 2, 1951, Rosenberg file.

225 *my unit, which prepared a memorandum for Ladd to give to the Director:* Ladd to Director, April 2, 1951, and April 3, 1951 (dated in error?), Rosenberg file. See also SAC Whelan to Director, April 3, 1951, Rosenberg file.

226 *The Director's final recommendation to Peyton Ford:* Director to Peyton Ford, April 3, 1951, Rosenberg file.

226 *later evidence shows that the FBI's recommendations:* See Michael

E. Parrish, "Cold War Justice: The Supreme Court and the Rosenbergs," *American Historical Review,* October 1977 (82), pp. 805–842. Also see Radosh and Milton, *op. cit.*

CHAPTER THIRTEEN

228   *whose code name was "Homer":* In *My Silent War,* Philby made this code name public for the first time. I believe he did so in a deliberate swipe at those of us who knew about the deciphered KGB messages; in effect, he was telling us that the Russians knew of our breakthrough.

229   *Philby . . . sizable party.* For more details, see David Martin, *op. cit.*

232   *All three were born in the years:* Of the many books on the subject of the three spies, I have used three main ones: Bruce Page, David Leitch and Philip Knightley, *The Philby Conspiracy,* New York: Ballantine Books, 1981; Andrew Boyle, *The Fourth Man,* New York: Dial Press, 1981; and Patrick Seale and Maureen McConville, *Philby: The Long Road to Moscow,* New York: Simon & Schuster, 1973.

233   *Walter Krivitsky:* His information on the double agents was not, of course, part of his memoir, *In Stalin's Secret Service.*

238   *Philby and Wisner had co-directed:* Martin, *op. cit.*

238   *Douglas MacArthur . . . Charles Willoughby:* William Manchester, *American Caesar,* Boston: Little Brown, 1978. By letter, Manchester asked Philby to comment on the charges that he or his compatriots leaked information on American plans in Korea to the Russians. In an April 1978 letter, Philby denied the allegations.

240   *Gold . . . received a typewritten envelope:* Summary Report, SA Jensen, June 31, 1950, *op. cit.,* and transcript of the interview with Gold by AUSA Myles Lane and SA's Norton and Harrington, August 1, 1950. Gold file.

241   *revelation to David Greenglass:* Report of SA John Harrington, June 27, 1951, in the Greenglass file, summarizes these warnings to Greenglass.

242   *first Sunday of February 1950, Harry Gold:* Lane et al., interview, *op. cit.*

242   *Gold . . . tried to persuade the prosecution team:* Radosh and Milton, *op. cit.*

244   *Roger Hollis:* Chapman Pincher, *Their Trade Is Treachery,* and Pincher, *Too Secret Too Long,* New York: St. Martin's, 1984 (p. 434).

245   *"We were told to expect":* Introduction to *My Silent War* by Graham Greene is © Greene, 1968.

PAGE   **CHAPTER FOURTEEN**

249 *Tartakow [said]* . . . *Rosenberg had described Perl:* Scheidt to
Hoover, March 24, 1951, *op. cit.*

250 *a new MiG fighter appeared:* See "Air Force Links Rosenberg Ring
to MIG Plans," Douglas Larsen, New York *World-Telegram and
Sun,* July 9, 1953.

251 *unknown fourth man lived with another young man:* Teletype,
Scheidt to Bureau headquarters, June 11, 1951. Rosenberg file (Tartakow).

251 *Klaus Fuchs had categorically denied:* Clegg-Lamphere report.

251 *Gary Pickard:* Summary Report of SA Robert F. Royal, August 7,
1951, Finestone file (Rosenberg file).

252 *Weinstein told . . . Ronald Radosh:* Radosh and Milton, *op. cit.*

252 *Russian diplomat told Rebecca West: The New Meaning of Treason.*

253 *John Gates:* Interviewed by Radosh and Milton, *op. cit.*

253 *Aronson and . . . Belfrage:* Cedric Belfrage and James Aronson,
*Something to Guard: The Stormy Life of the "National Guardian"
(1948–1967),* New York: Columbia University Press, 1978.

253 *"strong grounds for suspecting":* Guardian, August 15, 1952. The
seven Reuben articles begin with the issue of August 22, 1952.

253 *Belfrage had been described by Bentley:* Bentley signed statement
and Hoover-Stephenson letter.

254 *Judge Frank's twenty-four-page opinion: U.S.* v. *Rosenberg,* 195 F.
2nd 583 (1952), is appended to the microfilmed trial transcript. See
also Louis F. Nizer, *The Implosion Conspiracy,* New York: Dou-
bleday, 1973, and Parrish article, *op. cit.*

257 *Rabbi S. Andhill Fineberg: The Rosenberg Case: Fact and Fiction.*
New York: Oceana Press, 1952.

258 *the aging Stalin took umbrage:* See Adam B. Ulam, *Stalin/The Man
and His Era,* New York: Viking, 1973.

258 *Rudolph Slansky:* See Jiri Pelikan, ed., *The Czechoslovak Political
Trials, 1950–54,* Palo Alto, Calif.: Stanford University Press, 1971.

259 *"If we realize the true meaning": Ibid.*

260 *"The conviction of the U.S. atom spies":* Fineberg, *op. cit.*

260 *Shultz and Godson: Dezinformatsia—Active Measures in Soviet
Strategy,* New York: Pergamon Brassey's, 1984.

261 *"Public demonstrations are particularly useful":* Barron, *op. cit.*

261 *"diplomacy, information and disinformation":* Article by Sakharov
in the New York *Times,* June 5, 1980.

262 *Arkady Schevchenko:* Quoted in "Why American T.V. Is So Vulnera-
ble to Foreign Propaganda," by John Weisman, *TV Guide,* June 12,
1982.

262 *Bittman, . . . Levchenko, . . . Kaznacheev:* First two, in Schultz and
Godson, *op. cit.;* Kaznacheev, *Inside a Soviet Embassy,* Philadelphia: Lippincott, 1963.

PAGE

262   *Dorothy Thompson:* quoted in Fineberg, *op. cit.*

262   *"The nature of the crime":* cited in the New York *Times,* February 12, 1953.

263   *time has since proved that we were correct:* See Radosh and Milton, *op. cit.*

263   *hundreds of demonstrations:* See Nizer, *op. cit.*

264   *Albert Einstein:* Radosh and Milton, *op. cit.*

264   *Justice William O. Douglas:* James P. Simon, *Independent Journey,* New York: Harper & Row, 1980, especially pp. 299–311.

264   *Behind-the-scenes-maneuvering:* Parrish, *op. cit.*

CHAPTER FIFTEEN

270   *hollowed-out nickel:* James Donovan, *Strangers on a Bridge,* New York: Atheneum, 1964; and Louise Bernikow, *Abel,* New York: Ballantine Books, 1982.

271   *I constructed a memo about this unknown illegal agent:* Unfortunately, this memo has not surfaced in the more than 8,000 pages from the Abel file already made public by the FBI.

278   *book supposedly written by Lonsdale: Spy: Twenty Years in the Soviet Secret Service,* New York: Hawthorn, 1965.

279   *Katz had been re-identified:* See Gold references, *op. cit.* Tom Black named Katz to the Senate Internal Affairs Subcommittee in 1956; see "Ex-Spy Tells of Work for Soviet," the New York *Times,* May 18, 1956.

282   *"the most sensitive post [White] ever held":* Quoted in David Rees, *op. cit.*

284   *White had given the Russians printing plates:* According to Rees, *op. cit.,* Bentley probably overestimated White's sway in this matter, as the plates had previously been promised to the Soviet Government by the Treasury Department, with the cognizance of President Truman. I do not agree; and the FBI developed independent evidence that White influenced the Treasury Department position.

284   *"not yet in the Cabinet room":* Chambers, *op. cit.*

285   *Truman . . . said . . . he had first learned . . . in . . . February 1946:* At the end of November and the beginning of December 1945, the White House and top officials in other departments were alerted by Hoover about White and others named by Bentley. See letters in Bentley files, 61-3499, numbers 197–200, and 325.

287   *"The Director is testifying":* Both Hoover and Brownell testified on November 17, 1953, as reported in the newspapers of November 18. They released portions of the Hoover memoranda to the White House dated November 27, 1945, and February 1, 1946.

PAGE   **CHAPTER SIXTEEN**

291   *Yuri Rastorov:* A second secretary in the Soviet Mission in Japan, as well as a KGB man, Rastorov defected in 1954. He testified before the Senate Internal Security Subcommittee in 1956; this testimony is quoted at some length in Pierre J. Huss and George Carpozi, Jr., *op. cit.*

292   *false New Zealand passports:* See Chapman Pincher, *op. cit.*

293   *"veritable parody of impartiality":* article by Benjamin Stein in *Wall Street Journal,* February 8, 1974.

293   *"Guilt or innocence": Ibid.* Producer Goldstein wrote a letter to the *Journal*'s editor, insisting he had never said this to Stein (April 5, 1974); however, in Goldstein's book, *The Unquiet Death of Julius and Ethel Rosenberg,* New York: Lawrence Hall & Co., 1975, he makes virtually the same charges.

294   *Dr. Mark M. Kuchment:* See William J. Broad, "How a Soviet Secret Was Finally Pierced," the New York *Times,* June 26, 1984.

294   *Kuchment and I traded details:* Interview, Dr. Kuchment, January 8, 1985. See also Dr. Kuchment's paper for *Soviet Science and Technology,* Eyewitness Account Number 12, "The Life and Death of Alfred Sarant/Filip Staros and the Beginnings of Soviet Microelectronics."

Index

About the Authors

The son of a mining family from Idaho, ROBERT J. LAMPHERE graduated from law school and entered the FBI in 1941, at the age of twenty-three. Near the end of World War II he joined a squad in the New York office working on Soviet espionage matters, and from then until he left the Bureau in 1955, he was a specialist in counterintelligence and a pivotal figure in most of the important spy cases of the Cold War era. After leaving the FBI he took a position with the Veterans Administration and in five years rose to the rank of Deputy Administrator. From 1961 to 1981 he was a high-ranking executive in a major insurance company.

TOM SHACHTMAN is the author of a number of books, including *The Day America Crashed, Edith and Woodrow* and *The Phony War.*